Marketing Finance

D0488813

LIVERPOOL JMU LIBRARY

3 1111 01308 9162

Marketing Finance
Turning marketing strategies into shareholder value

Keith Ward

ELSEVIER
BUTTERWORTH
HEINEMANN

AMSTERDAM BOSTON HEIDELBERG LONDON NEW YORK OXFORD
PARIS SAN DIEGO SAN FRANCISCO SINGAPORE SYDNEY TOKYO

Elsevier Butterworth-Heinemann
Linacre House, Jordan Hill, Oxford OX2 8DP
200 Wheeler Road, Burlington MA 01803

First published 2004

Copyright © 2004, Keith Ward. All rights reserved

The right of Keith Ward to be identified as the author of this work
has been asserted in accordance with the Copyright, Designs and
Patents Act 1988

No part of this publication may be reproduced in any material form (including
photocopying or storing in any medium by electronic means and whether
or not transiently or incidentally to some other use of this publication) without
the written permission of the copyright holder except in accordance with the
provisions of the Copyright, Designs and Patents Act 1988 or under the terms of
a licence issued by the Copyright Licensing Agency Ltd, 90 Tottenham Court Road,
London, England W1T 4LP. Applications for the copyright holder's written
permission to reproduce any part of this publication should be addressed
to the publisher

Permissions may be sought directly from Elsevier's Science and
Technology Rights Department in Oxford, UK: Phone: (+44) (0) 1865 843830;
fax: (+44) (0) 1865 853333: e-mail: permissions@elsevier.co.uk.
You may also complete your request on-line via the Elsevier homepage
(http://www.elsevier.com), by selecting 'Customer Support' and then
'Obtaining Permissions'

British Library Cataloguing in Publication Data
A catalogue record for this book is available from the British Library

Library of Congress Cataloguing in Publication Data
A catalogue record for this book is available from the Library of Congress

ISBN 0 7506 5770 7

For information on all Elsevier Butterworth-Heinemann publications
visit our website at www.bh.com

Typeset by Integra Software Services Pvt. Ltd, Pondicherry, India
www.integra-india.com
Printed and bound in Great Britain

Contents

Preface

The objective of this book is to place marketing finance clearly within the context of the marketing strategy of a business. Strategic management, for the vast majority of commercially focused companies, is aimed at creating shareholder value. Nowadays, the creation of shareholder value for most of these companies is centred around their marketing strategies. This should mean that great emphasis is placed upon ensuring that these critically important marketing strategies do, in reality, create shareholder value.

Unfortunately, for many companies, developments in both information technology and management accounting have led to an increasing gap between the marketing strategies and the management accounting systems used within these companies. Relatively recently, I have been encouraged by the introduction into several leading companies of 'marketing finance managers'; typically these were financially trained managers who were physically moved to work alongside their marketing colleagues. In some cases, this role has been interpreted as 'accounting for marketing', which means deciding how to code up the marketing director's expense claim so it can be posted to the general ledger! This is not marketing finance as it is dealt with in this book.

The book does not attempt to deal comprehensively with all the detailed aspects of marketing strategies, marketing planning, etc.; these have each been the subject of many books already. Neither is this a book on detailed accounting rules (financial accounting standards, etc.). It deliberately tries to sit in the middle, exactly where the true marketing finance manager should sit; however, as you will realise as you read the book, sitting in the middle is not the same as 'sitting on the fence'. I have strong views on most issues relating to marketing finance and these are clearly expressed in the body of the book. These views have developed over the 30 years that I have spent being deeply involved in the interface between marketing strategy and finance.

The essential role for financial evaluation and control as part of the marketing planning process is now accepted by leading companies and, in some cases, the marketing finance manager works closely with the marketing research team to help develop a much more 'fact' based marketing strategy. For many companies, particularly in the fast moving consumer goods industries, this process started by measuring and managing brand values but the latest area of focus is on customer relationships. However for many companies, the marketing strategy is still product based; therefore each of these strategic thrusts is considered in detail.

The book is structured around the analysis, planning and control concept that underpins strategic management, marketing planning *and* management accounting. However, when properly applied in practice, these separate phases become somewhat blurred and overlapping; therefore it is no real surprise that the same has happened to the structure of the book. It seemed silly to talk about a brand evaluation process or valuing customer relationships without at the same time considering how to control such a marketing strategy.

Hopefully the book will stimulate some new thinking by both marketing and finance practitioners about how marketing finance should be implemented. My aim was neither to turn accountants into marketing managers nor vice versa. After all nasty definitions can be applied to both by the other side: an accountant is someone 'who knows the cost of everything and the value of nothing' while a marketing manager is someone 'who overvalues everything and doesn't care about the cost'. If a marketing finance manager can sit in the middle by understanding both shareholder value and customer value as well as the right costs to take into consideration for each strategic marketing decision, then it will be a truly value-adding role in any business.

I sincerely hope that the effort involved in writing this book proves worthwhile by providing you, the reader, with benefits that also outweigh the cost incurred in buying it. I would like to thank my wife, Angela, for doing all the figures, and my long-time secretary, Sheila Hart, for coming out of retirement to type the text (she can at least read my handwriting).

Keith Ward

Part One

Overview

1 Creating Real Shareholder Value

Overview

The overriding aim of a company is to create value for its shareholders on a sustainable basis over the long term. In order to create this value, the company has to develop and then exploit one or more sustainable competitive advantages, which will allow it to earn super profits on a continuing basis.

Most modern sustainable competitive advantages are the result of the successful implementation of marketing strategies (e.g. brand building, customer loyalty development, market segmentation). These marketing strategies normally require significant long-term upfront investments which must be regarded as high-risk expenditures by the business, because if they do not work, the expenditure is often irrecoverable.

It is therefore vitally important that these strategic marketing investments are rigorously financially evaluated prior to their commitment and properly financially controlled during their economic lives. This can only be effectively achieved by an integrated marketing finance approach. If, however, these marketing strategies are very successful they can create the most valuable assets owned by most modern businesses, which are represented by intangibles such as brands, marketing knowledge regarding customers and channels, technical know-how, patents and licenses. These intangible assets can produce very high rates of return for many years, if they are managed properly. Therefore a strategically oriented marketing finance system is needed to evaluate and control these assets, if the business is to optimise the shareholder value generated.

Real shareholder value is created by earning, on a sustainable basis, a rate of return exceeding the risk-adjusted required rate of return for any particular business. This can be measured in several interrelated ways: as the net present value of the future expected cash flows from the business, using the required rate of return as the discount rate; as the economic profit, or residual income, earned in a particular year (this is the excess return over the required rate of return for the business in that year); as the total shareholder return achieved by the investors in the company on an annual basis, this is the total of any dividend yield received from the company plus or minus the movement in the share price during the year.

The total shareholder return is the only truly externally based measure of value creation, but if it is not backed up by the internally focused value measures, the shareholder value creation may not prove to be sustainable. This has been clearly demonstrated by the spectacular but painfully short-lived boom in telecom, media and technology share prices at the end of the 1990s. Massive, but very speculative increases in these share prices (with correspondingly massive capital gains to their shareholders) were very rapidly followed by even more spectacular falls in many of these share prices, as it became clear that most of these companies were simply not capable of delivering, even in the long term, the levels of return on which their high share prices had been based.

If real shareholder value creation is to be sustained over the long term, the critical marketing assets must be fully developed and then properly maintained over their economic lives. A sensible approach in marketing finance is therefore to distinguish between development and maintenance marketing expenditures, as their objectives are significantly different. The objective of development marketing expenditure is to create a valuable long-term asset, and hence the returns from this type of investment will be received over the economic life of the asset. Conversely, maintenance marketing expenditure is designed to keep the existing marketing assets in their present valuable condition. Consequently the returns are much more short term, and it can be argued that the failure to spend adequately on maintenance is often reflected very rapidly in declining sales revenues and profit streams.

Introduction

At present many businesses feel themselves under attack from several sides. On one hand, investors often complain that their 'financial returns' generated from investments in these businesses are woefully inadequate, while financial markets and their regulators are becoming paranoid about the validity of the financial results being disclosed by large companies. On the other hand, environmental groups and even consumer associations are vociferously complaining that commercial corporations are achieving excessive profits at the expense of the environment and/or by cynically exploiting their consumers. These businesses may also feel oppressed by excessive government interference; many small businesses feel severely constrained by an increasing burden of government-imposed regulations, while multinational corporations face increasingly zealous tax authorities seeking to set aside their internal groupwide transfer pricing arrangements.

Inside these businesses, there is also great pressure for change and a correspondingly high level of stress and potential for conflict within the organisation. Marketing departments are increasingly being challenged to justify their expenditure levels in terms of 'economic added value'; growth in sales volumes, sales value or even market share is no longer a sufficient justification for an increase in this year's marketing budget. Indeed, some companies do not seem able to identify specific links between most of their marketing activities and their long-term strategic objectives; in such circumstances, it is not surprising that the marketing budget is being ever more rigorously challenged.

Similarly many finance and accounting departments are also struggling to define their future role within the new business paradigm. The staggering increases in the potential both for automating routine transaction processing and also for outsourcing to specialist suppliers the remaining workload has transformed the role of internal finance personnel. They are being challenged to change not only their focus but also their organisational structures. The strategic challenge for finance is to move from a transaction processing and management reporting focus located on the periphery of a vertically structured, functionally based organisation to a *strategic decision support focus integrated within the key horizontal business processes* of the new twenty-first century organisation.

Nowhere is this challenge more important than in the interface between marketing and finance. In many businesses, the marketing and finance functions can often find themselves in apparent direct conflict, often due to a lack of the close working relationship which finance has developed with other areas of the business, notably operations and production. Indeed, it can be the case, in some companies, that marketing managers feel that the main interest of their financial colleagues is to stop them spending money. Conversely, it can appear to these finance managers that the principal objective of their marketing colleagues is to spend as much money as possible on increasingly esoteric advertisements, very expensive trade and consumer promotions, higher customer discounts, etc.

This conflict can be disastrous for the business as increasingly the long-term sources of value creation result from the successful implementation of marketing strategies. For many industries, simply controlling the production side of the supply chain is no longer a sufficient condition to achieve long-term value creation. Indeed many businesses are deliberately exiting from the actual production of the products that they sell, as they see this business process as distracting their focus from the real sources of added value. These marketing led sources of value creation include market segmentation, branding, customer loyalty, and strategic partnering with selected channels of distribution. Clearly, if the business is to achieve its long-term objectives in this type of competitive environment, it is essential that its marketing expenditures are well directed and effectively controlled.

Such effective control can only be exercised if the marketing and finance areas work together in one integrated partnership. A significant challenge facing the finance function in many businesses, therefore, involves changing their perceived involvement in marketing activities from that of a cost-adding constraint to that of a value-adding, enabling partner. In an increasing number of businesses, this is being achieved by creating the roles of marketing finance managers, who are physically located in the marketing area and are seen as part of the marketing management team. As such, they should automatically be involved in the development of the marketing strategy, its implementation, subsequent modification and ongoing control. Ideally, they will share several management performance measures with their marketing colleagues, yet they have a clear financial responsibility to remain objective in their financial evaluations of proposed marketing expenditures.

Whether or not a particular business adopts this marketing finance manager role, this book argues for a very closely integrated link between marketing and finance. In far too many businesses, the marketing strategy and the financial plan are like a bad, jointly composed musical. The music is composed by one party, and the words are written completely separately by another person; then, and only then, the two are put together! The words of the marketing strategy can often seem to bear no relevance to the financial numbers in the business plan. Even more scarily for investors, there sometimes seems to be no marketing-based explanation for the actual financial performance of the company that is revealed to the world's capital markets in the company's published financial statements.

A marketing finance approach requires a financial involvement in at least two closely related but distinct aspects of marketing activities. *Prior to the actual commitment by the organisation to spend money, a rigorous financial evaluation should be carried out.* This is because true financial control can only be exercised in advance of any legally binding, financial commitment; once committed, the business will incur cancellation charges, or even have to pay the full cost, if it changes its mind. This financial evaluation compares the proposed expenditure against the potential benefits, taking into account the risks involved in the particular activity. This evaluation should include any other potential ways of achieving these particular objectives of the business.

The financial evaluation process should also indicate how the success/failure of the expenditure can be assessed, and how quickly this assessment can be made. It may be possible to improve the overall probability of success before having to commit the majority of the expenditure; this may be achieved by undertaking marketing research activity. This risk-reducing type of marketing expenditure should itself be evaluated financially, and any early warning indicators of success/failure should be identified. Any marketing activities where such early warning indicators can be identified are significantly lower risk than those where 'success' can only be assessed after all the expenditure has been incurred. If the initial expenditure has clearly failed, the business can avoid incurring the rest of the already doomed expenditure as long as early and effective financial controls have been identified.

Marketing finance can therefore be regarded as two interrelated processes of financial evaluation and control, and these processes are developed throughout the book. Much of the challenge relates to putting financial values to well-established marketing activities and objectives. Within the marketing area, many specific control measures have been developed to evaluate and control a wide range of marketing activities. Indeed, different marketing objectives are achieved by very specifically aimed marketing techniques. Unfortunately, far too often, these very different marketing approaches are financially controlled using a single financial measure, which is consequently often inappropriate. A key objective of this book is to highlight how appropriately tailored financial measures can be used when a marketing finance approach is implemented.

This is exacerbated because the most common financial performance measures consider *the efficiency* with which the activity has been carried out, rather than *the effectiveness with which it has achieved its pre-determined objectives*. An example using advertising expenditure may make this clearer. The 'efficiency' of purchasing media advertising (whether TV airtime, newspaper space, etc.) can be measured in terms of the 'cost per thousand' potential customers reached by the campaign.

EFFICIENCY IS DOING THINGS RIGHT
EFFECTIVENESS IS DOING THE RIGHT THINGS

However, such an efficiency-focused measure says very little about how 'effective' the advertising expenditure was in terms of achieving its pre-determined objectives. The specific marketing objectives for this advertising campaign could range from creating brand awareness, through changing the attitudes of potential customers or stimulating trial by new customers, to increasing the rate of usage by existing customers – each of which would probably use a different style of advertising communication.

In marketing terms, the achievement of any of these different objectives should be measurable, e.g. any increase in brand awareness can be measured by testing the level of brand awareness before the advertising activity, and re-testing afterwards. Thus, marketing can normally 'prove' whether it has achieved its marketing objective, e.g. raising brand awareness from 30 per cent to 40 per cent within the target group of consumers. The key marketing finance question is whether achieving this objective by spending £5 million on advertising was financially worthwhile.

The brand awareness both before and after the campaign could be tested in order to see if the marketing objective was achieved, and the efficiency with which the £5 million of advertising was purchased could be assessed. However, the money has not necessarily been effectively spent unless the benefit of increasing consumer awareness by 10 per cent has been financially evaluated as being worth well in excess of the £5 million cost that is to be incurred.

Clearly, to be of any value as a financial control, this financial evaluation must be carried out before the expenditure is committed, i.e. the advertising is booked, not actually run.

Even more clearly, such an evaluation, which relies on estimates of the future sales revenues that are expected to result ultimately from increased brand awareness, cannot be conducted by the finance function in isolation. It requires an integrated approach from both marketing and finance, as does the ongoing control process as the expenditure is committed. This is necessary as it may be possible to reduce the related risk by phasing the advertising expenditure in order to check that it is generating the increased awareness required (e.g. by doing a regional or segmented test first).

This integrated approach to the financial evaluation and control of marketing activities is at the very centre of marketing finance, but for this to be practical the strategic marketing objectives must themselves be integrated and aligned with the overall objectives of the business. This is considered in depth in the rest of this chapter.

A focus on shareholder value

The most common financial objective of modern commercial corporations is 'to create shareholder value'. Consequently, the differentiating elements within mission statements and long-term corporate objectives relate to the ways (i.e. the 'hows') in which this shareholder value is to be created on a sustainable basis.

Creating shareholder value will be broken down into several stages in this chapter, but the overall concept is quite straightforward. *Shareholder value is only created when shareholders achieve a total return that is greater than the return that they require from that investment.*

Shareholders can only achieve returns from their investments in companies in one of two ways: they can receive a dividend from the company and the value of their shares can go up (or it can go down). This total shareholder return (TSR) is shown in Table 1.1, with the capital growth element having a plus or minus impact on the dividend income element.

These two elements are inextricably linked as dividends represent profits and cash paid out of the company to its shareholders. Hence the higher the

Table 1.1   *Total shareholder return*

Annual total shareholder return (TSR) = dividend yield ± capital growth

$$\text{Dividend yield} = \frac{\text{Dividend per share}}{\text{Price per share}} \times 100\%$$

$$\text{Capital growth} = \frac{\text{Share price change}}{\text{Opening share price}} \times 100\%$$

---

dividend pay-out ratio (the proportion of post-tax profits paid out as dividends in any particular year), the lower the relative level of profits and cash which can be reinvested in the business. It is these reinvested profits that are the major source of the future growth of the business, and this future growth leads to increases in the share price. Not surprisingly, therefore some very high growth companies pay no dividends at all as they want to reinvest all their internally generated cash flows in order to grow as fast as possible in the future. This means that the only current source of shareholder return is capital growth generated from an increasing share price. If the high growth strategy fails, the share price may collapse spectacularly and suddenly, which highlights the key financial relationship between risk and return. This critical relationship will be emphasised throughout the book.

Risk and return

It is a fundamental principle of finance that investors will demand a return commensurate with the risk characteristics that they perceive in any investment. This is illustrated in Figure 1.1, which is known colloquially as the risk/return line as it shows the *required* return for any given level of risk. This deceptively simple relationship is critical to understanding the creation of shareholder value. The two axes are deliberately labelled 'perceived risk' and 'required return': *the return required by investors is driven by the risks they perceive in the investment.* If I do not fully understand the risk that I am taking, I may settle for a lower required return than a better informed investor. Alternatively sophisticated investors may accept a very low probability of a particularly disastrous outcome (as they have a well-diversified portfolio of other investments) and thus settle for a much lower required return than more

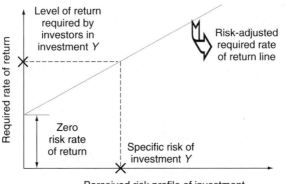

Figure 1.1 *Risk-adjusted required rate of return*

naive investors who are terrified of potentially losing most or all of their initial investment, even though this outcome is very unlikely. What is important is the risk perception of the investors, and this risk perception drives their required rates of return.

If risk perceptions are so important, we clearly need a definition of risk from the perspective of any investor. Risk is created by volatility in future expected returns. In Figure 1.1, a minimum positive required rate of return is shown; where the risk/return line cuts the vertical axis. This minimum required rate of return carries a zero risk perception, which means guaranteed, certain future returns. For investors in stable economies this normally means government guaranteed borrowings (e.g. US Treasury Bills, UK Government Gilts, European Central Bank debt). At the time of writing, the returns from these investments are low (i.e. interest rates in the USA and Continental Europe are being held down by the central banks in order to try to stimulate their economies) but these returns are at least not volatile. If the USA government promises to pay you a seemingly paltry 1.25 per cent p.a. interest, you can at least be confident of exactly how much interest you will receive and when you will receive it.

Accordingly a normally rational, risk averse investor requires an increase in the expected future return from any more risky investment in order to compensate for any potential volatility. Thus the cause and effect relationship is as shown diagrammatically in Figure 1.2; any expected volatility in future returns creates an increased perceived risk profile in investors that increases their required rate of return.

Of course, investors know in advance of making their investment in most government backed debt investments (Gilts, Treasury Bonds, National Savings Certificates, etc.) exactly what their return will be (i.e. the interest rate payable is stated on the debt offering). This is clearly not the case with most equity (i.e. stocks and shares in companies) investments, and this lack of certainty increases risk perceptions and hence required rates of return. Further, if the historical track record of a company's shares shows significant volatility in share prices and even dividend payments, most investors will require much higher returns from the company, as they will extrapolate this past performance as their best guide to the future performance of the company's shares.

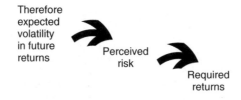

Figure 1.2   *Risk and return*

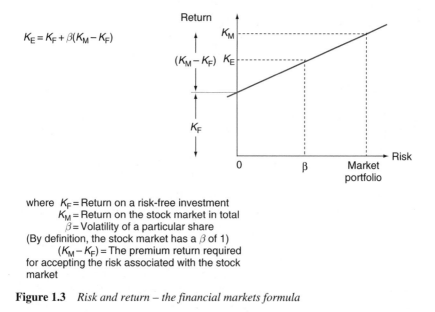

The Capital Asset Pricing Model (CAPM)

The return demanded by shareholders (often referred to as the cost of equity capital, K_E) increases with the perceived risk of the investment. (Risk is measured in terms of the volatility in the level of return over time.) Mathematically this can be represented as:

$$K_E = K_F + \beta(K_M - K_F)$$

where K_F = Return on a risk-free investment
K_M = Return on the stock market in total
β = Volatility of a particular share
(By definition, the stock market has a β of 1)
$(K_M - K_F)$ = The premium return required for accepting the risk associated with the stock market

Figure 1.3   *Risk and return – the financial markets formula*

Financial markets use various models to estimate the relative volatility of different industrial sectors and of the companies within each sector. The main formula is derived from our simple risk–return line and is known as the capital asset pricing model (CAPM), which is shown in Figure 1.3.

The CAPM calculates the beta factor for each company by comparing the correlation of the company's historic volatility with that of the stock market as a whole. If the stock market rises or falls by 5 per cent and share A moves by 7.5 per cent but share B only moves by 4 per cent, then share A is relatively much more volatile than share B; arithmetically share A has a beta factor of 1.5 while share B has a beta factor of only 0.8. This means that the required return (K_E) for share A will be significantly higher than for share B; a numerical illustration of this is given in Table 1.2.

Making a profit is not good enough

Table 1.2 indicates how much more challenging life is for a highly volatile company, caused by shareholders' natural dislike for risk. However, what is

Table 1.2 *Relative costs of capital (i.e. required rates of return)*

Base assumption: K_F = Return on a risk-free investment = 4% p.a.
$(K_M - K_F)$ = Equity market premium $\qquad$ = 5% p.a.
Share A $\quad \beta = 1.5$
Share A $\quad \beta = 0.8$
Using CAPM i.e. $K_E = K_F + \beta (K_M - K_F)$
For share A its's $K_E = 4\% + 1.5(5\%) = 11.5\%$
While for share B it's $K_E = 4\% + 0.8(5\%) = 8\%$

often forgotten, even by finance professionals is that the upward sloping 'risk-adjusted required rate of return line' of Figures 1.1 and 1.3 is, in reality, the shareholders' indifference line. In other words, moving from any point on the line to any other point on the line merely compensates the investor for a change in their risk perception; it does not, of itself, create shareholder value. Thus, using our numerical example of Table 1.2, investors who *require* a 4 per cent p.a. return for a risk-free investment, will *require* a 9 per cent p.a. return for taking on the overall stock market risk. Similarly, as is shown in Figure 1.4, they regard an 11.5 per cent p.a. return from share A as equivalent to (i.e. neither better than nor worse than) an 8 per cent p.a. return from share B, due to their differing risk profiles.

In financial terms, if shareholders receive, or expect to receive, exactly the level of return which they require from any investment, they have simply swapped a present capital sum (the purchase price of the investment) for a future set of cash flows (the future dividend streams from the company plus any expected ultimate sale proceeds from the investment) which have an equal present value.[1] Hence no shareholder value has been created. *Shareholder value*

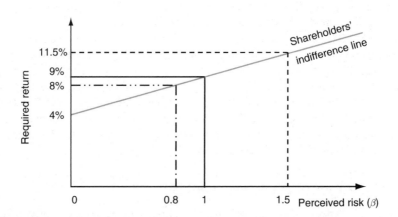

Figure 1.4 *Risk-adjusted required rate of return as shareholders' indifference line*

is only created when total returns are greater than the risk-adjusted required rate of return. Thus, a company can achieve positive accounting profits on a consistent basis without creating any real shareholder value at all. Hence, throughout the book, the term super profits will be used to describe shareholder value enhancing levels of profit; a super profit represents the excess rate of return over the required rate of return. This is defined more rigorously slightly later in the chapter.

In a perfectly competitive market, market forces would dictate that all investments would receive only their risk-adjusted required rates of return. If any business was generating super profits, new competitors would immediately be attracted into the industry, and their entry would drive down the overall achievable rates of return so that the super profits were eliminated. (Such is the theoretical world of perfect competition!) Consequently no shareholder value would be created. Accordingly, shareholder value can only be created by exploiting imperfections in the marketplace.

The greatest imperfections arise in product markets, i.e. the actual market-places in which specific products are sold to identified customers. For example, barriers to entry into an industry can be created by the existing competitors (or monopolist) to keep out any new entrants; thus preventing the rules of perfect competition from applying in that industry. This is diagrammatically illustrated in Figure 1.5. As a result, new companies cannot economically afford to enter this industry, even though the financial returns available are above normal levels. This restriction on potential new competition enables the existing players in the industry to sustain an apparently excessive financial return on their investments. However, in reality, the creation of an effective barrier to entry normally requires substantial additional investment (e.g. in very heavy market-

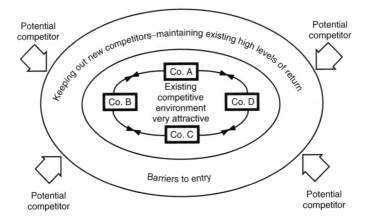

Figure 1.5 *A sustainable competitive advantage – developing an entry barrier*

ing expenditure to develop a strong brand). Thus, this apparent rate of super profits should first be regarded as providing the normal required rate of return on this additional investment. Only the remaining excess return, if any, represents 'real shareholder value creation'. This issue is considered in more depth in Chapter 2.

If companies are seeking to develop marketing strategies that will create shareholder value, then some simple evaluation guidelines should prove extremely helpful.

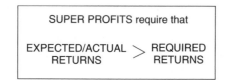

We have already established that *real shareholder value is only created from investment decisions where the expected return is greater than the shareholders' required rate of return*. However, any change in the shareholders' risk perception will create a corresponding change in their required rate of return. Thus, shareholder value-adding strategies can be diagrammatically represented as shown in Figure 1.6.

Any strategic move that takes the company to a position below the shareholders' risk/return line destroys shareholder value; i.e. the shaded area in Figure 1.6. As already discussed, moves along the risk/return line are neutral in terms of shareholder value; the higher or lower return being counterbalanced

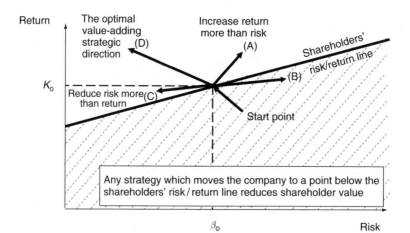

Figure 1.6   *Shareholder value-adding strategies*

by the change in the associated risk perception. Thus any shareholder value enhancing marketing strategy results in a move to a position above the risk/return line. It is not simply a question of increasing return or reducing risk, but of the level of increased return compared to the increased perception of risk, and vice versa.

From Figure 1.6, it is clear that strategy A is shareholder value enhancing while strategy B is value destroying. Both marketing strategies seek to increase both returns and risk, but for strategy B the increased risk perception more than outweighs the increased expectation of return. (It is possible that financial markets may be fooled for a while by the increased level of returns, but once the increased risks associated with the new strategy are realised, share prices will fall; often quite dramatically further than they had earlier risen.) Strategy A is a very common marketing-led strategy to try to create shareholder value, and many examples will be given throughout the book; the common theme across many of these strategies is the word 'growth'.

Almost any growth strategy (whether growing shares in existing mature markets, entering new markets with existing products, launching new products to existing customers, etc.) increases the risk of the business, and hence shareholders require an increasing return. The critical question therefore is whether the expected or predicted increased returns more than offset the required increase in returns due to the heightened risk perception. As discussed at length later in the book, the gap in the planning and control process of many businesses is the absence of this linkage between risk and return. Most financial evaluation processes focus exclusively on the changes in future returns, which assumes that the risk level is unaffected by the planned marketing initiatives.

In fact there is a very interesting shareholder value-creating strategy that actually sets out to reduce the level of returns in the future, but to make these lower future returns much less volatile and much more predictable (i.e. less risky); this is direction C in Figure 1.6. The simplest example of this type of strategy is the purchase of insurance by a company; the returns are reduced by the amount of the insurance premium paid. But the insured company hopes to avoid any future volatility in its financial performance that would have been caused by the adverse impact of the insured event. An extreme example is given in Practical Insight 1.1.

Practical Insight 1.1

Adding value through insurance

Many companies, particularly in the USA, have been forced into bankruptcy by ever increasing personal injury claims from contact with asbestos. T&N, a UK-based international company faced huge claims (estimated at over £350 million)

Adding value through insurance (*Continued*)

related to its historic association with the asbestos industry. The company's advisers estimated that this unquantified liability was reducing the group's market capitalisation by around £1000 million. By purchasing an insurance-based cap on its asbestos liabilities, the company was able to remove the excess discount even though it had to pay a significant premium to get this insurance cover. The premium reduced profits, but the reduced risk perception resulted in increased shareholder value.

There are a number of specific marketing strategies that seek to create shareholder value by reducing perceived risk proportionately more than they reduce future returns. A simple example is the negotiation of long-term discounts for loyal customers (e.g. 'overriders' or long-term agreements); the granting of a discount obviously reduces returns, but the objective is to make these lower returns significantly less volatile by 'guaranteeing' future sales from these more loyal customers. As discussed in Chapter 9, a shareholder value focus requires an understanding of how much volatility can be reduced for different levels of customer discount.

In Figure 1.6, it is clear that the optimal value-adding strategic direction (shown by strategy D) is to increase future returns while reducing the perceived risk of the marketing strategy. This reducing risk perception can result in a reduction in the required rate of return, so that the shareholder value-creating gap between expected and required rates of return can be substantial. Not surprisingly, because it is the most attractive strategic direction to take, it is the most difficult to achieve. In order to generate increased future returns with reduced levels of risk, the business must have developed a strong 'sustainable competitive advantage' (also often referred to as a 'differential advantage', a 'core competence', or, as above, an 'entry barrier'). Developing such a differential advantage is the main objective of modern marketing strategies. A strong sustainable competitive advantage should enable a company to increase its future rates of return to levels well above both its required rate of return and the rates of return achieved by its competitors.

However, its sustainable competitive advantage could also mean that, even in the event of a downturn in the market, its rates of return are less volatile in the future than those of its competitors. This lower volatility will result in a reduced level of perceived risk and a consequently lower required rate of return.

This means we can now expand our concept of super profits; a super profit is the excess return achieved by a business due to the development and maintenance of a sustainable competitive advantage. (As stated above, the excess return represents the surplus expected or actual return over the rate of return required by investors.)

Creating marketing assets

A key aspect of a competitive advantage in terms of its ability to create shareholder value is its sustainability. If competitors can match the competitive advantage immediately, or even relatively quickly, the company will be unable to exploit it to achieve a super profit. As already stated, any sustainable competitive advantage should act as an effective entry barrier, which stops competitors from coming into the financially attractive market created by the business. The sorts of entry barriers that can be erected are shown in Figure 1.7; the possible entry barriers shown are not meant to be totally comprehensive, but they illustrate a number of important issues relating to sustainable competitive advantages and their financial control.

It is clear that some potential entry barriers are the direct result of marketing activities (e.g. branding and control of channels of distribution), but several more can only be fully exploited through the implementation of the appropriate marketing strategy (such as low unit costs, technology barriers, licence protection, etc.). However all these entry barriers are normally only developed by substantial investment (i.e. upfront expenditures), and this investment must be regarded as high risk. If the entry barrier does not work, i.e. if competitors can find a way round it or through it, the company will be unable to generate a return on the substantial expenditure which was designed to develop the competitive advantage.

It should also be clear, from the illustrations of entry barriers shown in Figure 1.7, that they have a finite economic life. The clearest example of this is a patent that expires at the end of its 20 year life. The company

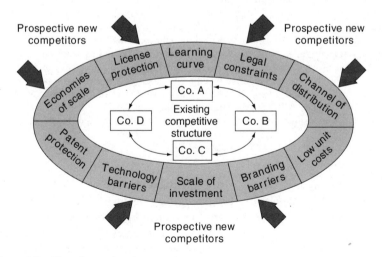

Figure 1.7   *Use of entry barriers*

may be able to extend the economic life of some entry barriers by carefully managing the sustainable competitive advantage (e.g. as has been done by certain very strong brands, such as Coca-Cola) but, as is discussed in more detail later in this chapter, this will normally require additional marketing expenditure in order to maintain the entry barrier. Alternatively, the business may decide to reinvest part of its current level of super profit in developing a replacement sustainable competitive advantage for when the initial advantage ceases to be effective. Good examples of this are ethical pharmaceutical companies (such as GSK) that often invest heavily in branding their patented drugs (such as Zantac). This actually reduces the level of super profits achieved during the patent period, as they are then effectively a monopoly supplier. However it can create strong existing customer loyalty and very good overall product awareness, which can work as a very effective competitive advantage once the patent has expired; particularly if new channels of distribution (such as the 'over the counter' market) are also exploited at this time.

The economic lives of these entry barriers can also be shortened dramatically due to changes in the external environment, as is illustrated in Practical Insight 1.2.

Practical Insight 1.2

The Cigarette Industry in the EU

The cigarette industry in most developed markets is very heavily branded and several of these leading brands have been very successful for many years – particularly Marlboro, owned by Philip Morris (PM). PM has managed the Marlboro brand very carefully and has changed the product attributes so as to appeal to successive generations of smokers. Thus originally Marlboro Full Flavour (i.e. the ubiquitous red chevron box) was dominant, but this is now smoked almost exclusively by older smokers. Younger adults are attracted to Marlboro Lights, which has a very strong share of younger smokers in most European markets.

However the new EU directive on cigarette labelling will ban all product references to 'light, mild, fresh, etc.', so that many of the leading brand names (e.g. Marlboro Lights, Mild Seven, etc.) face significant marketing communication challenges in maintaining their brand imagery, which has been developed over many years.

These entry barriers are the really important sources of shareholder value creation and *should therefore be managed as* the *key assets* of the business. Unfortunately, possibly because many of them are intangible and somewhat nebulous to most finance managers, many companies still regard their tangible fixed assets (factories, offices, plant and machinery, etc.) as the only real assets of the business. Without any intangible marketing assets to exploit, these tangible assets would probably generate, at most, the shareholders' required rate of return.

This means that many marketing activities, i.e. those aimed at developing a strategic marketing asset, should be financially evaluated and controlled as strategic investment decisions, irrespective of how they are treated for financial accounting purposes. Any financial investment involves spending money now in the expectation that, in the future, returns will be generated to more than recover this initial expenditure. Where the period over which these expected returns should be received is likely to be much longer than the current financial year, it is important that a proper long-term financial evaluation is carried out. This is particularly vital where these investment expenditures are regarded as high risk, due to the volatility associated with the potential outcomes. If the success of these investments is also critical to the achievement of the organisation's long-term objectives and overall mission, the need for a sound financial evaluation and control process becomes paramount.

In very many businesses, these factors are most obviously present in the key marketing investments that are being made in developing brands, entering new markets, launching new products and developing new channels of distribution such as the Internet. Thus, it is vital that these high risk, long-term investments are financially evaluated using the most sophisticated techniques available. Many companies would automatically calculate a full discounted cash flow for even the simplest, relatively small investment on labour saving machinery in their factory or operations areas. Yet these same companies often do not carry out such a long-term evaluation of much larger expenditures in the marketing area. Indeed it is still not uncommon to find almost no *financial* justification supporting many significant marketing initiatives. Perhaps this attitude is preserved due to the financial accounting rules of 'writing off' (i.e. expensing) all marketing expenditure in the year in which it is incurred; this may deter finance managers from considering any 'marketing expenditure' as creating an asset.

However, the proper definition of an asset is 'anything which will generate future net cash inflows into the business'; this clearly includes brands, trademarks, customers, channels of distribution, products, etc. Thus some marketing expenditure should be financially evaluated and controlled in exactly the same way as for other more tangible assets, but the way marketing itself classifies its expenditure is also very unhelpful. Many businesses still persist with the classification of marketing expenditures between 'above the line' (meaning mainly media advertising) and 'below the line' (meaning promotions for both trade and end customers, etc.). This distinction literally refers to where the expenditures tend to be shown in the profit and loss account but, in today's marketing environment, they have almost no relevance at all. The increasing power of many channels of distribution (such as supermarket retailers) and even consumers, let alone industrial customers, together with an increasing fragmentation in mass marketing media (e.g. TV channels), has led to a significant increase in the proportion of many marketing budgets which is spent 'below the line', i.e. directly to channels and end customers. If this is a more effective means of achieving the marketing objectives of the business, it is extremely sensible to do this. The change from ATL to BTL is irrelevant, the only relevant change would be in the objectives of the activity.

A much more important way of analysing marketing expenditure has unfortunately been ignored by most companies. As has already been stated, creating any valuable long-term asset requires the investment of substantial funds. This is also true for marketing assets, which require significant financial support during their developing periods. This *development expenditure* creates the attributes of the asset (such as brand awareness, distribution access, customer loyalty), which will generate the super profits of the future.

Once the marketing asset has been developed to its full potential, as with any asset, it must be properly maintained or it will decline in value very rapidly. A feature of many marketing assets (such as brands) is that some of their attributes (such as brand awareness) can decline very quickly if they are not properly maintained. Thus, another component of the marketing budget is *maintenance expenditure. Development expenditure is designed to increase the long-term value of the marketing asset by improving specific attributes of the asset, while maintenance expenditure aims to keep these attributes at their existing level.*

It has already been stated that all sustainable competitive advantages have finite economic lives and this is equally true for marketing assets. Thus, the mix of development and maintenance marketing expenditure will change over the life cycle. During the initial launch period, all the marketing expenditure will be development activity, as it is aimed at building the value of the asset; also, there are not yet any attributes to be maintained. Once the asset starts to be established, the existing attributes need some level of maintenance expenditure, but the majority of the marketing expenditure still goes to developing the asset to its optimum level. Once this optimal level is reached there is no longer a financial justification for more development expenditure; any excess marketing support will result in very small positive financial returns or, quite possibly, have a negative impact on the future earnings potential of the asset (this is discussed in Chapter 8). Consequently, for this fully developed, mature marketing asset, all the current marketing activity (which may be considerably less than was spent during the development phase) should be targeted at maintaining the asset's current position and strengths.

Eventually the marketing asset will approach the end of its economic life and, at this time, the business may, quite consciously, reduce the marketing support below the full level required to maintain properly the asset's attributes. In other words, the decline stage of the marketing asset's life is managed so as to maximise the cash flows received by the business. Indeed, this is the critical financial performance measure for any marketing asset, the objective is to maximise the super profits earned over the economic life of the asset. Due to the long life cycle of many of these assets, this has to be expressed in terms of the net present values of the cash flows that are expected to be generated over this economic life.

Also, because the economic life can, in certain cases, be extended, some marketing expenditure may be specifically targeted at extending the economic life of the asset. An alternative marketing strategy may be to transfer the existing strong asset attributes (such as from a brand) from a declining product to a new growing product. Even though doing so will accelerate the decline of the current product, it may extend the economic life of the 'brand' asset by associating it with another 'appropriate' product.

This distinction between development and maintenance marketing expenditure is very important, because the timing of the returns from each type of expenditure is very different. Development expenditure represents a long-term investment, and the returns may not be received until several years later. Thus, the marketing expenditure is incurred now, but the financial benefit is probably not felt in the current accounting year. The impact of reducing maintenance marketing expenditure is likely to be much quicker because, as many attributes can decline quite rapidly, there is likely to be a corresponding fall-off in sales revenues and profits. However for very strong brands such as Coca-Cola, as is discussed in Practical Insight 1.3, the accumulated strength of the brand attributes may keep sales levels up in the short term even if marketing support was significantly reduced; this does not, of course, mean that the long-term health of the brand has not been severely damaged.

In many companies, the marketing budget represents a very significant proportion of total expenditure. When the company comes under short-term profit pressure it is therefore very common for the financial director to look to marketing to make a significant contribution towards any required reduction in total expenditures. Under the traditional classification system, it is easy to predict where most of these cuts in marketing expenditure are likely to fall: on the long-term development activities. This is because reducing these development expenditures this year will have only limited impact on sales revenues and profits this year; so that the benefits of reducing marketing expenditure will drop to the bottom line.

Unfortunately the impact of this reduction in development marketing expenditure will be felt in future years, because the marketing asset will not become as fully developed as was intended. At least, by segmenting marketing expenditures into development and maintenance activities, the long-term consequences of such short-term action will be more clearly highlighted and the future expectations for the business can be appropriately modified. The best way of really focusing on these issues is through a well-designed marketing finance planning and control process, which is initially discussed in Chapter 2 and developed more fully in Chapter 6.

Practical Insight 1.3

Coca-Cola re-emphasises the long term

In December 2002, Coca-Cola announced that it would stop issuing quarterly and yearly forecasts. It argued that this process placed too much emphasis on the short-term financial performance of the company, rather than the more important long-term prospects. It said that it would instead offer details of its 'value drivers, strategic initiatives, and operating environment'. Douglas Daft, chairman and chief executive, said 'Establishing short-term guidance prevents a more meaningful focus on the strategic initiatives that a company is taking to build its business and succeed over the long run. We are managing this business for the long term.'

For a company like Coca-Cola, with very strong branding and a very high level of marketing support, the potential to manipulate profits in any one year is relatively easy by reducing its marketing expenditure. However in such a marketing-led business, this short-term focus could be severely damaging to the most important asset possessed by the company, i.e. the brand.

Defining shareholder value

We have now established that marketing assets are, for many businesses, the major source of super profits and that super profits are key to creating shareholder value. Now we need to define this concept of shareholder value more rigorously.

There are three slightly different, but linked, ways of measuring shareholder value: shareholder value analysis, economic profit and total shareholder return.

The shareholder value-added approach (popularised by Alfred Rappaport) uses discounted cash flow techniques to estimate the value of any potential investment, discounting forecast cash flows by the shareholders' required rate of return (i.e. the company's cost of equity capital). Rappaport stated that the value of a company is dependent on seven drivers of value, as shown in Figure 1.8.

The management of the business can use their expert insider knowledge to develop sales, profit and cash flow forecasts for the first five value drivers. The required time period for these forecasts is dictated by the time period of competitive advantage (i.e. value driver six), and this is determined by the relative strength of the competitive advantage. Thus a strong brand may generate high super profits for a much longer period than a small technical product innovation.

Discounting these cash flow projections at the company's cost of capital leads to a value being placed on the business by the management. This technique can quite easily be applied to individual divisions within a large group,

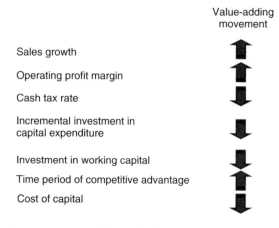

Value-adding
movement

Sales growth

Operating profit margin

Cash tax rate

Incremental investment in
capital expenditure

Investment in working capital

Time period of competitive advantage

Cost of capital

Figure 1.8   *Rappaport's seven drivers of value*

where the individual values can be aggregated to value the group. Alternatively the shareholder value impact of possible marketing strategies can be assessed using this technique.

The problem with shareholder value analysis is applying it from outside the company, which is exactly what current and prospective shareholders are trying to do. In order to arrive at an estimated company value, these outsiders require a great deal of information about the company, its future strategy, and the competitive environment in which it will be operating. Many serious investors (such as the renowned Warren Buffett of Berkshire Hathaway) and leading stock market analysts therefore use their own tailored versions of this shareholder value analysis technique.

Shareholder value analysis quite deliberately de-emphasises the short-term performance of the business (i.e. this year's financial results) in favour of focusing on the long-term potential of the company. Hence it is quite complicated to use shareholder value analysis as a periodic measure of performance; how to do this is discussed later in the book. Many companies therefore use economic profit (also known as residual income) as a periodic indicator of shareholder value creation. Economic profit is the surplus earned by a business in a period after deducting all expenses including the required rate of return on the capital employed in the business (i.e. it is what we have previously referred to as super profit). The calculation is illustrated in Table 1.3.

Economic profit has the major advantage that it teaches managers a great respect for capital – it is no longer seen as 'free' – and can encourage them to run their businesses so as to minimise capital employed. In many cases, this is beneficial to shareholder value creation because lots of high risk growth strategies do not generate sufficient extra return to service the extra capital

Table 1.3   *Calculating economic profit/residual income/super profit*

Operating profit after tax	£2 40 000
Capital employed	£2million
Cost of capital	10%

Calculation 1

Operating profit after tax	2 40 000
Less: cost of capital charge (£2m × 10%)	2 00 000
Economic profit	£ 40 000

Calculation 2

Economic profit = capital employed × spread of return

(where spread of return = return on investment –

$$\text{required return})$$
$$= £2m \times (12\% - 10\%)$$
$$= £40000$$

required to finance the growth. However, as economic profit is a single period measure, it can, if taken to extremes, lead to an under capitalised business which cannot grow to its full potential.

As stated above, there is a relationship between economic profit and full shareholder value analysis; shareholder value analysis shows the value of a business over its lifetime, while economic profit shows whether the company is creating value in any single period. More rigorously, the discounted value of all the projected economic profits of a business will equal the shareholder value analysis figure.

Both SVA and economic profit are 'internal' measures of shareholder value in that they show how well the company is using its competitive strategy to create value from the product-market mix it selects. The total shareholder return (TSR) measure, introduced earlier in the chapter, is externally focused; it looks at the value created for shareholders, whether through dividend income or capital growth. The TSR calculation is illustrated in Table 1.4.

Table 1.4   *Calculating total shareholder return*

Share price on 1 January	100p
Share price on 31 December	110p
Capital gain in the year	10p
Dividend paid on 31 December	5p
Total return	15p

$$\text{Total shareholder return (TSR)} = \frac{15p}{100p} \times 100\% = 15\%$$

From the perspective of shareholders, TSR is probably the most accurate measure of value – it *shows what they have actually received* from the company in the period. However, it can only accurately measure the past, and even this past financial 'performance' may not properly reflect the actual performance of the business and particularly of the managers running the business. Share prices, and especially movements in share prices, reflect the market's expectations, rather than actual corporate performance. Thus only adequate performance from a company expected to do poorly might increase the share price far more than superb performance from a company that was already a market favourite, and which had a correspondingly highly rated existing share price.

Creating sustainable and real shareholder value

Also a company could itself be doing well, but it could be in an out-of-favour sector and find that its own good financial performance is not reflected in the returns to its shareholders. Alternatively, a poor company could see its price rise for reasons unconnected with its underlying performance. When used as a measure of senior managers' performance, TSR is normally benchmarked against similar companies (e.g. those in the same industry or sector). This helps to eliminate some, but by no means all, of these difficulties.

This was very clearly illustrated in the dramatic split within stock markets during 1999 and 2000 between 'old economy' shares and 'new economy' shares. During the late 1990s investors became increasingly excited about the prospects for the new, high growth industries being created from the know-ledge revolution. Thus share prices of many new companies in the technology, media and telecoms (TMT) sectors rose dramatically, even though these companies were not yet trading profitably. All of the current share price was apparently based on the future super profits which would be generated by these companies. Indeed some long established companies (particularly in the telecoms sector) were re-invented as new high growth businesses (due to the potential of combining mobile telephony, Internet access, text and visual messaging, etc.).

As these share prices boomed, investors were desperate to raise funds to ride on the bandwagon; thus they sold their shares in the boring, old companies which were producing the same goods, profits and dividends that they had for many years. Consequently while overall stock markets soared to record levels, many sound, well-established, shareholder value-creating companies saw their share prices fall, and they dramatically under-performed the stock market in terms of the TSR generated during this period. Indeed, as explained in Practical Insight 1.4, the capital markets developed new valuation criteria for some of these businesses as their valuations could not be justified using traditional financial methods such as discounting expected future cash flows. Not surprisingly this 'irrational exuberance', to quote Alan Greenspan, has ended in tears and now we are, in general, back to more soundly based valuation models.

Practical Insight 1.4

Creating a 'bubble' effect!

The rapid growth potential of some 'new' industries led to some innovative methods of share valuation being used by many investors during the TMT boom. Unfortunately, but not surprisingly, this led certain companies to try to perform well in terms of the new valuation drivers being applied to them. As these drivers, in some cases, became more and more removed from the underlying shareholder value drivers, an inevitable valuation 'bubble' was blown up which subsequently burst with disastrous consequences for all involved; shareholders, employees, regulators and even the executives directly involved in 'manipulating' their own performance.

A simple example relates to both WorldCom and Enron, where sales revenue growth was seen as a key value driver by the financial markets. If sales grew rapidly then profits would eventually follow, seemed to be the logic. However, if sales growth for its own sake becomes the objective, then there is no certainty that these growing sales will actually be profitable at all. Thus both companies entered into extremely complex and technically convoluted ways of stimulating their apparent sales levels. Thus reported sales revenues grew exponentially from year to year, but net cash inflows did not grow at the same rates as most of this sales growth was an accounting charade.

If these published financial results had been analysed in terms of the long-term strategy being employed, the sustainable competitive advantage being exploited, and the expected competitive reaction, perhaps a more rational valuation for these companies may have been maintained and their eventual total collapse avoided.

Considering both business and financial risk

There is yet another dimension to shareholder value that we need to consider at the outset as it will reappear throughout the book. So far, we have considered the relationship between risk and return, with the shareholders' perceived risk as being the determinant of their required rate of return. Now we need to divide this concept of risk into two parts: business risk and financial risk.

As with all the other functional strategies (marketing, operations, human resources, etc.) that are now developed by most companies as essential aspects of their strategic management process, a company's 'financial strategy' must be tailored to the needs of the overall corporate and competitive strategies that are being implemented by the business. If the financial strategy is appropriately designed and properly implemented it can enhance shareholder value but, even more dramatically as is illustrated in Practical Insight 1.5, when an inappropriate financial strategy is applied, the entire business can be placed in jeopardy.

Business risk describes the inherent risk (i.e. volatility in expected returns) associated with both the underlying nature of the industry that the business is in and the specific competitive strategy that it is implementing. Thus a very new, focused, single product, high technology company (such as a business developing a specific aspect of biogenetic engineering) would have a very high intrinsic business risk. It must be remembered that, of itself, neither a high nor a low business risk is better; as long as the relative level of financial return matches the level of associated risk, either is acceptable.

However businesses with such dramatically differing levels of risk require fundamentally different financial strategies. Financial risk is the risk inherent in the company's choice of financing structure, and this involves both the sources of finance used and the ways in which investors receive their returns (e.g. primarily dividend yield or capital growth).

Funding for a company can, at its simplest, be raised by selling shares to investors who become part owners of the business or by borrowing money from a bank or other lender. The lender does not become a part owner, but remains a creditor of the company and requires both payment of interest on the debt and eventually the repayment of the amount lent. As such the lender has much more control over their expected future returns and they may increase this control (i.e. reduce their risk) by taking security over the assets owned by the business. The shareholders stand behind any lenders in terms of receiving any returns, but they can, if the business is successful, receive very high returns while the return to the lender is normally fixed. Our normal rule of a positive correlation between risk and return still applies to financial risk, so that the required return on debt financing (borrowed funds) is significantly lower than on equity funding (money raised by selling shares in the company).

This would appear to make it attractive for companies to raise most of their required financing by borrowing; if it is a much cheaper source of money. This is why we must consider the combination of business and financial risk. Lenders, such as banks, regard their loans to companies as relatively low risk because they effectively transfer much of the risk to the company. Failure to make interest or principal payments to your bank normally leads to the liquidation of your company. Thus any company with a high business risk, which will often show up as volatile financial results, should not rely on debt financing. The business and financial risk profiles combine together to give the overall risk profile for the business in the same manner as all sequential probabilities; i.e. mathematically the individual factors are multiplied together to get the combined result. To do this properly, we have to be sure that we are assessing financial risk from the right perspective. In this case, that is the perspective of the company raising the financing, i.e. the borrower or issuer of the new shares.

Debt financing is a high risk form of funding to the borrower, because the lender has transferred to them as much of the total risk as possible. Conversely because shareholders keep most of the total risk themselves (i.e. they cannot demand a dividend payment, and the company does not have to repay the

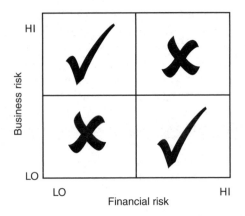

Figure 1.9   *Combining business and financial risk to create shareholder value*

money invested as long as it continues trading), equity financing is a low risk source of funding. The shareholder value enhancing combined strategies are illustrated in Figure 1.9.

Combining a high business risk strategy with a high financial risk strategy (such as would be achieved by funding our start-up bio-tech company with almost all debt financing) gives a very, very high total risk profile. Such a company might succeed spectacularly, but it is much more likely to fail completely and disappear. It is now well established that very high business risk enterprises should be funded with equity, and that this equity should be provided by investors who understand that their investment may be totally lost if the business fails (i.e. by specialist venture capitalists). This provides a logical combination of high business risk and low financial risk.

Another logical shareholder value enhancing combination is to put together a low business risk strategy and a higher risk financial strategy. A low business risk company will produce predictable profits and cash flows due to its low volatility, and these will enable it to pay both the interest and principal payments on its borrowings. If this low business risk enterprise uses primarily equity funding, it is missing out on a significant opportunity to add shareholder value through its financial strategy.

Practical Insight 1.5

Out of one wrong box into another

For its final years under Lord Weinstock, GEC plc was criticised by financial analysts for combining a low risk business strategy with a very low risk financial strategy. In the 1960s and 1970s Weinstock restructured the UK's electronics and defence contracting industries through take-overs and mergers. During the 1980s and early 1990s the group was highly profitable and cash generative but maintained a strong net cash position with a low dividend pay-out ratio. Consequently its total shareholder return was relatively poor as its share price under-performed the booming stock market.

In the late 1990s a new management team was brought in (Lord Simpson as Chief Executive and John Mayo as Group Finance Director). They very rapidly transformed the group, through very large scale disposals and acquisitions, from a well-diversified group involved in mature, relatively stable but low growth industries into a highly focused telecoms business mainly based around the USA markets (where GEC had never had any strong presence). Their acquisitions were financed by cash payments, using the existing GEC cash mountain, then the proceeds from selling GEC's original core businesses, and finally from raising large scale borrowings.

The renamed group (now called Marconi) subsequently suffered a dramatic crisis in the ensuing downturn in the telecoms sector. This resulted in a financial restructuring by the lending banks that left the original shareholders with less than 1 per cent ownership of the company, as much of the outstanding debt was converted into equity. There are people in the City of London who regard Lord Weinstock as dying, shortly after the collapse of the group he built up, of a broken heart.

This combination of business risk and financial risk can easily be applied in marketing finance, as will be illustrated throughout the book. Clearly high-risk marketing strategies (such as brand launches, new product launches and new market entries) should be regarded as being financed with venture capital type of equity funding, with its commensurately high required rate of return. Lower risk marketing activities, where the prospect of total loss is negligible and where the expected return is predictable within much tighter parameters, can utilise the much lower cost, debt type funding appropriate for these lower risk business strategies.

Note

1   The concepts of discounted cash flows and present values are considered below and in more depth in Chapter 7, when strategic investment evaluation techniques are discussed.

2 The Virtuous Circle of Analysis, Planning and Control

Overview

Strategic management is normally regarded as an integrated management approach drawing together all the individual elements, including the critically important marketing strategy, involved in planning, implementing and controlling a business strategy.

Thus it clearly requires an understanding of the mission and/or vision of the organisation (the 'why' it exists statement) and of its long-term goals and objectives ('where' it wants to go). There must also be a comprehensive analysis of the environment in which the business both is currently and will, in the future, be operating ('where it is'). This analysis process must include all the internal operations and resources (both existing and potential) of the organisation but, equally importantly, must cover the external aspects of its environment. This includes competitors, suppliers, customers, the economy, governmental impacts, as well as legal and other regulatory changes.

The combination of 'where the organisation is' and 'where it wants to go' will normally identify the need for a series of co-ordinated actions to bridge the gaps between the two, or even merely to maintain its current position if the external environment is changing adversely. These business 'strategies' must be developed in the context of the internal and external environments so as to ensure that they are practical; if not the goals and objectives will remain a distant theoretical 'wish list' rather than an achievable plan for the business.

A key element in achieving this is that the planning process must explicitly consider the responses of those stakeholders significantly impacted by the proposed strategies; particularly those competitors, customers and/or suppliers that are adversely affected.

For many large organisations it is also important that business strategies are developed at the appropriate levels within the organisation; thus an overall corporate strategy is needed for the organisation in total, with separate but linked competitive strategies for each subdivision of the business which is directly competing for identified customer groups with a specified product range against known competitors. However so far these business strategies are only plans, and the full process of strategic management includes the implementation of the selected strategies.

Some of the goals and objectives are long term, and the relevant strategies will be implemented in a dynamic and continually changing external environment. Therefore it is most unlikely that all the predicted outcomes from these action plans will be achieved. There is a need for a feedback process of evaluation, control and, where necessary, modification. Many such modifications will result in changes to those selected strategies that are not working effectively but, in some circumstances, the organisation may be forced to accept that its original goals and objectives are not attainable in the actual external environment or with its available set of resources.

Thus strategic management is a continual, iterative process of analysis, planning and control. Marketing finance must therefore follow a similar process if it is to contribute positively towards the sustainable creation of shareholder value.

However marketing strategies are also specifically tailored to the competitive environment in which each particular business is operating. The marketing finance process should be equally tailored to fit the environment and the ensuing marketing strategy. There are widely differing strategies that can be implemented, even in the same industry at the same time, and these differing strategies require suitably tailored control processes and performance measures. There is a need for a hierarchy of both economic and managerial performance measures for all businesses, but it is critical that some of these performance measures incorporate indications of how well the business is doing in terms of its long-term objectives.

It is particularly important that the performance measures are tailored to the key strategic thrusts of the business; if these change, the marketing finance process may need to be changed as well. One common strategic marketing thrust is to develop strong brands as a sustainable source of differential advantage. A branded strategy requires a good brand evaluation process if the resulting high brand expenditures are to be properly financially evaluated and controlled. Brands can be based on either customers or products, but other types of marketing strategy can be either customer led or product based.

In a customer-led strategy, the long-term customer relationship should be regarded as a critical asset of the business; thus, development expenditure is invested to win the customer, and maintenance expenditure is needed to retain the relationship for its full potential economic life. Life cycle customer account profitability analysis is therefore important in such a relationship marketing-oriented business.

Similar issues occur with product-based strategies and a suitably tailored response is required. Product life cycle costing is now quite a well-developed technique in some industries, using the dynamic cost reducing relationship of the experience curve to justify setting prices below the current level of costs in order to develop a sustainable cost advantage.

Introduction

A traditional approach to management accounting follows the same analysis, planning and control framework that is relevant to strategic management and is shown in Figure 2.1. One criticism of the truly traditional approach is that these individual stages are each carried out in isolation by separate parts of the organisation and are regarded as an end in themselves. As will be argued throughout this chapter and, indeed, through the whole of the book, much greater value is created from operating 'analysis, planning and control' as an integrated, iterative process, so that the dividing lines between any two stages become very blurred.

Financial analysis is required to establish *where* the business is today and to ensure that the strategic goals and objectives are realistic and meaningful. However traditionally management accounting has tended to focus on internal analyses, such as performance compared to this year's budget or last year's performance, etc. Also this financial analysis is often done for the business as a whole, whereas the business strategy may deliberately seek to create a number of differentiable market segments, which can be attacked with specifically tailored marketing strategies. The business strategy is very concerned with the external environment, and therefore the financial analysis process should itself be focused on external issues and particularly competitors and customers.

Financial planning is supposed to set out *how* the business intends to move from 'where it is today' to 'where it wants to be in the future', i.e. how it will achieve its 'realistic' goals and objectives. Unfortunately many traditional

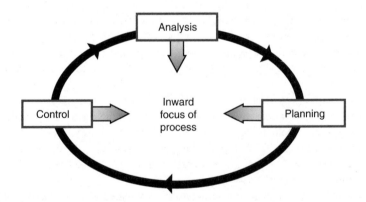

Figure 2.1   *Traditional management accounting process: analysis, planning and control as an iterative process*

management accounting planning systems are really simply extrapolations of the past (e.g. last year's sales plus a percentage and last year's costs minus a percentage) and take no account of the external environment in which the company is operating. Recent events (e.g. September 11, 2001) have shown the irrelevance of over-simplified plans based on extrapolations of the past. There are relatively few major industries in the world that have easily achieved any plans established prior to the destruction of the Twin Towers. Such a momentous event forces businesses to sit down and rebase their future plans; for some (e.g. USA airlines and other travel related businesses) their objectives will have changed (e.g. survival, rather than growth), for others the strategies required to achieve their previously agreed objectives may need amending in the light of a slowdown in global economic growth and dramatic falls in major capital markets.

Financial control seeks to monitor how well the agreed objectives are being achieved by providing feedback to the relevant decision-makers. However 'control' is much more than explaining how far away actual performance is from the planned level. The feedback should be used to make correcting decisions to put the business back on course or to change the aim of the business towards modified objectives. Financial monitoring and reporting, i.e. control, should therefore be regarded as a positive tool of management, acting as a much needed learning process for the difficult task of marketing planning. Far too often, the financial control process is seen as a way of apportioning blame for what went wrong, or as a means of claiming the credit for what went right. It is also vitally important that the financial controls used by the business are appropriate to the particular marketing strategy being employed and the stage of implementation that the strategy has reached. Unfortunately most large organisations still use only one method of monitoring financial performance (the most common being some form of accounting return on investment, i.e. profit divided by the investment tied up in the business) across all the disparate subdivisions making up the group.

A strategic marketing finance approach

The main problem with the traditional approach to management accounting is not therefore to do with the analysis, planning and control concept. It is the excessive focus internally within the business; what I have for years described as the 'budget, actual, variance syndrome'. Having established, with great effort and often much pain, the budget for the forthcoming year, management accountants will spend all year reporting in great detail how well or badly the business is performing against this budget. This detailed reporting will continue even though the budget may have been rendered completely irrelevant by some uncontrollable external event early in the financial year (or even before the new year actually started, but after the budget for the year had been finalised).

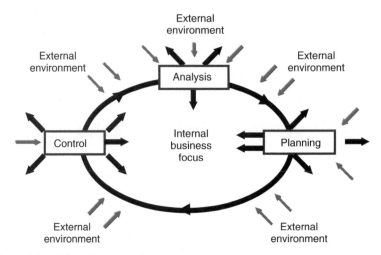

Figure 2.2   *Taking the external environment into account*

The only statement any of us can make with certainty about any business plan that we have ever been involved in is that 'it will be wrong!' Even if the financial objective was to make £10 million profit and the actual profit was exactly £10 million, it will, in reality, be a different £10 million; in other words, the sources of the actual profit will not be exactly those expected in the original plan. This is an inevitability of planning for the future in an uncertain, relatively volatile business environment.

Therefore, as indicated in Figure 2.2, it is critically important that the impact of the external environment is considered at each stage of the analysis, planning and control process. However, the main objective of Figure 2.2 is to highlight the relative importance and emphasis within each of these stages. This is done by the different black arrows emanating from each box in the diagram, while the external environment exerts a consistent pressure on the business throughout. The key objective of the analysis phase is to find out about and understand, as far as possible, the current and future external business environment; hence two externally facing arrows with only one looking inside the business. Most businesses have a lot of internal analysis, including all this year's management accounts, sales analyses, costing data, etc. What they need as a basis for planning for their future is information about *the specific environment in which they will be operating in this future*. This means that the greatest emphasis in the analysis phase must go on *predicting the future business environment*. Unfortunately this is not the case for most businesses; in many planning processes, the major external environmental analysis consists of a précis of the latest EIU (Economist Intelligence Unit) report for the country in which the business is operating. This is not meant as a criticism of EIU country reports as such but these are, fairly obviously, general statements of a best guess for the overall macroeconomics for particular countries. The report may give the view that inflation will be 2.5 per cent, the rate of exchange will be €1 to $1, unemployment will remain high at 8 per cent, the balance of trade will continue to be negative at 2.5 per cent of GDP, GDP growth will slow to 1 per cent and the government will run a fiscal deficit of 3 per cent of GDP.

The key, very powerful analysis question is '*so what*'? What would this macroeconomic environment mean for our business; in terms of market size, pricing opportunities, cost pressures from suppliers and employees, competitor initiatives both from existing competitors and any new competitors who might be attracted into our market place, etc.? Also, this set of EIU forecasts is a consensus, or most likely outcome, from an infinite range of possibilities. (Many readers will have seen the reviews that are done at the end of each year, when the forecasts of various experts are compared to the actual outcomes for that year. Not surprisingly, the maximum ranges between the extreme forecasts and the actual out-turns can be very great indeed.) Thus the analysis process should try to identify what sort of 'range' there could be during the plan period; this must be done for those most critical external factors having the greatest effect on the business. For example, in an export-led business, a forecast of €1 to US$1 may lead to an assumption of a relatively stable market place but, if the possible range for the currency is from €1 to US$ 0.75 cents or €1 to US$1.20, the future could be far less stable if either of these extremes were to happen. A failure to identify the need for contingency planning (which is considered in detail in Chapter 6) can have dramatic consequences for any business, as is illustrated in Practical Insight 2.1.

Practical Insight 2.1

Contingency planning for a devaluation

During the 1990s, Argentina staged one of the most amazing economic turn-arounds ever. From hyperinflation at the end of the 1980s, measured in '000s of percentage points (it peaked during 1989 at 20 233 per cent p.a.), by the mid-1990s Argentina had a lower inflation rate than the USA. During this period, the economy showed very strong growth in GDP, so that Argentine consumers began to feel much better off. This transformation was achieved by a new economic plan instituted by the Carlos Menem government elected in 1989 and re-elected (following a change in the constitution) in 1993. A key element of this economic plan was to fix the exchange rate of the Argentine peso to the USA dollar at parity (i.e. 1 peso = US$1).

This rate held from 1991 until the end of the 1990s, despite Argentina having massive foreign debts, very low foreign currency reserves and running a foreign trade deficit throughout this period. In December 1999 a new President was elected and he 'promised' to maintain the fixed exchange rate. This 'promise' was

> **Contingency planning for a devaluation** (*Continued*)
>
> reflected in the EIU country report, and hence the forecast exchange rate for 2000 and 2001 was 1 peso: US$1.
>
> Companies in Argentina based their planning on this critical assumption, despite the country already being in crisis talks with the IMF regarding new funding to finance the gap between foreign currency reserves and the foreign debt repayments to be made in 2000 and 2001.
>
> The ensuing economic crisis caused by the very substantial devaluation of the Argentine Peso was made much worse for many companies by the absence of any contingency plan for such a devaluation. The author has heard a number of senior company executives from this country state that the government 'said it would not devalue and the EIU did not predict it, so how were we to know'. No government has ever said in advance that it would devalue, and the EIU report very clearly stated that it was 'the government's stated plan to maintain the current exchange rate'.
>
> Externally focused analysis aims to identify those changes in the business environment that can have a material impact on the business. Predicting such a possibility does not mean that the business can stop it happening, but it does mean that the business can take steps *to minimise the impact should it happen.*

In Figure 2.2 both the planning and the control phases have five arrows coming out of their boxes, and this is to indicate that they are more important, and should therefore receive more emphasis than the analysis phase (which has only three arrows). However the balance between internally facing and externally directed arrows differs. The strategic planning exercise is carried out to devise action plans (strategies) which should achieve the corporate objectives; the analysis phase should have ensured that the objectives were realistic given the expected external competitive environment.

However any strategic initiative started by the business (such as launching a new product or entering a new market) is likely to trigger a competitive response; particularly if it starts to be successful. Alternative strategies to create shareholder value may have adverse impacts on other stakeholders who may also react; e.g. raising prices ahead of inflation or seeking to hold down input prices from third party suppliers. Thus the planning process needs to consider the impact of the proposed action plans on all those affected and to identify what possible counter initiatives they may launch.

The implementation of this game theory approach to marketing planning is considered in more depth in Chapter 4, but it should be taken one stage further. The output from the analysis phase should be used to identify what new initiatives would be in the best interests of competitors, as well as customers and suppliers. In other words, does the expected external environment enhance or diminish the relative competitive strength of our business? This can be particularly important where a range of potential future external environments has been identified if, in some of these, one business gains a significant competitive advantage while in others particular competitors do. Clearly the most appropriate marketing strategy will depend upon which of these alternative competitive environment scenarios proves to be correct. This means that a business cannot prepare one plan but must prepare a range of plans if it is to cope with an uncertain future external world.

Even more variants need to be developed if the response by competitors (or customers, or suppliers, etc.) to any proposed strategy is by no means certain. Obviously no business has the time or the resources to produce an infinite number of alternative plans, and so there needs to be a process for selecting the most important elements that need to be considered; this is discussed in Chapter 6. However the key issue is to focus back on the overriding objective to create shareholder value and the consequent need to develop some form of sustainable competitive advantage, if sustainable super profits are to be achieved.

All of these sustainable competitive advantages are, by definition, really relative statements in that they refer to things which one business does better, cheaper, faster, etc. than all others. They also need to be considered in the context of the customers who are willing to continue to pay a price for the goods or service that enables the supplier to generate a super profit. In other words, the customers must still perceive themselves as getting good value for money, even in the absence of direct, effective, viable competition. This means that the marketing finance planning and evaluation process must have this external focus in that it must include a comprehensive analysis of competitors and customers. This competitor analysis must not be limited only to obvious existing competitors, as new potential competitors may be attracted to any industry or sector that is generating super profits. Indeed, existing customers and even suppliers may be tempted to become competitors through vertical integration if the potential returns are high enough. It is essential that the company's current position is protected as far as possible by investing in creating strong entry barriers to deter all the identified potential competitors.

Finance managers are most unlikely to identify, on their own, all the potential novel marketing strategies that competitors may initiate to try to break through an existing entry barrier. Competitor analysis, as discussed in Chapter 4, therefore needs to be done as a co-ordinated effort, utilising all the knowledge and skills available within the business. Failure to identify these threats can transform the power base within an entire industry in only a few years, as is illustrated in Practical Insight 2.2.

Practical Insight 2.2

From commodity suppliers to dominant brands

In the very early 1980s the PC industry was starting and the dominant computer companies needed new suppliers for this very high growth potential product. This was particularly true for IBM which, although by far the largest and most profitable computer company in the world, was a late entrant into the PC market. In an

---

From commodity suppliers to dominant brands (*Continued*)

effort to get into this rapidly growing market as quickly as possible, IBM, unusually at the time, outsourced the operating system (to Microsoft) and the main processor chip (to Intel). It saw these items as necessary commodity inputs to a product that it would itself brand; thus IBM would take the dominant share of the total value chain. It could also switch its business to another supplier if it didn't get the price it demanded!

Over the succeeding years both Microsoft and Intel followed an aggressive branding strategy in a very successful attempt to turn themselves from subservient commodity suppliers to dominant branded goods companies. Indeed the key issues for most PC and laptop purchasers nowadays are that the machine supports Microsoft's latest version of Windows and contains an Intel Pentium processor; the name on the outside of the PC or laptop is largely irrelevant. Thus the once dominant branded computer companies have been turned into the commodity suppliers, which now need the branded components. Their relative profitabilities confirm the new balance of power.

The further changes in IBM's strategy are considered in a case study in Chapter 3.

This example of competitor analysis also illustrates the integrated, overlapping nature of a good analysis, planning and control process. Some companies regard competitor analysis as part of their pre-planning analysis effort and, indeed, once a year they analyse their competitors and issue a formal, glossy report covering their findings. Of course, if these competitors start new strategic initiatives just after this annual exercise is completed, the basis of the company's strategic plans is completely undermined. It is not important how or where you classify particular activities, as part of analysis, planning or control. These critical areas such as competitor analysis must be a continuous part of the equally integrated and continuous strategic marketing finance approach to planning and control.

The control element of this overall process has, as was shown in Figure 2.2, a greater emphasis internally within the business than on the external environment (i.e. three internal arrows compared to only two externally facing arrows). This is clearly because the focus of management control is on one's own business; we have already established that a lot of the external environment is beyond the control of any single business. What really needs justifying therefore is the continuing significant externally focused element within this control activity.

It is clearly necessary for all businesses to monitor the success with which their chosen strategies are being implemented. As already discussed, any business strategy is based on a large set of assumptions, many of which will turn out to be wrong. Contingency plans should have been prepared for the major foreseeable alternative scenarios but, for many businesses, their actual external competitive environment will contain a number of unpredicted elements. As already stated, monitoring performance against an already irrelevant plan *is not a real control process.* The control process itself therefore needs to provide a method of updating (often referred to by finance managers as 'flexing') the existing plan in order to incorporate the latest information on the real world in which the business is operating.

Once again, some businesses might argue that this is confusing control with analysis, but the key objective is to improve the decision-making within the business, not compartmentalise activities and responsibilities. This external element of control should certainly help to update the analysis element for next year's planning, as it keeps the external review up-to-date. Indeed for a few companies, where this continuous process is now well entrenched, it is almost impossible to state where analysis stops, and planning and control start. This is indeed how it ought to be, but it is not necessarily the case as is illustrated in Practical Insight 2.3.

Practical Insight 2.3

Planning managers prepare plans!

Many years ago (or at least it seems like it), soon after I had qualified as an accountant I moved into industry and was given the job of planning manager for a division of Mars Ltd. Basically the job involved working with sales and marketing managers and operational managers to prepare regular revised plans for the business. These proposed plans were presented to the top management team and, once approved, they were passed to line managers to be implemented.

As the business started to fall short of these plans, my job was to produce a revision to the plan; in fact, we produced a revised forecast every month, although some of the changes were quite small. Quite soon, the top managers decided that the planning process was quite good (after all they eventually approved each plan before it could be implemented). However the control process must be deficient as the business was not achieving these excellent plans.

Their solution was to promote me to Financial Controller so that I then had responsibility for both the preparation of the plans and their subsequent implementation.

Suddenly, the fun went out of life! I could no longer produce a superb plan to takeover the universe and then throw it over the wall of the organisational structure for my colleagues to try to achieve. Scarily, I still today come across quite a lot of companies that have planning managers whose entire role in life is to prepare plans. Even worse, as discussed in Chapter 6, there are planning managers in large organisations whose main role in life is to make sure other people plan!

The financial planning and control process

The main objectives of any financial planning and control process (whether or not it follows the continuous, integrated strategic marketing finance approach

Figure 2.3   *The very simple business model*

advocated above and throughout this book) are to enable the organisation to develop, implement and control a strategy that seeks to achieve its long-term objectives and overall mission. A good control process would indicate when modifications were needed in the overall strategy through short-term feedback loops and appropriate performance measures. Thus, as indicated in Figure 2.3, the long-term objectives must be consistent with the short-term budgets actually used by the company on a regular basis.

It is an obvious but important statement that the current year's budget must be the first year of the long-term plan but, in many companies, this does not stay the reality as the year unfolds. No plan is ever implemented without significant modifications not least because, as already discussed, there are always unforeseen changes in the external environment. Hence, during the year, the tactics and even the strategy may need to be changed. It is important that these required changes are, as far as possible, still consistent with the long-term objectives of the business. At least these long-term objectives should be taken into account as the possible modifications to the strategy are being considered. If necessary the objectives themselves may need to be modified, but the required supporting information for such an important decision must be readily available, as is shown by the feedback arrows in Figure 2.4. This feedback and modification process is developed in more depth in Chapter 6. Unfortunately, in many cases, changes are made during the year that enable the short-term budget to be achieved at the expense of these long-term objectives.

This can happen because the performance measures in use within most businesses focus almost exclusively on the short-term budget period (i.e. the current financial year). This would not necessarily matter as long as these performance measures included clear indicators of how the business

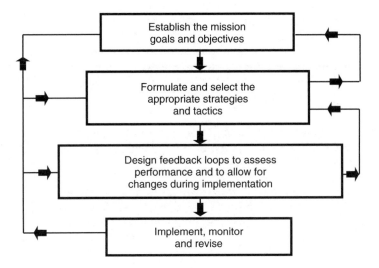

Figure 2.4   *The strategic management process*

was doing in terms of its long-term objectives (e.g. market shares, brand health indicators, penetration of new customers). In most cases these longer-term performance indicators are missing. It is, as already mentioned, quite common for the main performance measures to focus on sales revenues and profits this year, even though the marketing strategy may be based on the business developing new sustainable competitive advantages. This concentration on short-term performance increases the pressure on managers to compromise on longer-term investments in order to deliver the required financial performance now. Marketing activities often bear the brunt of this because, as mentioned in Chapter 1, marketing expenditure is regarded as an expense in the current year. Few managers would seriously consider stopping halfway through building a new factory, yet many companies curtail development marketing expenditures in order to hit this year's profit target.

It is therefore very important that businesses develop an appropriate set of performance measurements, which are both closely integrated with their long-term objectives and provide early indications when things are not going to plan. (This is the focus of Part Four of the book, where all of these issues are discussed in more depth.) A business needs performance measures at three different levels if it is really to stay in control of its long-term performance; these are shown in Figure 2.5.

The highest level of performance measure relates to the overall economic performance of the company, as this is of fundamental interest to its shareholders. In other words, is the business operating in attractive

Performance measures are needed at three levels to indicate:

❶ The economic attractiveness of the industry/sector
 ◆ Can shareholder value be created in this industry?
 ◆ Are entry/expansion strategies or exit/rationalisation
 strategies more appropriate?

❷ The relative competitive performance of the business
 ◆ Absolute performance is meaningless unless placed in its
 appropriate context.

❸ Internal measures of the key areas for this business
 ◆ The relative competitive positioning within the specific
 external environment will highlight the key areas for
 attention within the business if the strategic objectives are to
 be achieved.

Figure 2.5 *Strategically relevant business measures*

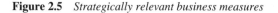

markets and industries where shareholder value can be created? If not, the long-term strategy should be either to improve the competitive environment (e.g. rationalise the industry or develop some new differential advantage) or to exit from this industry in order to invest in more attractive areas.

This top level of performance measure says very little about the relative performance of the business and its managers. In certain very financially attractive industries, the relatively few companies involved may all earn super profits and thus create shareholder value. Equally, in an over-supplied, extremely unattractive industry, the best management team in the world should lose less money than the rest, but they will find it impossible to create shareholder value. Thus, the second tier of performance measure is needed to put the absolute level of economic performance into an appropriate relative context; a 30 per cent p.a. return on investment looks decidedly less impressive if all the competition is achieving over 50 per cent.

This introduces a key issue for performance measures. Some performance measures are designed to reflect the economic performance of the total business or of a particular part, while others focus on the managerial performance of the people running the total business or specific parts of it. Few performance measures work well in both areas because, while economic performance measures *must* take into account *all* the factors affecting the business, managerial performance measures *should only* include elements where the manager whose performance is being assessed can exert some degree of control. It is unfair, and extremely demotivating, to hold managers accountable for something over which they have no control.

At the very top of the organisation, there may be very little need to distinguish between economic and managerial performance measures. As far as shareholders are concerned, it is the board of directors' responsibility to ensure that their company is involved in attractive markets; thus entry and exit decisions can re-position the company as necessary. At lower levels within the business, managers have increasingly less freedom of action or managerial discretion; i.e. a southern region sales manager cannot normally decide they would rather base their business in the north or sell a completely different range of products, manufactured possibly by a competitor. Hence different managerial performance measures must be used for different levels. The challenge, which is discussed in Chapter 12, is to ensure that each level of performance measure is consistent with the overall objectives of the total business. This concept, which is generally known as 'goal congruence', is based on the very simple but very true maxim of 'what you measure is what you get', i.e. people tend to try to achieve the objectives they are set. If, by achieving these objectives, they move the business away from its long-term objectives and strategy, it is the fault of the people setting the objectives, not the people doing the achieving; this is illustrated by Practical Insight 2.4.

Practical Insight 2.4

Achieve the measure, earn the bonus!

Having been promoted to the role of financial controller as discussed in Practical Insight 2.3, I now had much greater responsibility for achieving the key performance measures set by the group for the business division. Mars Group is well known for setting its businesses quite aggressive financial targets but these are always expressed in terms of 'Return on Total Assets' or ROTA. ROTA is calculated as profit before interest, tax and depreciation divided by the total assets invested in the business and expressed as a percentage. (Total assets is used to stop managers playing games with payment terms to suppliers, which can be done if return on net assets is used, as is the case with the majority of companies.)

This immediately means that there are two sometimes conflicting ways of increasing ROTA; profit can be increased by selling more goods, raising prices or reducing costs, or assets can be reduced. Sizeable bonuses are paid to the management team if ROTA targets are exceeded, so there is a strong incentive to do this. In many businesses, particularly where the target returns are high (e.g. over 40 per cent before bonuses are earned), it may be easier to achieve this by restricting investment in new assets, or even massaging the accounting treatments of certain items where possible (this is developed in the main case study in Chapter 6). This may be done even though the long-term strategy of the business is to go for growth while the markets it is involved in are themselves still growing, as is discussed later in this chapter.

The third level of performance measure should be very specific to the particular business and its long-term objectives. These measures must be appropriately tailored to the particular business and the level within the business at which they are being applied. It has already been established that there is a vast range of potentially successful competitive strategies, which are based on a specific set of sustainable competitive advantages. Several of these different strategies may be successfully implemented in various segments of the same industry at the same time. The performance measures used should be appropriate to the specific requirements of each different competitive strategy. This clearly means that different companies in the same industry may be using very different performance measures. Indeed the focus of their marketing finance planning and control system should probably have far more in common with a company in a completely different industry, but which is implementing a very similar strategy, than with a company in its own industry that is implementing a completely different strategy. This is illustrated in the case study described at the end of this chapter. A key issue therefore for a really good marketing finance process is that it is tailored to the needs of the business. This means that, if the needs of the business change because the strategy has changed, the tailored performance measures used in the business should also change. Unfortunately many companies are struggling to control their marketing activities because they are still using control systems and performance measures designed for previous competitive strategies.

One way of illustrating this problem uses a development of the well-known Ansoff matrix to highlight the different strategic thrusts that a business can have. The Ansoff matrix has been widely used for many years as a marketing planning tool, as it very simply illustrates the possible ways in which a business can try to fill the gap between its current level of performance and that required to achieve its long-term objectives. The beauty of the matrix is the clarity with which it describes these strategic options, i.e. increase the share of existing markets with existing products, sell new products to existing customers, sell existing products to new customers, or sell new products to new customers.

The Ansoff matrix illustrated in Figure 2.6 has only been modified from its original format in terms of the descriptions applied to the boxes for selling new products to existing customers and selling existing products to new customers. Before considering these, the other two possibilities will be briefly examined from a marketing finance perspective.

The implications of growing a business by selling more existing products to existing customers (the top left hand box of Figure 2.6) have been extensively researched over many years, with some amazingly obvious results. (One of the wonderful aspects of being an academic is that you can spend a lot of time researching something that is blindingly obvious to most practitioners.) Strategies to increase market share have been shown to create most shareholder value when the relevant market is itself growing strongly. This is because, if

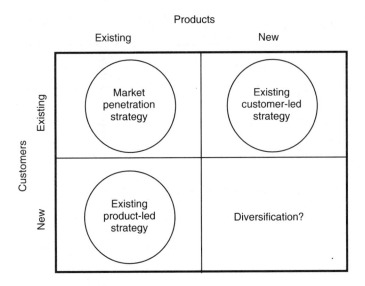

Figure 2.6   *Potential strategic thrusts of businesses (based on Ansoff matrix)*

the market is static or declining, any increase in volume by one company has to come at the direct expense of competitors. They are likely to respond aggressively, most probably through some kind of price cutting activity, which could reduce the total profitability of the industry. Thus the strategy may be successful in gaining market share but it will not necessarily generate a higher level of super profits. If the total industry is growing strongly, there is much less chance of such aggressive competitive reaction. Their own sales may still be increasing, even though they are, in fact, losing market share; the sales growth and consequent market share increase being achieved out of the new sales for the industry.

As discussed in more depth in Chapter 4, companies are increasingly using game theory-based strategic analyses in order to predict both competitive responses to their marketing initiatives and likely marketing initiatives of competition. From the marketing finance perspective, shareholder value can be separated into two phases: creating value and capturing value.

Creating value refers to marketing strategies that seek to increase the total value generated by the industry, e.g. increasing the total size of the market, adding value to existing products. Thus, it is possible for all competitors in the industry to benefit from these 'creating value' strategies, although they will not all benefit equally. Strategies aimed at creating value should result in less aggressive competitive responses; they can even be described as 'co-operative' ways of competing.

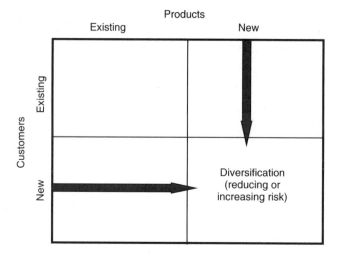

Figure 2.7   *Diversification using the Ansoff matrix*

Capturing value is all about gaining a greater share of the total value available within the industry. As a result, it tends to be a 'win–lose' game, and this can result in much more aggressive competitive reactions. In some disastrous examples these reactions resulted in dramatic price wars, which left everyone much worse off financially. The marketing finance process should therefore identify the type of shareholder value creation that should result from the proposed marketing strategy. This will help to predict the likely competitor response.

Selling new products to new customers (the bottom right hand box of Figure 2.6) has also been quite well researched, and the resulting shareholder value creation is also disappointing. A very common rationale for adopting this strategy is that it 'reduces the risk profile of the group'. However a 'new, new' strategic thrust is really an increasing risk strategy, because it is not normally built on any existing competitive advantage, as is shown in Figure 2.7.

The remaining two boxes are the modified headings for the original Ansoff matrix, because the key strategic thrust relates to the existing source of competitive advantage on which the growth strategy is based. In the case of selling new products to existing customers, this should be the loyal base of existing customers for which new products are to be developed or acquired. Correspondingly, the marketing strategy of finding new customers, segments or markets in which to sell existing products should be built on an existing successful product which is capable of generating a super profit in its existing market. These strategic thrusts are considered briefly in the remainder of this chapter but, in Part Three, each has a separate chapter that deals with the key issues in much more depth.

Brand-led strategies

Brands can be based either around products (e.g. Coca-Cola, Marlboro, Microsoft, Intel) or around customers (e.g. Tesco, Marks & Spencer, Wal-Mart, Citigroup, HSBC, Virgin). They are therefore considered before either customer-led strategies or product-led strategies, as a number of common issues can be more simply explained.

If a marketing strategy based on brands is to be shareholder value enhancing, the brand must enable the business to earn a super profit on its more tangible assets, i.e. the brand becomes an intangible asset of the business. However, brand assets can achieve such a super profit in different ways, and these different ways require appropriately tailored marketing finance processes.

A strong brand may enable the 'branded product' to be sold at a higher price than its unbranded equivalent. Alternatively, an equally strong brand could be sold at exactly the same price as other products, but command a significantly greater share of the market on a consistent basis. A third branding positioning would be to combine a slightly higher price together with a higher market share. It is important that the control process understands and focuses on the specific brand strategy.

There are a number of stages involved in developing, and then maintaining, a brand as a shareholder value enhancing asset. Some success, although not necessarily uniform success, must be achieved at each stage if the brand is to have a sustainable super profit generating capability. For a repeat purchase consumer brand these stages include awareness creation, propensity to purchase, ability to purchase (i.e. distribution), trial rates, repurchase rates, adoption rates, usage rates, and ultimately loyalty and advocacy rates. In many businesses, marketing research has developed specific effectiveness measures for each of these stages. The marketing finance challenge is to develop a comprehensive brand evaluation model that can incorporate these non-financial effectiveness measures. Several companies (such as BAT, Diageo, Cadbury Schweppes) are now using such overall brand evaluation models as key elements in evaluating and controlling their brand marketing expenditures. These models are based on the discounted cash flows that are predicted for the brand and on an assessment of the brand strength, which is used to determine the discount rate applied to these predicted cash flows (the stronger the brand, the lower the discount rate applied).

Clearly many assumptions have to be made to arrive at the eventual discounted cash flow result; i.e. the brand value, but this is not the point. Unfortunately many companies focus far too much on the resulting brand value, whereas the process should be regarded as a *brand evaluation* exercise. It is not the absolute value at any point in time that is important but the movements in the value and the directional trend in the key brand attributes, as discussed in Chapter 8. Such a model can be used in the marketing resource allocation exercise that has to be done in any planning process. It can financially evaluate proposed incremental development expenditure and ascertain the required level of maintenance marketing support. These evaluations are by no means simple and straightforward because the relative effectiveness of one company's expenditure is affected by the marketing spend of competitors.

Customer-led strategies

A customer-led strategy is designed to encourage existing loyal customers to try new products that are launched under the same brand. Retailing, particularly supermarkets, and financial services are two industries in which many companies have implemented customer-led strategies. To a large extent, they were forced to do this as it became increasingly difficult to build sustainable differential advantages around the products involved in either industry.

Thus, as shown diagrammatically in Figure 2.8, any customer-led strategy is built around the existing customers of the business. A critical question for evaluating such a growth strategy is therefore 'which customers should form the basis for future growth?' The shareholder value-focused answer is clearly to base the strategy around those customer groups from which the company can generate sustainable super profits.

This requires strategically oriented, long-term customer account profitability (CAP) analysis to be carried out. This CAP analysis should indicate the relative profitability of different groups of customers, but it should not be used as an attempt to apportion the net profit of the business among the different customers. Indeed, apportioning (or 'spreading') costs among customers can

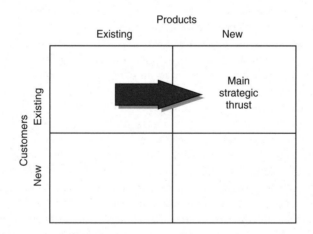

Figure 2.8 *Customer-led strategies*

destroy the main benefits from the CAP analysis, as is illustrated in Chapter 9. The analysis should support the important strategic decisions regarding which customer segments should be invested in, etc. Thus, the resulting information must be relevant to these decisions, and this is not achieved if a large proportion of indirect costs are apportioned to these customers.

The key phrase is *direct attributable costing*, where the real cost drivers for each major customer related cost are identified. These cost drivers are what causes the cost to be incurred by the business and what makes the level of the cost change. If they are accurately identified, this will indicate how customers should be grouped together. The idea is to group together customers who are treated very similarly and to separate groups where there are significant differences in the cost levels incurred and, hence, potentially in the rates of return achieved.

Many companies now operate quite sophisticated CAP systems of this sort but, if the *strategy* is to be based around customers, the analysis needs to be done on a long-term basis. Such long-term CAP analyses are less common. The idea is to evaluate which types of customers are financially worth investing in because, over their economic life cycle as a customer, the business expects to be able to generate a positive net present value from such an investment. This type of marketing strategy is commonly referred to as relationship marketing because the business tries to develop (i.e. invests in) a long-term relationship with the customer. If a relationship marketing strategy is being implemented, the marketing finance system needs to be appropriately tailored, so that these key customer relationships are managed as a long-term business asset. Thus development and maintenance marketing expenditures on customers are very relevant concepts.

Indeed, in a relationship marketing-based strategy, attention moves away from customer acquisition towards customer retention and development. The key priority is retaining and developing the most valuable long-term customers. However, in order to attract and then retain these very valuable long-term customers, the supplier must *create more value for these customers* than the competition; any sustainable long-term relationship must be mutually beneficial.

Customer value can be defined as the perceived benefit obtained by the customer less the price paid and any other 'costs' (e.g. time, inconvenience, effort) incurred in order to own the good or service. Customers who do not perceive that they are getting value from a relationship are likely to defect, probably without generating sufficient value to justify the original marketing investment.

Companies are now trying to assess customer lifetime value and are using increasingly sophisticated tools to do so. Data warehouses and data mining tools assist organisations in measuring the economic value of customers. Predictive modelling techniques can be used to predict the remaining lifetime of the relationship with the customer and the likely resultant future stream of profits and cash flows. *The economic lifetime value of the customer is the present value of the net cash flows expected to be generated from the customer.*

If the main strategic thrust of the business is based on customers, it is also important that these customers form an important element in the performance measures used within the business. If this is not done, many of the business support areas will focus on achieving their own performance measures, often to the detriment of the long-term development of these critical customer-based assets.

Product-based strategies

An alternative, but possibly equally attractive, marketing strategy is to base future growth around existing products, as is shown diagrammatically in Figure 2.9. These products may also be strongly branded, but the critical element in this strategy is that the growth opportunities are based on finding new markets, new segments or simply new customers to which to sell these existing products.

Not surprisingly, this marketing strategy should be built on those products that can achieve a sustainable level of super profit in their existing markets. Hence a focus for the tailored marketing finance system should be a decision-oriented long-term direct product profitability (DPP) analysis. As with the customer profitability analysis, the objective of DPP is to indicate the relative profitability of different product groups. Therefore, apportioning indirect costs in an attempt to arrive at a 'net profit' for each product can destroy the validity of the analysis and lead to disastrous resource allocation decisions being made; these are illustrated in Chapter 10.

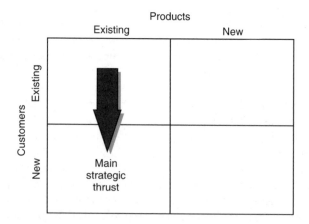

Figure 2.9   *Product-based strategies*

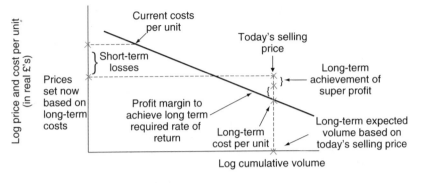

Figure caption and diagram labels:

Log price and cost per unit (in real £'s)

Current costs per unit

Today's selling price

Short-term losses

Long-term achievement of super profit

Prices set now based on long-term costs

Profit margin to achieve long term required rate of return

Long-term cost per unit

Long-term expected volume based on today's selling price

Log cumulative volume

The 'short-term loss per unit', if successful, is really an investment
in developing a long-term sustainable cost advantage

Figure 2.10 *Life cycle costing techniques. Strategic use of experience curves in setting prices*

For most businesses (and indeed for all of the large number of DPP analyses that I have personally been involved in), the allocation of directly attributable product-specific costs to appropriately grouped products can highlight significant differences in the relative profit contributions from these differing product groups. Once again if the DPP analysis is to be used to support long-term strategic decisions (such as to identify those products which should be launched internationally), the analysis must consider the long-term sustainable profitability of the products.

In some industries this requires the use of some product life cycle costing techniques because the product costs will change in a predicable way over time. It is now well established that the costs of producing many products (both goods and services) decline, in real terms, over time due to a number of factors. These include learning by employees that makes them more efficient, the introduction of new technologies and the economies of both scale and scope. These are combined together in the 'experience curve' concept, which enables businesses to predict the rate of decline of their real production costs per unit as cumulative production volumes increase.

This predictive knowledge can be used in the marketing strategy because the business could set its prices today based on its long-term costs rather than its current costs; this is diagrammatically illustrated in Figure 2.10. Such a pricing strategy would probably result in the business making a loss on its current sales, but these sales should increase rapidly as the low selling price stimulated demand. These increasing sales volumes should propel the business rapidly down its experience curve – towards its long-term cost level, at which point it should be generating a super profit. If it can gain a sustainable long-term cost advantage over its competitors by this strategy, it should regard the initial 'losses' as an investment in creating a sustainable competitive advantage.

The idea of having a sustainable cost advantage also indicates another important aspect of product-based strategies. The strategic marketing finance needs of a low cost-based strategy are fundamentally different to those of product-based strategies built on differentiated or value-added products. Thus the required competitor analysis focuses on the source of relative competitive advantage or disadvantage. Where the main basis of competition is on price, because there is no customer perceived difference among competing products, the relevant competitor analysis should concentrate on cost benchmarking. In such a commodity style, price conscious environment, the lowest cost supplier will normally win, and relatively small cost differences can be critical.

However, if the basis of competition is differentiation rather than price, an excessive emphasis on external cost comparisons or even internal cost reductions can be very counter productive. A cost difference no longer necessarily indicates a competitive advantage or disadvantage because it may be the source of the customer perceived differentiation that, in reality, creates the super profit. For these businesses, the focus needs to be on the value-adding elements rather than on the costs. Marketing finance therefore must become involved in the assessment of 'perceived use values' (where the perception is by the customers) of the differences between competing products. The perceived added value is then compared to the relevant incremental cost incurred in achieving the difference, with any resulting positive value gap being evaluated for sustainability.

Case study – Rudolph and the Elves

In an attempt to illustrate much of the above discussion, this chapter closes with a deliberately stylised and whimsical case study. However the case study is accurately based on the toy industry and has very many applications to any seasonally affected business. It aims to show how a marketing finance system must be tailored to the specific needs of each business.

Rudolph was beginning to regret his rapid rise up the managerial ladder; this time last year he had been head chauffeur but a continuing severe head cold had made him ask SC (as he was known in the business) for an indoor job. He had started as assistant stores controller but his skills and self-motivation had led to his promotion to Head of Production Scheduling and Controller Of The Corporate Headcount (HOPSCOTCH for short). One of his main roles was clearly to plan the production of the year's toy requirements, and to recruit and train the labour necessary to achieve this level of output. He had instantly identified one key problem: seasonality in sales! He had therefore approached the marketing department regarding ways in which this peak could be reduced. However, they felt that customers would be very averse to a change in delivery patterns, even if it were geographically organised. They had been trying for many years to generate additional purchase opportunities so that some spreading would take place but this had not really reduced the peak volume at Christmas.

They did accept that Rudolph's problems were increasing because their market research was becoming less reliable and was also being received later (very few letters now seemed to come down the chimney until October at the earliest). The lack of reliability and hence very late surges in demand for certain products were apparently due not only to the increasing sophistication of customers, but also to the greater product range availability which created shorter product life cycles than they had been used to in the past.

Thus, in recent years, they had been left with large unusable stocks of certain items. One potential reaction to this problem was to produce only low volumes of 'fashion' items early in the year and concentrate on making the mainly 'low risk' products in this period – this was complicated as fewer and fewer products could be classified as low risk. Such a seasonally based system did enable production to be matched more closely with demand, as the demand could be more accurately assessed, but it also increased production costs significantly.

Not only was overtime working required, but temporary labour was also hired. This meant increased training for short-term assistants. In spite of this training, Rudolph knew that wastage and rework costs would be significantly higher due to the temporary labour and tiredness on the part of the permanent employees. Offsetting this, of course, Rudolph had some savings arising from not having to rent vast outside warehouses and also in interest costs because he did not have to finance the higher inventory that would result from an even level of production throughout the year.

There seemed to be significant disadvantages to either seasonal matching or even production, but Rudolph had thought of one further option. If he invested in automated production facilities (in particular flexible manufacturing systems) then he could cope with the increased seasonal demand by running the machines for longer hours, and he shouldn't need to hire any temporary labour with all of its associated problems. If he didn't need the output he could turn the machines off and since the labour element involved would not be very great it wouldn't waste much money. Was this the answer to his problem?

Discussion of problem

Rudolph, in his employment for Santa Claus, has a number of very unusual competitive advantages which include an incredibly powerful brand name, a unique distribution system which enables deliveries to be made to all the children in the world on the same night of the year, plus the not unimportant fact that all these delivered products are given away free!

	Even production	Seasonably variable production
Advantages of system	Lower unit costs Better product quality Efficient, well-planned production – Stable well-trained workforce – Low wastage/rework Good machine utilisation	Production matched to sales – Low inventory – Low stock obsolescence – Low financing and storage costs Flexibility in manufacturing scheduling
Disadvantages of system	High inventory levels – Storage costs – Financing costs – Risk of stock obsolescence	Higher unit costs Poor quality Increased wastage & rework Poor machine utilisation

Figure 2.11   *Rudolph's initial options*

Therefore to analyse the main marketing finance issues it is sensible to place the problem in the more realistic setting of the toy industry. There are two existing strategies in use and a third, employing flexible manufacturing systems, has been proposed. Figure 2.11 summarises the advantages and disadvantages (strengths and weaknesses) of the existing options and it is clear, but not surprising, that the advantages of one system are the main disadvantages of the alternative.

In order to select the best alternative, each toy company should review its business strategy and then identify the critical success factors for that strategy. Clearly the chosen strategy should build on and emphasise the advantages of one system and minimise the impact of its disadvantages. Only then therefore can a decision be made as to whether even production, seasonally variable production or the flexible manufacturing systems should be selected.

If the toy company's marketing strategy was to concentrate on the more stable segment of the toy market (e.g. plastic toys for the 0–5 year age category) then it could logically implement an even production strategy. The risk of stock obsolescence is much lower than in the volatile high fashion segment of the market, where a strategy of seasonally variable production is thus more sensible. Also in the more stable product groups it may be more difficult to command any price premium against competition. Thus cost efficiency in production may be a significant competitive advantage, while the enhanced product quality is likely to be more relevant to these types of toys.

Should the marketing strategy emphasise the high fashion segment of the toy industry, where product life cycles are much shorter, it is much more important to have production matched to orders. This is much easier to achieve with seasonally variable production levels but, even in this manufacturing environment, there will be a need for very great production scheduling flexibility. A key focus of the marketing finance control system will be on getting very up-to-date sales information and translating this into revised production schedules. This requires information not on what is being shipped by the toy company to its wholesalers or retailers, but on what is being bought by consumers from these channels of distribution. One of the original keys to the success of businesses such as Benetton and Body Shop was excellent immediate feedback of information on what products were selling well; this has now become a critical part of most retailing strategies (e.g. using bar scanning at the check-out).

The more stable product strategy can use longer- term trend analysis to predict the demand for its products, e.g. demographics. (One of the delights of this segment is that it is actually very easy to predict how many 4 or 5 years old children there will be next year, or even in 3 or 4 year's time!) However this type of analysis is irrelevant to a very short life cycle product. Many high fashion toys are now linked to the latest blockbuster film (e.g. Harry Potter, Star Wars and Lord of the Rings) or a TV programme, and it is consequently almost impossible to predict the sales levels until the film has actually opened. This means that very, very fast marketing research is needed, and the operations of the business have to be tailored to this critical need for responsiveness and speed. Thus one good performance measure is to look at the 'cycle time' of the business (i.e. how long does it take to turn an order into a delivery); obviously reducing this cycle time by even a few days can enable more highly profitable sales to be achieved and/or avoid substantial inventory write-offs.

This emphasis on flexibility is much less important in the more stable strategy where, as already mentioned, cost efficiency is often critical. As the company is regularly producing the same product the use of standard costing and variance analysis can give good information on how efficiently the company is producing the toys, and some external cost benchmarking would provide useful additional information. This could be produced as part of the regular monthly management accounting pack, and trend information on costs could also be built up and comparisons made from year to year. In the volatile, high fashion business, some information would be needed much more rapidly than monthly, and long-term trends are not relevant; by the time the first sets of variance analyses had been prepared, the business may well have stopped producing the particular product. Thus this high fashion strategy requires fast, but approximate financial information. It can accept the necessary approximations because cost is not normally the critical success factor; product availability in time to satisfy this very short-lived demand is much more important. Many branded fashion products can achieve substantial price premiums so that cost inefficiencies can be recovered in the higher selling prices.

Figure 2.12 tries to summarise the main differences between the most appropriate marketing finance systems for these two very different businesses. As has been argued throughout this chapter, because the marketing strategies are very different their marketing finance systems, which should be tailored to the needs of the marketing strategy, should also be very different.

	Even production	Seasonally variable production
Key marketing information	Trend analysis on demand e.g. Demographics	Immediate feedback on final consumer demand and attitudes
Key operational performance measures	Standard product costing and in depth variance analysis	Cycle time Order fulfilment measures (e.g. On time in full)
Frequency and nature of management accounts	Monthly, detailed, accurate, full-pack (incorporating comparisons to last year, etc.)	Summarised, approximate, some issued daily, weekly (lots of reforecasts, no fixed budgets)
Style and nature of organisation	Stable, strong planning systems, good procedures and processes	Dynamic, flexible, chaotic – willing to change very rapidly and often

Figure 2.12   *Focus of Rudolph's marketing finance systems*

At first sight, flexible manufacturing systems would appear to have most of the advantages of both current strategies, and hence avoid their disadvantages. Various products could be produced without a drop in quality or requiring additional labour. Thus the fashion products could be produced at the end of the year, so that the marketing information was more reliable. However if the required output level can be produced in a very short period of the year (i.e. the run-up to the pre-Christmas sales periods), it is obvious that the machines will be dramatically under-utilised during the rest of the year. A major flaw in Rudolph's argument is that 'turning off these flexible machines when they weren't needed wouldn't waste much money'. Also the cost of acquiring really flexible manufacturing systems is normally much greater than traditional single function equipment. The last thing that a company wants to do is to leave very expensive plant and machinery idle: the return on investment will rapidly decline. Consequently any company will want to run its flexible machinery for 24 hours a day, 7 days a week. This may mean that the company has to expand its range of products in order to fully utilise the expensive investment in sophisticated plant and machinery. There are two possibilities and both have important strategic implications.

One commonly adopted choice is to expand the range of toys manufactured and sold by the company. The high fashion toys (whatever they may turn out to be this season) are produced late in the year, but much more stable demand toys are produced on the flexible machinery during the first 9 months of the year. This sounds very efficient but it is critically important that the company implements a strategically oriented costing system. The flexible machinery is very expensive and its high cost is recovered through a depreciation charge to the products it is used to manufacture. However the stable demand products that are produced for most of the year could have been manufactured using much cheaper, dedicated machinery in the even production strategy. If these products are charged a depreciation cost representing the extra investment required for 'flexibility', they will look very expensive and may be unprofitable – remember, it is unlikely that any price premium can be obtained for this type of product. The cost driver (i.e. the cause of the cost being incurred) of the extra investment in flexibility is the desire to produce high fashion toys and, therefore, all this extra cost should be charged to these specific products. Apportioning the total costs across all products destroys the decision support nature of the marketing finance analysis that is being prepared. Unfortunately very few companies seem to have product costing systems which directly allocate and attribute costs to products in this way.

The second way of expanding the product range is to produce products other than toys. If the flexible manufacturing system enabled almost any form of plastic injection moulded product to be produced, the company could produce high fashion toys in the run-up to Christmas but manufacture a wide range of other plastic goods during the rest of the year. This more clearly results in a very fundamental change in the business strategy as marketing toys is now only part of the business, and marketing would need to understand the requirements of many other customers. Indeed it is quite easy to see how the whole emphasis of the company's strategy could change from being a marketing-focused, toy company to a technology-oriented, plastic goods manufacturing company. In fact, it was observing just such a change in one company's strategy that led me to write Rudolph and the Elves as a case study!

An alternative strategic response would be to identify the key shareholder value process within the business and to concentrate on this. In the seasonally variable production strategy, the company needs to be very good at understanding its market and very, very fast both at getting information from this market and the products back to the market. What it doesn't have to be brilliant at is manufacturing the products, either in terms of their cost or, interestingly, their quality in many cases. Therefore what many such marketing-focused businesses now do, in the toy industry and in other rapidly changing industries, is to outsource the actual production of the products. In some cases this may be the total product while other companies retain some elements, such as final assembly. This enables the company to focus its key resources on the rapidly changing demands of its many customers, while its suppliers only need to focus on satisfying the requirements of one customer (our marketing-focused company).

This approach is followed throughout the rest of the book, where financial techniques and concepts are discussed in the context of the overall business strategy, but particularly the critical marketing strategy. Hopefully, by the end of the book, the reader will be able to carry out a much more exhaustive analysis of Rudolph's problems and suggest the optimum solution.

To send any suggested solution to Rudolph – write it out and then burn it on an open fire, so that the smoke goes up the chimney!

Part Two
Analysis and Design

3 The Strategic Management Process: Setting Goals and Objectives

Overview

Most modern businesses are quite complex and consequently need to develop and control strategies at several levels within their organisations; ranging from the overall corporate strategy at the top, down to the very detailed competitive strategies needed for each different product/market interface. The challenge for such groups is to ensure that each level in these structures makes a positive contribution towards creating shareholder value; achieving this may require changes to the organisational structure.

The strategic management process should start with a vision statement ('what the business is') and/or a mission statement ('what the business wants to be'). These unquantified statements are made increasingly more specific by the development of goals and objectives for the organisation. However different groups of stakeholders may need specific goals and objectives which are directly relevant for them; it is clearly important that these goals and objectives are all mutually compatible, and all in line with the overall mission statement.

For even simple, tightly focused businesses translating the mission statement into practically usable objectives and strategies can become quite complicated. Normally specific functional objectives and strategies need to be established. For larger, more diverse groups, the challenges are correspondingly greater. Each group needs to consider how its organisational structure impacts on the achievement of its overall mission and corporate goals and objectives. The most relevant structure is often to break the group into strategic business units, where each such division has responsibility for external customers and/or a specific range of products. However many large groups have now adopted mixed structures, where market focused divisions are supported by functionally based centres and some internally driven businesses (such as IT, marketing research). These mixed structures often create as many problems as they solve, but the key objective is to obtain economies of scale in the more general groupwide activities and processes while achieving clear market focus where specifically required at the divisional level.

In large groups, the costs incurred by the corporate centre can be significant and many such centres are consequently seen as destroying part of the shareholder value that has been created by the market-focused divisions. It is possible for corporate centres themselves to be shareholder value enhancing but in order to achieve this they need to have a very clear understanding of the role that they are fulfilling.

Another strategic issue for many businesses is their level of vertical integration. Industries almost inevitably start out being very highly vertically integrated but, as they mature, many go through a 'vertical disintegration' process. The strategic management process should enable sound strategic decisions to be made on whether the current or proposed level of vertical integration is appropriate for the stage of development of the industry. Unfortunately many companies failed to spot the potential transition from specialist supplier, helping to make the industry less vertically integrated, to potential competitor, taking over much of the shareholder value created by the industry, until it was too late. The transfer pricing system used within vertically integrated industries is critical in identifying those elements in the industry value chain that actually generate super profits. The value-creating elements must be protected against potential new entrants which may appear as specialist suppliers.

Organisations should focus on business processes so that they understand which processes truly add value. There are three different classifications of business process from this perspective. A few processes generate the super profits of the business and the strategic management process must identify these, so that they can be protected. There are some activities that do not add value and are not essential to the achievement of the company's objectives and these should be discontinued as soon as possible. However most business processes do not create shareholder value but they are essential; in other words, they need to be done but at the minimum cost possible.

Multinationals, and aspiring global businesses, face a number of additional risks and thus need to understand and effectively communicate across the organisation their risk-taking appetite; neither high nor low risk taking is necessarily very good or very bad, it is simply very different.

Introduction

Most financial investments should today be viewed as two-stage processes. Investors (i.e. primarily shareholders but including other providers of funding, such as banks) put money into a business in the expectation of receiving a more than acceptable future return relative to their perceived risk profile. As shown in Figure 3.1, the business invests these available funds in a range of business projects (products and markets, business divisions, etc.). These projects may involve a number of unrelated products being sold in a range of diverse markets. Indeed the complexity and scale of most modern corporations have

The two-stage investment process

In a perfectly competitive market, the portfolio of projects will always achieve exactly the return demanded by shareholders and other sources of finance, i.e. no value is created.

Figure 3.1 *Adding value*

effectively removed the investors from any possible direct involvement in, or even evaluation of, the detailed *competitive strategies* which are selected and implemented for each of these product-market-related investment projects.

As a result, investors have to base their investment decisions on a broader evaluation of the probable success of the *corporate strategy* for the whole group in which they invest. However, the development of such a two-stage process can significantly increase the costs of the investment process. Consequently there is a need for modern companies to demonstrate how their corporate strategies, as opposed to their detailed competitive strategies, create shareholder value, rather than merely adding cost. This means, that for the majority of today's complex organisations, strategic management should be a multilayered process that looks at the value-adding role of each level in the organisation.

Strategic management has already been defined, in Chapter 2, as an integrated management approach which draws together all the individual elements, including the critically important marketing strategy, involved in planning, implementing and controlling a business strategy; business strategy, however, now encompasses overall corporate strategies, detailed competitive strategies and all levels in between. In this part of the book, we are concentrating on the analysis and design phase of our iterative analysis, planning and control process. Thus the focus is on understanding the business environment in which the business currently is, and will be in the future, operating; although the overlapping and integrated nature of the process should be remembered. In Chapters 4 and 5 the areas of competitor analysis and existing position appraisal are considered, while this chapter looks at some of the key issues involved in designing a strategic management process for a modern company.

Many businesses start out as tightly focused, owner-managed organisations with a very restricted range of products serving an incredibly well-defined market. At this stage there should be little, if any, conflict between the corporate objectives, which have been defined from the overall mission statement, and the detailed competitive strategy which is actually being implemented. Except of course that, at this stage, very few businesses have clearly defined mission statements, corporate objectives or competitive strategies. Even so, the combination of controlling investors and senior managers as the same people means that there is not yet any gap between the aims of owners and the key internally based strategic decision-makers. Also the restricted product/market interface of the organisation normally means that the competitive positioning of the initial operation is quite easily decided. It is during the ensuing growth phase and beyond, for successful start-ups, that the complexity of larger group organisation structures appear and frequently threaten the continued success and shareholder value creation of the business; unless the strategic management process develops and adapts to *its* new environment. Hopefully it already comes as no surprise that the strategic management process should therefore be tailored to the specific needs of the organisation and the stakeholders who are involved in the business. These stakeholders are diagrammatically represented in Figure 3.2 and some of their conflicting needs are illustrated in Practical Insight 3.1 and throughout this chapter.

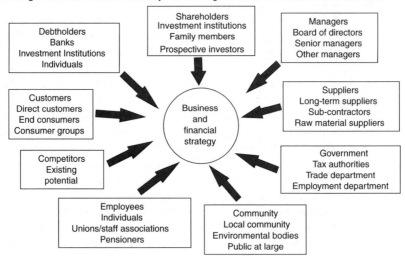

Figure 3.2   *Stakeholders versus shareholders*

Practical Insight 3.1

From public to private – an increasing trend

An increasing number of high-profile and very successful business people are coming to the conclusion that running a publicly quoted company adds far more cost and aggravation than it adds value. One of the earliest and most vociferous complainants was Sir Richard Branson. He floated his Virgin group on the stock market but very soon raised private funding to buy back all the shares that had been sold to external shareholders. He argued that the communication problems involved in talking to 'the city' and what he perceived as the 'short-term focus' of the stock market were having a significant adverse impact on his long-term strategy.

A much more recent example has been the spectacular success of Philip Green in his privately funded takeover and rapid turnaround of the previously publicly quoted BhS and Arcadia retail groups. He has attributed at least part of his success to his ability to communicate his key strategic focus directly to the key stakeholders (in this case, employees and suppliers) in the business. Having proved his abilities, he is, at the time of writing, in a position to mount a potential £3 billion plus bid for Safeway (the supermarket retailer) without needing to consider the use of the public capital markets.

Both of these entrepreneurs, plus an increasing number of others, are finding it easier to implement their long-term strategies without the involvement of a large body of external shareholders.

Mission, goals and objectives

These terms have already been used and it is therefore sensible to clarify their meanings. Unfortunately there does not seem to be universal agreement on the differences between these terms, but at least in this book they will be applied in accordance with their most literal interpretation and in the heirarchy shown in Figure 3.3.

Figure 3.3   *Hierarchy of business aims*

The most general and vague is 'the vision statement', which encompasses the way in which the organisation would like to impact its environment. This can become so lofty and altruistic as to be of no value; expressing how 'the world will become a better place due to the existence of this company'. More usefully, a vision statement sets out the long-term general aims of the business. By keeping the statement general and the timescale imprecise, the stated vision may be unachievable in practical terms but can still provide a target for the organisation to keep heading towards.

Many organisations regard vision statements as unhelpful and select 'the mission statement' as their most general expression of purpose. A mission statement should reflect the specific role that the business plans to fulfil over the long term. It therefore implicitly excludes areas of activity as well as expressly including others. The mission does not have to be prescriptive in terms of the goods and services supplied by the business as these products will probably change over time. However the mission statement should indicate the sectoral focus of the organisation (e.g. fast moving consumer goods, added-value convenience food products, business services, etc.). Despite this, it need not define specific direct customer groupings that will be targeted as these may also change over time as new channels of distribution are developed. For example, increasingly consumer goods companies can target their end consumers directly by using the Internet and other direct channels rather than selling through wholesalers and retailers; this has not changed their 'missions' which are still to be 'consumer' goods companies.

The major benefit of having a mission statement (and/or a vision statement) is to communicate the 'organisational purpose' to all the stakeholders who interact with the business. These stakeholders include employees, shareholders, customers, suppliers, etc. as was shown in Figure 3.2, and the mission statement should help them to understand what this particular business is all about. This means that the mission statement should be clear as to the critical, long-term positioning of the business with regard to quality, service, price, etc. Also, as discussed in Chapter 6, many companies now include statements regarding 'corporate values' and 'guiding business principles', which cover attitudes to employees and their working environments, customers and suppliers, as well as shareholders.

The mission statement should not contain specific financial objectives or target rates of return for shareholders, because these will change over time and with market conditions. However many companies do include relative adjectives such as 'leading', 'best', 'largest', etc.; if so, these adjectives must be placed in a proper context so that the meaning is not contentious. Does being 'the largest company in the washing powder industry' refer to sales revenue, profits, assets employed or the size of the actual packets of washing powder sold? Also is the 'industry' being considered global, regional, national or local? More seriously, given our focus throughout the book on turning marketing strategies into shareholder value, any reference to 'largest', 'best', etc. should be followed by indicating how this positioning would assist in increasing shareholder value. In some industries, economies of scale are so dominant that there is an obvious and direct linkage between size (i.e. having the largest sales revenue) and financial value created. However, in many industries the greatest shareholder value is generated by businesses occupying very well-protected niche positions, rather than supplying the greatest volume across all market segments. This necessary marketing focus in mission statements is now more common and many companies have even adopted the maxim that profit follows, rather than leads, the successful satisfaction of market requirements. For these companies long-term super profit generation, and consequent shareholder value creation, remains an integral part of their corporate mission but they accept that profits come from the business being successful. This can only be achieved by selling products that create satisfied customers.

Thus in general we can say that the vision statement describes 'what the business is', while the mission statement states 'what the business wants to be' in overall terms. These general statements that apply to all stakeholders in the business need to be translated into more understandable statements for the different groups of stakeholders; this is the role of the organisation's goals. Thus separate 'goals' may be established for customers, employees and suppliers, as well as for shareholders.

It is at this level of establishing more specifically relevant aims and targets that the organisation may come up against conflicting desires. All the different groups of stakeholders may be quite happy with the organisation's overall mission statement, but they may have very different emphases which only become highlighted when separate goals are developed for each group. For example if the mission statement referred to the 'development and marketing of high-quality products' in a specified sector, shareholders would probably assume that 'high quality' would result in high relative selling prices and consequently high profit margins. Customers may have interpreted this as 'good value for money' and resent any attempt to charge above average selling prices. Employees might be expecting the 'high-quality products' to lead to a dominant market share with consequent positive impacts on employment prospects and pay levels. The business has to develop mutually compatible goals for each of these separate groups of stakeholders which are in line with the overall mission statement so that these potential conflicts are minimised, but without creating confusion or communication problems in the future. Goals are established for shorter time frames than the mission statement, but they should not need to be changed dramatically in the short term.

This means that the strategic management process needs yet another, more measurable set of aims, and these are provided by the objectives of the organisation. These objectives will normally provide a more quantified statement of the goals of the business, and detailed strategies are then designed to achieve these objectives. This makes it critically important that the right objectives are established both in terms of the business direction which they set and the level at which the desired performance is established. Objectives have to be realistic and achievable, if they are to form a meaningful basis for monitoring actual performance against; this is developed in Chapter 6 in terms of different business attitudes towards objective setting. This is much less important when setting a vision or mission statement, as an 'idealistic' ultimate target can still be worth having, but as the aims of the organisation are made more definitive they should also become more practical. In order to achieve this level of practicality, the objectives should be set in the specific context of the external environment in which the business is, and will be, operating. This requires that both internal and external constraints are taken into account; these issues are discussed in Chapters 4 and 5.

It is also important that these quantified objectives focus on the correct strategic areas of the business. Far too many businesses still get this totally wrong; they establish a good mission statement aiming to be 'the best company in their chosen sector', they develop a well-focused, integrated set of goals which set out what being 'the best company' would mean for each key group of stakeholders, and they reduce all this to a single measurable objective which is to grow profits at 20 per cent per year! While it is true that it is much easier to assess whether profits have grown by 20 per cent year on year, than to decide if the company is getting 'better' or is actually 'the best'; it is obviously an inadequate single performance target on which to base the design of the company's competitive strategies. It is this excessive focus on purely financial objectives that leads to management behaviour that frequently results in the achievement of the objectives of the business at the expense of moving closer to the goals and mission of the overall organisation. The objectives must be more quantified, measurable (and hence possibly shorter term) derivatives of the organisation's goals; thus, each important group of stakeholders for whom a separate goal is established should be represented in these business objectives. The supremacy of financial objectives means that shareholders appear to dominate but, as previously stated, super profits *result from* the development of a sustainable competitive advantage and the creation of satisfied customers. An exclusive use of any financial measure can create major problems for even the most successful business, as is illustrated in Practical Insight 3.2.

Practical Insight 3.2

Hoist with its own petard!

Sir Clive Thompson, Chief Executive of Rentokil Initial plc, became known in the city of London as Mr 20%, because his group delivered this level of earnings per share growth for year after year.

Rentokil, as its name implies, started life as an 'infestation control consultant' (or 'rat catcher' to most of us) but grew into a widely spread business services group. The company's rapid growth coincided with an equally rapid expansion in the business services sector, as more and more companies looked to outsource non-core support activities. Much of this growth was by acquisition and these deals were financially engineered to assist in delivering the targeted e.p.s. growth. Mathematically, as any business grows and grows, it needs to find bigger and bigger acquisitions to create the same proportionate positive impact on its e.p.s. growth. Eventually, in other words, the business becomes dependent on more internally generated organic growth. The sector's rapid expansion was itself starting to slow by this time, and continuing to generate this rapid annual increase in earnings per share was becoming ever more difficult.

Unfortunately, but not surprisingly, for Sir Clive and Rentokil Initial, its shareholders had got used to 20 per cent p.a. growth. Consequently, when the group eventually failed to deliver 20 per cent (delivering a pathetic 17 per cent instead!) the share price fell significantly. It fell much further when Sir Clive re-based future growth expectations to the 'low double digits' level, even though this still represented significantly better performance than the business service sector in total.

Multilayered strategic management process

As discussed above, all organisations should have an overall vision and/or mission statement. For simple, tightly focused businesses, this statement can then be developed into a series of appropriate goals. These goals can themselves be translated into quantified corporate objectives so that the most suitable strategies can be selected and implemented. However, even for such a well-defined business, these overall objectives will almost certainly prove to be inadequate, because organisations simply do not function as total entities. In order to achieve the overall corporate objectives, strategic decision-makers will have to choose among alternative marketing strategies, different operational methods, various human resource policies, and a range of potentially innovative ways of financing the business. In other words, appropriate functional strategies have to be selected but many of these alternative *functional strategies* may be incompatible with each other. An early stage in the strategic management process, even in this simple business, must be to ensure that an internally consistent set of *functional objectives* is established; thus hopefully automatically ruling out mutually incompatible functional strategies. This requires feedback loops to allow for any required modifications to individual functional objectives or even to the overall corporate objectives.

There is, therefore, a hierarchical set of interdependent strategic objectives in even a simple organisation. Not surprisingly, in the case of a large, diversified group the problem of turning an overall mission statement into a set of specific measurable objectives can be much greater. While it may be possible to set out, for the organisation as a whole, goals and objectives that are appropriate for the corporate mission, this can be a meaningless, irrelevant exercise if the actual business is carried out by a group of smaller business units.

Historically, large businesses were normally organised on either a functional or a divisional structure. A functional structure obviously groups together all the functional skills and activities into one area ultimately under the supervision of one line manager (e.g. the marketing director, who has direct control over *all* the product and brand managers); this type of organisation is illustrated in Figure 3.4. The justification for this type of organisation structure is primarily that, by concentrating all the similar resources together, the greatest possible economies of scale can be realised; also better quality specialist managers may be attracted to, and retained within, these larger functional areas. However, such large functions may lack a close market focus and may see 'developing their expertise' as more important than serving the needs of the group's customers. This is a common criticism of centralised marketing functions and product development activities.

The best way of focusing managerial attention on specific markets is to subdivide the business into separate divisions that are given control over all the functions they need to make them almost autonomous businesses. Normally the central management of the organisation retains control over some key elements, such as funding, which stops the divisions being truly independent but can still allow a good degree of strategic discretion. It is also quite common to create divisions which only provide internal support services (e.g. marketing

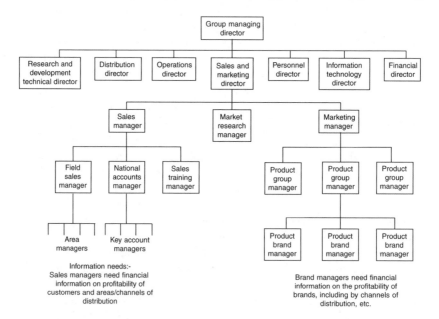

Figure 3.4   *Functionally based organisation structure*

research, information technology), or where one particular process/function (e.g. manufacturing) is grouped together to gain economies of scale (e.g. production efficiencies) but where all the output is sold within the group. (There are a number of control issues raised by the different methods used to charge for these services and these are considered in Part Four.)

The most relevant divisions of a group for strategic management purposes are, not surprisingly, called strategic business units (SBUs). SBUs are defined as being divisions of an organisation where its managers have control over their own resources, and discretion over the deployment of these resources within specified boundaries. In other words, the SBU has its own mission statement and set of goals; indeed, some groups have even re-named these as 'divisional charters'. Normally SBUs will have external customers and each SBU will focus on a particular market/sector and product group; consequently it will face specific competitors that may not be shared with any other divisions within the group. This divisionally based organisation structure is shown in Figure 3.5.

One very common way of implementing a divisional structure is to split geographic regions into separate divisions (e.g. Europe, Asia, Africa, etc.). This simple approach can create a wide range of problems at each stage of the strategic management process and can also lead to some very strange geographic linkages. Many large groups will have a range of products at different stages of development and with varying levels of success, and most or all of these products will be present in most or all of the regions. Thus each region faces the same range of strategic issues, but the organisation structures do not ensure that they all choose the same solution nor does it mean necessarily that the divisions share the best solution across the group. Also most large geographic

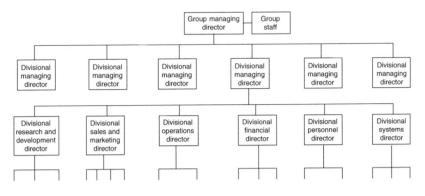

Separate functional organisations within each operating division
(replicated across all divisions)

Figure 3.5   *Divisionally based organisation structure*

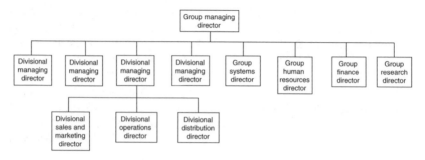

Figure 3.6   *Mixed organisational structure*

regions include some markets which have greater similarities with other markets located outside their region (e.g. Australia and New Zealand, for many products, share more similarities with North America and Western Europe than with most of the rest of Asia).

Obviously a divisional structure cannot achieve the economies of scale of a functional organisation, but the functional basis will not be as market focused. Not surprisingly, therefore, mixed organisational structures have been developed which try to obtain the benefits of both the traditional formats. A common form of such a mixed structure is illustrated in Figure 3.6, where the separate operating divisions concentrate on their existing products and markets. However, the centralised group organisation provides those overall support functions that can greatly benefit from the economies of scale that can only be achieved by carrying out these activities for the group as a whole.

Unfortunately this combined type of organisation creates almost as many problems as it solves. Although the groupwide functionally organised areas can achieve good economies of scale, there is now a high risk that they will lose the market focus that is achieved by locating smaller, less efficient units within the operating divisions. Thus the group may gain *efficiency* but lose *effectiveness* if the functional support areas do not concentrate on areas of most interest to the divisions, which they are supposed to be supporting; this is illustrated in Practical Insight 3.3.

Practical Insight 3.3

The worst of both worlds!

One very large multinational consumer goods company has a mixed organisation structure. It has six regional directors and eight global functional directors that, with one managing director, gives it an executive board of fifteen very successful, opinionated people. More importantly it creates some strategic ownership issues.

The group sales and marketing director strongly believes that the group's future success depends on the development of a focused portfolio of international brands; the area of its business where the group is currently a very poor second to its main competitor. The regional directors are responsible for delivering the current profit stream of the business and for achieving the group's short-term e.p.s. growth targets. This can be achieved from the existing mature local brands, but these have relatively limited long-term growth potential. However the international brands require significant marketing investments for several years if they are to deliver their long-term potential. This high marketing support would depress current profits: each regional director is unwilling to accept this negative impact on *their own regions*, although they all accept that *the group* needs to develop these brands.

Another increasingly popular way of trying to solve the economies of scale issue is by creating a matrix type of organisation structure. In its simplest form, this consists of most areas of the business reporting to two different managers, who have different types of responsibilities for the area. Typically an area will have a functional boss and a divisional line manager as well. Clearly this type of structure creates a number of complications in management reporting, which require that the differing managerial roles are clearly defined and understood by all those involved and affected by the matrix.

The major roles for the overall functionally based managers are to ensure the efficient utilisation of existing resources and the development of adequate future skills to serve the strategic needs of the group. Conversely, the divisionally based managers should concentrate on the effective use of the resources under their control, or available to their divisions, so that the selected competitive strategies can be implemented.

Matrix structures have been further refined by some types of companies in order to allow at least parts of the group to be managed as a series of projects, which are resourced and staffed as required. This project-based structure is frequently used by people-based businesses such as large firms of accountants, advertising agencies, investment banks and IT consultants, which regularly need to put together multidisciplinary teams for special projects. The various types of skill may be permanently organised on a functional basis, with managers who are responsible for people development and overall resourcing levels. When a particular project team is required, the project manager specifies the people skills and career background needed for the project, together with all the other resources, and these are supplied by the resource controlling functional managers. Once the need within the project is satisfied, the individuals are reallocated to their next assignments by the appropriate resource managers. Thus the projects are really a series of temporary subdivisions of the group.

Corporate centres

The range and complexity of organisational structures that are currently in use make it clear that the strategic management process must itself be flexible enough to cope with the implications of all these possibilities. However one aspect of organisational structure is facing almost universal challenge. Corporate centres are under attack! In the major developed markets of the world, not only is the truly diversified conglomerate seen as a dinosaur from a bygone corporate era, but also the corporate centres of very many other large corporations are seen as an endangered species, facing ever increasing demands and challenges to justify their continued existence.

Corporate centres are seen as adding costs not creating value. The next logical conclusion is that these corporate centres actually destroy part of the shareholder value created by the underlying business divisions; hence the trends towards demergers, management buy-outs, re-focusing initiatives, etc. Also many corporate centres have engaged in severe cost cutting exercises and dramatic head-count reductions.

However there is some new research that indicates that corporate centres *can* actually create shareholder value but only if they focus on the most relevant activities for their group. In the space available it is only possible to give a very brief précis of this new corporate configurations model, but it should be useful as it will be applied in the case studies discussed later in the chapter. Corporate centres can either interact with their business units directly or indirectly. Direct intervention means that the corporate centre does things on behalf of the business units, while indirect involvement means that the corporate centre leads, tells, guides, inspires or motivates, etc. the business units to do things themselves. Corporate centres similarly can create shareholder value in only two ways; they can reduce the total costs incurred by the group or they can increase the value generated by the group. In this model, we have described these sources of corporate advantage as economies of scale (i.e. reducing costs) and creating knowledge (i.e. increasing value). In Figure 3.7 the style of involvement (direct or indirect) and the source of corporate advantage are combined to generate a classic 2×2 matrix (the final version of the model uses a much more attractive 'rainbow' format, which is introduced in Chapter 6). The second matrix, shown as Figure 3.8, shows how a corporate centre can create value by operating in each of the four possible combinations.

This demonstrates that there is no unique way in which a corporate centre can create value, but the corporate centre must select the corporate configuration, as set out in Figure 3.9, which is appropriate for its group of businesses and their key strategic thrusts.

The Controls configuration, where the centre focuses on imposing financial targets and controls but leaves the business divisions to decide on the detailed competitive strategies needed to achieve these targets, is suitable for large

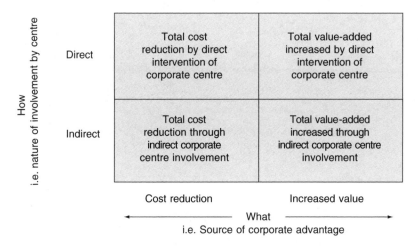

Figure 3.7 *Corporate centres: causal relationship of the model – the what and how*

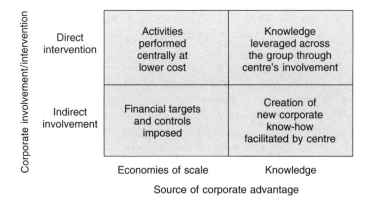

Figure 3.8 *The 'value-added' by the corporate centre*

diversified groups where the centre acts primarily as a shareholder only, such as Hanson was and Rentokil Initial may have become. The Scale configuration involves a much greater degree of direct intervention in the business units, because certain activities and processes are centralised in order to reduce total costs; this normally requires some standardisation across the group if the maximum economies of scale are to be realised. The most common areas for such cost saving centralisation are support functions (such as accounting, IT, etc.) but increasingly core processes (such as manufacturing, R&D, and even sales and distribution) are directly controlled by corporate centres. The key aspect of this configuration is that the shareholder value justification is cost reduction.

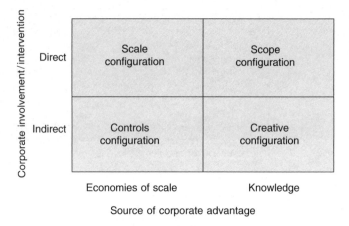

Figure 3.9   *The corporate configurations model*

The remaining two configurations are based on increasing value by either creating new knowledge or leveraging existing knowledge more extensively across the group. In the Scope configuration existing knowledge, which currently represents a competitive advantage for one division but which could have applications in other divisions, is more fully leveraged across the group. This normally means that the corporate centre needs skills in process and systems management because its role is in sharing the expertise that has been developed by the business unit. This is critically important particularly where, as is increasingly the case, this leveragable knowledge is in the marketing function of the business. The corporate centre does not 'manage the key brands centrally' or 'directly control key customers'; it makes sure that all the relevant divisions know what has proved successful elsewhere in the group and insists that this best practice is applied if appropriate.

Centralisation of brand management or customer account management actually fits into the Scale configuration as it is normally done to reduce costs by standardising advertising or sales processes, etc. For truly marketing-led groups, the Scope configuration is normally much more appropriate.

The Creative configuration is where the corporate centre acts primarily as a visionary leader, setting out the vision for the business and the way (in terms of beliefs, behaviour and style) in which this vision should be realised. The key roles are to motivate and facilitate (it has an indirect involvement in its business units) the business units to work together to create new competitive advantages for the group. Creative configuration groups are often highly innovative and there is a high degree of trust between the corporate centre and the business units; this 'trust' is often notably lacking in the Control configuration groups.

Our research demonstrates that lots of corporate centres do not really understand how they are trying to add value, while many others think that they are in one particular configuration, but their business divisions believe that their behaviour puts them in a completely different position. In some groups, the view of the corporate centre depends on which part of the business you are in, as is illustrated by both Practical Insight 3.4 and the IBM case study which follows.

Practical Insight 3.4

Confused signals

Returning to the very large multinational referred to in Practical Insight 3.3, its corporate centre manages to be in all four configurations at once. Not surprisingly, many of its divisional managers are confused about their relationship with their corporate centre.

The executive chairman and managing director consistently articulate their vision for the company as 'being the leader' in their industry globally and this includes a number of clear, but general, strategic statements. The central sales and marketing function is focused on leveraging existing knowledge by codifying several of the excellent processes, techniques and skills that have been developed around the group. The operations area is centralising several major core processes (such as manufacturing, sourcing and distribution) in order to achieve much greater economies of scale.

The group financial director is setting aggressive targets for cost reduction across the group, both at the corporate centre and within the regional structure, in order to achieve the profits growth required by the financial markets.

Each of these initiatives and emphases has been carefully thought through and is perfectly logical. The challenge is to communicate how all of these corporate centre roles come together at the product/market interface where the company ultimately has to compete successfully.

Case study – the rise, fall and rise of IBM

The rise of IBM

In 1914 the Computing Tabulating Recording Company was in some trouble and consequently recruited an outsider to sort out its problems; the next time this was to happen was in 1993. Tom Watson Sr took over a business making mechanical devices for processing data on punched cards and, from it, formed the modern IBM. In 1924 the company's name was changed to International Business Machines, and much of the famous IBM culture was established during Tom Watson Sr's period of control.

However the really dramatic growth came after the Second World War. IBM entered a period of consistently strong sales growth, with high profit margins and strongly positive operating cash flows. At first this growth was based on typewriters and, in the 1950s, IBM had 72 000 staff and sales revenues of over $500 million.

IBM did not actually pioneer the computer revolution, but it embraced it so emphatically that it rapidly came to dominate the new industry. Using its existing size, sales force muscle and marketing skills, it had taken an 80 per cent share of the USA computer market by the end of the 1960s. This growth continued even faster than its rapidly growing industry; sales revenues of $7 billion in 1970 grew to $40 billion by 1980. In 1980, IBM had a 38 per cent share of the *global* computer industry's sales revenues but a *60 per cent share* of *its profits*. This financial power enabled it to invest vast sums in R&D; at the end of the 1980s, IBM was spending $9 billion per year on R&D.

When John Akers took over as Chairman and Chief Executive Officer in 1985 (he was a lifetime IBMer), he publicly predicted sales revenues would grow from $46 billion in 1984 to $180 billion in 1994; this would actually have been a slower rate of growth than had been achieved in the previous 10 years. IBM expanded its organisation to cope with this expected growth; by 1986 total headcount was over 400 000. IBM's profitability continued to boom during the 1980s with profits after tax going from under $3 billion in 1980 to well over $6 billion in 1984 and 1985. Profits fell slightly in 1986 and 1987 but the share price continued to outperform the Dow Jones Index significantly. IBM's share price was obviously affected by the crash in 1987 but it still outperformed through the middle of 1989; the share price had been below $50 at the beginning of the 1980s, reached over $130 by 1985, peaked at $168 in 1987, but was well above $100 in early 1989.

IBM's success was built on its dominance of the mainframe computing market; at the end of the 1980s IBM had a 44 per cent global market share and an 85 per cent share in the USA of the compatible mainframe market. Mainframes contributed the vast majority of IBM's profits (60 per cent) due not only to their share of total sales but also to their very high profit margins; even in 1990 gross profit margins of 55 per cent were being generated on these hardware sales. IBM's total sales revenues in 1990 were $69 billion (including $10 billion of software, $11 billion support services and $4 billion of rentals and financing) and profits after tax were back up over $6 billion. When these results were announced, early in 1991, the share price climbed back to $130.

The fall stage

Unfortunately for IBM, the sector that it dominated (i.e. mainframe computing) was the one that was no longer growing in the still rapidly expanding computer industry. Since the mid-1980s, the trend had been towards client–server networks, and in the early 1990s this growth exploded; by 1994 client servers accounted for 50 per cent of USA total applications from well under 10 per cent at the start of the decade.

IBM was also late into the PC market and rushed its development programme by buying in the operating system from Microsoft and the microprocessor from Intel. (Subsequently IBM failed to retain exclusive rights to either of these products and the rest, as they say, is history!) Once it entered the PC market, IBM leveraged its market muscle and soon became the No.1 supplier of PCs. However even with $10 billion sales revenues, its PC business was only ever marginally profitable.

The mainframe market was not about to completely disappear overnight, not least because of the $1 trillion invested by customers in mainframe-based software systems. IBM developed parallel processor-based computers which would run these existing software systems but act as servers on networks; however these new products were not available until 1994. Also the USA economy went into recession at the end of the 1980s; it was neither a deep nor a long recession, as the economy started to grow again in 1991. However if companies are facing recession, they normally look to make savings and deferring a major expenditure item, such as replacing or upgrading the main-frame computer may look attractive.

The combined impact on IBM was substantial, its mainframe sales rev-enues fell 20 per cent in 2 years but the gross margins on these reduced sales were slashed from 55 per cent to 38 per cent. Actual gross profits on hardware sales fell from $25 billion in 1990 to $14.1 billion in 1992. Given IBM's very high fixed cost base (it still had almost 400 000 employees in 1990), this resulted in the company reporting after tax losses in both 1991 and 1992; it made significant provisions in both these years for cost cutting measures, including around 1 00 000 job cuts. Not surprisingly, the share price fell sharply and by early 1993 it was well under $50; this was not helped by a massive cut in the company's dividend payment and a credit downgrading by Standard & Poors (they downgraded IBM from AAA, the best there is, to AA-).

The second rising

On 1 April 1993, Lou Gerstner joined IBM as Chairman and Chief Executive. His impressive career had started at Harvard, followed by McKinsey (where he made principal at 28) and American Express, where he rose to President (No. 2 in the company). In 1989 he had been hired by KKR to run RJR Nabisco following its leveraged buyout, and it was from RJR that he came to IBM; thus, no high technology businesses in his background.

The first quarter results for 1993 continued the gloom; mainframe sales were down again, service sales revenues were again up sharply but they were still not significantly profitable. The share price fell to $40, which gave the company a market capitalisation of $25 billion, while its outstanding debt totalled $30 billion. (As an aside Intel and Microsoft both also had $25 billion market capitalisations at this time, but nearly 10 years before they had been worth very little while IBM had been worth $100 billion.) Within 18 months, Gerstner had changed the entire executive board and only one of the new members came from within IBM. He initially focused on reducing costs and at the end of 1994 headcount had been reduced to a total of 2 25 000, with more still to go.

The business mix continued to change; mainframe sales had fallen dramatically to $10 billion, with storage products also down to $5 billion, while the non-profit generating businesses of PCs ($10 billion) and services ($10 billion) continued to grow. However the company made a profit ($3 billion) again in 1994 on sales revenues of $64.1 billion. The big news was the $3.5 billion acquisition of Lotus Development but other than that, cost cutting and consolidation continued in 1995. In 1995 and 1996 demand for 'mainframe' computers (including IBM's new generation) re-bounded strongly and this further helped IBM's profit recovery. The major growth emphasis within the company was in the services area (systems integration, consultancy, outsourcing, maintenance), with a combination of acquisitions and organic growth. In 1997 this new focus was formally recognised with the creation of a Global Services Division; this new services business exposed IBM to a completely new set of competitors (systems consultancies including Accenture, Cap Gemini Sogeti, Sema, EDS), which applied a very different business model. The 1995 acquisition of Lotus had more explicitly opened up competition against software houses, including Microsoft, and IBM had also started to sell its technology to other technology companies (including competitors) and to buy in technology when strategically relevant or financially attractive.

During the first half of 1997, the stock market decided that the 'new' IBM was a very attractive investment and the shares, which until then had seen some good but volatile growth since Gerstner's arrival, nearly doubled in value. This took IBM's market capitalisation back over $100 billion as the shares reached record levels; there had been a 2 for 1 stock split in January 1997; so a 1997 share price of $90 was equivalent to $180 in the 1980s. (As a further aside, it should be noted that Intel and Microsoft were both, by now, capitalised at well over $100 billion.) By 1997, two-thirds of IBM's $76 billion of sales revenue came from fast growing areas such as PCs and services.

The dramatic growth in IBM's share values continued as the stock market got into its technology, media, telecoms (TMT) frenzy of the late 1990s. During 1999 the shares got very close to $200 which meant that Lou Gerstner's substantial package of stock options (granted when he joined in 1993, with a share price equivalent of around $20) had become very valuable indeed. Most IBM shareholders did not resent this because they had seen their own investments in the company transformed in one of the most amazing corporate turnarounds.

Strategic analysis

IBM's initial success in the computer industry was founded on a total focus on the needs of their major customers, together with good products. Its sales force had unrivalled access to the key strategic decision-makers in the major USA corporations and they acted almost as strategic consultants rather than computer sales people. Given IBM's emphasis on mainframes, it was very logical for it to concentrate on these largest customers that needed this scale of processing power (i.e. the big banks, airlines, car companies, etc.). This meant that IBM could develop an excellent understanding of the future systems needs of these customers and so build a strong long-term relationship; IBM was an expert in relationship marketing long before the term had been invented!

IBM also became recognised as a very strong brand, with the byline 'Nobody ever got fired for buying IBM'. In other words, it was a risk-reducing brand, in a period when decision-makers (such as financial directors) saw the new fangled information technology as a significant risk; i.e. what happens to my business if my new automated order processing system doesn't work! This enabled IBM to achieve premium prices for its products (particularly to its smaller, non-core customers) when its cost base, due to its massive scale, was potentially lower than its competitors. During its first rising, IBM was helped by these competitors, which all seemed to take 'Big Blue' as a role model and tried to copy its strategy. For example ICL, the UK-based computer company, tried to maintain a full equivalent product range despite having total annual sales revenues of $1 billion in a period when IBM was spending several times that amount on R&D.

This success had followed a classical pattern; IBM gained a dominant share of its domestic USA market when this market was itself growing rapidly, and it subsequently launched the now successful products internationally. In this second phase it was helped by many of its major USA-based customers who, during this period, were themselves undertaking significant international expansion. Its organisation structure therefore reflected the importance of its major customers (each really major customer had a main board member identified as the 'head' of its relationship management team) and its product development emphasis was on serving the future needs of these customers. The apparent profitability of mainframes was increased due to IBM's internal management system and structure. The most powerful salespeople sold the largest, most valuable systems (i.e. mainframes) and they would do almost anything to safeguard the relationship with key long-term customers. This meant that many add-on products and support services would be provided at low prices, or at cost, or even free, if it increased the probability of making the next big sale of a system upgrade. As long as mainframe sales continued to grow and their margins were very strong, this did not seem to matter.

The decline stage was triggered by several of these factors going into reverse at roughly the same time. The mainframe sector was not growing as fast as the rest of the industry because customers were buying replacement machines or upgrades, rather than being completely new purchasers. These replacement purchases will always be more volatile in demand as customers can defer the decision (the same is seen in many consumer markets). As the leader in the industry, with the closest customer relationships IBM should have been the most capable player of predicting, and hence planning for, this volatility. This highlights the biggest criticism of IBM's strategy during its period of market dominance; as Lou Gerstner put it, it started to believe that it knew what was best for customers, rather than finding out what customers really wanted and then giving it to them. In other words, as discussed in Chapter 5, arrogance and complacency were significant contributors to its decline.

Also these customers changed during this period. The mystique surrounding computers started to disappear as a new generation that had grown up with them moved into business. Customers were much less willing to pay a premium to buy the brand security offered by IBM. They wanted to pay for the best equipment to do each specific task and were now happy to have a range of IT suppliers; fewer and fewer companies are now exclusively supplied by one systems company. For IBM this created a large problem, if its brand no longer represented re-assurance then its premium pricing left it simply looking expensive in many industry segments. This was totally borne out by Financial World magazine which annually values the leading brands in the world; in the mid- and late 1980s IBM had been placed third behind only Coca-Cola and Marlboro, but by 1994 IBM had fallen to 290th (they only listed 290) with a negative valuation of $7 billion.

Competitors had also improved their strategies and were now attacking IBM on a whole host of different fronts; e.g. very cheap IBM cloned products, very expensive but incredibly specialised machines, integrated systems aimed at specific market segments. IBM was dying the death of a thousand cuts, rather than being beaten by a single full frontal assault.

The corporate culture and organisation structure did not help IBM during this period; it re-inforced the previously successful behaviour that was no longer relevant for its new competitive environment. Originally IBM's organisation allowed and effectively encouraged competition within the group, thus manufacturing businesses could produce any products within the range and quote prices to any of the sales and marketing divisions. The logic was that if we are forced to compete internally, we should be able to compete externally; given that many of IBM's divisions were bigger than its external competitors, this worked while the businesses were growing. However IBM's increasing dominance became a problem in such a rapidly changing industry. Each new generation of computers was both more powerful and cheaper than the previous one; this meant computer companies needed to sell more and more machines to get a financial return on the capital investment required for each new generation. Yet the rate of technological development was increasing, which resulted in shorter and shorter product life cycles. If IBM introduced a new generation computer, it effectively killed off sales of the existing generation that it already dominated; it was shooting itself in the foot. Therefore it wanted on one hand to extend each product life cycle until it had generated a healthy financial return, but on the other hand it needed to innovate to maintain its domination; it became harder and harder financially to justify introducing new products within the business. This explains why much of the output of IBM's massive R&D expenditure ended up being exploited by other companies; IBM could not see the financial return from introducing it itself.

Towards the end of the 1980s John Akers sought to change the organisation structure into four geographical marketing and sales units and nine manufacturing units, the thirteen units being known as 'Baby Blues'. The nine manufacturing units were 'product' or 'technology' based (e.g. storage devices) but only one (i.e. the PC division) was not heavily dependent upon mainframe sales for its profitability; as, of course, were all four marketing and sales units. Hence this re-organisation did not diminish the importance of mainframes; given this importance and the new power of these divisional managers, the proportion of R&D expenditure devoted to mainframe development actually increased prior to Lou Gerstner's arrival. Also the balance of power was still heavily towards the technologists in the company, with the role of sales to get the customer 'to buy what we have come up with'. It is self-evident that, towards the end of its first success phase, the corporate centre had no clear picture of what role it was trying to fulfil or of how the company needed to change.

Thus when Lou Gerstner arrived, with the significant advantage of no previously developed 'sacred cow' views of how high technology companies should be managed, he attacked the corporate culture and the management at the centre. He did not agree that IBM had 'poor products', he felt it had 'lousy management'. He made some seemingly minor, but symbolically important changes; he introduced casual dress to get away from the dark suit, white shirt and blue tie uniform that had previously made IBM employees so easy to spot. He encouraged IBM business groups to collaborate rather than compete; he opened up the company to buying technology if they hadn't got it and to selling their technology to other companies, including competitors. He also changed the organisation structure, and the managers heading up the organisation, so as to highlight the importance of the new growing areas of the industry and the needs of their key target customers. However most importantly he gave great clarity to the role of the corporate centre. For someone who quite famously repeatedly stated that 'the last thing IBM needs now is a new vision, mission statement or strategy'; he effectively gave the business a new vision, mission statement and strategy and a massively increased focus on shareholder value; he took IBM from a mainframe computer manufacturer back to the 'global solutions' company which it had really been during its first period of success.

Interestingly the new IBM is *still* heavily dependent upon mainframe computers for its super profits, despite the growth of its other businesses. It will be fascinating to see how well it survives the next significant downturn in USA corporate confidence and the probable resulting deferral of replacement mainframe purchases, which looks increasingly imminent at the time of writing. It will also have to do this without Mr Gerstner at the helm.

Vertical integration

It can be argued that IBM's turnaround strategy was substantially based on vertical integration with it moving further down its industry value chain towards the end customer. Such a deliberate strategic move towards becoming more vertically integrated raises interesting issues as is discussed below.

Initially the companies starting a new industry almost inevitably have to be highly vertically integrated as external suppliers of required components, etc., simply do not exist. This was certainly true to some extent for the computer industry, but even more so at the beginning of the oil industry and car industry, as is diagrammatically shown in Figure 3.10. Indeed a very famous example was Henry Ford's development of the Model T where pig iron entered one end of the manufacturing process and finished cars left at the other; the only part not produced on site were the tyres but if rubber trees could have been grown in Detroit no doubt this might have happened as well.

However as industries develop, more and more specialist suppliers become available and provide the opportunity for the original players to become less vertically integrated. These specialist suppliers can often develop sustainable competitive advantages due to their greater focus on one single segment of the

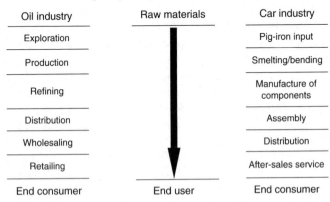

Figure 3.10   *The inevitability of vertical disintegration*

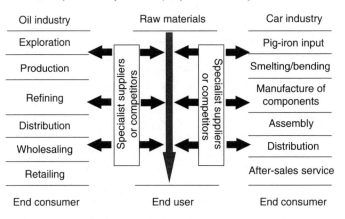

Figure 3.11   *The inevitability of vertical disintegration*

industry value chain. By supplying other companies in the same industry or in other industries requiring a similar input, these specialists can often generate significant economies of scale that can reduce the total costs incurred in the industry supply chain. As always, how this value enhancement is shared amongst the potential beneficiaries is determined by their relative competitive strength, and this can present a serious threat to the originally vertically integrated companies.

Ultimately, the industry can become dominated by focused specialist companies and this is often at the expense of these creators of the industry if they do not identify, until it is too late, whether these specialist suppliers can turn into *potential competitors*, as shown in Figure 3.11. When an industry is completely vertically integrated it is very difficult to establish which activities/processes in the total value chain really create the shareholder value generated by the industry.

Does finding oil create all or most of the value? If it is left under the desert or sea, it is much less valuable than when properly extracted, refined and distributed to a final end user. It is relatively easy to establish the total value created by the total industry, but much more complicated to break it down into its component stages. Many vertically integrated companies try to do this by introducing systems of transfer pricing from each stage to the next. Unfortunately, far too often, such transfer pricing systems are merely attempts at 'fairly' apportioning the total profitability of the industry across these stages. A major contributor to this abuse of transfer pricing is the international tax system because most tax authorities around the world will accept transfer prices based on a mark-up on the cost of the operation (for example, cost plus 10 per cent is quite common); for the tax authorities in any country, this at least ensures that they receive some taxation from vertically integrated activities carried out in their jurisdiction.

Transfer pricing systems should seek to indicate which segments of the industry value chain generate the real super profits, as these must be defended against potential competitors, including specialist suppliers. As has already been discussed, entry barriers only act as a deterrent against *potential* competitors and therefore it is important that they are erected before the specialist suppliers become established in the industry. A classic example from the computer industry relates to the development of the PC sector, already referred to in the IBM case study and in Chapter 2.

PCs were developed and launched by the existing computer companies plus a few new entrants into the sector (such as Apple Computers). These companies saw the major value creation activities as being the box manufacture and the associated branding, but they clearly needed other things to make the PC work successfully. They considered the operating system and even the core micro-processor as commodity components within the overall value chain; it was easier to get someone else to produce them, so these computer companies could focus on the really important areas of the industry. Of course it was too late to react once Microsoft and Intel had developed their own incredibly strong branding and grabbed most of the industry value share, reducing the computer manufacturers to largely commodity suppliers themselves.

Transfer pricing should therefore focus on the strategic choices facing the vertically integrated business and is another key element to be considered in designing the organisation's structure. As well as indicating which value-creating activities must be protected, a good transfer pricing system should highlight non-value-adding activities, where an exit strategy (such as actively encouraging specialist suppliers to enter) would increase shareholder value.

This really argues that organisations should focus on business processes so that they understand which processes truly add value, i.e. positively contribute to shareholder value. In practical terms this means that all business processes should be classified into one of only three categories:

1   Critical value-added processes
2   Non-value-added but essential processes
3   Non-value-added and non-essential processes.

The critical value-added processes generate the super profits of the business and the focus of the strategic management process must be to protect them and to develop them to their full potential. This means that these processes *must be kept in-house* and be managed as the key assets of the business. Any outsourcing of these processes will, over time, give away the company's source of competitive advantage; it is therefore essential that the corporate centre knows what these critical value-added processes are.

Fortunately these critical value-added processes are normally very few in number; in my experience, 90 per cent of the super profits are contributed by 10 per cent of the processes and, for most businesses, most of these processes are in the sales and marketing area. This means that most business processes fall into the non-value-added but essential classification; they need to be carried out but they add cost rather than value. The key objective for these processes should therefore be to achieve the required outputs at the minimum cost possible.

This minimum cost may be achieved by outsourcing this activity from a third party supplier and, for these non-critical non-value-adding processes this is not a significant strategic risk. However, there is a lot of research evidence to suggest that a major source of cost savings from outsourcing comes from re-defining (i.e. reducing) the expected level of the activity or process; this is particularly true for internal support activities. Interestingly many otherwise sophisticated organisations do not have service level agreements (SLAs) for *internal* support activities, but would automatically insist on them if an outside supplier were providing the service. SLAs provide a key benefit of forcing the customers (the recipients of the service) to specify exactly what it is that they require and are prepared to pay for. SLAs also provide a major benefit of enabling responsibility and accountability to be properly assigned, as is discussed in Part Four.

The non-critical, non-value-adding and non-essential processes should be discontinued wherever possible and minimised everywhere else. A key problem of many re-structuring initiatives (such as business process re-engineering) is that these processes are made more efficient, when they should be stopped altogether. Many financial control measures emphasise the efficiency with which a company's strategy is being implemented, rather than focusing on the effectiveness; this area is also developed in Part Four.

Multinationals and risk-taking appetites

There are an increasing number of companies that have expanded their mission statements and corporate objectives to include the word global, thus giving the impression that they intend to extend their presence and influence to all parts of the world. To date, I still prefer the description 'multinational' for even the most international of these companies. To be truly global, a company should not really have a home base that is significantly more important to it than any other area. Thus its businesses should be spread around the world in proportion to the relative shares of relevant purchasing capability but, more importantly, its ownership and management team should also be drawn from, and be representative of, this global base. Most companies, even very international ones like IBM, Coca-Cola, Citigroup, etc. still have a dominant home investor base and a restricted source for their senior managers.

Therefore, although there are already several truly global markets (particularly financial markets such as currencies), which do not worry about international borders and time zones, and several global brands (such as Coca-Cola, Marlboro, Microsoft and Intel), these global markets and products are serviced by multi-national companies. These multinationals do worry about the currency in which they earn their profits because, if your shareholders are predominantly based in the USA, they will want to see their financial returns expressed in US dollars. This specific risk aversion can have important consequences for the design of the multinational's strategy as is illustrated in the next few case studies based around the car industry and Ford Motor Company in particular.

Case study – multinational strategies

Overseas investments

Ford Motor Company was started in the USA and its main shareholders are still based there; hence its profits are reported externally, expressed in US dollars. However it manufactures and sells cars and trucks all over the world and this can raise significant long-term, medium-term and short-term issues for the group's central management.

The first fundamental strategic management issue is how it should regard its long-term investments in these different countries in terms of the exchange risk involved. One of Ford's earliest overseas investments was in the UK and this can be used to illustrate the issue; for simplicity and obvious confidentiality issues all the numbers in this case study have been modified but the rationale and conclusions are still completely valid. Assuming that its initial investment in the UK cost £250 million when the exchange rate was $4:£1 (yes, it really was at this level, once!), this represented a cost to its USA shareholders of $1 billion; on which they required a return of, say, 20 per cent *in US dollars*. However with the subsequent depreciation of sterling against the US dollar, this original investment would now have a converted value of only $400 million (£250 million at a spot rate of exchange of $1.60:£1). This looks disastrous at first sight, but does not necessarily represent a real economic loss to the USA multinational; it expected to generate the return on its investment through the profits and dividends produced by selling cars, not by selling the factory at some time in the future. This is illustrated in Figure 3.12, which shows that as long as profit margins on UK sales can be maintained in real terms and the sales volumes are in line with those planned at the time of the initial investment, the required US dollar denominated financial return can still be generated from the UK business.

Sterling has fallen in value relative to the US dollar because of the higher level of inflation in the UK than in the USA over this long-time period; relative differences in inflation are the primary causes of long-term movements in

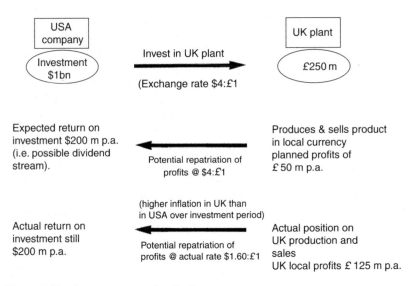

Figure 3.12 *Long-term cross-border investments*

currency values. Higher inflation means that UK incomes rose in terms of their sterling values relative to incomes in the USA. If the rate of exchange between the two currencies stayed the same, people with £ sterling incomes could travel to the USA and bring back (import) the cheaper goods. When the gap became large enough, arbitrageurs would export goods from the USA to the UK and effectively guarantee themselves a profit, as is shown in Figure 3.13. As more people did this, there would be an increasing demand for US dollars in the foreign exchange market and an increased supply of sterling; as importers into the UK sold sterling to buy dollars to pay for their imports. In any free market, such a shift in relative supply and demand leads to a compensating change in price, i.e. sterling depreciates against the US dollar until supply and demand are back in equilibrium.

	Price of goods		Rate of exchange		
	USA	UK	US$	:	£
1 Initial situation	$10 000 Car	£5000	2	:	1

The equivalent price of the product in the two markets is the same: thus no gain can be achieved by transfer.

	Price of goods		Rate of exchange		
	USA	UK	US$	:	£
2 Inflation in UK 20 per cent higher than in USA – no change in exchange rate	$10 000 Car	£6000	2	:	1

Arbitrageur can now buy the car in the USA for equivalent of £5000, take it to the UK and sell it at the new UK price of £6000.

	Price of goods		Rate of exchange		
	USA	UK	US$	:	£
3 Inflation higher in UK – exchange rate adjusts	$10 000 Car	£6000	1.6667	:	1

Buying the car in the USA for $10 000 now costs the equivalent of £6000, which is its UK selling price.

Figure 3.13 *Purchasing power parity*

Clearly this position can remain out of balance in the short and even medium term due to government interference through monetary or fiscal policy, or even regulatory impact on capital or trade flows. Eventually however market pressures will force governments to move into line with the underlying economic reality. Consequently it is valid to argue that in the long term, all relative purchasing powers in local currencies are equal; this concept is known as the theory of purchasing power parity. Higher inflation in one country will ultimately result in a decline in the value of that country's currency. The critical issues for the economic return on an investment in such a country (e.g. the UK) are whether the specific local currency selling prices will rise proportionately to the inflation differential and whether the company can maintain its profit margin during such an inflationary period. If it can, its sterling profits would be sufficiently increased so that they would convert back into the required US dollar return on the original investment, as was shown in Figure 3.12.

For the car industry and many others, this analysis was also valid for many other long-term investments. Many multinationals (including Ford) decided to build manufacturing plants in Spain in the early 1970s based on its entry into the EU in the post-Franco era of industrialisation. At the time Spain had much lower labour costs than most of Europe (particularly Germany and the UK), even after allowing for relative labour productivity. During the following decades Spain experienced much higher relative inflation levels and, consequently, local labour costs in pesetas increased dramatically. However this local currency increase was almost exactly offset by the depreciation in the relative value of the peseta, so that the relative labour cost advantage for the Spanish production facilities was actually achieved as predicted in the original financial evaluations.

In the long term, purchasing power parity works but the short-term fluctuations can create significant volatility in profits for a multinational group such as Ford; as was discussed in Chapter 1, volatility in profits increases risk perception which in turn causes increased required rates of return. A truly 'global' company might not worry about this, but most multinationals certainly do. The introduction of the Euro across most European countries has, of course, changed this, but it has also forced each of the Euro denominated countries to keep its inflation rate the same as all the rest; they cannot now devalue or depreciate their way out of trouble.

Cross-border sourcing decisions

Ford faced another cross-border problem for many years that also illustrates the complexity of strategic management in multinationals. Its production capacity in Germany exceeded its sales levels in Germany but it possessed an efficient, cost-effective plant that it wished to fully utilise. Exporting cars from Germany to other countries is one obvious solution but what if Ford also has a plant in that country (like the UK). For several years Ford was exporting cars from Germany to the UK, even though its UK plants were not working at maximum capacity. The strategic evaluation of such a sourcing decision will obviously need to be done well in advance and consequently will normally be done at planned or budgeted exchange rates. This is a good illustration of the need for the corporate centre to ensure that all divisions use a common planned exchange rate; if each business could choose its own rates, no decision would probably be reached. If the actual rates of exchange differ from these, the group must be able to change the decision if necessary, while trying to reduce the risk that such exchange rate volatility could invalidate the original decision. The logic of the initial decision is set out in Figure 3.14, using the illustration of the same car produced and sold in the UK and Germany, with the equivalent impacts being shown in US dollars (which, as previously discussed, is how the corporate centre will view the outcome); the financial analysis uses deutschemarks because the analysis of this situation related to a period prior to the launch of the Euro.

The important thing about the logic of this decision is that there are two prerequisites before it makes economic sense to manufacture cars in Germany and ship them to the UK, while leaving capacity idle in the UK. The first obvious point is that the German production costs must be relatively lower than the British equivalent; this is satisfied in Figure 3.14 with German costs of $10 000 and British costs of $12 000. This cost differential must be large enough to cover both the physical costs involved in shipping the car from Germany to the UK and any increased manufacturing costs in Germany (e.g. of producing a British specification, right hand drive car).

However the second prerequisite is that selling prices for the equivalent car in Germany must be lower than in Britain; as the group would avoid the on-costs by selling all its German production in Germany, and UK demand could still be satisfied profitably from UK production facilities. From Figure 3.14 this is also true as the German selling price is $12 000, while the UK selling price is $15 000. Indeed this lower German selling price means that, despite its superior manufacturing efficiency, the group makes a lower profit in producing and

	UK		US dollar equivalents		Germany
Budgeted rates of exchange	£1	:	$2	:	4DM
UK selling price	£7500	@$2: £1	$15 000		
UK production cost	£6000		$12 000		
Profit	£1500		$3000		
			$12 000	German selling price	DM 24 000
			$10 000	German production cost	DM 20 000
UK selling price	£7500		$2000	Profit	DM 4000
German production	£5000	@ 4DM:£1 ←		Export production	DM 20 000
New profit	£2500	@$2:£1 ⇒ $5000		◄ (Improved group profits)	

Figure 3.14 *Sourcing decision – exchange rate impact*

selling a car in Germany ($2000) than by *producing and selling* the same car in the UK ($3000). However, by combining the lower production cost base with the higher selling price, the group profit is substantially increased ($5000); this is clearly potentially a source of super profit, as long as it is sustainable. The rationale for this situation is that the UK selling price is dictated by domestically based manufacturers, that all face the higher UK production costs, while the German selling price is driven down by the more efficient, domestically based, and even more market dominant, producers. The relative selling prices in each market were also affected by the market shares of the group in each country (high in the UK and much lower in Germany).

Thus, at the budgeted rates of exchange (£1: $2: 4DM), the decision to produce cars in Germany and export them to the UK makes sound economic sense. However, it introduces an additional foreign currency exposure for the group. If the rates of exchange fluctuate, as they almost certainly will, the decision may no longer be valid and the group could end up financially worse off. If the actual rates of exchange are as shown in Figure 3.15 (£1: $1.667: 3.25DM), the decision outcome can be re-calculated. These actual rates of exchange could be caused by different rates of inflation, as discussed above; i.e. in the USA 0 per cent inflation, while the UK had an extreme level of 20 per cent. The strengthening of the deutschemark can be explained by productivity gains in excess of price rises, i.e. real cost deflation in the manufacturing sector.

If the German business could maintain its local selling price, it would show a small gain in its US dollar profits, but if it had to pass on its production cost reduction to its customers it would merely maintain its equivalent profitability. As long as the UK company is able to increase its selling prices in line with inflation, thus maintaining its real margins, it will generate the same US dollar profit. This is true for both locally produced cars and imported sales; therefore there is the same economic logic for importing cars as there was originally.

However, as argued above, purchasing power parity only works in the very long term, and in the short term exchange rates do not move directly in line

	UK		US dollar equivalents		Germany
Actual rates of exchange	£1	:	$1.667	:	DM 3.25
Increased UK selling price	£9000			Unchanged German selling price	DM 24 000
Increased UK production cost	£7200 (Converted @ £1: $1.667)				
Profit	£1800 Same US$ profit $3000				
	Increased profit on German production and sale		$2307	Reduced German production cost ← Profit	DM 19 500 DM 4500
Imported product					
Increased UK selling price	£9000	←		Reduced German production cost	DM 19 500
Imported cost	£3000 ← @ £1:DM 3.25				
Profit	£6000 Same US$ profit $5000				

Figure 3.15   *Sourcing decision – (contd) actual rates of exchange*

with relative rates of inflation. Consequently there is a risk that the actual rates of exchange given in Figure 3.15 are not caused by differential inflation rates. A further review of the sourcing decision is needed to highlight the key implications and risks involved.

If the group decides to export cars from Germany to the UK, it will leave UK capacity idle, while additional resources may be committed in Germany to meet this increased demand. There is a physical planning period during which it may be impossible, and certainly would be very expensive, to reverse this decision once taken and implemented. It could therefore be very costly if, during this physically committed timescale, exchange rates suddenly changed so as to destroy the economic logic of the sourcing decision. For example if the exchange suddenly moved to £1:3DM, the group could find itself committed to importing cars from Germany which were now *more expensive* than those it could produce locally (i.e. 20 000DM @ 3DM: £1 gives an imported cost of £6666.5 against a local cost of £6000). It would be sensible for the group to consider hedging against the possibility that a previously sensible decision becomes economically disastrous due to a change in external circumstances, as long as the hedging cost itself does not affect the logic of the original decision.

In this example this could be done by fixing the rate of exchange for the imported cars through a forward purchase agreement for the deutschemarks required. If the rate on the forward contract was better than 3.33DM: £1, the company has effectively guaranteed that the imported cars will be cheaper than the locally sourced alternative. However the group has also given up the possibility that these cars could be substantially cheaper if the rate stayed still or even went the other way! An alternative hedging strategy therefore tries to safeguard the downside risk associated with an adverse exchange rate movement but to retain the potential benefit if the exchange rate moves favourably. Thus if the exchange rate moved to 4.25DM: £1, the cost of the imported cars is reduced still further; but not if the company is committed to a forward rate agreement. This upside potential can be retained if an option (an option is a right, but not an obligation, as is explained in Chapter 7) to buy the required deutschemarks is purchased; a premium is paid to buy such an option. If the actual rate declines, the option is exercised and the downside can be avoided, but if the rate improves, the option is allowed to lapse and the required currency is bought directly in the spot foreign exchange market. Therefore the insurance type of option contract would not be used, but the premium paid has still reduced the potential volatility in future financial results.

This example shows how a large group can manage its international sourcing issues but the challenge remains; how does such a group implement this type of strategy. It is clearly in *the group's* interests, but not necessarily in either of the individual division's (i.e. Germany and the UK) interest, to undertake the hedging strategy. Some groups would enforce this from the centre, often by centralising these activities, but this direct intervention leads both to a large corporate centre and the strong possibility of demotivated business divisions as they lose managerial discretion. Other groups seek to motivate all divisions to act in the best interests of the group, so that the corporate centre should not need to get involved in refereeing or legislating for this type of issue. Another way is to set target profits for all divisions expressed in US dollars so as to 'encourage' divisional managers to look for ways of ensuring, not only their local currency, but also their US dollar equivalent earnings streams. For some multinational companies, a downside of this can be a tendency for divisions to speculate in foreign currency markets with very disastrous consequences. The last alternative is for the centre to show how best practice within the group has created value and to leverage that best practice (e.g. by using options) more widely across the group.

Therefore the way in which a multinational approaches this type of problem should be dictated by the strategic role of the corporate centre (i.e. which corporate configuration they are in). The specific managerial performance measures that should be used for each of these corporate centre strategic roles are considered in Chapter 6 and Part Four.

Strategic opportunity

This exchange rate problem for Ford actually helped in an acquisition opportunity within the automotive industry. For all of its life as an independent car company, Jaguar had a reverse position on currency exposures to Ford Motor Company. Jaguar produced cars in the UK but sold many of these cars in the USA, generating large US dollar revenues against its predominantly £ sterling cost base. Its management could, and did, hedge this foreign currency risk by entering into forward rate agreements for its expected US dollar income. This strategy reduced its volatility but also took away the potential upside on currency movements.

However Jaguar faced a more fundamental strategic problem because its main competitors in the USA car market were actually also importers, but primarily from Germany (i.e. Mercedes Benz, BMW, Porsche and Audi). Consequently their foreign currency exposures were between the deutschemark (now Euro) and the US dollar, not £ sterling and US dollars. From a competitive perspective, Jaguar could find itself significantly worse off if exchange rates moved the wrong way. If sterling was to strengthen against the US dollar, Jaguar would, if not hedged, need to increase its USA selling prices in order to maintain its UK-based margins (its £ sterling denominated selling prices for these exported cars would otherwise fall). However if, at the same time, the deutschemark was to weaken against the US dollar, its German-based competitors could, if also unhedged, actually reduce their US dollar denominated selling prices and still make as much local currency profit as before. This means that, if it wanted to

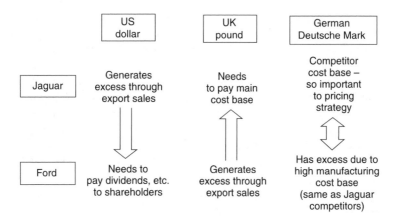

Figure 3.16 *Natural hedging strategy opportunities*

be sure of being competitively priced in the USA market, Jaguar had to look at its competitors' cost base and their hedging strategies as well as its own position.

If we now add together Ford's net position and Jaguar's, as is done in Figure 3.16, the offsetting exposures give a 'combined group' a natural hedge. Jaguar generates US dollar revenues that are attractive to Ford's USA-based share-holders, while Jaguar's UK-based costs would partially balance Ford's excess UK sales revenues. This still leaves Ford with excess German production costs but this now puts Jaguar in the same position as its direct competitors. Obviously there would be many other strategic reasons for such an acquisition, but the value of such a natural hedge could enable one bidder to justify paying more than other potential bidders. Once acquired, the corporate centre would need to consider how it set the managerial performance targets for Jaguar's top management team; it would no longer be sensible for them to continue their previous hedging strategy to safeguard sterling profits.

One such other strategic reason for the acquisition is the relative brand positioning of the products within the groups' portfolios. Ford would strongly argue that it could never recover the full 'value' of its top of the range products (e.g. the Ford Scorpio). Consumer testing indicated that, if the product could be branded as a BMW or a Mercedes, customers would be willing to pay a significantly higher price. In other words the current brand image was inappropriate for the actual engineering quality of the car. Conversely Jaguar had, for several years, retained a very good brand image, particularly in the USA, despite a poor reputation for manufacturing quality. If, following the acquisition, Ford could merge its engineering and production skills into Jaguar's imagery, the combined product offering could potentially generate significant super profits and hence create shareholder value. Thus what Ford actually purchased was a brand, as it had to invest heavily in upgrading Jaguar's existing manufacturing facilities.

This had to be seen as a significant risk because if consumers perceived the new Jaguar models as really Fords they would be unlikely to be willing to continue to pay the same premium pricing as before. If however Ford could improve the product quality, while maintaining the distinct and separate branding of Jaguar, the acquisition should have proved very successful. This type of financial impact could be even more dramatic if Ferrari and Maserati customers perceived themselves as actually buying a very expensive Fiat. This is why it is essential that corporate centres really understand what their role should be and how their organisations should be structured if the chances of achieving their overall goals and objectives are to be increased rather than reduced through its indirect involvement or direct interventions. The importance of understanding your competitors has also been highlighted and the key issues involved in competitor analysis are considered in the next chapter.

4 Future Competitive Environment Review – Competitor Analysis

Overview

A marketing finance approach requires a greatly increased emphasis on externally oriented analysis and a key element in this is a soundly based competitor analysis.

The first stage in any competitor analysis is to establish exactly who are the company's competitors. Competitors can only be realistically defined by customers – your competitors are your customers' alternative suppliers. This definition of competitors should include both existing competitors and new potential competitors. However the focus of the competitor analysis is different for each type of competitor. Potential competitors may be deterred from entering the market (i.e. actually becoming competitors) if sufficiently strong entry barriers are erected in time, existing competitors cannot, by definition, be deterred. Aggressive competitive activity may drive existing competitors out of the industry, but this may not be practical if these existing competitors face high exit barriers.

This identification of either entry barriers or exit barriers highlights that competitor analysis should be used as a decision-making aid. Thus it is not enough to produce an annual analysis of a competitor's published financial results; competitor analysis needs to be forward looking and focus on relative differences between the businesses. This relative analysis means that the competitor analysis process must be tailored to the particular needs of each company and its competitors; thus the focus of the competitor analysis process will be very different depending on whether the basis of competition is selling price or value-added differentiation.

A good competitor analysis system really involves a two-stage process. The first stage consists of placing each competitor's business into its correct context, and this can be facilitated by classifying the competitors into a series of non-mutually exclusive categories. These highlight the key role of the competitors and the types of strategic thrusts that they are likely to employ. A major objective of competitor analysis is to predict strategic initiatives by the competitor and their responses to moves made by the company.

Not surprisingly therefore, an increasing number of companies are utilising game theory as a basis for their competitor analysis and strategy development. The most sustainable, shareholder value-enhancing scenario is where the industry is a positive-sum game that can allow all the players in the industry to create shareholder value. This means that the analysis should distinguish between 'creating-value' and 'capturing-value' strategies. Creating-value strategies increase the total value generated by the industry, while capturing-value strategies simply take a greater share of the existing total value available. The worst result is where competition becomes value destroying (i.e. the industry becomes a negative-sum game) so that there is less value to be shared among all the competitors.

The second stage of competitor analysis involves a detailed, but tailored, comparison of the differences between the company and each of its competitors. Such an analysis must produce readily usable information rather than masses of irrelevant data. If the main basis of competition is selling price, a key element of competitor analysis will be relative cost benchmarking. In order to obtain the required information, the company may need to use some quite sophisticated and creative analyses but normally a sufficiently accurate cost comparison can be obtained. However an overemphasis on cost benchmarking can be unhelpful if competition is based, not on selling price, but on product quality or service levels, etc. In such cases, the competitor analysis must try to place values on these differentiating attributes and compare these values with the costs incurred in achieving the differentiation.

There is a wide range of sources of information that can be used to provide competitor information, but most of the required data is normally already available within the company. The challenge is to turn this data into usable management information and to incorporate it into the company's strategic decision-making process.

Introduction

One of the major distinguishing features of a marketing finance approach is the concentration on providing comparative financial information on other businesses. The main area of interest is obviously to gather, analyse and disseminate information on competitors, but this chapter also considers briefly the other elements of the value chain, namely suppliers and direct customers. Clearly, a better understanding of their possible alternative competitive strategies can be of great assistance to a business in selecting its own strategy.

As discussed in Chapter 2, traditional management accounting has concentrated on analysing the internal cost structure of the organisation, and then planning how this structure will change in the future so that a long-term plan and a short-term budget can be developed. The actual cost base is then compared against this budget as the year unfolds. In more sophisticated businesses, the original budget can be flexed to take account of significant changes in the external environment so that the comparisons with actual results are more meaningful.

This traditional type of management accounting system provides two main types of benefits to the organisation:

First, the analysis and planning process sets out the forecast financial outcome of the proposed business strategies for the planning period. This enables the managers to decide whether this planned outcome is satisfactory or not. If the outcome is not acceptable, the plan can be modified until the best potential result is obtained. Also, if the critical success factors have been properly highlighted in the analysis process (as discussed in Chapter 5), the sensitivity analysis on these critical success factors can be applied to the financial plan so that managers can identify the key risks and opportunities that may occur. This can again enable the plan to be modified prior to implementation, or the business may try to reduce its exposure to a particular key risk by adopting some appropriate hedging strategy.

Second, once the plan has been implemented the control process provides a method of comparing actual performance against planned performance. This comparison can enable changes to be made to the plan as necessary in the light of the actual outcomes of the initial strategic decisions. These subsequent decisions should, as always, be based on the latest information available and this requires that the plan should be updated to take account of material changes since it was formulated; hence many businesses now use a rolling forecast system as the basis against which actual performance is compared (as discussed in Chapter 6).

The benefits of this type of management accounting are unquestionable, but such a system does not explicitly address some of the major issues facing businesses when they are trying to develop a competitive strategy. Competitive strategies have already been defined as specific courses of action that are designed to create sustainable competitive advantages which should enable the business to generate super profits, from which shareholder value is created.

A competitive advantage can only, by definition, be created by comparison to competitors and this comparison should be as precise and clearly defined as is practicable. Thus, in most good traditional management accounting systems, such competitive comparisons are *implicitly* included in the essential forecasts of market share gained and pricing levels that are assumed for the planning period. However, unless these competitive assumptions are made clear and explicit, it can be very difficult during the monitoring and control process to identify the real reasons for any diversion from the planned results. For example, if forecast price increases cannot be implemented or made to stick because competitors do not increase their prices, the planned profitability of the business can be seriously affected. In such circumstances, it is vitally important that the managers of the organisation can determine if competitors are holding down their prices as a short-term marketing tactic in order to try to gain market share, even though they themselves may be suffering significant cost increases with a consequent adverse impact on their own profitability. Should this be the case, these competitors will need to increase their selling prices in the short term to restore their required profit levels, whether the market share growth tactic has worked or not. Alternatively, and much more seriously, the competitors could have a relative cost advantage that could enable them to maintain these lower price levels over the much longer term.

Clearly the appropriate competitive response to these alternative causes of the same market situation should be dramatically different, but the ability to identify the appropriate response depends on the quality of the competitor analysis that has been carried out.

Defining the competition

YOUR COMPETITION IS DEFINED FOR YOU BY YOUR CUSTOMERS. COMPETITORS ARE YOUR CUSTOMERS' ALTERNATIVE SUPPLIERS.

The first stage in defining who are a company's competitors should have been done as part of establishing the mission statement of the business carrying out the competitor analysis. Competitive strategies have to be developed at the level where the business sells products in distinct markets and against identifiable competitors. If this identification is not relatively simple and straightforward, the business is either inappropriately structured or has not yet defined a sufficiently clear competitive strategy.

However many businesses adopt an internal perspective to identifying competitors based on the industry sector within which they operate. This often brings in too wide a spectrum of 'competitors'. As discussed in Practical Insight 4.1, a car manufacturer need not consider all other car manufacturers as competitors, but should focus its analysis on those companies providing a similar product offering as its own to the same types of customer. Indeed, as illustrated later in the chapter, the competitive product analysis carried out by leading car companies has been taken to a very sophisticated level.

Practical Insight 4.1

A very segmented industry

Ford Motor Company is one of the leading volume car manufacturers in the world and has, for many years, placed much emphasis on having good competitor analysis. Historically this analysis sometimes suffered from an internal 'wish-list' of competitors, rather than an externally focused, real world-based, customer-driven definition of competitors. Thus, to anyone working in the car industry, the leading companies to which one would like to be compared would be Mercedes Benz, BMW and Porsche. Unfortunately if one's product range actually aims at a lower priced market segment, such a competitor analysis is not as relevant as it should be.

However, following the acquisition of Jaguar that was discussed in Chapter 3, part of Ford became a potentially viable competitor against these luxury car manufacturers (i.e. with its other luxury car marques, Aston Martin and Volvo). The basis of the relevant competitor analysis in this segment of the car market should be significantly different to that used in the volume-oriented, middle-price categories, where the bulk of Ford's business has been traditionally (i.e. cost efficiency is still important, but branding and quality perception are much more important).

The VW group face a different competitor analysis problem, due to their multi-branding strategy (i.e. ownership of Audi, VW, Skoda and Seat brands). Originally these brands were in highly differentiated market segments but Skoda, for instance, has undergone a transformation in production and design quality. Also the desire for manufacturing efficiencies has led to the sharing of major elements across the group's product range. For example, the Skoda Octavia's top of the range model shares its chassis with the Audi A3 and has a slightly detuned version of the engine in the Audi TT. There is clearly the potential for customers to associate these products as competitive (as the author has done by switching from an Audi to a Skoda!). In response the group is trying to make the channels of distribution (i.e. the dealers) appear very differentiated by focusing each one on only part of the group's offerings.

Customer-led definitions of competition can also highlight some less obvious but very important competitors. Once the business focuses on alternative suppliers to its prospective customers (i.e. its chosen market) as its competitors, it is forced to define what the customer is actually buying. In some cases the actual good or service may not adequately define competitors because the customer is actually purchasing a group of attributes or benefits rather than the specific product. Hence, competitors will be other businesses providing what the customer perceives as a comparable group of benefits even though the product may appear physically very different.

COMPANIES SELL FEATURES.
CUSTOMERS BUY BENEFITS.

For example, cinemas show films to the public and thus compete directly against other cinemas. Video rental shops, satellite and cable television channels, and increasingly the Internet are competitors which use a different channel of distribution for the same genre of product. However, cinemas are really also in competition with other leisure service businesses, as their customers may choose to spend their leisure time and money in alternative ways; competitor analysis may therefore need to incorporate 'live' theatre, spectator-based sporting events and other forms of passive entertainment.

Identifying competitors consists of finding other businesses that supply alternative *competing* products to the *same end* customer, even though they may use different strategies, including very different channels of distribution. Analysis should attempt to identify not only the existing competitors but also, and often even more importantly, the potential new competitors that may be attracted into the company's area of operations. If potential competitors are not identified in advance, it may be very difficult to compete successfully against them once they are established.

In many cases, new competitors can only enter a market because of some significant change in the external competitive environment. New sources of competitive advantage may emerge which the new players are better placed to exploit. Alternatively the change could destroy or substantially reduce the strength of the existing competitive advantages held by the original players. These issues are illustrated in Practical Insights 4.2 and 4.3.

Practical Insight 4.2

The milkman doesn't knock anymore

In the UK, retail dairies had established fierce competitive strategies against each other (the obvious visible, direct competition). This competition was based on service levels with some dairies emphasising the time of delivery, while others extended the range of products delivered by the milkman. However, a new form of competitor has taken an increasingly large proportion of the market for milk which is *consumed* in the home.

Large supermarkets entered the retail milk market using their bulk buying power (as the supply side of the milk industry changed considerably), new technological developments (which increased the shelf life of the product) and new packaging developments (which made bulk packaging acceptable and practical). Their move to out-of-town superstore locations and the consequent increase in car usage for shopping made home delivery of bulky products such as milk, bread and soft drinks, etc. less of an issue for consumers. The competitive environment was changed from one focused largely on service to one dominated by the issue of price; many consumers are not now willing to pay the price premium required for the delivery service offered by the retail dairies.

Practical Insight 4.3

From key assets to expensive liability

In the retail financial services industry, a key competitive advantage was, for many years, the national network of branches that the large players in the industry all had. This served as a significant entry barrier to new entrants. However technology has now transformed the industry and almost removed the need for branches. Customers can transact their business over the Internet, the telephone and through automated teller machines (ATMs). A number of completely new businesses have entered the industry, and the big players have been forced to launch their own 'branchless' equivalents. The cost advantages of not having large branch networks are substantial and consequently the original large banks are desperately searching for new added-value ways of re-utilising their branches or exiting from them as cheaply as possible.

Focusing on customer-defined competitors and including both existing and potential competitors is very useful in identifying the main purpose of any competitor analysis, namely to assist the development and implementation of the company's competitive strategy. In other words, competitor analysis is a strategic decision-support process.

Competitor analysis as a decision-making aid

THE KEY ISSUE IS TO UNDERSTAND WHERE COMPETITORS ARE NOW BETTER OR WORSE THAN YOU ARE, AND HOW THIS IS LIKELY TO CHANGE IN THE FUTURE.

It is only after the appropriate set of existing and potential competitors has been identified that the required analytical information can be determined. Thus, like most other aspects of marketing finance, competitor analysis has to be tailored to the specific needs of each company. Also, although strategically important, good competitor analysis is relatively expensive and should itself be subjected to some form of cost-benefit analysis.

The initial objective is to understand exactly what significant differences exist between the company and each of its main competitors. This means establishing where competitors are *better* or *worse* than the company; it must always be remembered that a sustainable competitive advantage is a relative concept. A sustainable competitive advantage enables an organisation to do something that cannot be matched by anyone else in the eyes of its customers. Thus, a strongly branded product can create very strong customer loyalty because its users do not believe that any competitive offering is as good. Hence a company that employs a strategy of always having the lowest selling price in its market does not have a sustainable competitive advantage unless it is also the lowest cost supplier. If not, its competitors can immediately match its low selling prices without being at a relative commercial disadvantage. Indeed, at least one competitor may be able to undercut the company!

Sustainable competitive advantages must therefore be described in terms of 'better', 'cheaper', 'faster', 'more reliable', etc. This requirement for a *relative* comparison with competitors removes the need for absolute precision in assessing every cost incurred by all competitors.

HAVING A *GOOD* PRODUCT WILL NOT ENABLE YOU TO CREATE SHAREHOLDER VALUE IF YOUR COMPETITORS HAVE A *BETTER* PRODUCT.

The ultimate objective for competitor analysis, however, is not to establish the current position, but to indicate the relative competitive positions in the future. The challenge is to project where competitors are heading in terms of costs, value offerings, quality gains and product innovations, etc. Again, such analysis can be complex, time-consuming and correspondingly expensive. It should not, therefore, be done for all aspects of all competitors.

Competitor analysis should concentrate on the strategically important aspects of each targeted existing and potential competitor. For example, an in-depth cost comparison with a competitor may be of no value if the basis of the competitor's strategy is either perceived quality of product, responsiveness of service levels to customer needs, or a highly attractive image-oriented brand. The focus of the analysis must be on whether any cost premium incurred by the competitor increases its total economic added-value by allowing a substantially greater price premium or by creating a high degree of customer loyalty.

Where the basis of competition is primarily on price, an in-depth cost comparison is clearly important; no company can justify its claim to be 'the lowest cost supplier' in its industry if it has not done an external cost benchmarking exercise against its competitors. Similarly a company which claims to have 'better products' than any of its competitors should have done customer research to validate the perceived extra value of the product, and analysed this extra value against any extra cost incurred in delivering it to the customer.

Accordingly, competitor analysis processes differ significantly in different industries and even within an industry if different competitive strategies are being employed. This means that, for many companies, the competitor analyses within the organisation may need to be tailored if it is competing in different ways against different competitors in different market segments. Each analysis should provide the appropriate information to support the different strategic decisions that the company and its competitors will be facing.

Competitor analysis cannot therefore be carried out by any form of historical reconciliation of competitors' financial results with the company's own. It must be focused on the future and must try logically to predict competitors' desired positions and to highlight their weaknesses, so that these can be attacked.

Competitor analysis as a two-stage process

DETAILED COMPETITOR ACTIONS AND REACTIONS CAN ONLY BE PREDICTED WHEN THE COMPETITOR'S BUSINESS IS PLACED IN ITS CORRECT CONTEXT.

For large complex competitors, it is important to understand the competitor's overall corporate and financial strategy, and where this particular part of their business fits within this strategy. Many large companies comprise a large number of business units competing directly against a quite diverse range of external businesses, which are often themselves part of similarly complex groups. Competitor actions/reactions from any particular part of such a business will be significantly affected by the position of this business unit within the group's overall portfolio and how the other businesses within the group are performing.

With this in mind, competitor analysis must place the particular competitive business unit into its appropriate context. This should assist in identifying the most likely goals and objectives that will be established for the competitor by the group centre. Not only will these goals and objectives drive the competitor's own strategy but they will also have a tremendous impact on the competitor's responses to any strategic initiatives appearing in the marketplace.

The strategic positioning of competitors is facilitated by classifying competitors into a number of non-mutually exclusive categories; the idea being to build up a picture of each competitor which can be easily and clearly communicated within the company. One obvious such classification is between existing and potential competitors, and it has already been stated that competitor analysis must consider both classifications. However, the issues that need to be addressed are significantly different.

Potential competitors are, by definition, not yet present in the particular marketplace (e.g. market segment) and they may be deterred from entering if sufficiently strong 'entry barriers', as described in Chapter 1, are erected in time. Existing competitors cannot, also by definition, be kept out of the industry by such entry barriers but they may face 'exit barriers', which may prevent them from leaving the industry.

It is economically irrational for any company, under perfect conditions (remember our brief discussion on perfect competition in Chapter 1 when entry barriers were introduced!), to stay in an industry if it is unable to achieve its required rate of return. (If it does so, it continues to destroy shareholder value year after year.) Competitors could therefore be forced to exit from an industry by a company with a strong sustainable competitive advantage, if this was used to force down the rate of return achieved by these less well-positioned businesses. However, in the real world, companies do not automatically leave an industry even though their rate of return is less than that required by their shareholders. Indeed, some competitors will stay in an industry where they are making losses. Exit barriers, which are diagrammatically shown in Figure 4.1, can mean that there are significant costs associated with leaving an industry.

If the barriers to exit are substantial, it may not be economically rational to try to drive out existing competitors. In this case, the company's competitive strategy must take into account the strategic intentions of all existing competitors. In other circumstances, the optimum competitive strategy may be to try to improve the economic attractiveness of the industry by driving out the weakest competitor; here the key role of competitor analysis is to identify which is the weakest competitor and what is the best way of forcing them to exit from the industry.

As can be seen from Figure 4.2, there is a wide range of possible exit barriers and they must be fully understood before any aggressive competitive action is initiated. It is quite common to see a large business start a price war in an industry with significant excess capacity. This will only work to increase the profitability of all the players in the industry if the price reduction stimulates total demand very significantly so as to outweigh the immediate reduction in

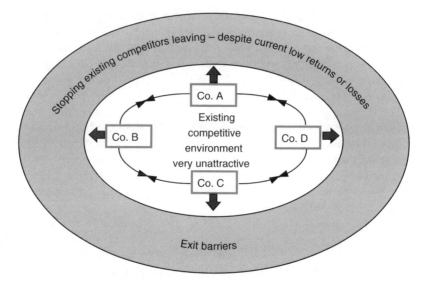

Figure 4.1 *Maintaining the unattractive status quo – exit barriers*

the contribution per unit. More commonly this strategy is used to try to force out the weaker players and therefore reduce the total outputs of the industry; thus enhancing the longer-term financial return of those remaining. This strategy is much less likely to succeed if the weaker players face significant exit barriers, such as having a very high fixed cost structure with long life specialised fixed assets and high costs of physically closing down their operations; this is

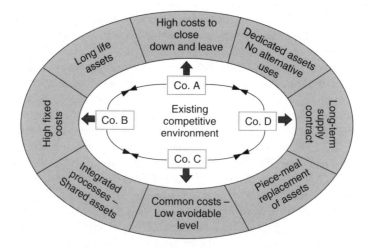

Figure 4.2 *Exit barriers*

illustrated in Practical Insight 4.4. Their response is much more likely to be to match the price decrease, or even to take it one stage lower again. Should this happen, the effect of the competitive strategy will be to reduce the overall profits of the industry without necessarily improving the overall long-term competitive environment.

Even if the competitor could be forced out, their likely method of exit also needs to be predicted. Some companies may leave an industry gradually over many years, perhaps by not reinvesting in their long life fixed assets. The price-cutting initiator would therefore have to be prepared to continue its aggressive marketing strategy until the competitor finally left. If financial returns started to increase while the competitor was still in the industry, the decision to exit could be reversed. A further alternative strategy is therefore to accelerate the required rationalisation of the industry by acquiring or merging with one or more competitors even though, quite rapidly after the companies come together, the total capacity of the weaker business is closed down.

The competitor analysis required in this type of competitive environment should indicate the ideal time to initiate this type of 'exit forcing' strategy and the probability of its success. Clearly, any such initiative should be implemented when the exit barriers are at their lowest. For example, in an asset-intensive industry, acting just before the competitor commits to a significant reinvestment is likely to have a much more positive impact (in terms of increasing their likelihood of exiting) than waiting until after the competitor has made its reinvestment, when the competitive reaction will normally be the exact opposite of that desired.

The competitor analysis information required includes a life-cycle analysis of the competitor's existing asset base, its required rate of return on this type of reinvestment, and its capital investment decision-making process so that the strategy can be implemented in time to influence the reinvestment decision. Such strategically focused information differs considerably from that generated by many operationally orientated competitor accounting systems, where the main sources of analysis are the published financial statements of direct existing competitors. It should also be clear that this information differs significantly from that required in an environment where the company is currently earning super profits and the key issue is how to develop very quickly, strong entry barriers in order to keep out potential competitors.

Practical Insight 4.4

The ultimate exit barriers?

Mining companies, and the extractive industries in general, have a set of business parameters that can leave them locked in to their businesses even though the prospects of earning a reasonable rate of return, let alone generating super profits, are bleak in the extreme.

The ultimate exit barriers? (*Continued*)

Most mines operate with high fixed costs; even if they can keep some of their labour costs variable, they normally have high overheads. They also have very dedicated fixed assets, with long economic lives and virtually no alternative uses. However, in many such industries the value of their output (e.g. gold, nickel, coal) is controlled by the external environment and can be extremely volatile. This would make it very attractive to be able to close down temporarily when prices are depressed or, at least, to reduce the level of output. Their high fixed costs would make this difficult enough but, in reality, the major problem is the very high financial cost of closing down. In most countries, mining companies are not allowed simply to close down a mine. They must not only make the site safe, and pay off the workforce, but also repair any damage done to the physical environment; this can make it cheaper to continue operating the mine at a loss than to incur the costs incurred in closing down!

We now turn to consider the other non-mutually exclusive ways of classifying competitors, which are set out in Figure 4.3. The degree of resistance from a competitor will often be dictated by whether the particular business that is being attacked is regarded as a core part of the group's activities, rather than a peripheral activity. Not surprisingly, most competitors will defend their core areas of business as vigorously as they can, but they may not put the same resources or commitment into defending non-core parts of their group.

Similarly, the ability and willingness to defend a peripheral business will depend upon the performance of the core business. If the core business itself is already under severe attack, it may be a good time to attack one of the group's

Competitors can be grouped into a number of non-mutually exclusive categories:

❐ Core business or peripheral.

❐ Position of this business unit within their group's portfolio
   e.g. development unit versus main profit generator.

❐ Degree of concentration/focus on this business unit
   e.g. vertically integrated versus dedicated to one area.

❐ Key performance measures used
   e.g. profits/cash flow versus growth/market share.

❐ Principal decision-makers
   e.g. professional managers versus family shareholders.

❐ Risk-taking appetite
   e.g. risk averse versus high risk-taking.

Figure 4.3   *Classifying competitors*

peripheral businesses in an attempt to force a quick exit decision. Conversely, if the core businesses are all highly profitable, cash generating but mature operations, it may not be such a successful strategy aggressively to attack the only high growth, but cash consuming, business in the competitor's portfolio. Thus it is also important to understand the main role within the competitor's overall strategy that is played by the particular business being analysed.

Another way of classifying competitors is by reference to their relative levels of vertical integration. In many industries, it is quite common to find competing businesses that have very different levels of vertical integration, as is the situation in the case study on the cigarette industry at the end of this chapter. BAT plc is much more vertically integrated than Philip Morris; BAT has tobacco leaf growing interests around the world while Philip Morris buys its tobacco from dealers. This will significantly affect their business strategies and potential responses to changes in the competitive environment. Consequently, it is important that companies carefully analyse their competitors from this perspective – particularly when one competitor, or small group of competitors, has a structure that differs from the rest of the industry.

A major potential problem faces any vertically integrated organisation which has competitors dedicated to only one section of the industry value chain; such a dedicated competitor can easily identify the contribution generated by its focused business, whereas such fundamental analytical information may not be so readily available to the vertically integrated company. Indeed, many internal management accounting systems make it very difficult to establish the 'true' profitability of the different parts of the business. As discussed with reference to the computer, car and oil industries in Chapter 3, it is critical that the company's internal transfer pricing system highlights which areas of the business really generate super profits. These areas must be safeguarded against competitive threat; however, far too often, transfer pricing systems are merely cost or profit apportionment processes.

The oil industry is also a good example of another element of competitor analysis. The major oil companies are all highly vertically integrated with businesses ranging from exploration to retail outlets. Many of these companies would regard themselves as quite good at competitor analysis, but most of their analysis was traditionally directed towards other similarly vertically integrated oil companies. Relatively recently large supermarket chains entered the retail fuel market in several countries. The oil industry faced a new group of competitors with very different business strategies developed from a completely different attitude to the industry and its need to be vertically integrated. These supermarkets, particularly in France and the UK, have successfully gained share in the retail end of the oil industry, but show no signs of moving into oil exploration or refining. This example is developed in more detail in Chapter 5.

It is also important to understand what performance measures are used by competitors as this will also affect their behaviour; under our already stated maxim of 'what you measure is what you get'. If a business wants to grow, it should normally have growth as one of its key performance measures, rather than focusing on measures of profits or cash flow. Where competing businesses have fundamentally different focuses, their behaviours and responses to specific opportunities and threats may be equally different. Indeed they may both regard themselves as winning in a particular competitive environment. (For example, if one company emphasises growth while its competitor focuses on profits, both could be happy if one is gaining market share but the other is increasing its profits because it has a relatively reduced rate of marketing support – one is certainly more short-term oriented than the other, and may well need the maxim of a short life but a happy one!) It is therefore critical that the competitor analysis does not stem from any potentially false assumptions regarding the strategic objectives of competitors. Many businesses have fallen into the trap of assuming that all their competitors have the same objectives as they do, and hence that these competitors will use similar performance measures; the competitor analysis must establish the real competitive situation.

The remaining two classifications (i.e. the types of principal decision-maker and the relative risk-taking appetites) are reasonably self-explanatory and can best be illustrated by a linked extreme example. There are two competitors in an industry, both of which have very recently appointed new chief executives. In one company, the new chief executive is 62 years old and has worked for the company for 41 years, joining straight from University. He is also the third generation of his family to hold this job; not too surprising as his family are the largest shareholders in the publicly quoted group, which also bears the family name. The other company has hired in its chief executive from outside. She is 35 years old and has a very successful career record to date, but this is her first appointment at this very top level in a group. In her previous sales and marketing roles she had achieved significant growth in market shares, sometimes through very aggressive competitive strategies including starting severe price wars on occasions.

Clearly the attitudes and risk-taking profile of these two executives are likely to be poles apart and it is very important that this information forms part of the competitor analysis process. Leading companies in this area, such as Philip Morris that is the subject of the case study at the end of the chapter, maintain a database on the key executives in its competitors so that they know what to expect when they move into a new managerial role.

A game theory view of the industry value chain

ANY STRATEGY WHICH AIMS TO CREATE INCREASED SHARE-
HOLDER VALUE SHOULD ALSO IDENTIFY WHERE THAT
INCREASED VALUE IS GOING TO COME FROM. IF IT CANNOT,
IT IS NOT A STRATEGY – IT IS A WISH LIST.

The continual emphasis throughout the book on shareholder value should lead to a consequent focus on the sources of the super profits that generate this shareholder value. In fast-growing industries, the total value-added produced by the industry can be increasing rapidly. More end users may be buying the good or service, existing users are buying more and may be willing to pay increased real prices for enhanced levels of benefits. It can be possible for all the companies in such an industry to generate shareholder value. This can be true but it is not normally the case, even in high growth markets.

The most logical long-term competitive strategy in a growing market is to try to increase market share during this growth phase. As discussed in Chapter 2, much empirical evidence exists to suggest that the greatest shareholder value is produced by the companies with dominant market shares in their industries and that these dominant market shares are most economically developed while the market is itself growing. Hence, part of the successful company's growth, even in a rapidly growing market, comes at the expense of competitors. The competitor may still be growing, but at a slower rate than the industry; i.e. they are losing market share.

In a slow-growth or static-mature industry, almost any growth in sales volume or revenue by one company has to come at the expense of a competitor. It is of course likely that the competitor will try to defend their existing levels of sales and profits. Hence, if such a gain is to be sustainable, the aggressive growth company should be utilising a strong competitive advantage, against which the competitor has no defence.

However, increased levels of financial return can be generated, not at the direct expense of competitors, but from squeezing the other elements of the industry supply chain, as is shown in Figure 4.4. This means reducing the value-added by either suppliers to the company or the direct customers of the company, so that the company takes an increased share of the total value added by the industry. Again, this type of strategic thrust should be based on a sustainable competitive advantage and may depend on a fundamental re-structuring, or re-engineering, of the current business processes applied within the industry. Really good examples of business process re-engineering result in the total value added by the industry being increased so that all the parties involved could benefit; once again, there are many fewer examples where *all* parties do actually share in these benefits.

These ideas are shown diagrammatically in Figure 4.4; a competitive strategy should be clear as to the source of any expected increase in super profits. Further, the competitive strategy process should explain why such an increase is sustainable – in other words, why the affected competitors, suppliers or customers cannot do anything about it. Unless this process is carried out, the company has developed more of a 'wish list' rather than a properly evaluated and financially justified competitive strategy.

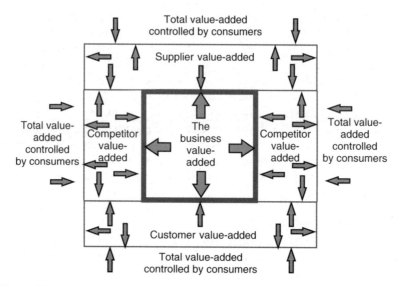

Figure 4.4   *Game theory view of industry value chain*

It is quite normal for the sum of the strategic plans of all the players in an industry to be much greater than the total value generated by the industry; i.e. they cannot all be achieved. Hence many companies have introduced game theory concepts to build in the dynamic interactions among themselves, competitors, customers and suppliers.

The basics of game theory are very easy to state, but its practical application can become very complicated. As in any competitive game (such as bridge or chess), developing a successful strategy is considerably assisted by predicting the future actions and reactions of the various players. In other words, you have to look forward to potential outcomes and then reason backwards to develop the most successful strategies. However in business there are a range of different types of game, as is shown in Figure 4.5. Most other normal 'games' have a simple win–lose outcome (if I win then you lose, and vice versa); they can be described as zero-sum games.

Industries can degenerate into negative-sum games where all the players lose out; this can be the result of many destructive price wars, as discussed earlier. It is therefore important that the company assesses the risk of this type of result ensuing from its proposed competitive strategy. Conversely, it is also quite possible for an industry to produce a positive-sum game, where all players in the industry win; also as discussed earlier, in a very financially attractive industry all companies involved may create shareholder value. Such a position is potentially much more sustainable than a win–lose game; as no competitor

(1) Zero-(or constant) sum games

◆ Win–lose or lose–win outcomes

(2) Positive-sum games

◆ Win–win strategies possible

(3) Negative-sum games

◆ Lose–lose strategies quite likely

Figure 4.5   *Different types of games*

should want to risk destroying the shareholder value which they are creating. This should still be true even if the win–win is 90:10 in one party's favour. Thus the strategic intent should be as shown in Figure 4.6 as this is the most sustainable way to create shareholder value. If the industry remains as a zero-sum game, particularly one that the company is continually winning, there is a risk that competitors become more willing to take greater and greater risks (i.e. implement increasingly aggressive strategies) because of their continuing poor financial performance. This could push the industry back into a negative-sum game, where all parties lose; yet this risk does not seem to be acknowledged in many macho, 'winner takes all' strategies! It is still better obviously, as shown

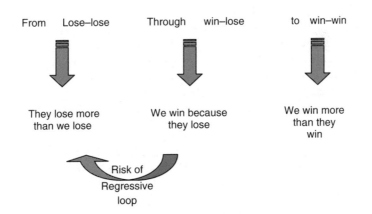

Figure 4.6   *Different types of games – strategic intent*

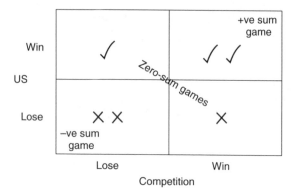

Figure 4.7   *Different types of games*

in Figure 4.7, to be the winner in a zero-sum game, but the long-term sustainability of such a position must be considered.

We need therefore to distinguish between *destructive competition* and *constructive competition*. Destructive competition reduces the total value created by all the players in the industry, whereas constructive competition seeks to increase the total value created. As discussed in Chapter 2, the link between shareholder value and competitive strategy is also a two-stage process; stage one seeks to create value within the total value chain, while stage two tries to capture as much of this total value as possible. This is shown diagrammatically in Figure 4.8.

The value creation type of competition can often be viewed as a co-operative form of competition vertically within the total industry value chain. Indeed the term 'co-opetition' was coined by Ray Noorda to describe this, and the concept has been developed by USA academics Brandenburger and Nalebuff. However the logical responsibility for managing this value creation competitive spirit rests with the dominant player in the industry. If a competitor with a 10 per cent market share increases the total value created by the industry, it is likely that 90 per cent of the value they have created will go to other industry players. Unfortunately, in many industries, the dominant player adopts a strategy that focuses exclusively on capturing more of the existing industry value chain.

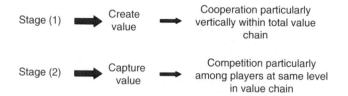

Figure 4.8   *Link to shareholder value and competitive strategy*

This can still be true even when this strategy results in very destructive competitive responses; this type of dominant company simply becomes even more aggressive!

Other industries suffer, interestingly, from the lack of a dominant player that is able to manage the total value created by the industry. There are many examples of industries with four or five relatively evenly balanced competitors that quite regularly degenerate into value destroying price wars. Such price wars are most unlikely to force any of the competitors out of the industry, and thus total profitability in the industry is dramatically reduced. This position is often triggered because the total aspirations of all the competitors cannot be met by the total industry; e.g. where five competitors all have objectives to achieve 25 per cent market shares.

Detailed but tailored analysis

MOST COMPETITOR ANALYSIS EXERCISES PRODUCE A MASS OF IRRELEVANT AND CONFUSING DATA, BUT VERY LITTLE APPROPRIATELY TAILORED, USABLE INFORMATION.

Having defined who the competitors are and placed each of these competitors in their appropriate context, the second stage of our competitor analysis process involves analysing all the specific competitive advantages and disadvantages relative to each competitor. This should enable an appropriately tailored competitive strategy to be developed.

That competitor analysis should be tightly focused and have clearly defined objectives should by now be clear. The best objectives are built around competitive strategy decisions, so that competitor analysis is forced to act in a decision-support manner. However all competitor analysis should be tailored to suit the particular environment in which the company is operating. This can mean that, even within one company, the competitor analysis process may be differently structured for separate categories of competitors.

The analysis must produce readily usable information, rather than lots of standard regular reports on all competitors. The key phrase for all management information, which is 'the right information at the right time to the right people', can be applied very readily to competitor analysis. The timing of competitor analysis should not only be geared to the company's strategic decision process but, as already mentioned, should respond to changes in the competitive environment.

For example, in the car industry, most players conduct extremely in-depth analyses of directly competitive products. When a new competitive product becomes available, it is, quite literally, taken apart and examined in detail to try to establish not only what each modified or new component costs the competitor, but also what it would cost the company to incorporate into their equivalent offering. Additionally this analysis will try to establish the value of the innovations to the competitor's customers. This well-developed value-in-use pricing analysis can be seen from the focus put by direct marketing comparisons used in their product advertising, on differences in levels of equipment, performance (e.g. acceleration, top speed, etc.), fuel efficiency, boot and interior space (they even value knee room, shoulder height, etc. for passengers). The practical application of this technique is considered in more depth slightly later and again in Chapter 11.

As already established, cost benchmarking is essential if the primary basis of competition is selling price, but it may give false signals if competitors are selling differentiated products. The cost benchmark that is required is where competitors *are likely to be in the future*, rather than merely where they are now. Thus concentrating on internal costs and planned improvements may give a completely wrong impression of the company's competitive position; if competitors are improving at a faster pace from a better starting position, the company is falling further and further behind.

The best cost benchmark is therefore against the *lowest cost direct competitor* both in terms of comparing current cost levels and future expected improvements. Such direct comparisons may be difficult to make, although a very good approximation of relative cost levels can normally be assessed. Hence many companies now do cost comparisons with carefully selected non-competing businesses. A sensible approach is to select non-competitors that are considered excellent in a key strategic area (e.g. operational efficiency or customer service) and to carry out comparisons against them in this area. This can be used to set an initial internal standard or target but also, because such comparisons can be beneficial to all the participating businesses, they can be *updated regularly* and can even incorporate planned improvements.

For many large companies, a start point for any relative cost comparison exercise can be to use its internal business units as benchmarks. This can establish existing and planned *best practice* within the group; less well-performing business units can be asked to develop plans to bring themselves higher up the league table. Such internal comparisons are only productive if the group can properly make allowances for all the unavoidable differences across its operations, as is illustrated in Practical Insight 4.5. If this can be done, it should be possible to build up a very good picture of competitors' relative positions; using similar techniques, if not such certain knowledge. A simple initial competitor positioning can be achieved by deciding where they would be in the group's own internal league table of cost efficiency.

Practical Insight 4.5

Flexibility versus high volume

One very large, 'global' FMCG company has carried out a comprehensive cost benchmarking exercise on all its factories worldwide. This highlighted the very wide range of cost levels for producing the same product. Many of these cost differences had obvious causes: much lower labour rates in one country, much higher volumes generating economies of scale in another.

However, within Europe, there was also one plant that had much higher per-unit costs. Eventually it was decided to close down this 'inefficient' plant and transfer the production volumes to other lower cost factories, which had adequate spare capacity. Unfortunately the unit costs in these plants subsequently increased significantly, rather than reducing as had been expected.

The more detailed analysis revealed that the closed factory had been the European source for all the small production runs required. Thus it had emphasised flexibility and responsiveness in order to cope with its customers' demands. The 'lower cost' plants had focused on long runs and stable operational planning; they were now struggling to cope with the complexity of a much increased product range and much shorter production runs.

If the basis of competition is not largely selling price, then detailed cost bench-marking will not provide the whole answer. What is required is an analysis of the specific sources of value-added in each competitive offering, i.e. identifying the differentiators across the products. For each significant difference, the competitor analysis should seek to establish three things:

1   What value is placed on this element by the customer?
2   What does/would it cost the competitor to incorporate?
3   What would/does it cost your company to include?

(Numerical examples of this analysis are given in Chapter 11 to show when a sustainable competitive advantage/disadvantage is achieved.) This analysis highlights the true value-adding elements of the product, as opposed to those that add cost, as well as indicating the sustainability of the competitive position.

Sources of competitor information

IN MOST CASES, 80 PER CENT OF THE REQUIRED BASE DATA IS ALREADY AVAILABLE WITHIN THE COMPANY. THE CHALLENGE IS TO PULL IT ALL TOGETHER AND IDENTIFY THE REMAINING 20 PER CENT.

The car industry illustration shows that, in many industries, a great deal of the information required for competitor analysis can be obtained from direct examination of competitive products and observation in the marketplace. Many companies find that, when they implement a comprehensive competitor analysis process, they already have available most of the inputs that they require.

Drawing together from, and sharing the information across, different parts of the business is the key. Sales divisions come up against competitors every day and will also have a mass of information about how customers rank their different suppliers. Equally the sourcing side of the business should have a lot of

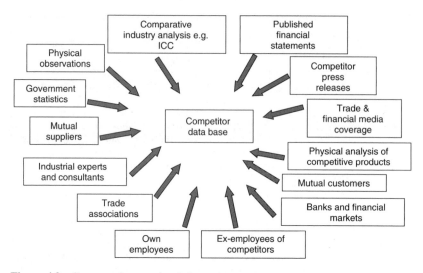

Figure 4.9   *Sources of competitor information*

information from suppliers regarding competitors' supply strategies, while operations and R&D departments should regularly be analysing competitive products.

In addition to these 'internal' sources of competitor information a large number of other available sources exist, as is illustrated in Figure 4.9. Consequently finding the required base information is not normally the main problem. This is particularly true if it is remembered that relative rather than absolute figures are needed.

Competitor analysis should have the objective of enabling the company to predict the major actions and reactions of its competitors. This is illustrated below by an examination of a major strategic change in one of the world's most profitable industries.

Case study – Marlboro Friday

On 2 April 1993, Philip Morris staggered the business world by announcing a significant price discounting promotion across the USA of what was then the world's most valuable brand, Marlboro cigarettes. On 20 July 1993, this promotion was turned into a permanent price reduction, which was extended across all Philip Morris' premium price tobacco brands in the USA. This move, now generally referred to as Marlboro Friday, is likely to go down in history as one of the most dramatic strategic brand management decisions ever taken.

The USA cigarette market had for a long time been the world's most profitable market (total profit pool of over $10 billion) in which Philip Morris (PM) held a dominant volume share (42.3 per cent in 1992) and an even greater value share. However the industry faced some major problems. Although very large (507 billion cigarettes in 1992), consumption was declining in volume terms at 3 per cent a year as the industry faced an increasingly hostile business environment. USA-based manufacturers had maintained production efficiencies through taking advantage of increasing export markets, as previously closed markets opened up (Japan, South Korea, Eastern Europe, the former Soviet Union and even China); but some of these faced medium-term challenges as pressure mounted for localised production.

Perhaps most significantly, domestically there was a marked change to the previous price segmentation of the market during the late 1980s and early 1990s. In order to understand this, we need to go back to the development of Marlboro.

Market background

Unlike Coca-Cola, Marlboro has not always dominated its market in the USA. Philip Morris only entered the USA cigarette market in 1934 when volumes were already over 100 billion per year. Marlboro was launched in 1937 and peaked at 2.3 billion cigarettes in 1945. In 1953 Marlboro had a negligible share of the market and was targeted at female smokers. It was re-launched in 1955 as a filter-tipped cigarette aimed primarily at male smokers; then in the late 1950s an advertising campaign featuring a cowboy and wide-open spaces was introduced! At this time the leading USA brands (Lucky Strike, Camel and Chesterfield) were all plain cigarettes, i.e. non-filtered, and these brands did not launch filtered versions until the 1960s, by which time Marlboro was well established.

Marlboro's growth was steady rather than spectacular and was fuelled by very high marketing support (i.e. brand development investment) so that in 1975 Marlboro became the largest cigarette brand in the USA market, and in 1983 PM became the largest USA-based cigarette company, selling 205 billion cigarettes out of 597.5 billion, of which 120 billion were Marlboro. This was interesting because the market volume peaked in 1981 at 638 billion cigarettes, and then went into a slow but continual decline. Thus PM had followed our shareholder value-enhancing strategy of gaining market share while the market was itself growing.

Once it had the leading position in the now mature market, its strategy changed and it looked to increase the profitability of the market. Accordingly, as the price leader with the dominant brand, PM took retail selling prices up significantly faster than inflation; through the 1980s, price rises averaged 7 per cent p.a. in real terms. Consequently, although total industry volumes were declining at 3 per cent p.a., the total profit pool was still increasing; what should be a win–win game for all the players. (Even with these high real price increases, cigarettes were still highly affordable in the USA due to the relatively low, by international standards, excise taxation.)

As both prices and profit margins grew substantially, there were increasing opportunities for industry players to launch lower priced cigarettes, which still generated perfectly acceptable margins. To PM this did not make any sense as it risked turning the industry into a commodity where competition was based on price alone. There was no evidence that lower prices would reverse the downward trend in cigarette consumption; thus industry profitability would be decreased. They wanted consumer choice to be dominated by brand equity and image; not surprising since they were winning hands down under these rules of the game, with Marlboro having 25 per cent market share while no other brand had over 5 per cent share. Therefore although low-priced cigarettes were launched back in 1981, PM stayed out of the sector until 1992.

The first competitor to try to change the game by launching very cheap cigarettes was the smallest industry player, Liggett. Back in the 1950s and even earlier, Liggett had been a major player but it had fallen to around 2 per cent market share with no really viable brands. Unfortunately for the other players, the sheer profitability of their industry meant that Liggett was only dying very slowly; 2 per cent of $10 billion is still more than most companies make in annual profits. It felt it had nothing to lose from a high risk, aggressive strategy, as it was not able to compete against the big boys on brands; also, it had just been taken over by a corporate raider with no background in the cigarette industry. Its initial launch of a cheap commodity cigarette (called Black & White) was immediately successful and in 18 months it had doubled its total sales volumes. However by the end of the 1980s its sales were back to where they had been before the launch of Black & White.

In a declining market, Liggett's volume growth had to come at the expense of its competitors. The biggest losers were R J Reynolds (RJR), American Tobacco (AT) and Brown & Williamson (B&W), the BAT subsidiary, as they all had sizeable positions in the less strongly branded mid-price segment. During the 1980s PM and the other player, Lorillard, were largely unaffected as their most important brands were in the high-price segment (Marlboro for PM and Newport for Lorillard). RJR, with Doral, and B&W, with GPC, entered the low-price segment aggressively to try to stop Liggett's growth. Not only did they stop Liggett, but they were in fact too successful and also grew this segment quite significantly.

Not surprisingly, the profit margins on these much cheaper cigarettes were substantially lower than those achieved on the high-price segment, despite the much lower level of marketing support. Also during this period a number of retailer brands were launched, supplied by the major manufacturers who had plenty of spare capacity. (This strategy of filling spare capacity while effectively shooting yourself in the foot is discussed in more detail in Chapter 11.) The result was that, by 1989, the total mid- and low-price segments represented nearly 30 per cent of the total market; not too surprising when the price gap between high and low segments represented over one-third of the retail selling price of the high segment.

However through the 1980s PM continued to deliver high profits growth to its shareholders and still stayed out of the low-price segment. To understand this, we need to put its USA tobacco business into the context of the group's overall corporate strategy.

Understanding Philip Morris

Philip Morris Inc., the publicly quoted group, has a stated mission of being 'the most successful consumer packaged goods company in the world' and its main strategy to achieve this is through 'building and protecting' very strong consumer-based brands. This goal had been translated into a financial objective of delivering 20 per cent p.a. growth in earnings per share; an objective which PM achieved in each of the 15 years from 1977 to 1992. However, in the latter years of this period, analysts had noted that earnings per share had grown faster than sales revenues and notably faster than sales volumes; this is the impact of the real price increases in the US tobacco market.

The success of Marlboro in the USA and its consequent very strong cash generation enabled PM to launch its cigarette brands internationally and to acquire other branded product companies; Miller brewing, General Foods (Maxwell House coffee), Kraft Foods, and Jacobs Suchard. However, as shown in Table 4.1, although those other businesses were growing strongly and were highly profitable compared to their direct competitors, they could not match the profitability and cash generation of the USA domestic tobacco business. Indeed the group had become more, rather than less, dependent upon

Table 4.1 *Philip Morris – extracts from published profit and loss accounts*

$ billions	1992	1991	1990
Sales revenues			
Domestic tobacco	12.0	11.6	10.4
International tobacco	13.7	12.2	10.7
Food	29.0	28.2	26.1
Beer	4.0	4.0	3.5
Financial services	0.4	0.4	0.4
	59.1	56.4	51.1
Operating income			
Domestic tobacco	5.2	4.8	4.2
International tobacco	2.0	1.7	1.4
Food	3.3	2.9	2.6
Beer	0.2	0.3	0.3
Financial services	0.2	0.1	0.2
	10.9	9.9	8.7

USA tobacco for its profits growth during the late 1980s; by 1992 PM's domestic tobacco business generated $5.2 billion of operating income on sales revenues of $12 billion.

Clearly a logical long-term strategy for PM would be to reduce this dependence by growing the profits of its other businesses, but the relative profit margins involved highlight the scale of the challenge. To generate the same total profits from its combined food businesses, it would need sales revenues of around $80 billion; making it the world's largest food company by a long way. The need to continue to grow profits in a declining market was creating major competitive pressures for the group, so could PM change the expectations of its shareholders; particularly as BAT plc (the second largest international cigarette company) had an earnings per share annual growth target of high single digits, i.e. 8 per cent p.a.? Unfortunately, at the publicly listed company level, PM does not compete primarily with BAT, which has its main listing on the London Stock Exchange. USA-based investors, who are considering whether to hold PM shares, would see their main alternatives as being other USA-based fast-moving consumer goods (FMCG) companies, such as Procter & Gamble, Kellogg, Coca-Cola, Anheuser-Busch (brewers of Budweiser). It may come as no great surprise to learn that, during this period, these 'competitors' were delivering 20 per cent p.a. earnings per share growth to their shareholders; thus PM was virtually pressured into setting an aggressive and challenging financial target. For these other FMCG businesses, the target was less challenging as their main markets were still growing!

Another piece in this puzzle is that PM had recently appointed a new Chairman and Chief Executive, Michael Miles. For the first time, he did not come from the cigarette side of the business. In fact Miles had been acquired with Kraft Foods, where he had been Chief Executive Officer. Interestingly Kraft had faced severe price competition in the USA cheese market from retailer brands and it had responded to a loss in market share by reducing the price of Kraft's brand leader by 20 per cent. This price reduction had worked, in that the share had been regained! The group maintained that it would act whenever necessary to protect its brands, as is evidenced by the following statement in its 1992 published financial statements: 'After our people, our brands are our most important assets. To ensure that every one of our brands is a leader in its category, we invested approximately $11 billion in world-wide marketing activities. Many of our products faced intensified price competition in 1992. When necessary, we maintained our market position by adjusting our prices and expanding our discount alternatives.'

The price reaction

The continued growth of the very low-price segment eventually forced PM to respond. In 1992 they launched Basic into this segment and it sold 11 billion cigarettes in 1992 and 24 billion in 1993; i.e. it took a sizeable share immediately. However this really increased the level of competition at the bottom of the market and competitors became more aggressive in their price discounting. (PM was already producing cigarettes for retailers as their own private labels; in 1992 they sold 12 billion of these.)

The real crisis point was reached towards the end of 1992 when previously loyal Marlboro smokers started switching to these very low-priced alternatives. Some competitors actually celebrated gaining Marlboro switchers into their 'brands', but the competitive reaction from PM was rapid and predictable. This switching indicated that the price premium for Marlboro was now above its brand equity value and logically this gap had to be closed before an increasing exodus from the brand began.

In order to validate this price elasticity issue, PM undertook a market test in Portland, Oregon during December 1992. The price of Marlboro was discounted for 4 weeks by 40 cents a pack of 20 (or $4 for a carton of 200), which was approximately a 20 per cent price reduction to around $1.75. The very cheap cigarettes were selling for between $1.10 and $1.30 and so this reduced the price gap significantly. During the test market, Marlboro regained market share while elsewhere it continued to decline and, at the end of the test market, its share in Portland fell back once the price discounting stopped. It is fascinating that competitors either did not see this activity or did not realise its significance; had they been properly focused on competitor analysis they should have predicted some aggressive response as soon as Marlboro started to lose share and thus would have been watching for exactly this kind of market test.

Following this risk-reducing marketing research, PM was able to go nationwide with the same 40 cent price reduction on Marlboro on 2 April 1993. By March 1993, Marlboro's market share had fallen to 22.1 per cent from a peak of 26.3 per cent in 1989 and 24.4 per cent in 1992. The price reduction was introduced initially as a price promotion rather than a reduction in future selling prices for a number of reasons. During the previous 3 years, the cigarette industry in the USA had been shipping more cigarettes into the trade than consumers were actually buying; what is often referred to as 'stuffing the pipeline'. This meant that sales and profits looked slightly better at the financial year-end (much of this extra shipping took place at the end of the financial year and involved offering wholesalers and retailers discounts for taking extra deliveries), but it also meant that the trade was holding excessive stocks of cigarettes. If PM merely reduced *its selling price* of Marlboro, it would be quite a while before *consumers saw the new lower price* because the existing higher price stock would have to work its way through the system.

PM cut straight through this problem and actually *reduced the price of all the inventory* in the channel of distribution by physically sticking the discounted price on the packs or cartons already in the trade. This made the impact of the promotion immediate and gained a lot of media coverage, but it cost a lot of money (PM had to pay the trade the whole value of the discount) and took a lot of sales and marketing resources. (PM had an advantage because it had a large field sales force for its USA food business as well as its cigarette business.) Marlboro's share rose quite rapidly and by July it was back to 25 per cent, while the very low-priced competition lost share. On 20 July 1993 the promotion was confirmed as a permanent price reduction and was extended to all of PM's high-price brands. At the same time PM also adjusted the prices of its mid-price brands and its own very low-price product, Basic; it raised the selling price of Basic by around 6 cents per pack and dropped its mid-price cigarettes to exactly the same selling price. This was trying to force the whole market back to only two selling price points, high and mid, and was a clear signal of PM re-establishing control over the market, and reducing price as a key decision-making input for consumers.

Competitor reactions

The much lower profitability of the cheaper cigarettes made it impossible for competitors to reduce their selling prices sufficiently to maintain the original price differential. Also the small increase in prices at the bottom of the market gave some profit gain to offset what they would all lose from their high- and mid-price offerings.

It might have been possible for some competitors to keep their high-priced brands at their original selling prices (e.g. Lorillard with Newport, which is a menthol cigarette and thus in a distinct niche in the market) so that they would have been at a premium to Marlboro. This could have implied to consumers that the only brand that was in trouble was Marlboro as it had had to discount its price. However unless most of the other premium brands also did this, there was a major risk of being out-of-step with the rest of the industry.

Also it appears that PM had thought of this as well because at the same time as they reduced the price of Marlboro they also significantly increased their marketing expenditure on the brand. This was a marketing masterstroke, although it further reduced the profits generated in 1993. PM had a very good understanding of the strategic thrusts of their main competitors in the USA tobacco industry. Most were totally focused on generating profits and cash flow from the USA cigarette market. R J Reynolds had been the subject of a massive leveraged buy-out in 1989 and was looking for profits and cash flow to service and repay their substantial debt mountain. BAT plc, B&W's parent company, had fought off a similar leveraged buy-out attempt and had promised its shareholders increased earnings per share and dividends; its major single source of profits and cash flow was B&W. American Brands, which owned American Tobacco, had a publicly stated policy of increasing its dividends at a rate of 10 per cent per year and it relied on its tobacco division for much of this.

As a consequence, it was predictable that these competitors would seek to restore, as quickly as possible, as much of their profit streams as they could. Hence they immediately looked for cost savings and slashed their discretionary spending in the second half of 1993. By far the largest item of discretionary expenditure in this industry is marketing support and there were severe cutbacks by all these competitors in the second half of 1993. This meant that the impact and effectiveness (when measured in terms of share of voice, as discussed in Chapter 8) of Marlboro's increased brand expenditure was increased significantly. PM was therefore able to achieve two objectives during the second half of 1993 and in 1994; first, it was able to re-inforce the brand image of Marlboro in the minds of its existing smokers and, second, it was able to increase its share of new smokers during this period.

PM needed to re-inforce Marlboro's brand image as there was a real risk associated with the price reduction. The lower price was aimed at winning back those smokers who had already switched out of Marlboro to a lower priced alternative and to stop further price-motivated switching. However up to this point Marlboro had lost around 4 per cent market share but still had over 22 per cent; thus 22 per cent of the market had just seen the price of their regular brand reduced significantly. This may sound great but, for a number of premium positioned brands, it could be disastrous as it implies that the brand is no longer worth its premium price; i.e. its image is somehow tarnished and less attractive. In order to avoid this, PM spent substantial money on Marlboro's imagery through the Marlboro Adventure Team (white water rafting and sky diving, etc. – all the things you do while smoking a cigarette!).

The resulting impact

Marlboro Friday resulted in Marlboro regaining market share during 1993 and 1994 and the increased marketing support gained it a significantly higher share of new smokers. However the short-term financial consequences were dramatic; PM's operating income in 1993 from domestic tobacco fell by $3 billion and it only got back to its 1992 levels in 2000. Thus the immediate financial gain from regaining market share was swamped by the negative impact on the total value of the market and its increased marketing support. The competition was all badly affected financially, despite their attempts to reduce marketing costs and, in the longer term, several have lost significant market share as well.

The immediate stock market response to Marlboro Friday was one of shock, with share prices down significantly. The stock market had already anticipated some bad news, with the share price falling since October 1992. Despite 1992's results showing the normal 20 per cent growth in earnings per share, analysts knew that Marlboro was losing share, and that the company was 'stuffing the pipeline'. Thus share prices had fallen from a peak of over $80 to well below $70 by the beginning of April.

On 2 April 1993, the share price fell over $13 to close at just over $50; this dragged the whole Dow Jones index down by 50 points. During the next week, the fall slowed and the price levelled out at $46; the decline in PM's market capitalisation from its peak in 1992 was an amazing $36 billion. Therefore, in terms of shareholder value, it looks like a disastrous move! Yet most observers and analysts (myself included) now believe it to be a great marketing move by PM!

The dramatic decline in the share price was created by a classic 'double whammy'; at exactly the same time, the company *reduces* the expected future returns *and increases* the perceived risk of the investors. Risk is about volatility and suddenly nice regular 20 per cent p.a. growth disappears and much lower profits are now predicted for future years. However, if you compare the likely outcomes for PM in the USA cigarette industry with Marlboro Friday and without, i.e. with a do-nothing alternative, Marlboro Friday generates significantly greater shareholder value (the present value of the future expected cash flows) than the 'do-nothing' alternative over the longer term. This is because 'doing nothing' would result in continued loss of market share by Marlboro as more and more of the market traded down to the very low-priced cigarettes. Reducing the price of Marlboro now, reduces profits dramatically in the short term but these may grow in the future as Marlboro regains share and PM can return to managing the total profitability of the market.

Thus, with the benefit of hindsight, the stock market had not reduced PM's share price sufficiently prior to Marlboro Friday but they panicked and completely over-reacted. As Marlboro regained share, PM's share price did appreciate considerably through the rest of 1993 and early 1994. One impact of the panic was particularly interesting; as well as reducing the share prices of PM and its cigarette competitors, the stock market also marked down the share prices of the other FMCG branded companies, i.e. Coca-Cola, etc. The argument was that if Marlboro, as a leading consumer brand, was under threat then all the other leading brands must be as well. There were 'learned' academic journal papers and newspaper articles talking about 'the death of the brand', etc., because some people thought that Marlboro as a brand must be dying if PM had to discount its price.

This reaction is particularly worrying because, if Marlboro really was dying, PM's strategy should have been the opposite. Instead of reducing the price, they should have held the price or even increased it so as to obtain the maximum cash flows before the brand finally died. Obviously this is a critical question, if it makes so much difference to the strategic response. Accordingly it should form the focus of marketing research prior to the implementation of any price changes. The key questions are which type of smokers are being lost and why; these are, of course, classical marketing-research questions?

If Marlboro is losing previously loyal smokers (i.e. older age profile smokers) who are leaving because the brand is perceived as relatively too expensive, then reducing the selling price could regain some or all of these lost consumers. However, if Marlboro is no longer winning its share of new smokers who feel that the brand attributes are no longer relevant or appropriate to them, then dropping the price is simply likely to re-inforce the impression that the brand is dying. PM's market research confirmed that the problem was selling price elasticity because its market share of new smokers was still greater than its overall market share; this shows that the brand still has long-term growth potential. Its exit interviews and switching data also highlighted that it was losing older smokers to the very low priced commodity style products.

It should by now be clear that PM understood most, if not all, of this at the time but one key problem was their inability to communicate, in advance, with their shareholders without giving away critical information to their competitors. However their management team did build up significant credibility with the stock market through their handling of Marlboro Friday. As a result, when, in 1996, PM did a similar price reduction on its branded products to regain market share once again lost to retailer brands and much cheaper commodity style products, the stock market believed in their strategy from the start. This was despite the fact that in this market, the USA breakfast cereal market, PM was only the No. 3 in terms of market share, not the leader.

5 Existing Position Appraisal

Overview

The existing position appraisal should provide the basis for developing the future strategies and plans with which the organisation aims to achieve its goals and objectives. A major objective of this appraisal is therefore to highlight relevant constraints and opportunities that may impact on either these objectives or the appropriate strategies.

A number of techniques have been developed and subsequently refined to help this process. The SWOT analysis (strengths, weaknesses, opportunities and threats) is a good example of these techniques. It requires very careful implementation but, if properly used, can provide very helpful insights into the current relative positioning of the company (its strengths and weaknesses) and how this may be affected by potential future developments in the external environment (the opportunities and threats). Ideally, the selected strategies should build on and develop the organisation's existing strengths so that they reduce the impact of the threats, while enabling the opportunities to be exploited and the significance of the weaknesses minimised or removed. In other words, the existing position appraisal should highlight those areas of the business and its environment that are critical to the achievement of its goals and objectives.

Porter's '5 forces model' is a good diagrammatic way of representing the relative strengths of the various competitive forces within any industry; internal existing rivalry, buyer power, supplier power, threat of new entrants and threat of substitute products. The key to applying this technique is to focus on which force is the most important, rather than producing a balanced view on all five; whereas it is important to produce a more balanced SWOT analysis. Another very popular Michael Porter model outlines generic strategies that could create shareholder value if successfully implemented. A company has to be either the lowest cost supplier in its chosen market or have a sustainable differentiation advantage that enables it to command a higher selling price. These alternative strategies may be implemented industry-wide or by focusing on a smaller niche or market segment. Increasingly many businesses now talk about needing to achieve both lowest cost status and a differentiated position; what they normally really mean is that one particular advantage can no longer sustainably offset any significant disadvantage in the other!

Another very popular analytical technique is the product life cycle, particularly when applied with some form of the Boston Matrix. The Boston Consulting Group's Matrix considers the key drivers of success for a product as it moves through its life cycle. This makes it very useful provided that an organisation can determine both where its products currently are in their respective life cycles and when they are likely to move to the next stage. Unfortunately, in practice, it is only relatively easy to state, with the benefit of hindsight, *where* a product *was* several years ago and to establish *when* it *changed* from growth to maturity, etc. It is much more difficult to use the product life cycle in an 'ex-ante' predictive way which is clearly what is needed as a basis for developing strategies and plans.

The consideration of the practical application of this technique is deferred until Chapter 12, where the appropriate tailored control and performance measures are also considered, although its use within branded and customer-led strategies is discussed in Chapters 8 and 9 respectively.

Introduction

The logical start point for the strategic planning process is to review the current situation of the organisation in terms of its internal resources and the external environment. This existing position appraisal utilises and builds on the strategic management process and competitor analysis discussed in Chapters 3 and 4 and therefore provides the link into the planning process which is considered in Part Three. Strategic management has already been developed as a multi-tiered process and this means that the situation review will normally also need to be done at several levels for most modern businesses.

However even for today's complex groups, there is often a large degree of commonality in the external environment faced by all its operating units. If this is so, it is more efficient to undertake this external part of the analysis on a group-wide basis, thus establishing a common view on forecast rates of inflation, etc. Carrying out this situation review at the highest common level not only avoids duplication of effort but also ensures that all levels of the organisation are basing their strategic decisions on the same view of the outside world.

Even though this common view may be proved to have been wrong, it should reduce the chances of completely opposite strategies being adopted by different parts of the business. For example, in the multinational groups used as case studies and examples in Chapters 3 and 4, it would normally be sensible for one forecast of future exchange rates to be used by all the business divisions. If each division was allowed to make its own forecast it is quite possible that their individual teams of economists would come to completely opposite conclusions (after all, the collective term for economists should be 'a disagreement'). This could have ludicrous consequences for such a group, whereby if the USA-based division expected the dollar to strengthen against the Euro they would plan on increased imports from Europe. If the continental European division forecast the dollar to weaken relative to the Euro they would probably be forecasting lower exports to the USA. There are obvious potential implications for resource allocation decisions across the group; e.g. capacity planning and marketing expenditures. In many cases these conflicting views will ensure that the group is put at a *competitive disadvantage whatever the actual outcome* of the particular environmental factor.

The internal part of the position appraisal will have to be conducted at the level in the group that has control over the resources concerned, and which can really make decisions regarding their effective deployment. Normally this will be at different levels in the group's structure for different areas and, as with competitor analysis, the strategic planning process must allow for this complexity of analysis and design.

SWOT analysis

A major objective of the existing position appraisal process is to highlight constraints and opportunities that need to be taken into account when planning for the future. Consequently an out-of-date analysis is of no value. Information is needed on the present, and on likely changes over the planning time horizon. However the historical perspective can often provide the best basis for assessing these likely future developments, and the appraisal must be made in the relative context of competition. This relative competitive grading is most easily carried out in the form of a SWOT analysis. SWOT stands for strengths, weaknesses, opportunities and threats, and is normally shown as the 2×2 matrix format of Figure 5.1.

The strengths and weaknesses refer to the internal aspects of the organisation compared both to the competition and to the expectations of the market place; i.e. what the business is relatively good and bad at doing. This internal analysis therefore utilises the output of the competitor analysis process that

Figure 5.1   *2 × 2 matrix format for a SWOT analysis*

was discussed and illustrated in Chapter 4. It is essential that this review is done realistically and honestly; fooling yourself is a stupid and sometimes fatal mistake, as is illustrated in Practical Insight 5.1. It must also be done against the aims of the organisation as set out in the mission statement and corporate goals, which were discussed in Chapter 3, as these will indicate which areas of strength or weakness are likely to prove important in the future. This highlights the differences between the very long term, unchanging mission statement and the more definitive, practically achievable objectives; objectives may need to be modified in the light of the organisation's current strengths and weaknesses, whereas, the organisation may need to change these existing strengths and weaknesses in order to move towards its long-term mission statement!

Practical Insight 5.1

An honest SWOT analysis

Some years ago, I was conducting a strategy workshop for the UK's leading electrical retailer and started by getting the group to develop a SWOT analysis for their business. Quite rapidly, a large number of strengths were identified but no weaknesses were forthcoming. Despite considerable encouragement they were unable to identify any relative weaknesses and therefore I unilaterally added 'complacency' to their SWOT chart. This prompted one manager to leap up and declare that he'd identified a 'weakness'. He then said, 'our main weakness is that we don't know how good we really are'. I quite rapidly added 'arrogance' to the weaknesses side of the SWOT chart!

More recently, I was working with a building services business that was preparing to float on the UK stock market. Their top management team identified a wide range of weaknesses and threats, partially offset by some opportunities; what were missing were the relative strengths of their highly successful organisation. I suggested 'modesty' and 'humility' could be 'strengths'; at least this 'stimulus' resulted in a more balanced final matrix.

The modification of objectives may be particularly necessary as a consequence of the analysis of the external environment. This seeks to highlight external threats (i.e. potential constraints) and opportunities for the business. Previously established objectives may be clearly seen as unachievable in the light of this analysis, or the identification of new future opportunities may reveal that the existing objectives are set at far too low a level. As shown in Figure 5.2, there is a broad range of external factors that need to be taken into account. There is a resulting danger that the SWOT analysis becomes an unmanageably long list of apparently equally important items. If the situation review is to be of assistance to strategic planning, these factors must be ranked in order of importance so that only the main priorities are included in the

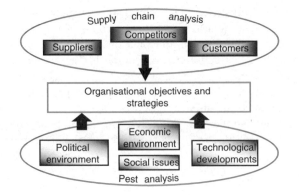

Figure 5.2   *External environmental factors: affecting organisational objectives and strategies*

matrix. This can best be demonstrated by using a real case study example; for confidentiality reasons, the name of the company has been omitted from the case study.

Case study – example of a SWOT analysis

The company is a well-established leading branded biscuit manufacturer, which had key strengths in its strong brand franchises developed over many years and a very good distribution network. This had been built up by its large national sales force that sold directly to the major retailers and gained access to smaller outlets through a network of wholesalers. Both of these strengths created barriers to entry for potential new competitors, and consequently in the past the company *had* generated *super profits*.

However, more recently, the company had experienced increased competitive activity in its marketplace as the industry matured and total sales growth slowed significantly. Another weakness was its dependence on retailers for access to consumers; if total sales are static, retailers will want to reallocate their shelf space to products where sales are growing. The largest retailers were also using their increasing buying power to take an increasing share of the total industry supply chain (i.e. by raising their margins) and were looking to develop their own retailer brand versions of some of the company's leading brands. Thus there was heavy competition among existing manufacturers, as companies fought to retain their access to the consumer and their share of the static total market. Increasingly this competition was being based around price, thus putting increased pressure on profit margins, with consequent pressure on marketing expenditure and product innovation. If insufficient marketing support was provided to their brands, a principal strength of the company would be eroded quite rapidly.

Although the total market was static there were, as always, some segments which were showing quite strong growth; unfortunately the company was not well represented in many of the highest growth areas. It had regarded these as peripheral products (e.g. snack bars) being sold, initially at least, through alternative channels of distribution (e.g. health food shops, petrol stations, confectioners) that were not the traditional strengths of its sales force. Indeed several of these innovations were not even launched by biscuit companies! Consequently when these new products gained distribution through supermarkets, the company found it difficult to gain shelf space for its own 'late to the market' versions. It had tried umbrella branding to link some of the new products to its well-established mainstream biscuits, but the brand association had seemed illogical to consumers; it had actually had an adverse effect on its mainstream brand.

The company had large scale production facilities, but so did most of its competitors. Indeed the industry in total had excess capacity and this had led some players to go into contract manufacturing for the large retailers and even for some wholesalers and voluntary association groups (i.e. producing biscuits branded by the retailer). So far the company had refused to go down this strategic option but it accepted that the potential use of this fact in its advertising ('if it doesn't say "X" on the packet, it didn't come from our factory') had been weakened by recent strategic moves by some very large food companies (such as Kelloggs, Heinz and Nestle). (This is discussed in more depth in Chapter 11.) The company had maintained its total focus on the biscuit industry while several of its competitors were now parts of much larger, more widely spread food businesses. This 'diversification' into other related products had enabled these competitors to gain some economies of scale and scope from some significant costs within the industry supply chain such as sales force, distribution and packaging costs. Since biscuits (like washing powder) are a relatively low-value item compared to their physical bulk (compared to razor blades and cigarettes) and also need protective packaging during shipment, these costs can be quite significant and had been rising faster than the price increases which could be obtained given the external competitive environment.

A consequence of all this was that the historic profit and cash generation achievements of the company were unlikely to be maintained in the future. However there was the potential opportunity for the company to acquire related products or brands which could benefit from its strong sales and marketing skills; the historic lack of successful product innovation made organic developments significantly more risky for this company unless it made changes internally. Conversely, the company could itself have become the target for an acquirer that believed it could reduce associated costs or rationalise the production capacity of the industry. This analysis is summarised in Figure 5.3.

The rationale for a SWOT analysis is easy to say but much more difficult to do in practice. The selected strategies should build on and develop the

	Positive	Negative
Internal	**Strengths** Strong brands Focused company Good distribution National sales force Barriers to entry	**Weaknesses** Static market Heavy competitive pressure Dependent on more mature products Stronger customers
External	**Opportunities** Strong position in market Good financial record Strong sales and marketing skills Funding for new investment Possible acquirer of other products/brands	**Threats** Retailer brands Commoditisation of market New growth segments New focused entrants Possible acquisition target

Figure 5.3   *SWOT analysis for a branded biscuit company*

organisation's strengths so that they eliminate or minimise the impact of the potential external threats, and the externally identified opportunities should be exploited if possible to reduce the significance of the weaknesses while the organisation improves its performance in these areas. If looked at in this way, the existing position appraisal should highlight those areas of the business and its environment that are critical to the achievement of its goals and objectives. The available analysis and planning resources should be concentrated on these critical success factors, and the business strategies should be selected accordingly. Many organisations seem to forget that their relative competitive positions can change considerably over time and that the external environment can be extremely volatile. Consequently, the critical success factors may also change and this may require a corresponding adjustment to the main strategic thrusts of the organisation and to its strategic positioning. What makes this particularly complicated in practice is that the same piece of information may result in inputs to at least two apparently conflicting sides in the position appraisal; as is illustrated in Practical Insight 5.2.

Practical Insight 5.2

The good news and the bad news

Paul Adams, Managing Director of BAT plc, made a very balanced comment in 2002 when he said, 'The good news in Germany is that Philip Morris is losing market share and the bad news in Germany is that Philip Morris is losing market share'.

Clearly, for a company with a mission statement 'to regain leadership of the international cigarette business', increasing market share in such a large and profitable market as Germany should be good news. This is particularly true when it reflects increasing success for brands that have significant potential in other major markets. Also, if the market is not growing, this growth has to come at the direct expense of competitors. It is therefore not unexpected that a large loser in such a situation is the current market leader, who also happens to be the No.1 global competitor.

However, when this competitor is also losing market share to other competitors through pure price competition, this may be very bad news. As was illustrated by the Marlboro Friday case study discussed in Chapter 4, Philip Morris has shown itself to be quite prepared to reduce the selling price of Marlboro when it believes that this is necessary to restore 'branding as the principal basis of consumer choice'. The loss of Marlboro market share to very low price commodity style products thus increases the possibility of a very expensive price war in the market. Even without a severe pricing response, any increasing emphasis on price as the main basis of competition in a previously brand-based market should be seen as a significant threat.

The most important part of the analysis is the cause of the change rather than simply noting the change; thus a movement in market share may well be both good news and bad news.

Other techniques

There are many other techniques that can be used to provide a comprehensive analysis of the current position and only some are introduced in this chapter. One very neat diagrammatic way of representing the relative strengths of the competitive forces in an industry was developed by Michael Porter during the 1980s and is shown in Figure 5.4. Porter's '5 forces model' has

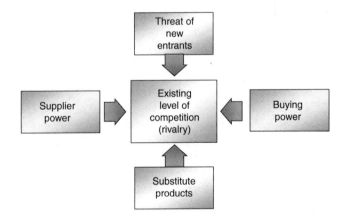

Figure 5.4 *Industry analysis: competitive forces model – Porter's '5 forces model'*

been widely used across many industries and it can be usefully applied with his later technique, a development of the added-value concept, which he called the value chain. The value chain, as was illustrated by the zero-sum game diagram shown as Figure 4.4 in the previous chapter, looks at the total value added by the industry and by the particular organisation within the industry.

Further it tries to identify both the source of any increases in this added value and its corresponding level of sustainability. Porter's development of the value chain breaks down the contribution of each primary and support activity carried out by the organisation. The objective of this analysis is to highlight the activities which contribute most significantly to the total value added; to this extent the technique mirrors the business process classification referred to in Chapter 3, and is illustrated in Practical Insight 5.3. The strategic planning process seeks to improve on or defend the current share of this value added that is gained by the organisation; these strategy models therefore tend to focus on capturing value, while Porter's model of generic strategies can highlight opportunities to create more value.

Practical Insight 5.3

Sustainable strength or threat?

A very successful marketing consultancy company would certainly have included its team of consumer promotions consultants as a major competitive strength. They had developed an excellent reputation in the market for innovative, tailored and highly productive promotions, which gave them continual repeat business from a range of major clients.

What they failed to recognise, and thus to remove through granting sizeable equity participation, was the threat to their continued success that suddenly materialised when the whole of this management team left to start their own company. Within a very short period, the 'loyal' major clients had followed the team to their new business.

Michael Porter, in his 1980 book 'Competitive Strategy', outlined the generic strategies that could create shareholder value if successfully implemented; over 20 years later these generic strategies are still widely used by companies in their strategic planning processes, but have not surprisingly been developed somewhat during this period. As is shown in Figure 5.5, to be successful across its chosen industry, an organisation must either be able to supply the product from the lowest cost base within the industry or be able to command a higher price in the market by differentiating its product in the minds of its customers. The business may not be able to sustain either of these strategies across the whole industry. It should then adopt the third strategic category that is to focus on a particular segment of the industry (often referred to as a 'niche'

Figure 5.5   *Porter model of generic strategies*

strategy), where it can command a sustainable competitive advantage. Logically, this sustainable competitive advantage can be achieved in each niche by either being the low-cost supplier or differentiating the product so as to achieve a higher selling price.

Porter made much of the problems caused by being 'stuck in the middle' of an industry (i.e. being neither 'lowest cost' nor 'properly' differentiated) but he always refers to these strategies as *alternatives*. Many companies now believe that, in their very competitive industries, they should be *both* the lowest cost suppliers *and* differentiated to be successful; however, there are no good examples of companies that have achieved both in one industry. What is now true is that even companies selling differentiated products must ensure that they are as cost-competitive as possible; in other words, any relative cost disadvantage must be caused by their differentiation, and hence value-adding, attributes. Also even companies selling 'commodity' style products, where selling price and consequently relative cost levels are critical, must ensure that *their* commodities continue to provide their potential customers with an equivalent set of benefits. Thus Porter's generic strategies are not now seen as extreme alternatives but as integral parts of the need to develop competitive advantages in order to achieve sustainable levels of super profits. This can most clearly be illustrated by another case study highlighting how the changing external environment dramatically impacts on the basis of competition.

Case study – petrol retailing – is it part of the retailing or oil industries?

Background

As discussed in Chapter 3, the oil industry, like many others, was started by a few very highly vertically integrated companies. Indeed the 'oil' industry is still dominated by the major multinational or global players (they used to be referred to as the 'seven sisters', but recent industry consolidation has sharply reduced the size of the family). They have faced increasing levels of competition in their 'up-stream' operations (i.e. exploration and production) from the 'national' oil companies (often state owned or state backed; like PDVSA of Venezuela, PEMEX of Mexico, PETROBRAS of Brazil). These 'national' oil companies, not surprisingly, have tended not to be so geographically diversified, although several of them are becoming more vertically integrated by moving into downstream operations (such as oil-derived chemicals, plastics, aviation fuel and petrol retailing). Some of the original oil majors have taken a strategic decision to curtail their direct involvement in some of these 'downstream' activities, e.g. by exiting from 'chemicals'. However these oil majors now face increasingly severe competition in the petrol retailing element of their down-stream businesses.

This newer competition from supermarket retailers has been most successful in France and the UK, where retailers have gained combined market shares of over 50 per cent and 30 per cent respectively. This case study will focus on the development in the UK market, but this mirrors what happened in France.

Supermarkets first sold petrol in the UK in 1974 and this move coincided with the opening of out-of-town superstores. Their marketing of petrol was consistent with their normal retailing strategy; the petrol was retailer branded and sold at a discounted price relative to the normal pricing of the oil majors. The initial share gains were quite modest but as their new store openings accelerated in the 1980s so did the inroads into the shares held by the established petrol retailers.

The oil majors had different forms of involvement in petrol retailing; some sites were directly owned and operated, others were owned but managed by a third party, still more were franchised (i.e. owned and managed externally but exclusively supplied by the oil company).

By the early 1990s, the supermarkets in total had taken a 20 per cent market share and had around 600 petrol stations between them. This was a very small proportion of the total number in the UK (just under 20 000 at the end of the 1980s), but this total was reducing quite rapidly. Despite the supermarkets opening new petrol sites, this was more than offset by the closures by the oil majors and particularly the independents; thus 600 sites closed in 1993 and 1000 in 1994.

In the mid-1990s the supermarkets took their petrol retailing strategy into its next more aggressive stage. The first stage had been to open petrol stations only on the site of their major new stores, but the second stage involved open-ing petrol stations with small supermarkets attached. Tesco Express, of which there were fourteen at the end of 1996, is the best example; a Tesco Express outlet consists of a 200 square metre supermarket selling a range of chilled and fresh goods located next door to a petrol station. In their published financial statements to the end of 1996, Tesco highlighted the growing importance of petrol as a source of profitability; it had contributed over 10 per cent of the retailer's profits. The trend has continued with more supermarket chains opening smaller stores, many of which are based around petrol stations. The most recent move has been for joint ventures between an oil company (supplying the fuel) and a supermarket (supplying all the non-oil goods).

Not surprisingly there have been significant changes in the competitive strategies of the oil majors. Esso, the largest UK petrol retailer with 2100 petrol stations at the time, test marketed a 'Price Watch' campaign in September 1995. This went national in 1996 and aims to make each Esso service station *price competitive* against its local competition, including any supermarkets.

Shell, the second largest with around 2000 sites in total, focused on its 'Select' stores (of which there are around 800) and developed them as convenience retail outlets; for example, 'Select' is in the top five sandwich retailers in the UK. This total convenience retailing market is certainly large and the share of petrol stations is growing. Petrol station forecourt shops have around a 10 per cent share of the more than £30 billion UK convenience retailing market; also in some service station shops, more than half the turnover comes from 'non-petrol buying' customers. Shell has also gone quite heavily into customer loyalty technology with its SMART card concept; this has been given broader appeal by bringing in other companies. However competition in this area is also growing as BP is now involved in 'nectar' collectibles with Barclaycard, Sainsbury's and Debenhams.

BP, the third largest petrol retailer in the UK, had already redeveloped some of its sites with 'Express Shopping', providing hot foods and bakery products; this concept has become much more widely spread across their sites. Thus all the oil majors are trying, in different ways, to become much more retail oriented in their service station operations, in an attempt to compete effectively against the supermarkets. Part of this response is also to learn what works best so that it can be applied to build entry barriers in those markets around the world where the supermarkets, or other new entrants, have not yet become the serious threat they are in the UK.

Strategic analysis

So, how did it come to pass that long established, very sophisticated, global oil companies find themselves losing out to a bunch of 'pile 'em high, sell 'em cheap' ex-market traders? The easiest way to describe this is to personalise the analysis by looking at Shell and Tesco as examples of the developments in petrol retailing.

Shell have, for over 100 years, been very proud of how they have developed their corporate brand; their logo has been seen on all their petrol stations around the world and has come to stand for quality, applied technology but, more importantly, oil-based products. In other words, the Shell brand is based around the product and this brand awareness has helped Shell in building retail market share in developing markets (such as Asia and Latin America). The key attributes of the Shell brand when applied to petrol were originally risk reduction through consistent product quality and national/international availability. Consumers became loyal to Shell petrol because they believed it reduced the possibility of damaging a very expensive asset, their car, which they perceived could result if they bought a cheaper petrol from the very early discounters in this market. They were therefore prepared to pay a premium price for the known branded product. Also the highly visible national network of Shell petrol stations continually reinforced the brand awareness and reassured motorists that, wherever they were, they would always be able to buy their preferred brand. The oil majors all looked for appropriately highly visible sites (on major road intersections, on routes used everyday by motorists going to and from work), which were correspondingly expensive. Also because they were now 'in retailing', the oil majors had to set up organisational structures both to manage all these sites (2000 spread all over the country) and to source and distribute all the other products sold through their forecourt shops. As a result, they had relatively high overheads and *their* shops were relatively expensive; this did not matter as long as they were not primarily competing on price. In the past, forecourt shops were widely regarded as being expensive but they were convenient, particularly when they were the only shops open late at night and at weekends.

Tesco opened its first out-of-town superstore in 1974 and this represented a major strategic risk for the company. Its previous successful stores had been in town centres but now customers would need to travel *out* to get to the new store; the clear risk was that nobody came. A key difference was that many more customers would use their cars to get to these new stores, hence vast car parking had to be provided but also an opportunity was created. If cheap petrol was made available on site there would be an added incentive for customers to bring their cars to the new superstore; the supermarkets were perhaps particularly fortunate that 1974 was the year of the first major increase in oil prices, as this made motorists far more conscious of relative petrol prices. The supermarkets utilised this low-price petrol idea even more cleverly because, initially, they gave motorists a voucher for each litre of fuel purchased which entitled them to money off in the superstore; in most cases, the value of the voucher represented all of the gross margin made by the retailer on the petrol sales. Thus the supermarket's strategy with petrol was, at first, simply to use it to reduce the business risk associated with their move to out-of-town locations. As a product in its own right, it certainly would not generate a super profit because it was being sold at a discount and the supermarkets initially had no buying power.

However a longer-term strategy was already being developed and this involved using the very high customer visibility of petrol stations to develop the retailer brands that supermarkets were building during the 1970s. If Tesco had no interest in the branding potential for petrol, the easiest solution would have been to get Shell, or another oil major, to provide a petrol station on the site of each new superstore. Tesco had no relevant product knowledge prior to 1974 and there are quite important risks involved in storing in bulk and selling a product like petrol; these risks could easily have been passed back to the existing experts. The key difference is that the branding strategy of Tesco is built around the customer rather than the product; thus, a Tesco retailer branded product should be perceived as being good value for money while providing perfectly acceptable quality. By the 1970s petrol had become a commodity for most consumers; the grades of petrol were standardised and the car manufacturers specified what octane-rating petrol should be used (e.g. 95 RON for most standard cars). Consequently consumer loyalty was being eroded and the oil majors were finding it increasingly difficult to maintain consumer-perceived product differentiation in their branded petrol; this meant that petrol had now become an ideal product to be used within the retailer-branding strategies.

The sustainability of the discounted selling price now becomes a key element in this strategy; the oil majors are much bigger and should therefore be able to match, or even undercut, the selling prices of the supermarkets. At this time the supermarkets are buying their petrol in the international spot markets, where the price is highly volatile. However their other costs are significantly lower than for the oil majors. The attributable land and building costs are quite low if the petrol station is located on an out-of-town superstore site; particularly as, in most cases, the land would otherwise have been used for additional free car parking. The supermarket chains already have all the required infrastructure to supply and manage their store networks, all they require in addition is one or two people to actually buy the petrol. On the actual site, their costs are also much lower because each superstore site already has over 100 employees and needs an additional two or three till operators per shift in the petrol station, while the oil company has to staff up each location from scratch. Thus their fixed costs are lower and their investment is lower but their key input purchasing price is volatile and should potentially be higher.

This raises the critical question of how the vertically integrated oil companies set the transfer price to their downstream petrol stations. In order 'to assess the economic viability of each business', most oil companies used an externally set value for their internal transfer price; they used the spot price in the inter-nationally traded oil market! As just stated this price is very volatile and, as these input prices are translated into output prices by the oil industry's retailing businesses, this inevitably results in equally high volatility in retail petrol prices. For the oil companies this still causes great volatility in their overall profits because, to a very large extent, their upstream internal costs for exploration, production, refining and distribution are unaffected by this spot price for oil and petrol. However, for the supermarkets this meant that a volatile input price was compensated for by an equally, and exactly matching, volatility in the selling price. This left the supermarkets with a relatively low but stable gross margin on each litre of petrol sold; the low margin meant that sales volumes became critical but the superstore locations and discounted retail prices could almost guarantee high-volume sales (remember supermarkets have achieved over 30 per cent market share with less than 10 per cent of the total sites) through each outlet. This consistent total margin, after deducting the much lower attributable fixed costs and allowing for the required rate of return on the lower attributable investments, could still produce a super profit once the supermarkets gained sufficient market share. Hence petrol rapidly became a key strategic product for supermarkets.

The oil companies faced a further competitive problem during this period as supermarkets extended their opening hours; they had always opened their petrol stations for 24 hours a day, 7 days a week where it made economic sense. This highly visible retail competition made it virtually impossible for other retailers, including forecourt shops, to justify having much higher prices due to their convenience of 'being open when everyone else is closed'. This has forced them to become much more efficient retailers; how effective they have become is an interesting question.

The changes in the external environment (changing opening hours, changing outlet locations) and the significant changes in the customers' perception of the product (a reducing interest in product 'quality') meant that the entry of a new set of competitors has transformed the competitive arena for the original players. As was mentioned in Chapter 4, the fact that the competitive analysis of the oil majors previously focused on the other oil majors meant that they lacked any useful information with which to counter the new arrivals, before it turned into a battle for survival. Conversely, because the petrol retailing arms of the oil companies sold other consumer goods (Coca-Cola, Marlboro, Cadbury's, etc.), the supermarkets had always included them in their competitor analysis, even before they moved into petrol retailing.

Product life cycles

It has been a well-established idea for many years that products follow a 'life cycle' which affects both the current rate of sale and more importantly the appropriate strategic options for the future. The petrol retailing case study, as well as the earlier Marlboro Friday and IBM case studies, is an example where an industry is significantly affected by the maturing of the main product within the industry. It is very common to find that the basis of competition changes as a product moves through the stages of the life cycle. This means that there are different critical success factors in each stage and these should result in differing

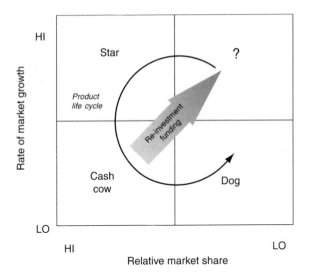

Figure 5.6   *The growth share matrix (product portfolio, Boston Consulting Group)*

strategic thrusts and focuses from companies involved in the industry. These varying strategies require different, suitably tailored control measures (these are developed in Chapter 12).

The product life cycle has therefore been developed by many organisations into a general strategic planning concept; for this to work effectively it is essential that the existing position appraisal identifies both where the product currently is in its life cycle and when it will move to the next stage. It is often very difficult to obtain sound answers to either of these questions but the use of the Boston Matrix, developed by the Boston Consulting Group and illustrated in Figure 5.6, can make the analysis both easier and more meaningful. The technique attempts to relate critical strategic issues to the different phases of the product life cycle and to show how successful strategies must be appropriately tailored to the changing needs of the business. Many organisations have developed their own more sophisticated versions of the basic matrix, but for simplicity this discussion will use the original format developed by BCG.

Figure 5.6 shows the matrix with rate of market growth on the vertical axis and relative market share on the horizontal axis, with the circular arrow depicting the direction of the product life cycle. Rate of market growth is taken as a key indicator of the attractiveness of the industry, because most businesses would prefer to be involved in a rapidly growing market than a static or declining one. Relative market share is used to show the competitive strength of the company in the industry, because a great deal of empirical research has shown that companies with dominant market shares tend to produce higher financial returns. Much of this evidence has been produced from analysis of a large database (over 3000 mainly USA-based businesses) known as PIMS, which stands for profit impact of market strategies; this is run by the Strategic Planning Institute and allows businesses to compare their performance with similar organisations.

The analysis of the database seems to indicate that three sets of factors are predominantly influential in determining the relative financial performance of an organisation. One major element is, as mentioned above, the relative competitive position of the business, as represented by relative market share in Figure 5.6. However increasingly other representative factors such as relative product quality and customer service levels are seen as more important in some industries. Another set of factors takes into account the relative attractiveness of the market and this is included in Figure 5.6 as rate of market growth.

However the relative attractiveness is also affected by the degree of competition within the market and this is impacted by the level of entry and exit barriers, etc. The third set of factors describes the investment intensity (need for capital in the industry) and the operational productivity (level of profit margins, cost structure and spare capacity in the industry) of the industry. One of the key elements of Porter's 'niche' strategy is that a focus on a smaller market enables the business to develop a much larger, and hence more profitable, relative market share. The Boston Matrix also highlights once again the need to do this analysis at the appropriate level within the business, i.e. the detailed competitive strategies must be developed at the SBU level because products can be at various stages of their life cycles in different markets at exactly the same time. This means that each such market could require a differently tailored competitive strategy; particularly when, as is quite common, the overall group has widely varying relative market shares in most of these markets.

The popularity of the Boston Matrix has undoubtedly been aided by the adoption of short emotive titles (wildcat/problem child/question mark, star, cash cow and dog) for each of the four boxes in the matrix. It is unfortunate that these titles carry such obvious qualitative connotations as is evidenced by the use of three such titles for the launch phase of the life cycle; 'problem child' sounds much more negative than 'wildcat', which itself is clearly very risky, but more exciting than a neutral 'question mark'! At first sight, to an ambitious marketing management team, it may seem much more challenging and interesting to run a business/brand portfolio that is in the 'star' phase rather than a 'cash cow', yet risk averse shareholders may prefer the boringly predictable stream of super profits which flows from a successful 'cash cow' business. As already mentioned, the implications for designing performance and control measures are discussed in Chapter 12, where each phase of the life cycle is analysed.

Case study – Ebenezer Scrooge meets Miser Shylock

In an attempt to draw together the material included in this chapter, and the other two chapters in Part Two, another reformatted case study is now analysed. The case study has again deliberately been set in a fictitious environment (as with Rudolph) but, once again, the statements included are all real quotes; these particular quotes come from senior managers in the car industry, the electrical white and brown goods industry, and supermarket retailing, which are all industries where such strategies have been employed.

Ebenezer Scrooge had, at last, found employment that gave him true job satisfaction. As Accounts Payable Manager of Cratchett, Critchett and Crutch he was able, on a daily basis, to refuse to pay suppliers, even though they were genuinely owed money for goods delivered to, and services performed for, the company. Of course he only refused outright in extreme cases but the use of broken promises ('the cheque's in the post'), being devious (e.g. requesting very small credit notes, but holding up the entire payment as a result), and even outright lies (the computer's broken down, so we can't print any payments), etc. meant that each day at work was a complete delight.

What added to his pleasure was that the more cunning he became in avoiding paying money out, the more money he got paid by his employer. The company ran an overall management incentive scheme based on return on investment, whereby outstanding creditors reduced the net investment element. However they also set targets for individual managers and Ebenezer's was geared to creditor days outstanding; the longer he took to pay, the more bonus he got paid. Obviously he added all these bonuses to his existing hoard of money that was hidden under his bed.

In previous companies, Scrooge had always faced pressure from colleagues in the sourcing and supply departments and the operations areas. They complained that suppliers would refuse to deliver because they hadn't been paid, or that quality and service was deteriorating. He considered this as a poor buying strategy as they should have identified alternative suppliers to whom they could turn. At last he had found a purchasing manager who shared his aim in life.

Miser Shylock had learnt his negotiating skills in Continental Europe and claimed to have been responsible for closing down at least thirty companies by refusing price increases or cancelling orders, and even contracts, at short notice. He found recessions and downturns as a particularly productive environment for his style of negotiations. At the beginning of the current year, he had written to all their major suppliers informing them that, due to the severe competitive pressures CC&C was facing, he required a 5 per cent price *decrease* for the forthcoming year. Miser believed in always having at least two current suppliers plus one more submitting quotations for all new contracts. He felt that by doing this, he could obtain the lowest possible input prices and normally keep them, below the full costing of suppliers (i.e. 'There will always be one supplier willing to price on a marginal basis in order to get our business. The mistake they make is to believe that once they are established, they can increase prices in order to restore their profit margins. I always go for competitive tendering to keep their prices down.')

Scrooge and Shylock worked closely and happily together (though their colleagues never seemed to see them smile), helped by CC&C's dominant position in its industry. 'It is very difficult for most of our suppliers to stop deliveries because we are late in paying them. Miser has always got alternatives waiting and so we remain relatively unaffected even if we have to switch suppliers. My staff are now very good at paying just before we get taken to court; although, obviously, we do occasionally wait too long and incur court costs, etc. However we can offset these collection costs against the interest we have earned by keeping the suppliers' money. I have, in fact, argued that my department should be run as a profit centre by properly crediting us with the interest earned on the creditors' money that we place on deposit. After all, it is free money so we should get as much of it as possible.'

Bob Cratchett, CEO of the company, felt distinctly uncomfortable about these views expressed to him by Shylock and Scrooge. He was not sure that they were in the long-term interests of the business but he could not dispute the short-term profit improvement since they had both joined the company.

Case analysis

A sensible start point for analysing this case is to consider the competitive environment in which such a supply strategy could be implemented. The key element is, of course, that there is a dramatic imbalance between the relative powers of supplier and customer; the analysis also considers some examples where the power resides with the supplier. This discussion will therefore highlight where it will not work and the significant problems that can be caused by such significant imbalances in power when they are abused.

The suppliers that most commonly face this hostile competitive environment are those in industries made up of many, relatively small businesses selling to few, much larger customers. The buying pressure from these limited, powerful customers is increased when the products involved are effectively undifferentiated commodities; this enables customers to switch suppliers easily and makes 'selling price' the key buying criteria. However the absolutely critical factor for this situation to exist is that there must be excess capacity at the supplier's level in the industry value chain. Such excess capacity can mean even very large suppliers have almost no negotiating power with much smaller customers. The key elements in this analysis are summarised in Table 5.1.

If these commodity producing suppliers are competing on price, they may well set their selling prices below full cost simply in order to gain volume; but

Table 5.1   *Competitive environment*

Supplier	Customer
Many, smaller	Few, larger
Commodity style products	Added value products
Excess capacity	Strong stable demand
No economies of scale	Low switching costs
High exit barriers	High entry barriers
Low entry barriers	Differential advantages
Cannot add value	Can control quality
Can't differentiate	Don't value relationships

they only need to do this if there is not enough demand to go around! This position is exacerbated when the suppliers also face high exit barriers because, although none of them is doing well financially, the excess capacity is likely to exist for a long time. The most common exit barriers involved are dedicated, long life fixed assets that are replaced on a progressive, piecemeal basis allied to a very high fixed cost structure; e.g. coal mining, power stations, steel, basic chemicals, flour milling, paper and board mills, etc. The situation is even more likely to persist when there are no substantial additional economies of scale to be gained once the normal operating scale has been achieved; this makes it very difficult for any single supplier to gain a sustainable cost advantage that would enable it to drive out its competitors. It also makes it economically difficult to justify rationalising the industry's capacity through merger or acquisition.

At the other end of the scale, the excess capacity in the industry may be preserved due to very low entry barriers and a poor flow of information across the fragmented industry. This occurs in many service industries (such as office services businesses and many types of specialist retailers) where, despite a high level of business failures, there always seem to be enough new entrants to maintain an overall excess capacity position; the power is normally exercised by the dominant supplier, not by the customer (e.g. consumer). In both these extremes, these companies must also find it very difficult to create any meaningful differentiation in their output or to add significant value in other ways; thus the power remains with the other party in the negotiation.

Turning to the dominant customer position of CC&C, this strength is most easily maintained when they are transforming these commodity inputs into a much more added-value product, e.g. one that is itself highly differentiated in its market. This means that the customer can erect strong entry barriers in order to maintain its high level of super profits; particularly to prevent the suppliers from trying to move further down the value chain. The car companies and electrical goods manufacturers have been extremely good at achieving this; it is a massive strategic move to go from making small components for a car to producing the whole car! Another way of achieving this is by branding the 'commodity' product before selling it on; a key part of some retailer branding, such as is done by Marks & Spencer, is that the 'product' supplied to them gains value simply because it carries their brand name – the consumer neither knows, nor cares, which supplier actually made the product. Again car companies have increased their power by effectively de-branding most car components. Years ago, many consumers did know and care what brand of lights, starter motor, battery, fuel injection system, etc. was in their car; but not any more.

It is clearly helpful for these customers if they incur low switching costs when they change suppliers, as they frequently will. This regular switching may require them to hold additional buffer stocks to allow for any delay in obtaining new deliveries, or they may take supplies from several sources at the same time. Clearly this either means that product quality is not important or that it can be economically controlled by the customer; this is much easier with commodity style products. What *is* particularly important is that the customer is *not* interested in developing *long-term relationships* with its suppliers; i.e. it does not place any value on continuity, possible innovation and new product development, etc.

This highlights one increasingly common strategy where Scrooge and Shylock could do dramatic damage; if customers want to build increasingly close, mutually beneficial relationships with a limited number of key suppliers, they cannot continue to 'screw them down on price' and 'take excessively long payment periods'. A classic example is the 'just-in-time' delivery strategy, which relies on 'as required' responses from suppliers. Very few suppliers would continue to deliver 'within 4 hours' of receiving an order if they have not yet been paid for the goods that they delivered within 4 hours *over 90 days ago*; particularly if they were also forced to use marginal pricing to get the orders in the first place.

Even if customers do not want such responsive relationships, they must be aware that their suppliers will be desperately keen to change the nature of the current trading relationship. Thus, if the demand for their product is growing, the key excess capacity condition may be removed and their negotiating power will be considerably reduced. Normally they will, not surprisingly, find that they are the last customer to be supplied if and when there is a shortage; suppliers often have long memories and do bear grudges! Hence this type of supplier strategy is most commonly found in relatively mature industries, where customers see input prices as very important to maintaining their own existing dominant share of their market. It is very interesting to find that there are many companies that state that they now do 'value relationships' with their suppliers but where Scrooge and Shylock look-alikes are still running their accounts payable and sourcing activities. The marketing finance approach to creating value really does require a fully integrated approach across the whole organisation.

Part Three

Planning

6 The Planning Process

Overview

The planning process requires a multitiered structure that matches the strategic management process discussed in Part Two. Most large organisations have a corporate philosophy and culture that has a significant impact on how they plan. Some businesses develop very conservative plans that they intend to exceed while others set extremely stretching targets that they will do well to get near to. Neither planning style is right or wrong, but they each have important implications for the tailoring of their associated planning processes.

Gap analysis and contingency planning are useful planning techniques, but they need to be very carefully put into practice. The business should decide which of the four potential ways of filling the gap between extrapolated current performance and the desired objectives builds on its existing core competences. Contingency plans should be developed for those unlikely external events that could have dramatic implications for the organisation. The focus of strategic planning should be on the most important, most likely external business environment.

The planning process should be fully linked with the control process and the performance measurement system, with all of them being consistent with the business objectives and strategies. Organisational structures should be designed to be consistent with competitive strategies and, if strategies are changed significantly, the structures should be reviewed to make sure that they are still appropriate.

Corporate planning of the portfolio of businesses comprising the group should only be done at the very top of the organisation, while detailed competitive strategy planning can only be effectively done at the very bottom of the organisation. Therefore all other levels of the organisation should help to make the drawing together of the myriad of small business unit plans easier; this suggests that a structure based around commonality of strategic thrust and competitive environment may be value adding.

The planning process will inevitably be partly top-down (i.e. targets driven out from the centre) and partly bottom-up (i.e. issues and opportunities proposed from the business units). The dominant element has implications for the size of, and the information needed by, the corporate centre. The planning process should be an integrated part of the ongoing strategic management of the organisation, and not seen as a 'one-off' annual event that distracts managerial attention away from running the business.

One increasingly popular way of achieving this is the use of rolling forecasts that force the business regularly to update its view of the future. By making the planning process more continuous and integrated within the normal management role, the emphasis on the annual plan is reduced, and planning becomes seen as what it must be, a critical line management responsibility.

Introduction

Part Two considered the various elements involved in conducting a thorough analysis of the current situation of an organisation. If this is properly carried out many of the key issues regarding planning for the future will already have been considered. Indeed the situation review aims to show not only where the business currently is, but also where it is likely to go if no changes are made to the current strategies. Similarly a good SWOT analysis should highlight the critical success factors for the business and hence where changes to the existing strategy are likely to have the most beneficial effect. Further the competitor analysis should predict the most likely marketing initiatives by competitors so that appropriate responses and counter initiatives can be developed.

The planning process, which is the focus of this chapter, should therefore concentrate on *choosing among the alternative courses of action* (i.e. strategies and tactics) that could improve the likelihood of achieving the organisation's goals and objectives. (This direct linkage has already been discussed in Chapter 2 and is re-shown diagrammatically as Figure 6.1 for completeness.) Obviously a key part of the planning process is to provide information on the range of possible outcomes for these alternative courses of action. However an equally important element is to assess the risks associated with each of these

Figure 6.1   *The very simple business model*

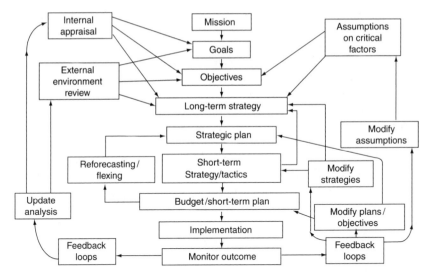

Figure 6.2 *The planning process in context*

alternatives; as already stated, most businesses still fail to incorporate an adequate risk assessment process within their planning and control models. Their principal focus is on assessing the expected returns from new strategies, which carries an implicit but unreasonable and unrealistic assumption that all these alternatives have similar risk profiles.

Another very common problem of planning processes is that our very simple planning model of Figure 6.1 becomes transformed into the monster shown in Figure 6.2. Even worse is that this complex process is then reduced to a 'planning timetable' with specified dates by which each separate activity must be completed. This is normally achieved by working backwards from the requirements for the ultimate approval of the final plan; e.g. if, as was the case for one company, the relevant main board meeting is scheduled for 6 December, then the divisional plans must be finished and approved by 10 November to allow for group review and consolidation into an overall corporate plan that can be circulated to the board members at least one week before the actual meeting. In this large, very sophisticated group the annual planning process had started in early July with the issue from the corporate centre of the basic macroeconomic assumptions to be used for the next planning period. This enabled all the underlying business units, whose individual plans would then initially be consolidated into divisional plans, to work out their own planning timetables. First they had to agree their own objectives with their divisional managers, as well as translating the overall global group assumptions into a specifically relevant detailed set for their external environment. Then they had to agree the review process that their plans would go through so that an agreed deadline for submissions was established. In practice this meant that their critically important 'strategic plan' needed to be agreed during one week in late September. Many of the divisions attempted to *focus* on this 'planning exercise' by taking the top management team away from the office for *two days*, often a weekend, in order *to consider their strategy for the next few years!*

This incredibly bureaucratic approach to planning, which is very common in large groups, explains the cynicism expressed in Chapter 3 regarding the role of most planning managers. Most planning managers do not 'do planning'; they 'manage' the 'planning process', by establishing and monitoring the planning timetable. In many companies it is considered much more important to have met the planning timetable's deadlines than to have developed a meaningful business plan. The good news is that we should not want planning managers to do the planning; planning is a critical line management responsibility! The bad news is that planning and control must be completely integrated into the organisation's overall strategic management process, rather than being seen as an administrative imposition from the group's centre.

The objective of this chapter, which is then developed through the rest of Part Three, is to set out a more logical planning process, which builds on the in-depth analysis and design advocated in Part Two. At the beginning of the book, the overall strategic management process was broken into four stages, as was shown in Figure 2.4. These four stages can now be linked into the key marketing finance activities, as is done in Figure 6.3. The existing position

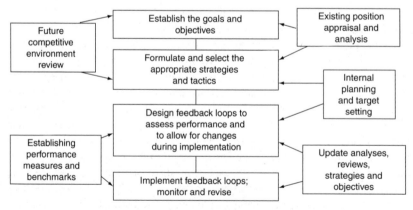

In other words planning and control should be completely
integrated into the strategic management process.

Figure 6.3   *The planning process and its marketing finance interfaces*

appraisal and future competitive environment review that were discussed in Part Two, clearly affect the goals and objectives that are established for the business. They also have a significant impact on the appropriate strategies and tactics that should be adopted in the future. The planning process also affects these strategies and tactics but must drive the design of the feedback loops that are needed to facilitate control once the plan is implemented. These feedback loops should incorporate appropriate update analyses and reviews of both the strategies and, where necessary, the objectives. The establishment of appropriately tailored performance measures and benchmarks is considered in part in this chapter but is dealt with in depth in Part Four.

Corporate values

As discussed in Part Two, strategic management in most complex modern organisations must be multitiered and the planning and control processes need to be similarly structured. The detailed planning process at the individual business unit level should be tailored to the specific needs of each such unit and its particular competitive environment. However most large groups have an overriding corporate philosophy and corporate culture that has a strong influence on both the corporate goals and objectives and also the strategic thrusts that seek to achieve them, as shown in Figure 6.4.

Corporate philosophy refers to the key fundamental attitudes and beliefs that pervade the whole organisation and can constrain some types of behaviour, as well as empowering other actions by even quite junior employees. This overall philosophy may have originally been created or stimulated by the organisation's founders or early leaders (e.g. a founding family such as in the Mars family-owned group that is used as the basis of the case study at the end of this chapter).

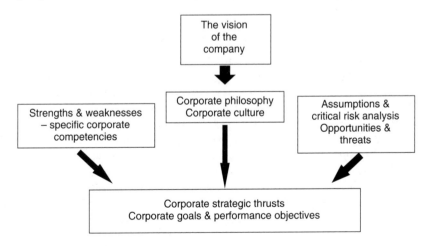

Figure 6.4   *Corporate visioning*

Similarly corporate culture can be viewed as the sum of the *shared* values and beliefs, the shared assumptions and philosophies; i.e. *the norms* to which people within the organisation can all relate. Increasingly large publicly quoted corporations and many other organisations are seeking to make their corporate philosophies more explicit by communicating them both internally and externally. The external communication aspect has received a significant boost through the relatively new emphasis on corporate social responsibility, which requires businesses to explain how they relate to and impact on their total set of stakeholders (as was shown in Figure 3.2) rather than just their shareholders. Internally, corporate philosophies are often described as 'guiding business principles', or something similar, and are used to set out what the senior managers in the company both believe and/or want their organisation to be. As shown in Figure 6.4 therefore, it is logical for the corporate philosophy to be derived from and to be consistent with the organisation's vision statement. However what is even more important for the future success of the business is that the corporate philosophy is consistent with the corporate culture. Culture shows the beliefs and values that are actually 'shared' across the organisation, rather than those that top managers would like to be held! All the research in this area highlights how difficult it is to change culture and that it is strongly based on informal systems and routines, with stories, symbols and rituals being very important factors; e.g. what sort of behaviour gets 'rewarded' in this organisation. However it is also clear that the corporate philosophy must be consistently reinforced by the performance measures used within the company and by the style of its planning process.

Corporate style was introduced in Chapter 3 as it relates to the way in which the corporate centre interacts with its underlying businesses and the overall nature of the group, as is shown in Figure 6.5. Thus at one extreme, a large group could consist of a wide range of unrelated businesses where the primary role of the corporate centre is to manage the portfolio of disparate businesses so that decision-making is highly decentralised. At the opposite extreme the group could be highly centralised with the corporate centre taking a highly involved role in decision-making across its tightly focused group of businesses. Clearly there is a continuum of types of groups in between these extremes. Another element that has a significant impact on the overall planning process is the organisational structure within a large group. As discussed in Chapter 3, the most common structure revolves around geographic groupings of the business units comprising a group. Alternative structures emphasise the industries in which business units are based, or the technologies they utilise, or the competitive environments they face. Within groups comprising closely related businesses, the structure can be based on the stage of development of the market or the particular competitive strategy that is being employed. Encouragingly, more large groups are now moving away from geography to a strategically more relevant way of grouping their component businesses; two interesting relatively recent develop-

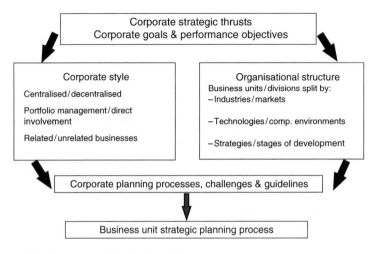

Figure 6.5 *Corporate visioning (contd)*

ments are to classify business units according to 'the rules of the game' that they are playing by and by 'the particular role of their market' within the group.

Clearly the combination of the organisational structure that is implemented and the corporate style of the group will have a significant impact on the corporate planning process that should be used, and on the challenges faced by and guidelines required for this process. However, corporate style also refers to the way in which the group is managed from the centre and this was also introduced in Chapter 3. The Corporate configurations model shown in Figures 3.6, 3.8 and 3.9 can be developed into the more sophisticated Rainbow Diagram shown in Figure 6.6. The vertical axis still represents the style of corporate involvement (i.e. direct or indirect) and the horizontal axis shows the source of corporate advantage (i.e. cost reduction through economies of scale or value-adding through knowledge). This rainbow format of the model highlights the different requirements for the planning and control processes within the four previously discussed configurations.

The Controls configuration normally has a tight formal planning process with targets set for the business units by the centre. A common control system for such groups is to compare actual *business unit* performance against the budgeted level of performance, with the consequence that the focus of the business units' management teams is exclusively on their own financial performance. The most common performance measures used in these types of groups are therefore profits, some form of return on investment (e.g. return on capital employed), and cash flow at the business unit level. A key potential risk in this environment is the use of 'budgeting game playing' by the business units to try to negotiate lower financial targets for the forthcoming planning

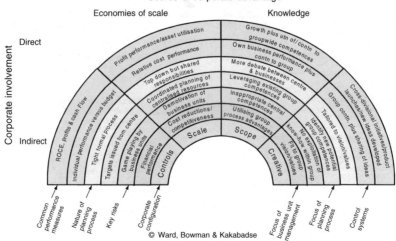

Figure 6.6   *The rainbow diagram: the planning and control process*

period. This type of planning process is consistent with the lack of detailed business unit knowledge at the corporate centre in the highly diversified and decentralised groups that typify the 'shareholder' corporate style of the Controls configuration. It also reinforces the common lack of trust between the corporate centre and the business units, and the absence of collaboration among the businesses comprising the group.

This can be contrasted with the other indirect corporate style of involvement, namely the Creative configuration with its 'leadership' corporate style. In this configuration the focus of corporate planning is to identify potential new group-wide competences or sources of corporate advantage, and the actual corporate planning process should be tailored to the particular group vision and values (such as 'innovative leadership of the industry'). This should make business unit managers concentrate on how well their individual business objectives and strategies fit with the group's specific values, rather than focusing exclusively on their own financial performance. This requires the control system to incorporate some measure of the contribution made by the business unit to the overall development and growth of the group; a key element is therefore sharing of new innovative ideas across the group. This 'sharing' should be facilitated by the corporate culture of openness and trust that is vitally important to this Creative configuration. Common performance measures used correspondingly reflect a group approach plus the key aspects of the corporate vision/values; e.g. cross-divisional initiatives, new ideas developed and new products launched. A good practical example of this is 3M which, in order to maintain its innovative culture, sets a standard that at least 50 per cent of sales revenues should be generated from products launched in the last 5 years.

The direct involvement configurations (i.e. scale and scope) should have similarly tailored planning and control processes, as is detailed in Figure 6.6. The research on which the Rainbow model is based indicates that it is possible to change from one configuration to another, but that this is most commonly achieved alongside (if not caused by) a change in the top management team. This is illustrated by several of the practical insights in this chapter, including Practical Insight 6.1.

Practical Insight 6.1

Why change a winning formula?

GE, the USA-based conglomerate, was widely regarded as having a very comprehensive planning and control process before the now world famous Jack Welch was made Chairman and Chief Executive at the beginning of the 1980s. However the rigid and somewhat bureaucratic planning process obviously did not suit the style in which Jack Welch intended to manage the group. Accordingly a completely new process was instituted across this vast multinational, whose businesses ranged from power plants and jet engines through aeroplane leasing to investment banking and consumer credit.

The continued growth in sales revenues, profits and shareholder value creation through most of Jack Welch's long period of leadership showed the long-term value of such a complete change. Following the departure of such a unique leader, it will be interesting to see if GE's planning process is transformed again to suit the style of its new top management.

Gap analysis and contingency planning

One very well-known planning technique that can be used at either the corporate or the individual business unit level, is gap analysis. This takes the gap between the projected performance of the business, if it continues as it is (e.g. as is shown by the situation review), and its objectives and tries to indicate how this gap can be filled. Diagrammatically the possibilities are shown in Figure 6.7 and these are, not by coincidence, very similar to those included in the Ansoff Matrix in Figure 2.6 (as the Ansoff Matrix shows all the possible ways of generating sales growth; sell more existing products to existing or new customers, or sell new products to existing or new customers).

The problems with gap analysis are, once again, with the ways in which it is normally practically applied. The corporate (or business unit) objectives are often defined in some ideal form, with the result that the apparent 'gap' is huge; requiring very aggressive and correspondingly very risky strategic initiatives if such a gap is to be filled. As already discussed, all objectives *should* be

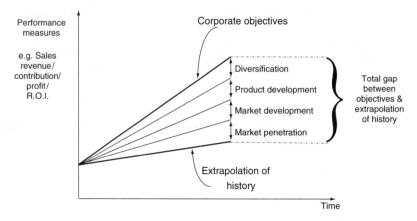

Figure 6.7   *Gap analysis*

established in the context of the particular relevant external environment that should already have been comprehensively analysed. However, even if this is done, businesses still have very different planning styles in the way in which they set such objectives. Some businesses quite deliberately take a prudent approach to establishing their targets and objectives, as their corporate culture is that 'targets should be met or even slightly exceeded'. At the other extreme targets can be set that are severely stretching and may only be achieved if *everything* goes really well; however, by aiming at such BHAG's (big, hairy, audacious goals as these have now become known), the business may greatly exceed normal expectations even if it falls a little short of the stated objective. Neither behaviour is right or wrong, but they are very clearly different and correspondingly require different planning processes and particularly tailored feedback loops.

In the very cautious planning environment, it is to be expected that the vast majority of objectives will be achieved, and the emphasis of the planning process is on ensuring that these achievable objectives contain acceptable levels of both economic return and management stretch. The variances from the conservative plan are likely to be relatively small and will probably be, on balance, slightly positive as the culture is one of over-achievement, even if this is created by consciously under-promising during the planning process. The much more aggressive 'let's go for it' style of planning will result in much more significant deviations from the highly stretched targets included in the plan, and most of these variances will represent shortfalls against the 'planned' performance. The feedback loops and the performance criteria used in these differing styles of business must be tailored to their separate requirements; otherwise managers may feel very badly treated when their performance is appraised. It can be a very salutary experience to move from one style of company to the other, which means that managers can go down a very steep, and often painful, learning curve; as is illustrated by Practical Insight 6.2.

Practical Insight 6.2

Game-playing in planning

The new sales and marketing director of a large FMCG company set the tone for the forthcoming planning round in his initial address to his new company's sales conference. He said, 'Let me make it clear that, in my career to date in several other companies, I have never failed to achieve any sales target or marketing objective that I have been set. I expect this standard of performance to be applied throughout this organisation.' Somewhat amazingly, he was very surprised at the low sales plans that were initially submitted to him shortly thereafter, particularly as this company had had a reputation for aggressive forecasting.

In a similar FMCG group, I once worked with a sales and marketing director who was an expert at game playing when it came to agreeing objectives. As an ex-rugby playing, prematurely bald, very large man, Dave regularly fooled senior executives by being able to cry to order during planning meetings. Once he felt the targets being talked about were getting even slightly difficult, he would let a few tears roll gently down his cheeks to show 'how seriously he viewed the task he was being set!'

The main benefits to be gained from using gap analysis, as with any of this type of planning technique, are to do with resource allocation decisions. As stated earlier, the key focus of planning is to make decisions (i.e. exercise choices) about how, and how much of, the identified 'gap' (i.e. the required improvement in performance) should be filled. It is now generally accepted that more focused businesses create greater shareholder value than very widely spread and highly diversified ones. Yet, in most marketing textbooks, managers are still recommended to use *all* the possible ways in gap analysis and the Ansoff Matrix to grow their businesses. It is clearly impossible to be highly focused on several things at the same time. It is also most unlikely that any business has strong core competences in each of the areas, i.e. growing share in existing markets, developing new customers and new markets, developing and building new products, and diversifying into unrelated products sold in new markets. If the strategic choices are not building on established strengths the risks associated with these strategies are significantly increased which, of course, means that the *required* rates of return are also higher. Yet the *sustainable* levels of *expected* returns are unlikely to match these increased requirements, unless strong entry barriers have been erected based on sustainable competitive advantages developed by the business. The planning process should therefore highlight the most appropriate source(s) of future growth, so that the available resources can be focused in this area.

Another increasingly popular planning technique is contingency planning, which is also sometimes known as scenario analysis. The whole basis of planning is that the future is 'unknowable' and that many of the required base assumptions will prove to be wrong. Consequently organisations ideally need to develop a range of plans that will enable them to succeed in whatever future environment they find themselves. Clearly no business can, or should, have the capability to develop the infinite range of plans that are needed to cope with the possible combination of future events. Thus a prioritising process is required and this is diagrammatically shown in Figure 6.8. The axes represent the probability of an event or potential outcome occurring and the potential impact on the business if that does happen. Logically the main focus of *strategic planning* is based on the most likely future environment and the most important events, i.e. the top right hand corner of Figure 6.8. However, in the top left hand corner, there are some future circumstances that, although not very likely to come to pass, would have very significant impacts on the business if they actually happened. These require contingency plans to be prepared, so that the organisation knows what it should do as soon as the 'unlikely' but material event happens, such as, a possible currency devaluation, the launch of a new or improved product by a competitor, the entry of a new competitor, the loss of a major customer, the start of a significant price war. Of course, the assessment of the 'probability of occurrence' is much easier if a comprehensive assessment of the future business environment has been carried out.

Scenario analysis became much more popular after it became widely known that Shell, by using the technique, had identified the possibility of a massive rise in oil prices prior to the first OPEC led oil crisis in the early 1970s.

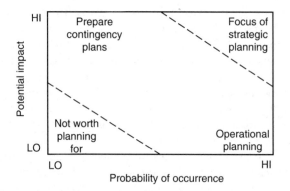

Figure 6.8   *Contingency planning/scenario analysis techniques*

An integrated process

Therefore the outcome of a sound, strategically oriented, planning process is a base plan, based on the most likely future business environment, supported by a number of contingency plans which indicate how the business should respond to significant differences from its expected situation. These contingency plans should cover both positive and negative changes because, if the organisation has not considered the upside potential, it may not be able to respond quickly enough to take full advantage of the 'surprise good news'. This is illustrated in Practical Insight 6.3.

Practical Insight 6.3

Unexpected and unplanned

Around 30 years ago, I was working as a management accountant for Mars Confectionery when value-added tax was about to be introduced on consumer goods in the UK. The company ran lots of planning models trying to assess the impact of various possible rates of tax that might be applied to their products.

At this time, confectionery products faced some adverse pressures based on health concerns and particularly dental concerns among children. Therefore most of the planning alternatives considered relatively higher rates of tax on sugar- and chocolate-based products than on other foods, which were widely expected to be zero rated. It came as a great surprise when the UK's finance minister announced, as part of his budget speech, that all foods, including confectionery, were to be zero rated for VAT.

The sales and marketing and finance teams did an excellent job of responding very quickly to this completely unplanned for, but nonetheless very good, business opportunity. However, in their industry, Shell would have had a much better potential for exploiting their sudden external change, which happened around the same time.

This overall planning process needs to be integrated into a full planning and control system, as shown in Figure 6.9, in which the planning process links fully with the control process and the performance measurement system, with all of them using the same management information system. It is quite astonishing to me that, at the beginning of the twenty-first century, there are still many organisations that prepare plans outside their normal accounting systems. Some of these businesses then spend a lot of time trying to reconcile (e.g. inputting into the 'general' ledger) the inputs to their planning processes with those used by their monthly 'control'-focused reporting systems, so that the performance measures (which are normally based on their plans) can meaningfully assess the relative actual performance against these plans. Other businesses in this position have actually given up trying to reconcile their plans with their actual results, which means that the performance measures

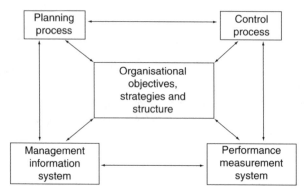

Figure 6.9   *An integrated process*

they use are based on one or the other or, in some cases, something else altogether!

All of these elements should be driven by, and be consistent with, the organisational objectives, strategies and structures. Readers may already have gathered that I am a firm believer that organisational structure must follow the strategies selected by the business; if you change your strategy you should review your structure to check that it is still relevant. This is also true if the organisation changes its objectives significantly and this may be caused by the external environment or by internally driven changes, such as is the case in Practical Insight 6.4.

Practical Insight 6.4

Old mutual – no longer old or a mutual!

Old Mutual had been a leader in the life assurance industry in South Africa for many years but, like several locally dominant such companies, it looked to take advantage of externally imposed restrictions being lifted. Thus at the end of the 1990s it changed dramatically; it demutualised and became a publicly quoted company with a listing on the London Stock Exchange as well as in South Africa. Its top management team was strengthened and moved to London, from where it made several large acquisitions, particularly in the USA, primarily of asset management, rather than life assurance, businesses. The acquisition of large institutional shareholders, rather than the policyholder members it had had as a mutual, required a much clearer focus on shareholder value and a rigorous financial evaluation of resource allocation decisions.

Not surprisingly the group rapidly developed a new more integrated planning and control process to meet these dramatically changed requirements. Obviously developing and implementing such a significant change only added to the already high pressures on management that were caused by the other sizeable changes in a previously relatively stable organisation.

Strategic planning levels

Having stated that organisational structure should follow strategy, we now need to return to the issue of the multitiered nature of strategic management and, hence, of the planning process. As shown in Figure 6.10 there are two absolutely imperative levels of planning in any large complex organisation. Corporate planning, which primarily consists of deciding upon the composition of the portfolio of businesses that comprise the group, must be done at the very top of the organisation, for the whole organisation. If separate parts of the group are allowed to make their own independent decisions on dynamic acquisitions/divestments or organic moves into new areas of activity, the group is really running a 'portfolio of portfolios', in that the overall group is built up from several 'independent' sub-groups beneath the ultimate parent. There is a mass of research and academic theory to show that this is *always* sub-optimal from a shareholder value point of view, and hence *should* be avoided. As it *can* be avoided quite easily by the design of the planning process implemented within any group, it is surprising how often it is still found to be a problem.

The second planning imperative is that detailed competitive strategy planning can only be meaningfully carried out at the level where specified products are sold to identifiable customers with known competitors, i.e. at the lowest practical sub-division of the organisation. As stated in Part Two, many different competitive strategies may be in use at the same time within any one large business, and the detailed planning process needs to be focused on the specific requirements

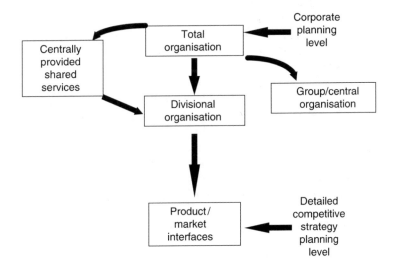

Figure 6.10   *Strategic planning levels*

of each such individual competitive arena. For many large groups this would create an administrative nightmare, and their planning managers could find it unacceptably complex to go directly from lots of relatively small planning units to the total group; hence the use of intermediate divisional structures in which to bring together these detailed competitive strategy plans.

As soon as the intermediate, 'grouping together' role of divisions is clearly stated, I believe it becomes fairly obvious as to the best way to do this administratively required 'grouping'. The separate business units should be grouped by commonality of competitive strategy and key strategic thrusts, as this should highlight the relative strengths of their planned strategies more easily. It should also enable divisional managers to develop specialist skills and in-depth knowledge in a particular type of strategy (e.g. growing market share in rapidly growing markets), and would make discussions and interchange among the business units within any division much more productive and value enhancing. The common divisional groupings by geography, industry, etc. are simply administratively convenient and may make for more *efficient* consolidations of business plans, but they do not make the planning process more *effective*; as stated very early in the book, we should be much more interested in improving effectiveness (i.e. doing the right things) rather than doing the wrong things more efficiently.

Figure 6.10 also contains two different sorts of activities coming out of the top 'total organisation' box. This relates to activities carried out by the group's centre and raises an important question as to whether they should be charged out to the divisions, and hence ultimately to the underlying business units. These centrally provided activities can be split into two distinct categories; the first represents centrally provided shared services where the group's centre carries out activities that would otherwise have to be done by the divisions for themselves. The second covers those activities that the corporate centre needs to do simply because it is a group or decides to do because *it* thinks that it is a good idea.

There is a very common economic justification for any group carrying out activities centrally; economies of scale, as is the justification for the centre's directly intervening role in the Scale configuration. In other words it costs less to do something once for the group as a whole, or at least for a large part of the group, than for each division to do it for themselves (e.g. setting up a global accounts payable centre rather than having one in each country, or even several in many countries). If the centralisation of activity is justified on the economies of scale basis, the appropriate share of the total cost should be charged to each benefiting business unit within the group. The transfer prices for this centrally provided service should be, by definition, less than it would cost the business units to do it for themselves, and so they should not argue about the amount they are charged. Yet as soon as any discussion on centrally provided services in a large group starts, the business units always complain that 'the centre's charges are excessive' and that 'they could do it for less themselves'! Either the economies of scale are not being realised, in which case the shared services should be reviewed, or the centre is including in its charges costs that relate to other irrelevant activities that the business units do not see as necessary or directly worthwhile, i.e. they would not do it themselves if it wasn't done for them by the centre.

These group activities that are carried out by the centre for the centre should be financially justified at the centre and paid for directly by the centre. Including these costs in the transfer charges made to operating divisions, as is done by most large groups, creates distrust and antagonism within the business units and destroys a key linkage between accountability and controllability; this is developed in Part Four. I accept that many groups want to recharge to their divisions all the costs incurred at the group centre for tax or fiscal reporting purposes; this can easily be done in the financial accounting system, but such non-controllable charges from the centre must not form any part of the financial measures that are used to judge managerial performance at the divisional or business unit level. However financial transfers must be made for any services provided by the centre for the benefit of, and on behalf of, the divisions because, without the inclusion of these costs, the economic performance of the divisions cannot be properly assessed. Hence critically important resource allocation decisions may be wrongly made as the supporting information could be fundamentally flawed. The complexity of this process in many large groups is illustrated by Practical Insight 6.5.

Practical Insight 6.5

Separate internal service centres

A large firm of insurance brokers had, some years ago, made a conscious decision to centralise the majority of its administrative services and had in fact set this up as a separate division of the group. Thus the group contained some operating divisions that were organised according to particular product areas (e.g. aviation insurance, marine insurance, etc.), while other operating divisions were organised according to customer groupings (e.g. UK retail broking, which was itself geographically segmented). All of these divisions were provided centrally with their administrative support, which included accounting, human resources management, information systems and facilities management.

The costs incurred were allocated to the users via a transfer pricing mechanism. As with most businesses, the charging system led to frequent and violent complaints from the operating divisions, particularly as the services division's costs represented around 20 per cent of group revenues. The issue came to a head as a result of one strategic planning exercise where profit improvement across the group was identified as critical.

The senior management of the centralised management services division could quite easily cut their costs significantly, but this would have a detrimental effect on the level of service provided to the operating divisions. Two possible areas

Separate internal service centres   (*Continued*)

identified for substantial savings were systems development (but competitors were already ahead in this area and known to be investing heavily) and a move to cheaper offices away from the main business centres.

It was clear that this support division could not make sensible strategic decisions in isolation of the operating divisions, even though it had been set up as a separate 'business'. Consequently *its* strategic planning exercise necessitated very close involvement from its 'customers', with respect to both the level of service that they required to achieve their own divisional objectives and the level that they could afford. This question of affordable cost meant that centralised services were split into two types:

1   a group standard (e.g. conditions of employment), that was considered essential for all divisions to adhere to if the group image was to be maintained;
2   discretionary levels of service, that were negotiable between each division and the admin division.

Within the discretionary areas, the operating divisions had the right to opt out if they felt the service was too expensive or not necessary for their type of business. This obviously made the admin division much more customer focused with a greater emphasis on adding value to the group rather than just reducing its cost base. Indeed, as a result of this iterative planning process, the centralised systems development budget was not only significantly increased but also re-focused on the areas of potential competitive advantage that the operating divisions highlighted.

Top-down versus bottom-up

Another very common issue in developing a practical planning process is the directional flow of objectives, situation review and outline plans. A top-down planning process establishes goals and objectives for the business units at the corporate centre and the task of the planning process is to show how these targets can be achieved. Fairly obviously, in most such groups, the business units all initially complain that their targets are unrealistically high and the planning round can be subjected to a great deal of 'game playing'. There may be some 'back pocket' hiding of accruals and reserves that can 'very reluctantly' be released when 'the centre demands an additional 10 per cent profit growth'. This top-down process is most commonly found in the Controls configuration style of group where the lack of detailed knowledge at the centre about the individual businesses means that such groups tend to be managed by using a few financial performance measures.

A bottom-up planning process initially builds the overall plan up from the lowest levels within the business units (i.e. individual product sales to specified customer groups). This resulting plan is reviewed for acceptability against the group's overall objectives and required modifications are then discussed with the individual business units. If these individual discussions are to be value-adding, they need to be tailored to take into account the specific situation of each business unit; as opposed to a more top-down approach that would demand a uniform '10 per cent' increase from everyone. This means that the corporate centre requires much more detailed information from its businesses if it is to be able to have meaningful strategic discussions with each one; once again, this is a good justification for making the intermediate groupings (i.e. divisions) based around commonality of strategies and external environments.

Any good planning process, not surprisingly, contains elements of both 'top-down' and 'bottom-up' approaches; a key way of assessing the group's planning style is understanding which approach is the more dominant. However a challenge facing many large groups is that on one hand they want their corporate centres to become more value-adding in their interactions with the business units, i.e. less of 'do this because the centre says so'. However this requires more information at the centre, and either more resources at the centre or more effort by the business units to provide the required information to the centre in a readily usable format. On the other hand, most of these large groups are also desperately trying to reduce the size of their corporate centres! Yet again, there is a need to identify what activities actually add value and what merely add cost. In many groups, their multitiered organisations (e.g. business units to areas to regions to the centre) create what I refer to as a 'civil service approach to Prime Minister's Question Time'. This means that managers at each level spend a great deal of time and effort working out answers to questions that 'might be asked' by the level above; quite often, regular reports are prepared because once, on a whim, the sales and marketing director asked for some type of analysis that hadn't then been prepared!

It is very important that all levels in the group are using consistent (but not necessarily the same) ways of assessing the opportunities and risks facing the businesses during the planning process. Ideally there should be a sufficient degree of trust and self-confidence within a group, that business unit managers are able to respond, to a question from the centre, that they do not know the answer because they do not believe they need to know that to be in full control of their business; unfortunately, in some groups, this would be a potentially very high risk and very low return strategy! However it must be emphasised that detailed competitive planning is primarily done for the benefit of the business units and not for the corporate centre; hence it must not be regarded as something imposed on them from above.

Also the planning process should not be regarded as an annually occurring event where, for a limited period each year, a vast amount of business resources are tied up in 'completing the planning process'. Once over, these resources can then be re-directed 'to running the business again', with the obvious implication that the planning process has nothing to do with actually running the business.

To avoid this, the planning process must not be allowed to become a mechanistic, centrally prescribed, bureaucratically driven process where, once finished, the plan is filed away and not referred to again, until the start of the following year's planning process.

The overlapping phases of our analysis, planning and control iterative process should mean that planning is regarded as a continuous and essential element in running the business. How to achieve this in practice is discussed below, after another practical insight illustration of planning in a large group.

Practical Insight 6.6

A top-down approach in practice

Although he has been heavily criticised by some commentators, Lord Weinstock implemented a very focused planning process across GEC during his years in charge. Financial objectives were centrally set and tended to incorporate strong elements of management stretch; the focus was on improving profit, returns on investment, and cash generation from year to year, with a consequent risk that businesses within the group shied away from making long-term investments. All the business units submitted summarised monthly accounts direct to the corporate centre and each general manager knew that they could expect a direct telephone call from Lord Weinstock to question any significant deviation from their plan. The corporate head office of GEC could be kept very small because the chief executive knew all the (around) 150 businesses well enough to have a relatively detailed discussion on each one's performance. This is possible when one individual has been largely responsible for building up the group and has been involved in the development or acquisition of most businesses within the group.

It is, of course, much more challenging for a new top management team coming in from outside, who will normally require much more support at the centre and more information from the business units. The business units will probably find such a dramatic change in the group's planning processes very challenging indeed, as proved the case with the transition to Marconi.

More than a budget

A budget can be defined as an agreed quantified plan designed to try to achieve an agreed set of objectives in a given short-term period, which is normally one year. Logically the budget should be *the first year* of the longer-term strategic plan that is the focus of this chapter. Hence the budget objectives should be completely compatible with the objectives of the long-term plan.

However, far too often, the short-term budget objectives, such as this year's profit target, are achieved at the expense of the long-term plan objectives, such as brand building or increasing customer penetration. This is normally caused because the budget objectives do not contain any early indicators of movement towards the longer-term objectives; e.g. the first steps towards brand building may be increased brand awareness, improvements in potential customers' attitudes towards the brand and initial trials of the brand by new customers. If these linkages are not included it is too easy for managers, when they come under short-term profit pressure, to cut back on their development marketing expenditure in order to achieve this year's key performance measure.

This short- and long-term conflict can still arise even if there is no initial incompatibility between the relative sets of objectives. All plans, and hence all budgets, are based upon a set of assumptions, some of which will inevitably turn out to be wrong. The actual competitive environment may require a modified strategy and even a change in the long-term objectives of the business. Many sophisticated companies accept this but still regard the short-term budget, once it is agreed, as 'a fixed-in-stone contract between the business unit and the centre'. If this is the case, there may develop a significant conflict between achieving these now out-of-date, false budget objectives and the modified long-term objectives.

This is frequently referred to as a 'no surprises' culture but no surprises does not mean 'no changes'; it means no surprising changes! What large groups find completely unacceptable is when a business unit continues to predict that it will achieve its budgeted profit and cash flow for the year until, suddenly in the final 1 or 2 months, it flags up a significant shortfall in performance. At this stage it is impossible for the centre to do anything about this under-performance but, if it had been forewarned much earlier in the year, it may have been able to institute changes, either in this business unit or elsewhere in the group, to compensate for the performance gap. At least it would have been able logically to consider the tradeoff between short-term and long-term performance, and to manage the expectation of its external shareholders. Thus, no surprises means warning about changes to plans as far in advance as possible.

Of course, if a range of contingency plans has been developed, the impact of the changed competitive environment should already have been assessed and reviewed to some extent. This makes the incorporation of such changes much easier, but anyway they are often taken into account by 'flexing the budget'. Most companies that use flexed budgets only take account of changes in sales volumes, but flexing should be applied to all the uncontrollable elements of the competitive environment so that the plan reflects what would have been included if these elements had been correctly predicted. Although the elements themselves (e.g. rate of inflation, exchange rates, etc.) may be uncontrollable, the business should be able to predict both their possible levels and the impact of such levels on their strategy and possibly on their objectives.

The problems caused by the fixed static nature of budgets have led an increasing number of businesses to prepare rolling forecasts throughout the year. Thus at the end of the first quarter of the year, the business re-forecasts to the end of the current year and adds in the first quarter of the following year.

Consequently the business is always looking a full year ahead; there should always be an initial basis for this rolling forecast in the existing strategic plan, so the additional workload involved is not massive. Also if a rolling forecast process is in place, the extra effort needed to produce the more formal 'plan' each year is much less, as the business is regularly updating its look into the future and always basing it on the latest available information on the external environment. Hence a rolling forecast system is a major way of making the planning process fully integrated into the strategic management of the business as it takes the emphasis off the 'annual plan'.

Case study – Knight Foods

Background

'Knight Foods' is the European convenience foods division of a very large, family-owned, fast-moving consumer goods group. It has been one of the fastest growing divisions within the group in recent years, as the two main world-wide divisions (confectionery and pet foods) operate in relatively mature industries. The group uses return on total assets (ROTA) as the principal financial performance measure for its divisions, and ROTA is measured against the target set in the plan and that achieved in the previous year. Senior management within the divisions have a significant bonus linked to the relative financial performance of their business.

Much of the future growth of Knight Foods was dependent upon the success of existing and potential research and development initiatives. This case study tracks the development of one such initiative over time and considers how the successful launch of this range of new products led to changes in the business strategy and thus its structure.

Canned meat products

Originally, the division had no involvement in meat products, being focused primarily on rice- and potato-based technologies. However, by applying variations to existing proven group processing technologies, the division had developed a new meat-processing technology that should enable less expensive cuts of meat to be presented in an attractive form. The most immediately obvious form of presentation to the consumer was as convenience/cooked meats, e.g. canned meat pie fillings, etc. A particularly attractive market opportunity was in the catering market where the existing products did not contain a guaranteed number of 'chunks' of meat, which led to significant problems of portion control. Thus the marketing specification for the new product included a very consistently sized chunk, which would enable each can to contain a specified number of pieces of meat.

Consumer research had identified reluctance to buy existing canned meat products that were seen to contain lumps of fat or gristle and chewy meat. Thus the marketing brief was to enable an advertising message of 'no lumps of fat or gristle' to be used for the new brand. The technology underlying the new product consisted basically of bowl chopping, mixing and blending into an emulsion, before extrusion into strips for cooking. The cooked strips were then chopped into chunks and canned. The emulsifying and extrusion process ensured 'no lumps' of fat or gristle in the product, while the extrusion and slicing process ensured a consistent chunk size, and provided precise control over the number of chunks per can.

The sustainable competitive advantage

The market opportunity was assessed as significant enough to generate super profits provided that the company could generate a high volume of sales. The financial evaluation was based on gaining share of the existing market, even though it was felt likely that the improved product would also attract new consumers or regain lapsed users. It was also decided to base the financial projections on selling the new product at the same price as existing products, thus planning to pass all the product benefits on to the consumer.

A key part of the risk evaluation was that the process technology involved was not a realistic competitive advantage as, once the product was launched, competitors would be able to analyse the product and reverse engineer their own version quite quickly. Therefore the potential sustainable competitive advantage was in being first to market and building the brand identity that owned the 'no lumps of fat or gristle' positioning; thus, if competitors launched their 'me too' versions, their marketing action would not only increase the sector but also reinforce Knight Foods' existing position so that its early dominant share of this growing sector would mean their sales would continue to grow.

The product development challenge was therefore quite easy to define. It was already possible to meet both aspects of the marketing brief without any sophisticated technology; you simply started with prime cuts of meat, trimmed off all the fat and gristle, and then chopped it into regular chunks. The problem was therefore one of cost; i.e. producing a good quality product at a raw material cost that enabled the finished product to be sold at the same retail price as the existing product in the marketplace. A further problem was that market prices of the various cuts of meat required for the process varied significantly over time. Thus there was a need for substantial flexibility in the formulation of each product in the range to ensure that the total raw material cost objectives were to be achieved consistently. The product development team were set the challenge of producing product formulations that would have coped with the range of raw material input costs that had been experienced in recent years, while matching both the quality and cost standards set for the new proposed range.

Another significant planning risk related to the commitment of the significant capital investment required for a national scale meat plant; as stated earlier, the division had no existing meat-based production facilities. In order to reduce this risk, an evaluation was carried out to see if the major investment could be deferred until the success of the product launch was established. This could most easily have been achieved by initially launching in a relatively small test market, getting consumer feedback and, if successful, launching nationally once the new national plant had been constructed. Unfortunately this would have provided competitors with a wonderful opportunity to develop and launch their own improved products at almost the same time, potentially destroying the key branding advantage.

Therefore the initial launch had to be on a national basis but it could be done with a limited product set from within the full planned range. A very labour-intensive, scaled up pilot plant was used to manufacture the initial volumes required for the launch. This resulted in very high variable product costs initially, which meant that early sales volumes generated virtually no contribution. However forgoing this contribution means that the capital investment could be deferred until the success of the initial launch had been evaluated. The longer-term financial evaluation was obviously done using the variable cost structure predicted once the new national meat plant had been completed.

Post-launch development

The new products were successfully launched and the national plant was constructed on the same site as the existing business, but it was established as a separate business division. This was done to create focus within its management team on the existing new meat products and some other potentially exciting related technologies that were under development.

However the new business was not totally self-sufficient, as it relied upon certain shared services (such as steam generation, effluent treatment, site security and general administration including payroll, etc.). It also utilised the existing Knight Foods' national sales force and distribution network, although it had its own brand marketing team. There was obviously a need to establish a transfer pricing system between the two investment centres for these services.

The first principle is that it should make economic sense for both parties to continue to work together in these areas; i.e. if the new meat division could have provided its own services for less than it was being charged then it should have gone off and done so. However the meat division's sales were expected to grow very rapidly as it gained market share and launched new variants under the newly established brand umbrella. This made forecasting its demand levels, particularly for highly volume-sensitive items like steam and effluent treatment, very difficult; a key question was, who should pay for the meat division's forecasting inaccuracies? The logical answer was clearly the meat division but the scale of the problem could be minimised once the nature of the costs incurred was analysed.

The costs for raising steam or processing effluent can be clearly broken into a fixed element and a variable per unit element. The fixed cost levels are determined by the way in which such facilities are set up to run (e.g. running them 24 hours per day, 7 days a week or 16 hours per day, 5 days a week). Once this decision is taken and the size of the facility has been established these costs should not change significantly during the year. Thus the meat division could establish its planned requirements and should receive an appropriate annual fixed cost recharge. The expected volatility would be caused by the actual volumes of product produced by the meat division and the corresponding volumes of steam used and effluent produced. However such a service provider should be able to calculate a 'planned' variable charge per unit, given that their fixed costs had already been taken into account. The meat division would then pay this variable charge per unit for all the units that it actually used. Any inefficiencies in the provision of the service by the providing business unit were borne by it, as they were clearly outside the control of the new meat division. This transfer pricing system needed to be covered by a service level agreement (SLA) between the two divisions, so that both divisions were absolutely clear about their responsibilities in this area. As stated before, no sensible organisation would enter into such a deal with a third party without such an SLA, but many businesses still do so when dealing with other businesses within their own groups; it nearly always ends in tears!

Resolving the sales force charge used slightly different logic (the distribution costing problems are considered in Chapters 9 and 10). The meat division general manager wanted to ensure that the sales force were properly motivated to get distribution for his new and expanding range of products. If they only received a small contribution per unit sold, he was concerned that they might prefer to spend their time selling Knight Foods' other more established products. As they were part of the Knight Foods' organisation they effectively 'received credit' for all of the contribution generated from these sales. However if the sales force were given too high a contribution rate on meat sales, the performance of the meat division would itself look very poor. The General Manager had initially assumed, not surprisingly, that the two divisions had to share the available total contribution between them.

However in the case of motivating and assessing managerial, rather than economic, performance this does not have to be the case. As far as the group is concerned, the production and sale of meat products have arbitrarily been split between two divisions; if this split adversely affects the behaviour of either or both parties, the *group* will suffer. Therefore, the group's interests are served by having the sales force focus its resources on those products that will generate the greatest long-term benefit for the group. This is most easily determined if the comparative profit contributions on all the products to be sold by the sales force are calculated on the same basis. Hence the Knight Foods' sales force was credited with the full contribution from the meat sales they achieved, while the meat division was also credited with the same full contribution. (The important thing about management information is that it should be relevant and useful, not that it necessarily adds up!) The meat division was also charged with the equivalent cost of the sales resources that were occupied developing its business, so that its economic performance assessment and future decision-making were not distorted.

These resource allocation decisions are so important to the planning process that they form the focus of the next chapter before, in the remaining chapters of Part Three, we consider in depth the three main types of marketing strategy, namely brand-based, customer-led and product-based strategies.

7 Strategic Investment Evaluation and Control

Overview

Strategic investment decisions often are one-off opportunities that have a very wide range of alternative potential outcomes and may depend on a sequence of successful outcomes to earlier stages in the total investment programme.

The payback method of evaluation is a good indicator of the risk involved in an investment opportunity, particularly if expressed as a proportion of the expected economic life of the project. The discounted payback calculation allows for the time value of money by applying a negative interest rate to future cash flows to bring them to their equivalent present values.

This is also done in the full discounted cash flow technique, but the discount factors are applied to all the future cash flows. In the net present value method, a criterion rate of discount is selected and applied to all the cash flows so that a net present value is computed; the higher a positive net present value is, the more financially attractive is the project. If the criterion rate is very close to the shareholders' required rate of return, the net present value is a very good indicator of the shareholder value creation potential of the investment opportunity.

The internal rate of return (IRR) method applies alternative rates of discount to all the expected cash flows, until one is found that generates a net present value of zero; this discount rate is the project's IRR. Although it is very popular, the IRR does have several flaws and problems, with the result that the net present value method is to be preferred. The net present value can be turned into a percentage or ratio by dividing it by the value of the original investment; this is called the profitability index. The profitability index can be used to rank possible alternative investments if companies wish to maximise the net present value generated from any finite capital investment budget (a process known as capital rationing).

The wide range of potential outcomes and sequenced stages of many strategic investment decisions mean that the use of probability estimates can be very useful. The probabilities of success of each stage are assessed and these can be used to compute the cumulative probability of the ultimate cash inflows. This process takes account of the specific project risks so that these probability adjusted cash flows can be discounted using the company's cost of capital.

If the 'success'-based cash flows are used, a much higher discount rate must be applied to take into account the risks involved in the project. Applying a very high discount rate creates some problems because it can heavily discount some relatively certain cash outflows in the early years of the investment project.

Many strategic investment projects can also be viewed as containing options which can themselves be significantly valuable. These real options have the same value drivers as the more familiar financial options, but the practical application of the sophisticated option valuation models requires sound common sense if the value of any flexibility is to be accurately reflected. The use of real option valuations is particularly relevant in phased, high-risk strategic investments that have very low, or even negative, net present values under normal discounted cash flow techniques. The value of the option can frequently more than outweigh the negative net present value of the underlying cash flows.

Introduction

In the previous chapter, the main focus of the planning process was highlighted as 'making choices among the available strategic alternatives'; i.e. making strategic investment decisions. Not surprisingly therefore this chapter examines how such important decisions should be made.

A strategic investment decision is any *long-term expenditure that is specifically aimed at achieving the key strategic objectives of the organisation*. Thus they are not restricted to the traditional view of capital expenditure appraisal processes, which normally focus exclusively on expenditure relating to the acquisition or development of tangible fixed assets. Indeed, in most organisations, the really important strategic investment decisions try to develop a sustainable competitive advantage from which the company can generate super profits and consequently create shareholder value.

This means that strategic investment decisions can involve expenditure on any of the following:

- Brand development
- New market entries, new segments and new customer groups
- Customer relationship development
- Product innovation and development
- Research and development
- Sales and distribution development
- New channel development
- Acquisitions, joint ventures and strategic alliances
- Business process re-engineering programmes
- Information systems and technology

(As previously stated, it is the purpose of the expenditure that is important and not how it is treated for financial accounting purposes.)

As with any long-term expenditure, strategic investment decisions should be subjected to a very rigorous financial evaluation prior to approval and an appropriate financial review and control process during the commitment period. Thus, as discussed slightly later in this chapter, all the normal capital project evaluation techniques can be applied, but certain modifications may be appropriate due to the specific characteristics of strategic investment decisions.

There are several characteristics of many strategic investment decisions that distinguish them from the more common *operational* investment decisions that managers face on a regular basis. Thus strategic investment decisions often are *one-off opportunities* that consequently require *specifically tailored* financial evaluations. These financial evaluations require forecasts of future sales revenues and costs, as for all long-term decisions, but these forecasts should be based on the *specifically appropriate set of assumptions* that are relevant for this particular strategic decision. Further, the *potential alternative outcomes* of such strategic investment decisions frequently have a *very wide range* (e.g. from strong success to complete and total failure) and long-term ultimate success may depend on a *sequence of successful outcomes to earlier stages* in the total investment programme.

The uniqueness of most strategic investment decisions makes it most desirable that they can be predicted sufficiently far in advance so that the required evaluation can be collected or developed. The identification of the most likely future strategic investment decisions that the organisation will face is made much easier if the key value-added processes within the business have been identified as discussed in Chapter 3. For many companies, the failure to do this means that their most critical strategic decisions have to be made with the least supporting analysis of any decision taken by the company. Unfortunately it is still the case that most ongoing decision-support processes are based around the much more predictable, but much less value creating, routine operational decisions that businesses regularly face.

All long-term investment evaluation techniques are trying to compare the future expected returns from current expenditures where the decisions differ as to the size and timing of both the investment and the expected returns, the relative certainty (i.e. the risk profile of the investment) of these expected returns, and the overall economic life of the project. It should be remembered that all financially based decisions must be evaluated using only the future cash flows that are directly associated with that decision; i.e. sunk costs that have already been incurred must be ignored in the financial evaluation. The principal methods of financially evaluating capital projects are based on this fundamental premise and these are each briefly explained and then put into the context of strategic investment decisions where the potential source of shareholder value creation is some form of intangible asset. However, for reasons of pressure of space in this chapter, the initial illustrations have deliberately been kept very brief and the major, in-depth examples are given, as usual, in the extended case study at the end of the chapter.

Payback period

The payback method of financial evaluation calculates how long it is expected to take to recover the original investment made in the project; i.e. in cash flow terms when the cumulative cash inflows equal the cash outflows required for the investment. The calculation is shown in Figure 7.1. The shorter the time needed to payback the investment the better the investment looks, at first sight, to the business; so that in both Figures 7.1 and 7.2, project A (payback period of 2 years) looks better than project B (payback period of 2.5 and 3 years).

The advantages of the payback calculation are that it is very simple to calculate and it does, to some degree take the timing of cash flows into account. Thus a large cash inflow in Year 1 will probably result in a shorter payback than if this cash inflow was deferred until Year 3. However the main advantage, and thus focus, of the calculation is that it highlights the risk associated with an investment; i.e. the longer the time taken to recover the initial investment, the greater the risk associated with the investment. Unfortunately in its simplest form, the payback technique does not allow projects to be ranked by their true relative risk profiles. This is illustrated by looking at Figures 7.1 and 7.2 in slightly more depth.

In Figure 7.1, project B has a slightly longer payback than project A, but it has a *much more* stable expected annual cash inflow, which actually indicates a lower level of risk, unless somehow A's very *volatile* (remember that volatility is our key indicator of risk) expected cash inflows can really be very accurately predicted! Figure 7.2 illustrates an even more common issue in

Comparing two projects: both require an initial investment of £1 million but cash inflows differ

Year	Project	A	B
0	investment	(£1m)	(£1m)
1	inflows	£1 00 000	£4 00 000
2	"	£9 00 000	£4 00 000
3	"	£ 50 000	£4 00 000
4	"	£7 00 000	£4 00 000
5	"	£2 00 000	£4 00 000
	Payback period (i.e. time to break even)	2.0 years	2.5 years

Figure 7.1 *Payback period*

Project	A	B
Payback period	2 years	3 years
Prefer project A on payback period alone However: expected economic life of project	4 years	10 years
Proportion of expected life required to payback original investment	50%	30%

Figure 7.2   *Payback*

strategic investment decisions because although project B has a longer pay-back period, it is expected to continue to generate financial returns for 10 years while project A is predicted to end after only 4 years.

The prediction of the economic lives of long-term investments is clearly not only vitally important to their valid financial evaluation but also very difficult in many cases. One simple way of making the payback technique much more relevant to assessing the true risk profile of strategic investment decisions is therefore to express the payback period in terms of the expected economic life of the investment. As shown in Figure 7.2, if only 30 per cent of the project's expected life is used up to recover the initial investment, the risk profile is lower than when 50 per cent of a relatively short expected economic life is needed to do this. For short economic life projects, this revision to the simple payback calculation is particularly valuable; encouragingly some companies are now using this method as a key risk indicator for their strategic investment decisions.

However, the payback method can never be the sole decision criteria because it does not take full account of any cash inflows that are expected to be received after the initial investment has been recovered. It is also very difficult to set a maximum payback period, or even a maximum proportion of economic life before payback must be achieved, for most real strategic investment decisions that involve developing a sustainable competitive advantage. This is possible for many other investment projects such as cost-reducing labour-saving activities, but becomes more problematic when the investment requires ongoing expenditures over several years before any sizeable cash inflows are generated, such as is often the case with developing new brands, entering major new markets, or launching completely new products.

Another problem of the simple payback calculation is that it does not adequately reflect the importance of the expected timing of the cash flows because, in Figure 7.1, the expected £4 00 000 cash inflows in Years 2 and 3 for project B are both seen as worth the same as that expected in Year 1. This problem can be readily solved by using the discounted payback technique.

Discounted payback

It is very clear that the passage of time affects the value of money, and any long-term decisions that include spending funds now in the anticipation of receiving benefits in future years cannot be properly evaluated without taking into consideration this impact of the decreasing value of money with time. Thus the £400000 cash inflows expected in Years 2 and 3 for project B in Figure 7.1 are not worth the same as that expected in Year 1 because of the time delay in receiving. It is quite possible to calculate how much each year's delay 'costs' by applying a compound interest rate to the earliest sum to be received. If the £400000 received in Year 1 was invested at a 5 per cent p.a. interest rate, it would have grown to £420000 in Year 2 and to £441000 in Year 3; the reducing purchasing power of money due to inflation clearly shows that money received sooner is more valuable than later. This simple value of money impact can still have quite dramatic impacts on investment evaluations even in a period of relatively low inflation and correspondingly low interest rates.

However the time gap between making an investment and receiving the returns from it can also affect the risk perception of the investor, as a longer time delay means that more things may change and potentially go wrong. This is reflected in financial markets by what is described as an 'upward sloping yield curve' over time; this simply means that normally investors require a higher rate of interest for holding a long-term investment than they do for holding a short-term one. This means that investors require to be compensated for more than the inflation-based loss of purchasing power over time.

The discounted payback version of the technique acknowledges the true value of the timing of cash flows by applying a discount factor (i.e. a negative compound interest rate) to all the future expected cash flows. Thus all future cash flows are translated into their equivalent present values so that they become directly comparable. This means that the adjusted present values can be meaningfully added together. The simplest analogy is probably to think about trying to add up financial values expressed in several different currencies such as US dollars, euros, yen and £'s sterling. The original answer to the calculation would be meaningless but, if all the separate currencies are converted to a single base, they can then be added together. It doesn't really matter which common currency base is used but, being British, I would automatically convert currencies into £'s sterling as this would make the resulting value more meaningful to me. Similarly the cash flows from different time periods could be converted into any common period, but it is most logical to convert the future expected inflows back to today's present equivalent value

Year	(£000's) Discount factor	Project A		Project B	
		Gross cash flow	Present value	Gross cash flow	Present value
0	1	(1000)	(1000)	(1000)	(1000)
1	0.909	100	90.9	400	361.6
2	0.826	900	743.4	400	330.4
3	0.751	50	37.5	400	300.4
4	0.683	700	478.1	400	273.2
5	0.621	200	124.2	400	248.4
	Net present value		+474.1		+516.0
	Break even period		3.27 years		3.02 years

Figure 7.3   *Using same projects but introducing time value of money (10%)*

as this is both most readily understood by managers and also directly comparable to the proposed investment outflows. The actual mechanics of the discounting process are illustrated in Figure 7.3 where the cash flows for the projects A and B of Figure 7.1 are discounted to their present values using a discount rate of 10 per cent per year. The basis for selecting the rate of discount is discussed in the next section of the chapter.

Not surprisingly, the discounted paybacks for both projects A and B in Figures 7.1 and 7.3 are increased to over 3 years as the present values of the later cash inflows are reduced. However the decision ranking from using the discounted payback technique is still the same; the shorter the payback period the better. While the introduction of discounting removes one major objection to the simple payback calculation, the technique still suffers from the other disadvantage as it takes no account of any cash flows that occur subsequent to breaking even in cash terms. This disadvantage can be removed by using the full discounted cash flow technique.

Discounted cash flows

This concept adjusts all the cash flows expected to result from a strategic investment decision to their present values by applying an appropriate discount factor to all future items. This calculation is also shown in Figure 7.3 and shows net present values of £4 74 100 for project A and £5 16 000 for project B when a discount rate of 10 per cent is applied. Under this method a criterion rate of discount is selected and applied to all cash flows appropriately, so as to give a present value for all items. The net result of these cash outflows and inflows is called the *net present value* of the investment; the higher the positive net present value the better.

The criterion rate of discount that is used should reflect the risk associated with the proposed investment, so that many companies use their shareholders' required rate of return (i.e. their cost of equity capital discussed in Chapter 1) as their normal discount rate. One major advantage of using the shareholders' required rate of return as the discount rate is the direct linkage that is achieved to shareholder value. Any positive net present value for a proposed investment indicates that the expected cash inflows, if achieved, would be shareholder value enhancing. As this is the main financial objective of commercially motivated organisations, the net present value version of the discounted cash flow technique is very widely used.

There are some differences in the way companies implement the technique relating to the cash flows that are used and the resulting discount rate that is applied. Without getting too bogged down in the technicalities, companies can discount the net cash flows resulting from the project, after deducting the impact of any debt-based financing used, by the company's equity cost of capital. Alternatively the overall cash flows, before taking account of these debt-based funding impacts, can be discounted at the company's weighted average cost of capital. The weighted average cost of capital takes account of the required returns on both equity capital and debt funding and the proportion of each that is used by the organisation.

It is often argued that the criterion rate of discount should take account of the specific risk of the particular activity being undertaken. This means that, while the company's cost of capital can be used as a starting point, the actual discount rate applied may be increased or decreased to adjust for specific risk issues. There are strong arguments for not using discount rates that are materially different to the cost of capital and it can be preferable to allow for the investment's specific risks by adjusting the project's expected cash flows, as is explained later in the chapter. These arguments are based on the actual computational basis used in the discounting calculation and also apply to the alternative full discounted cash flow technique, the internal rate of return.

The internal rate of return method applies alternative rates of discount to all the expected cash flows (inflows and outflows), until a discount rate is used that causes the investment's discounted cash flows to break even (i.e. the net present value is zero). This break even discount rate is called the internal rate of return of the project; the higher the internal rate of return the better. The basis of the technique is illustrated in Figure 7.4, where a 20 per cent discount rate still gives a positive net present value for the cash flows of project B from Figure 7.3. However a 30 per cent discount rate gives a small negative net present value, the break even rate must consequently be between the two rates, and linear interpolation (or more computer-based calculations!) tells us that the internal rate of return (IRR) is at 28.8 per cent. This IRR is then normally compared to the company's required rate of return; again shareholder value should be created if the IRR expected from the investment is greater than the company's cost of capital for this level of risk.

IRR is becoming increasingly popular as the basis of evaluating strategic investment decisions, and research questionnaires and anecdotal evidence

The overall break even for the project is given by the discount rate which results in an NPV of 0

For project B (£000's)

Year	Cash flows	Discount rate 20%		Discount rate 30%	
		Factor	P.V.	Factor	P.V.
0	(1000)	1	(1000)	1	(1000)
1	400	0.833	333.2	0.769	307.6
2	400	0.694	277.6	0.592	236.8
3	400	0.579	231.6	0.455	182.0
4	400	0.482	192.8	0.350	140.0
5	400	0.402	160.8	0.269	107.6
	Net present value		+196.0		−26.0

$$\text{Break even point} = 20\% + \frac{196.0}{222} \times (30\% - 20\%)$$

(using linear interpolation)

$$= 28.8\% \text{ (i.e. IRR for project B)}$$

Figure 7.4 *Numerical example of internal rate of return calculation*

indicate that this is primarily because it generates its answer as a percentage, while the net present value is an absolute number. This can be easily understood as we all tend to think of financial returns in terms of percentages (e.g. the cost of capital, the rate of interest, the return on investment). However it is somewhat worrying as the IRR technique does have conceptual flaws to do with its actual computation. One flaw is relatively minor in that each time the annual cash flows expected from the investment change signs, the computation can produce an additional answer (i.e. two IRRs are calculated); this can happen quite frequently, such as if another burst of development expenditure is needed in Year 2 or 3, or if the capacity of the investment is planned to be increased significantly following a successful launch. It is actually normally quite easy in practice to identify which of these multisolutions is the relevant one and which can be ignored.

The second flaw is more fundamental as it can make the solution generated an inaccurate reflection of the true expected shareholder value-creation potential of the investment. The computation applies the same (often high) discount rate to all the cash flows involved in the strategic investment opportunity. This can mean that *expenditures* that *will* take place in Years 1, 2 and 3 (say) may be discounted by a high-rate IRR so that they are included in the computation at significantly lower present values; yet these expenditures will definitely take place as they are the basis of the expected much less certain future returns. Equally, in most *strategic* investment decisions, the ultimate generation of high sustainable cash inflows is dependent on a series of earlier steps that have to be successfully completed first. It is not logical to apply very high discount rates to these earlier activities, simply because the overall risk of the investment is high; this is the reason for not wanting to increase the criterion discount rate, when using NPVs, dramatically away from the company's cost of capital. (This is illustrated in the calculations used slightly later in the chapter.)

A further problem of the IRR calculation is particularly important for many long-term marketing-led strategic investments where the cash inflows, if the investment is successful, may continue for many years but will take several years to become significantly positive. The IRR calculation gives much higher relative results for shorter-term investments that became cash positive in the early years of the project; this is again due to the application of the 'high' break-even rate of discount that is applied to all the cash flows. This excessively decreases the impact of long-term cash inflows from successful brands, new market entries and new product launches.

Another significant problem of the IRR technique is that it does not lead to the optimal allocation of resources when businesses are capital rationed. The theory of finance says that companies should undertake all investments where the expected return is greater than the required return, as this will maximise shareholder value. However most organisations have limited resources in terms of capital and management, etc. so that an important element of their planning and investment processes is to ensure that they undertake the *most attractive* available opportunities. In financial terms, this means maximising the net present value that can be achieved from the available investment funds; unfortunately, this is not necessarily achieved by investing in the projects that generate the highest IRRs.

However, if the net present value of each strategic investment is divided by the investment required to undertake the project, this does provide a ranking criterion that will maximise the shareholder value generated from available investment resources. The resulting profitability index, which is shown in Figure 7.5, highlights the proportionate super profits potential of each available investment; in other words, how much shareholder value should be generated for each £ million invested. In Figure 7.5 project A would be preferred

Project	A	B
Net present value	+ £10 m	+£1 m
Original investment	£100 m	£1 m
Profitability index	10%	100%

Note:

Profitability index is simply the net present value divided by the original investment and expressed as a percentage or a number. A few companies use the average investment rather than the original investment

Figure 7.5   *Profitability index*

to B on the basis of net present value alone (£10 million compared to £1 million), but project A ties up £100 million of investment funds in order to generate its £10 million NPV. In a world of unlimited access to capital, the company should do both A and B, but B should be higher up the investment priority ranking due to its much better profitability index. Therefore, the preferable net present value version of discounted cash flow can be turned into a percentage measure of shareholder value creation without introducing the conceptual flaws of IRR.

Accounting return on investment

Another common investment evaluation technique is the accounting return on investment (ROI) calculation. The calculation compares the average annual profit expected to be made by the project with the average value of the investment (normally the net book value of the assets employed) over its economic life. The major focus of the ROI technique is to compare this average ROI achieved by the investment over its economic life with either the current ROI achieved by the company or its target rate of return. The logic is that if the company only invests in projects that beat the target ROI then the company must in time also beat its target; unfortunately such logic, when based on average rates of return, is very over simplistic.

The technique is again apparently very popular because it produces a financial result that is expressed in a percentage format, and this percentage can be easily compared to the most common financial measure of performance used by businesses, i.e. actual ROI. However, such an annualised projected performance measure does not enable managers to choose among alternative investment opportunities; would you prefer an investment that is expected to generate an average 30 per cent ROI for 5 years or one that should deliver 25 per cent ROI for 8 years?

A relatively simple adjustment to the calculation makes the comparison of relative ROIs more meaningful and helps to rank competing projects more appropriately. The accounting ROI in a specified year of the project (say Year 5) is compared to the company's required ROI. This modification removes all the problems associated with calculating averages, and sets a 'comparable' standard for when all new projects should be generating value-adding returns; i.e. it tries to introduce some assessment of risk. However, it still penalises long-life investments if the same specified year of evaluation is used for all projects. A better modification is therefore similar to the change proposed to the payback technique where a maximum proportion (e.g. half) of the investment's economic life is allowed before the project is required to achieve the company's required accounting rate of return.

Even after this adjustment, there are still problems associated with using accounting ROI as a basis for evaluating strategic investment decisions. The main one is that the whole technique is obviously based around *accounting* measures rather than the more objective cash flows required for net present values and discounted paybacks. This means that the results of the evaluation are affected by the accounting treatment applied to the expenditures incurred and inflows generated by the investment opportunity. For example, if marketing development expenditure is capitalised as an asset on the organisation's balance sheet, rather than being expensed as it is incurred, the resulting accounting ROI would be significantly altered. This is self apparently nonsensical as the same amount of money has been spent to try to achieve exactly the same objectives; hence the financial evaluation should generate the same result!

A personal approach to strategic investment evaluation

Normally an organisation will be attempting to rank or grade a diverse range of investment opportunities, so as to decide how it will invest its available funds. Due to the diversity in timescale, size, scope and nature of these possible investments, it is normally sensible to use a combination of measures if the most appropriate choices are to be selected. Over many years of involvement in such processes, I have developed a personal set of criteria that I use for this purpose.

The most important criteria, not surprisingly from what has previously been written in this chapter, are the profitability index of the investments and the net present value method of discounted cash flows. Another useful and important measure of risk is the discounted payback calculation but, in addition, I include the maximum cumulative cash outflow required by the investment; this measures the maximum downside that the organisation is becoming exposed to, if the project goes wrong at the worst possible time. It indicates whether the investment is 'affordable', in terms of not running the risk of either dragging the whole company down or at least forcing the deferral or cancellation of other value-adding opportunities.

In addition, I prefer to prepare the cash flow projections using the most appropriate financing package for the specific investment opportunity and then use a discount rate based on the company's cost of equity capital. This means that if the investment involves the acquisition of major re-saleable tangible assets (such as freehold land and buildings) a significant proportion of debt financing may be utilised. However, if the investment is primarily on brand marketing expenditure this should be financed exclusively with equity. Thus I do not like to use the weighted average cost of capital averaging concept as I have yet to come across an 'average' strategic investment opportunity.

Another important element in the ranking process is to understand the existing portfolio of investments within the organisation. If the business currently consists primarily of very mature products that have no significant growth prospects, long-term investments that do provide strong growth potential may be more highly attractive than another short-term investment with similar financial returns.

Practical implementation issues

There are a number of practical issues that have to be addressed in applying these capital project evaluation techniques to strategic investment decisions. The most important of these is ensuring that the investment will, if successful, increase shareholder value and this brings us back to the issue of selecting the appropriate discount rate and technique.

One issue that regularly causes problems for many organisations is how to take account of inflation in these long-term financial evaluations. The basic solution is very simple, as is shown in Figure 7.6. There are two ways of preparing future cash flows and two ways of setting a discount rate and it is essential that a consistent approach is adopted in both areas. Future cash flows can either be forecasted including a prediction of future inflation or they can be done in real terms (i.e. excluding inflation). This does not mean that all future cash forecasts are based on today's levels, because the forecasts should show any expected relative changes in these *real* values. In other words, if labour, or other significant, costs are expected to increase in future in real terms this change should be included and an assessment then has to be made as to whether selling prices are expected to be increased in line with future inflation, or faster than inflation, so as to maintain contribution margins in real terms. Similarly discount rates can be calculated to include expected inflation or at the real required return rate that excludes predicted inflation.

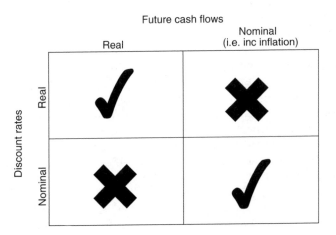

Figure 7.6 *Implementation issues: impact of inflation on DCF analysis*

What is clearly unacceptable is to build inflation into future cash flows and then discount those inflated cash flows at a real non-inflation related, discount rate. Future investments will all tend to look ridiculously attractive, while conversely if inflation is excluded from the cash flow forecasts but included in the discount rate applied, the business will find it impossible to financially justify any new investments. If inflation is allowed for in the cash flow forecasts, a compatible rate of inflation should be included in the discount rate, and it is this need for compatibility that is *currently* causing problems in many organisations.

Most businesses in the developed countries have now got used to the relatively low inflation rates that have persisted for several years, in terms of only incorporating very low inflation into their new cash flow forecasts. For example the normal rate of inflation used for strategic investment decision forecasting in the UK is, at the time of writing 2.0 per cent to 2.5 per cent p.a., which is exactly in line with the inflation target set for the British Central Bank by the UK's government. However a large number of these same companies are then discounting these cash flow projections by double digit discount rates (e.g. 10 per cent to 12 per cent p.a.); this automatically implies that they are looking for an 8 per cent or even 10 per cent real rate of return on their new strategic investments! This is far higher than these organisations have ever achieved in the past!

Other companies use a *real* discount rate (rather than the nominal one that includes inflation) and inflation-exclusive cash projections on the logic that this makes it unnecessary to forecast future inflation. Unfortunately it is still necessary to forecast the relative net impact of inflation on the cash projections as, otherwise, the totally unrealistic assumption is implicitly included that *all* future cash flows are index linked; i.e. are unaffected by future inflation. I personally find it much easier to do all discounted cash flow calculations using nominal projections and a nominal discount rate, ensuring that the same rate of inflation that is included in the cash flow projections *is also included* in the discount rate.

This discount rate is, as already discussed, based on the shareholders' required rate of return but, as shown in Figure 7.7, this cost of capital is determined by the company's existing risk profile. All strategic investment projects have their own risk profiles and therefore have their own required rates of return. This means that a low-risk project like project A, in Figure 7.7, would create shareholder value because it is above the project risk/return line, even though it generates a rate of return that is less than the company's existing cost of capital. The theoretical argument is that if the company undertook such a low-risk project, it's more predictable cash flow returns would over time reduce the overall risk profile of the total company. However I know many chief executives and chief financial officers who are not prepared to wait for this reduction in their risk profile (which would be seen in a lower beta factor being

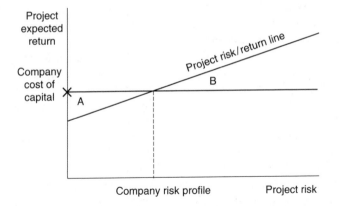

Figure 7.7   *Implementation issues: project risk and return*

applied to their company), because they believe that investors would be immediately upset at the lower rate of return being generated by the new investment. Therefore these companies often set the minimum required rate of return (often referred to as 'the hurdle rate') at, or even slightly above, their current cost of capital, as shown in Figure 7.8.

Unless these companies implement the kinked return line shown in Figure 7.8 they will find project B from Figure 7.7 financially attractive. Although project B generates a projected return that is greater than the company's current cost of capital, it also has a higher project risk than the company's current risk profile. From Figure 7.7 it can be seen that it would indeed be shareholder value destroying. If organisations want to ensure that projects like 'B' are rejected, they can insist on increasing rates of return for all projects

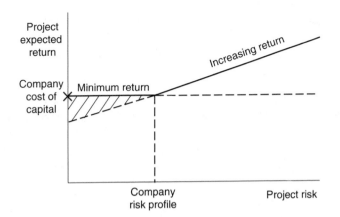

Figure 7.8   *Minimum reinvestment return requirements*

with higher risk profiles (i.e. by assessing the project beta factors) than that of the overall company; hence the common 'kinked' hurdle rate requirement for strategic investment decisions.

Unfortunately this process tends to introduce a skewed distribution into the portfolio of strategic investment decisions that gain financial approval. The shaded segment area in Figure 7.8 shows low-risk investment opportunities that will be rejected because of the company cost of capital minimum required rate of return. Unless this company identifies some high-return but low-risk investments, most of its *new* investments will have risk profiles that are greater than the company's current risk level; i.e. they will be above the upward sloping portion of the line, as it is very unlikely that many projects can be found that fit above the horizontal portion of this kinked risk/return line. This results inevitably in the company's risk profile increasing over time, which is not necessarily a bad thing but I have *never* seen any organisation state this as one of its *strategic objectives*. If the business wants to maintain its current overall risk profile, it should accept that its portfolio of new strategic investment projects should contain both higher and lower risk profiles. The lower risk investments should be financially evaluated against a correspondingly lower required rate of return; i.e. the straight line project risk/return line of Figure 7.7 is to be preferred to the kinked line of Figure 7.8.

Probability estimates

As mentioned at the start of this chapter, a common feature of strategic investment decisions is that they consist of several quite high-risk stages that need to be successfully completed before the potential high financial returns can be realised. This introduces another challenge into the strategic investment evaluation process that can partially be handled by incorporating the probability estimates of success for each of these stages.

Figure 7.9 shows two projects with the same expected value but very different risk profiles, due to their dramatically different ranges of possible outcomes. Project A is expected to have a value of 1000 or nothing, while B is only

| | Project A | | | Project B | |
Value of outcome	Probability of outcome	Expected value	Value of outcome	Probability of outcome	Expected value
1000	10%	100	80	25%	20
–	90%	–	100	50%	50
			120	25%	30
	100%	100		100%	100

Figure 7.9 *Implementation issues: use of probability estimates*

expected to vary between 80 and 120 at the extreme (i.e. very close to its expected value of 100). Indeed 50 per cent of the time, B should actually generate its expected value, while A cannot achieve its expected value of 100, always having a high variance (10 per cent of the time, it will over perform by 900, but 90 per cent of the time, it will under perform by 100). It is clearly this volatility in possible outcomes that drives the assessment of the risk profile, but it should also indicate where the focus of financial control should be placed.

Many businesses would spend most of their effort in trying to refine their assessment of the value of the successful outcome of project A; is it really 1000 or 900 or 1100? This is a waste of time for such an unlikely outcome; this high-risk project has a small likelihood of delivering a very high return. The focus should be on making it more likely that this high return will be achieved. As shown in Figure 7.10, if the probability of success could be increased from 10 per cent to 20 per cent the expected value of the project is doubled; the remaining 80 per cent probability of total loss still means that the project has a high-risk profile. However in the already low-risk project B, increasing the probability of actually receiving 100 from 50 per cent to 60 per cent does nothing at all for the overall expected value; in low-risk projects, the focus of the financial evaluation *should be* on the assessment of the value of the outcomes rather than on refining still further their probability distributions.

This simple illustration highlights how the use of probability estimates can help, but it becomes much more powerful when there are a series of high-risk stages, as is shown in Figure 7.11. In this highly simplified version of a real strategic investment case, the company identified a phased investment programme for the development and launch of a high-risk new product. In Year 1, some marketing research costing £2 million was to be undertaken. This would be

Project A			Project B		
Value of outcome	Probability of outcome	Expected value	Value of outcome	Probability of outcome	Expected value
1000	20%	200	80	20%	16
–	80%	–	100	60%	60
			120	20%	24
	100%	200		100%	100

In project A a 10% increase in the probability of success to 20% results in the doubling of the expected value of the element, although the remaining 80% probability of total loss means that this element still has a high risk profile.
In project B, a 10% increase in the probability of the most likely outcome has no effect on the expected value of the project.

Figure 7.10   *Implementation issues: revising initial probability estimates*

	① Expected annual cash flow (£ ms)	② Probability of success of previous stage	③ Cumulative probability factor (2 × previous Year's 3)	④ Probability adjusted expected annual cash flow
Years				1 x 3 (£ ms)
1	(2)	100%	100%	(2)
2	(4)	50%	50%	(2)
3	(4)	60%	30%	(1.2)
4	(6)	70%	21%	(1.26)
5–15	11	80%	16.8%	1.85

Figure 7.11   *Use of expected values in high-risk strategic investment decisions*

reviewed at the end of the year and was assessed as having an initial probability of success of 50 per cent; if it was unsuccessful, the rest of the project would be cancelled. The next stage in Year 2 involved product feasibility testing and more marketing research, costing £4 million and a probability of success rating of 60 per cent. If this worked, Year 3 involved pilot scale production and test marketing requiring a net cash outflow of another £4 million with a success expectation of 70 per cent. Year 4 was the full national launch with consequent negative cash flows of £6 million but a higher probability of success of 80 per cent due to the successful outcomes of all the previous stages. Following a successful national launch, the company expected to generate £11 million cash inflows per year (representing £10 million annual profit plus a depreciation add-back of £1 million) for 11 years from Year 5 to Year 15.

The cash flow items shown in column 1 of Figure 7.11 represent the cash flows that will occur if each stage is successful; hence they are often referred to as the success cash flows. However given the probabilities associated with each stage it is 'relatively unlikely' that the company will actually receive its £11million in Years 5–15. Mathematically the cumulative probability of success of each subsequent stage can be calculated by multiplying together the probabilities associated with all the prior stages; this is done in column 3 of Figure 7.11. This shows that it is only 16.8 per cent likely that the ultimate national launch will be successful. Put another way, as is done in column 4 of Figure 7.11, the probability adjusted expected inflow each year from Year 5 to Year 15 is not £11 million but only £1.85 million (i.e. £11 million×0.168). Each of the cash outflows has similarly been reduced by its appropriate cumulative probability of success, or *individual risk factor*.

Thus for our project we now have two very different looking cash flow projections and we need to decide which one we are going to discount in order to evaluate the project. Different companies would choose either of these but the key issue is that the discount rate used must be very different. The whole purpose of using the probability estimates is to identify and focus on the specific risks associated with each stage of the strategic investment project. Therefore the probability adjusted expected cash flows should be discounted at a lower rate, and normally the company's cost of capital is reasonably appropriate. Some companies use the risk-free rate of return to discount these cash flows but the risk-free rate is only appropriate for 'certainty equivalent' cash flows; i.e. where all the risk has been removed. Our exercise does not make it *certain* that the company will receive £1.85 million per year for 11 years it has merely taken account of the sequential risk process involved in this long-term strategic investment.

If the success cash flows are used in the financial evaluation, a much higher discount rate must be used to take account of the higher risk profile that is still included in these cash flows. As shown in Figure 7.12, a discount rate of 35 per cent per year has a similar impact as applying the cumulative probability factors and then using a discount rate set at the level of the company's cost of capital. The problem with this method is that it means that a very high discount rate (35 per cent) is applied to all the projected cash flows even though they obviously have very different risk profiles; ranging from the certainty of spending £2 million this year to the much less likely receipt of £11 million in Years 5–15 (assessed as 16.8 per cent probable).

Another advantage of using the probability method of assessment is that it enables almost automatic updates as the project moves from stage to stage. Thus if, as is shown in Figure 7.13, the first year has been successfully completed on budget and no other estimates or probability factors have changed, each of the annual cash flows has become 1 year nearer and twice as likely to

Comparison of net present value calculations

	Probability factor adjusted cash flows			Unadjusted cash flows		
Year	Expected annual cash flows (£m)	Discount factor @ 15% (i.e. Company cost of capital)	Present value	Original annual cash flows (£m)	Discount factor @ 35%	Present value
1	(2)	0.870	(1.74)	(2)	0.741	(1.48)
2	(2)	0.756	(1.51)	(4)	0.549	(2.20)
3	(1.2)	0.658	(0.79)	(4)	0.406	(1.62)
4	(1.26)	0.572	(0.72)	(6)	0.301	(1.81)
5–15	1.85	2.992	5.53	11	0.828	9.11
	Net present value		+0.77	Net present value		+2.00

Figure 7.12   *Use of expected values in high-risk strategic investment decisions*

Increasing present values as project success becomes more likely

Update on project

The first investment stage (Year 1) has now been successfully completed on budget. No other estimates have been changed and the same probability factors have been applied to the expected remaining future cash flows.

Year	Annual cash flow (£m)	Probability of success of previous stage	Cumulative probability factor	Probability adjusted expected annual cash flow
1	(4)	100%	100%	(4)
2	(4)	60%	60%	(2.4)
3	(6)	70%	42%	(2.52)
4–14	11	80%	33.6%	3.70

Figure 7.13   *Use of expected values in high-risk strategic investment decisions*

occur (the 50 per cent probability of success of the original Year 1 is no longer applicable). These new cash flow forecasts can now be re-discounted at the same discount rate (i.e. the company's cost of capital) as was originally used. If the success-based cash flows are being used, the subsequent years' values have not changed but the risk profile of the project has reduced; thus, the discount rate should be reduced somewhat. In this project a rate of 30 per cent rather than the original 35 per cent gives an equivalent assessment of the project, as is shown in Figure 7.14.

I find it very strange that many companies have trouble with the idea of assessing probabilities of success for each stage of a major strategic investment

Recomputing net present values

	Probability factor adjusted cash flows			Unadjusted cash flows		
Year	Expected annual cash flows (£m)	Discount factor @ 15%	Present value	Original annual cash flows (£m)	Discount factor @ 35%	Present value
1	(4)	0.870	(3.48)	(4)	0.741	(2.96)
2	(2.4)	0.756	(1.81)	(4)	0.549	(2.20)
3	(2.52)	0.658	(1.66)	(6)	0.406	(2.44)
4–14	3.70	3.441	12.73	11	1.118	12.30
	Net present value		+5.78	Net present value		+4.70

As the total risk associated with the project has now reduced, the discount factor used on the gross unadjusted expected cash flows should be reduced; approximately 30% would generate a similar NPV as produced by the probability adjusted cash flows.

Figure 7.14   *Use of expected values in high-risk strategic investment decisions*

because they see the process as 'subjective'. Yet these same companies see nothing subjective in projecting cash flows for the next 20 or 30 years and then choosing a 'high' discount rate to reflect the risk associated with the particular project. The use of probability assessments means that the appropriate line managers can be totally involved in the process, and innovative ways of assessing, or even improving, the chances of success may be identified. In most companies the choice of the risk-adjusted discount rate is solely under the control of the finance function.

Real options

Even using cumulative probabilities in these sequential strategic investment decisions does not fully reflect the potential value of some high-risk opportunities, as it does not apply a financial value to any flexibility that may exist regarding subsequent investment decisions. Each decision point in the investment programme may create an option for the company to continue or not, and these options can have significant value. This is particularly true where additional information can be gained during the intervening period for which the rest of the expenditure can be deferred.

An option is *a right*, but not an obligation, *to buy or sell* an asset *within a specified period* of time *at a given price* (the exercise or striking price of the option). A call option is the right to buy an asset, a put option is the right to sell an asset. Over the last 30 years, finance theory has developed very sophisticated models for valuing financial options (e.g. those relating to stocks and shares, foreign currencies, etc.). More recently, there has been a growing awareness that this methodology can be applied to valuing the real options created as part of major strategic investment decisions. Space in this book does not allow a comprehensive discussion of option valuation techniques, but all the normal valuation models are based around the five basic value drivers of options. These are set out in Figure 7.15 and are amazingly logical. Options are valuable only where the value of the asset involved is volatile; thus an

Five parameters

1) Current price of the underlying asset (P)

2) Exercise price of the option (E)

3) The instantaneous variance of the asset returns (σ^2)

4) The time to expiry of the option (t)

5) The risk-free interest rate (r_f)

Figure 7.15 *Option value drivers*

option to defer for a year, the decision to buy a house or a share, etc. is valuable if you think house prices, etc. may change significantly during this year. This makes volatility a key driver of option values, but the volatility *must* make the option exercisable if it is to generate value. Therefore the relationship between the current asset price and the exercise price is another key driver of option value; the closer the exercise price is to the current asset price, the more valuable is the option, as it is more likely that it will ultimately be exercised. If the exercise price of a call option is already below the current asset price, the option is said to be 'in the money'; for a put option, this happens when the exercise price is above the current asset price. Logically an option with 2 years to run is more valuable than an option with an unexpired life of 2 weeks and therefore the time to expiry of the option is also important as an option value driver. The last factor, the risk-free interest rate, relates to the fact that the exercise price does not have to be paid until the option is exercised, which is normally at the end of its life. If the asset was actually bought or sold, the value would be paid immediately; therefore, the comparison should be made between the asset price and the present value of the exercise price. This means that the exercise price of the option is discounted back to its 'certainty' present value by using the risk-free discount rate.

Each of these option value drivers has an equivalent for strategic investment decisions so that the methodology can be applied to real options, as is shown in Figure 7.16. In strategic investment decisions, the option does not relate to buying or selling an asset but rather to carrying on with the investment programme. Hence the current asset price is normally the present value of the investment's expected cash flows, while the exercise price of the option is the subsequent expenditure required to finish the project and consequently generate these expected cash flows. The life of the option is clearly the potential length of deferment for these subsequent expenditures and the time value of money is

Option value drivers ~ applied to real options

Five parameters

1) Current price of the underlying asset (P)
   – present value of investment's cash flow

2) Exercise price of the option (E)
   – subsequent expenditure required to acquire the total investment

3) The instantaneous variance of the asset returns (σ^2)
   – volatility of the investment's returns

4) The time to expiry of the option (t)
   – length of deferment period

5) The risk-free interest rate (r_f)
   – time value of money

Figure 7.16 *Valuing the real options*

the same as for financial options, although several companies seem to prefer to use their own cost of capital rather than the more appropriate risk-free rate. The most difficult issue in most cases is the volatility of the investment's returns but this can be quite simply assessed by considering the range of the potential outcomes. It is not necessary to try to get over-sophisticated to generate continuous ranges and statistical distributions; like many practitioners in this area, I prefer to exercise common-sense judgements rather than spurious complex calculations. A logical frame of reference for volatilities in high-risk strategic investments can be gained by considering the annual volatility of the relevant stock market sector; the overall USA stock market index has had an annual standard deviation (which is the square root of the variance) of ±26 per cent over the past 5 years. Most individual strategic investment projects will therefore have annual volatilities significantly in excess of this!

The main advantage of incorporating the real option value drivers is that it can highlight how *flexible and phased*, but high-risk investments can be financially worthwhile even if the current net present value of the investment is negative, using the probability-adjusted expected cash flows. The cumulative volatility value impact from the real options built into the investment *may more than offset* the current negative net present value. This type of investment would not be accepted under traditional discounted cash flow analysis, even using cumulative probability factors. A very simple initial example may make this clearer and this is given in Figure 7.17.

Under traditional discounted cash flow analysis, this investment would not be started since it shows a negative NPV of £4 million. At first sight, it looks even more absurd to spend £1 million to acquire a 1-year option on a negative NPV project. However, Figure 7.17 also shows that the expected returns have quite a high volatility (assessed to be 30 per cent per year) and could therefore

A simple example

Present value of expected, but volatile, returns (P) = £100 m

Present value of required investment (E)   = £104 m

Volatility of returns (per year) (σ)   = 30%

Risk-free interest rate (r_f)   = 6%

*It is possible to defer the investment for 1 year (t) at a cost of £1 m. Should the £1 m option fee be incurred?

The company's cost of capital is 10%

Traditional DCF analysis

NPV today = £100 m − £104 m = −£4 m

Figure 7.17 *Valuing the real options*

A simple example (contd)

However the investment of £1 m purchases an option to go ahead, or not, at the end of 1 year.

This option can be valued by using option tables:

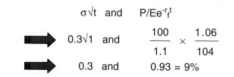

$$\sigma\sqrt{t} \quad \text{and} \quad P/Ee^{-r_f t}$$

$$0.3\sqrt{1} \quad \text{and} \quad \frac{100}{1.1} \times \frac{1.06}{104}$$

$$0.3 \quad \text{and} \quad 0.93 = 9\%$$

This represents the option value as a percentage of the underlying asset value.

Thus the option value is   £100 m × 0.09 = £9 m

Figure 7.18   *Valuing the real options*

be significantly higher than the current 'expected' present value of £100 million. This means that the investment *could* have a substantial positive net present value (e.g. £130 million minus the less volatile investment costs of £104 million). Equally the cash inflows could turn out to be much less valuable than the expected £100 million, but it could be worth spending £1 million to find out.

The 1 year deferral option is valued in Figure 7.18 by applying the well-known Black and Scholes option pricing model to these particular values. As stated before, the details of the valuation are beyond the scope of this book, but it should be clear that it is well worth spending £1 million to acquire an option that is valued at £9 million. It must be clearly understood that paying the £1 million option fee does not mean that the £104 million investment will automatically be undertaken in 1 year's time. This investment will be reassessed prior to the expiry of the option when a better assessment of the likely returns may be possible.

The use of real options is therefore particularly relevant where the total investment will be made on a phased basis and the subsequent investments depend on the situation at the particular time when they are to be made. The company is effectively creating its own real options and these need to be valued appropriately. There are several common types of strategic investment decision-created options and these are summarised in Figure 7.19. One of the most common examples is a new market entry where the initial entry can be done on a phased basis while much greater information is gained about the particular market; thus the benefits of phasing and learning by waiting are obtained. A slightly more detailed example of such a decision is given before ending the chapter with an in-depth case study.

Type of decision	Real option created
Phased investments	Call option on subsequent stages
Abandonment	Put option on value of abandoned assets
Learning by waiting (timing/deferment)	American call option, but with dividend flows (i.e. early exercise may be worthwhile)
Varying outputs/methods (e.g. dual fuels/ sourcing/location)	Flexibility options (values dependent on volatility of fuel costs/supplier prices/ exchange rates & labour costs, etc.)

Figure 7.19   *Examples of real options*

Real option example

An initial market entry requires an up-front investment of £10 million and losses are expected for the *first 2 years*. If the sales growth targets and other success indicators are being met, a significant second phase investment of £150 million will then be made in Year 3. Subsequently significantly enhanced profits and cash flows are anticipated. These are shown in Figure 7.20.

There is a currently assessed 50 per cent probability that the second phase investment will be made; probabilities on all subsequent cash inflows are ignored to keep the analysis relatively simple. The volatility of the second phase investment's cash flow projections is estimated to be 40 per cent per year.

Project cash flows – expected results if second phase goes ahead

£m

Year	0	1	2	3	4	5	6–15 (p.a.)	Perpetuity (p.a.)
Investments	(10)	–	–	(150)	–	–	–	
Cash inflows – from first phase	–	(4)	(2)	–	2	2	2	1
– from second phase	–	–	–	(10)	8	14	20	15

N.B. Company cost of capital = 10%

Figure 7.20   *A simplified phased investment example*

Overall DCF evaluation (applying 50% probability factor to second phase)

£m

Year	0	1	2	3	4	5	6–15	Perpetuity (p.a.)
Investments	(10)			(75)				
Cash inflows	–	(4)	(2)	(5)	6	9	12	8.5
Net cash flows	(10)	(4)	(2)	(80)	6	9	12	8.5
Discount factors @ 10%	1	.909	.826	.751	.683	.621	3.82	2.39
Present value	(10)	(3.64)	(1.65)	(60.08)	4.10	5.59	45.84	20.32

NPV = £0.48 m   i.e. the overall project generates a nil NPV

Figure 7.21   *A simplified phased investment example (contd)*

The discounted cash flows for the combined project are shown in Figure 7.21 using a 10 per cent discount rate (the company's cost of capital) and applying the 50 per cent probability factor to all the second phase cash flows. This shows that the overall project generates a nil net present value (i.e. it has an IRR of 10 per cent), but there is a potential real option as to whether to undertake the second phase of the investment.

A better way therefore of evaluating this investment is to consider it as a first phase investment of £10 million that acquires for the company an option to make a subsequent £150 million investment. The financial evaluation is consequently the sum of the net present value of phase 1 plus the net present value of the option to do phase 2.

Phase 1 can be evaluated using conventional discounted cash flow and this is shown in Figure 7.22; the resulting negative net present value (£2.66 million) means that phase 1 is not worth doing just for itself. To this, we need to add the value of the option and this uses our five option value drivers as shown in Figure 7.23.

The expected present value of the cash flows resulting from the second phase investment can be calculated from a discounted cash flow as is done in Figure 7.24. Care is needed to ensure that the present value of these cash inflows is then compared to the present value of the required second phase investment (the £150 million is the amount to be spent in Year 3) discounted at the risk-free rate of 6 per cent. This discounted present value of the investment (£125.94 million) is higher than the expected present value of the inflows but this is not critical because these expected inflows are highly volatile, and we are going to value that volatility as is done in Figure 7.25.

Introducing option values

Phase 1 can be evaluated using conventional DCF

Year	0	1	2	3	4–15 (p.a.)	Perpetuity (p.a.)
Cash flows	(10)	(4)	(2)	–	2	1
Discount factors	1	.909	.826	.751	5.12	2.39
Present values	(10)	(3.64)	(1.65)	–	10.24	2.39

NPV = £(2.66) m   i.e. Phase 1 is not worth doing as a stand-alone project

Figure 7.22   *A simplified phased investment example (contd)*

Introducing option values

To evaluate phase 2 as an option, we need the five option value drivers:

P = the present value of the cash inflows from the extra
    investment

E = the required new investment (£150 m)

σ = the volatility of this investment's returns (assessed to
    be 40%)

t = the deferment period (3 years)

r_f = the risk-free interest rate (6%)

Figure 7.23   *A simplified phased investment example (contd)*

Cash inflows (for phase 2)

Year	0	1	2	3	4	5	6–15 (p.a.)	Perpetuity (p.a.)
Cash inflows	–	–	–	(10)	8	14	20	15
Discount factors @ 10%	1	.909	.826	.751	.683	.621	3.82	2.39
Present values	–	–	–	(7.51)	5.46	8.69	76.4	35.85

Present value = £118.89 m

[N.B. This is still less than the true present value of the required new
investment (£150 m); if this is discounted at the risk-free interest rate (6%) it has
a present value of £125.94 m. If discounted at 10%, this is reduced to £112.7 m,
which is how the overall project evaluation was done to generate the combined
NPV of £0.48 m.]

Figure 7.24   *A simplified phased investment example (contd)*

Valuing the option

Applying the option value drivers and option tables

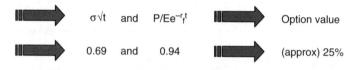

$\sigma\sqrt{t}$ and $P/Ee^{-r_f t}$ Option value

0.69   and   0.94   (approx) 25%

Therefore the option has a value of 25% of £119 m = around £30 m
This significantly outweighs the small negative NPV on phase 1

Figure 7.25   *A simplified phased investment example (contd)*

Re-assessing the investment

The revised evaluation of the current investment shows a positive
NPV of £27.4 m (£30 m option value – £2.6 m phase 1 NPV)

When this is placed in the context of an initial investment of £10 m,
by calculating the profitability index, the attractiveness of this
flexible investment is highlighted.

$$\text{P.I.} \quad = \quad \frac{\text{NPV}}{\text{Original invt}} \quad = \frac{£27.4\,m}{£10\,m} \quad = 2.74$$

$$\text{Adjusted P.I.} \quad = \quad \frac{\text{NPV}}{\substack{\text{PV of}\\ \text{cum. invt}}} \quad = \frac{£27.4\,m}{£15.3\,m} \quad = 1.79$$

Figure 7.26   *A simplified phased investment example (contd)*

The high volatility (40 per cent p.a.) and the long deferment period (3 years) when combined with the relative closeness of the current asset value and the option exercise price make for a very valuable option. The £30 million option value easily outweighs the small negative NPV (£2.6 million) generated by phase 1 of the investment. Thus the £10 million investment should be undertaken as is shown in Figure 7.26.

Figure 7.26 also shows how the profitability index can still be applied to these types of investment decisions; however, using the original investment overstates the attractiveness of projects that also have negative cash flows in their early years. It is much better to use the present value of the maximum cumulative investment that is required by the project; this is shown as the adjusted profitability index and this is how it is also described in the following case study. Even after this adjustment, the profitability index (at 1.79) is still incredibly good but this still does not mean that the second phase investment will be undertaken. This will depend upon a reassessment of the financial evaluation using the improved understanding of the expected returns that should be gained during the first 3 years of market entry.

Case study – Peter Piper is puzzled

Peter Piper was puzzled and perplexed, so he picked a particular portfolio of proposed projects to present to his colleague, Suzy Seller, whose support he sought as he searched for the single supreme solution to the evaluation and control of strategic investment decisions.

Peter Piper's large diversified group used ROI as the principal financial measure of performance but used discounted cash flow (calculating both IRRs and NPVs) as the main method of approving capital expenditure proposals. The divisional ROI targets were based on the previous year's achievements and the current external environment. The IRR criteria were based on the group's current cost of capital (assessed to be 15 per cent) and the level of risk associated with each project.

Peter Piper's European division was achieving 35 per cent ROI against a group average of 30 per cent, but it was well aware that a number of its products were very mature. These three potential projects had recently been put up to the divisional board for possible approval. The impact on the future profitability of the division differed dramatically and the decision regarding which, if any, should be put up to the group as part of the division's strategic plan did not seem, to him, obvious.

Project A

An existing retail business unit within the European division (one of the few relatively new and growing businesses) had identified new branches that would enhance profitability significantly, but required investment in freehold property plus additional stock levels. The net cash flow after tax from these new branches was forecast at £3 million per year and the economic life of the project was taken (under group guidelines) to be 10 years. The property investment should have a high, but unknown, residual value and in the absence of better information this had been assumed to be the same as original cost, i.e. £10 million. The stock investment of £4 million was assumed to be recovered at the end of the 10 years. If the properties were leased, rather than being bought, an after tax annual rent of 5 per cent for a 10-year lease would be payable.

The basic financial evaluation is shown in Table 7.1.

Table 7.1   *Project A – DCF calculation IRR = 21.4%*

Timing	Cash flow item	Amount	Discount factor @ 15%	Present value
Yr 0	Investment	(£14 m)	1	(£14 m)
Yr 1–10	Profit stream	£3 m	5.019	£15.06 m
Yr 10	Return on investment	£14 m	0.247	£3.46 m
			Net present value	£4.52 m

Profitability index = 0.32

Accounting return

	Year	
	1	*10*
Net book value of investment	10 m	10 m
Working capital	4 m	4 m
	14 m	14 m
Profit after tax	3 m	3 m
Return on investment	21.4%	21.4%

Project A analysis

Project A is relatively low risk because the group is already in this retail market and should be able accurately to assess both the investments required and the expected returns. The key risks involved are that the new shops are in poor locations and consequently do not generate the expected rate of return. However if this was the case, the company could rapidly close these failing shops down, sell the properties and transfer the inventories to their remaining shops, thus recovering most of their original investment. This exit strategy option highlights how low the risk associated with the project is. The project is also shareholder value enhancing as it generates a positive NPV when discounted at 15 per cent, the company's cost of capital.

Unfortunately the divisional management team is unlikely to put the project forward as, in each of the next 10 years, it shows an accounting return of 21.4 per cent p.a., compared to the current divisional level of 35 per cent and a group average of 30 per cent. This shows the potential conflict between shareholder value measures based on long-term cash flows and costs of capital, and accounting-based measures based on historic costs of assets. Clearly it is in the group's interest for this project to be invested in, and it probably should be done even if the IRR was slightly below the company's current cost of capital, due to the low risk involved.

However if the project is properly evaluated, both the divisional manage-ment and the group should want to invest in the new retail outlets. The invest-ment can really be divided into two projects; one based in retailing and one in investing in freehold property. The reason for the low accounting ROI is the £10 million cost of the new shops, where the financial return is the saving of the £5 00 000 rental cost if they were leased; i.e. a 5 per cent annualised return. The only financial justification for buying freehold property is that it is expected to increase in value but in this evaluation it has been assumed to be worth what it cost at the end of the 10 years. Interestingly one strength of the discounted cash flow technique, using the time value of money, is that chan-ging the residual value (even by ±100 per cent) makes very little difference to the net present value of the project; it is still worth doing the project even if the shops have *no* residual value at the end of 10 years!

Once the freehold property investment is removed, the remaining £4 million investment in inventories generates an annual expected return of £2.5 million; an annual accounting return on investment of 62.5 per cent, which is well above the division's targets. Also the amended project has an IRR of 62.5 per cent and NPV at 15 per cent discount rate of £9.54 million, giving a profit-ability index of 2.38; making it a very attractive project indeed! The potential landlord of the freehold property will be quite content to generate a 5 per cent after tax yield on its investment, as this should cover its financing costs and give it all the potential long-term increase in the value of the property. Ultimately this would be reflected in the rental values charged to the tenant, so that Peter Piper might want to spend part of the increased financial return on buying an option to limit the rent increases at the end of the initial 10 year lease.

Project B

A manufacturing business unit within the division had proposed a spin-off from one of their main product lines (i.e. a range extension). The new products would be linked to the existing product range through umbrella branding and should therefore become profitable straight away. However the expected economic life of these high cash flows from the investment project was only 5 years due to the maturity of the main product range. The investment required was £10 million for plant and equipment with a further £2 million for both stocks and debtors. The residual value of the plant was negligible and the fashion nature of the product indicated a risk of not recovering the inventory value at the end of the project. The annual profit stream was projected to be £3 million for each of the 5 years, which translates into an annual cash inflows of £5 million, given the annual depreciation charge of £2 million.

The basic financial evaluation is shown in Table 7.2.

Table 7.2   *Project B – DCF calculation* IRR = 25.1%

Timing	Cash flow item	Amount	Discount factor @ 15%	Present value
Yr 0	Investment	(£14 m)	1	(£14 m)
Yr 1–5	Profit (add back deprecia- tion)	£(3 + 2) m	3.352	£16.76 m
Yr 5	Debtors recovered	£2 m	0.497	£0.99 m
			Net present value	£3.75 m
	Profitability index = 0.27			

Accounting return

	Year				
	1	*2*	*3*	*4*	*5*
Net book value of investment	8 m	6 m	4 m	2 m	0 m
Working capital	4 m	4 m	4 m	4 m	4 m
	12 m	10 m	8 m	6 m	4 m
Profit after tax	3 m	3 m	3 m	3 m	3 m
Return on investment	25%	30%	37.5%	50%	75%

Project B analysis

At first sight, project B looks financially attractive. It generates a good net present value and a high IRR, thanks to its high cash inflows from Year 1. Also its accounting return on investment is good, due to the rapid depreciation of the investment in plant and machinery; by Year 3, it is beating the current ROI performance of the division.

However the key risk associated with this project is actually the length of its economic life and this is not under its own direct control due to the umbrella branding strategy. As discussed earlier, a good risk assessment technique in this situation is to calculate the discounted payback as a proportion of the expected economic life of the project. For this project, this can be shown to be almost 80 per cent of the 5-year life, as the discounted payback period is almost 4 years at a discount rate of 15 per cent. This means that if the estimate of economic life was wrong by 1 year, the project would generate almost no shareholder value; if the project actually lasted 2 or 3 years longer, the value created would be substantial.

In such cases, it is important to do as much research as possible to refine the estimate of this critical factor. If no satisfactory reassurance can be gained that the existing umbrella branding would remain strong for *at least 4 years*, this project should be rejected on the grounds of risk.

Project C

Another business unit within the division had already spent £5 million on developing an exciting new product concept that could eventually take the business into new market segments, although the product could be tested and launched in existing markets and to existing customers of the group. This phased development plan meant that high initial expenditures would need to be followed by additional years of negative cash flows before, if the project was ultimately successful, high profits and cash flows would be generated.

An investment of £10 million in plant and machinery was required (nil residual value) and £4 million was estimated as needed for working capital (all treated as spent in Year 0 and reclaimed in Year 10). Additional expenditures on further R&D and then launch marketing would result in cash outflows in Year 1 of £2 million, then £1 million in Year 2 and a small £1m inflow in Year 3. From Years 4 to 10 a successful launch in Year 3 would generate annual cash inflows of £11 million.

The probability of future success for each year was as follows:

Success of Year 1 net expenditure	= 78%
Success of Year 2 net expenditure	= 85%
Success of launch in Year 3 and Years 4 to 10 projections	= 90%

The financial evaluation of the probability adjusted cash flows is shown in Table 7.3.

Table 7.3 *Project C – Applying probability forecasts to original cash flows* IRR = 18.1%

Year	Gross cash flow	Probability for year	Cumulative probability	Expected value	Discount factor @ 15%	Present value
0	(£14 m)	1	1	(£14 m)	1	(£14 m)
1	(£2 m)	1	1	(£2 m)	0.870	(£1.74 m)
2	(£1 m)	0.78	0.78	(£0.78 m)	0.756	(£0.59 m)
3	£1 m	0.85	0.66	£0.66	0.658	£0.43 m
4–10	£11 m	0.90	0.60	£6.60 m	2.736	£18.06 m
10	£4 m	1	1	£4 m	0.247	£0.99 m
					Net present value	£3.15 m

Profitability index = 0.22
Adjusted profitability index = 0.19

An alternative proposal was to do some additional market research and product concept testing before committing the £14 million on plant and working capital. If the results were positive, the cumulative probability of overall success would be improved to 80 per cent from the current level of 60 per cent $(0.78 \times 0.85 \times 0.90 \times 100$ per cent) by spending an additional £5 00 000 now. The financial evaluation of this additional expenditure is shown in Table 7.4.

Table 7.4   *Project C – Using additional market research spend of £5 00 000*

Evaluating incremental activity:

Year	Gross cash flow	Probability change	Expected value	Discount factor @ 15%	Present value
0	(£500 k)	1	(£500 k)	1	(£500 k)
4–10	£11 m	20%	£2.2 m	2.736	£6.02 m
				Net present value	£5.52 m

In other words, it is worth spending up to £5 m now to increase the ultimate probability of success from 60% to 80%.
The overall project's net present value would increase to £8.67 m and the profitability index to 0.60 (or 0.52 on an adjusted basis).

The project could be financially evaluated using the 'success' cash flows, as discussed earlier in the chapter, and the discounted cash flow calculation is shown in Table 7.5 so as to indicate some of the potential problems. If the cost of capital is used as the discount rate, the net present value is increased significantly, but this figure is clearly misleading because of the risk factor that is still included in these 'success' assuming cash flow forecasts. The higher IRR (28.0 per cent versus the 18.1 per cent shown in Table 7.3) needs to be compared to a higher risk-adjusted required rate of return; as discussed earlier, the key question is by how much should the required rate be increased to reflect the associated risk?

The accounting ROI calculation is shown in Table 7.6 and this highlights the problem of using this method on this type of project. Where the annual accounting return has a range from highly negative through zero to a maximum of 250 per cent, any calculation of an 'average' has to be seen as completely meaningless. Indeed as soon as this project moves into significant success it starts to generate an incredibly high 100 per cent rate of return on investment.

Table 7.5   *Project C – DCF calculation: 'Success' cash flows* IRR = 28.0%

Timing	Cash flow Item	Amount	Discount factor @ 15%	Present value
Yr 0	Investment	(£14 m)	1	(£14 m)
Yr 1	Loss add back depreciation	(£2 m)	0.870	(£1.74 m)
Yr 2	Loss add back depreciation	(£1 m)	0.756	£(0.76 m)
Yr 3	Breakeven add back depreciation	£1 m	0.658	£0.66 m
Yr 4–10	Profit add back depreciation	£11 m	2.736	£30.10 m
Yr 10	Recovery working capital	£4 m	0.247	£0.99 m
			Net present value	£15.25 m

Profitability index = 1.09
Adjusted profitability index = 0.92

Table 7.6   *Accounting return calculation*

	Year							
	1	*2*	*3*	*4*	*5*	-----	*9*	*10*
Net book value of investment	9 m	8 m	7 m	6 m	5 m		1 m	0 m
Working capital	4 m	4 m	4 m	4 m	4 m		4 m	4 m
	13 m	12 m	11 m	10 m	9 m		5 m	4 m
Profit after tax	(3 m)	(2 m)	–	10 m	10 m		10 m	10 m
Return on investment	(?)	(?)	0	100%	111%		200%	250%

Project C analysis

The relevant financial evaluations are those included in Tables 7.3 and 7.4. It is obviously sensible to spend the additional £5 00 000 on marketing research *before* committing the high initial investment of £14 million and then investing a further £3 million in the two subsequent years. This demonstrates that the funds 'at risk' peak at £17 million in Year 3 and the present value of this £17 million is used in calculating the *adjusted* profitability indices shown in the tables.

The critical impact on the net present value from this project is once again different from the previous two projects discussed in this case study. There is very little impact if the cash inflows last 1 year more or less than the predicted 10-year life assumed in the evaluation, because of the impact of discounting on the cash flows in Years 10 and 11 (e.g. the present value of the £11 million expected in Year 10 is only £2.72 million). Also a relatively small change in the value of the annual cash inflow is much less than a similar proportionate change in project A; this is because of the delay in receiving the cash inflows until Year 4. The most important impact is made by the year in which the cash inflows start; if they are delayed even until Year 5, the net present value becomes negative. However if the high cash inflows can be started 1 year earlier, the net present value is more than doubled.

The focus of the financial evaluation should therefore be on the development of the sales levels following launch and the time control over the activities that need to precede the launch. In this type of project it is often possible to accelerate the launch date by carrying out several activities simultaneously rather than sequentially. Obviously this may have implications for the risk profile associated with each item of expenditure that is affected, but another potential way of improving the financial evaluation would be to defer the major investment items if this is possible. This was a major way of improving the project in the Knight Foods' case study discussed in Chapter 6.

8 Brand-Based Strategies

Overview

Brands can be based on either products or customers. A product-based brand strategy, such as Coca-Cola and Marlboro, enables the business to grow and create shareholder value by finding new customers for the existing product. On the other hand a customer-based brand enables shareholder value to be created by new products being sold to existing customers. All strong brand strategies are self-limiting in that if the brand is stretched too far its strength can be irreparably weakened.

If a competitive strategy that is based on brands is to be shareholder value enhancing, the brand must enable the business to earn a super profit on its more tangible assets. In other words, the brand is itself an intangible asset of the business.

There are only limited ways in which a brand can generate a super profit. A strong brand can enable the underlying 'product' (whether good or service) to be sold at a higher price than would be obtainable without the brand. Alternatively more of the underlying 'product' can be sold at the same price, either by increasing the market share gained or by increasing the size of the total market. It is clearly possible for a brand to generate a super profit by a combination of slightly higher price and higher market share.

In all these cases, the 'brand' increases the financial return that can be generated from the 'product', but a strong brand can also reduce the volatility of the cash flows produced by the underlying product. This reduced volatility reduces the perceived risk of investors and can result in a lower required rate of return.

There are a number of stages involved in developing a brand into a long-term asset. This development process requires considerable financial investment by the brand owner. Marketing has now developed quite sophisticated research techniques and methodologies that can evaluate the effectiveness of activities at each stage in the brand development process. The challenge for marketing finance is to turn these purely marketing measures into financially relevant measures that can ensure these successful brands are shareholder value enhancing.

In order to develop a brand to its 'full potential' value, significant market-ing investments are required. In order to financially evaluate and control these investments, marketing budgets should be split between development and maintenance activities. Development marketing expenditure aims to increase the long-term value of the brand asset; its financial return may only be realised some years into the future. Maintenance marketing expenditure is designed to keep the brand attributes at their current level. Some marketing expenditure may also be aimed at extending the economic life of the brand.

Brands can be positioned to reflect how well the underlying product works (functional attributes) or to emphasise representational attributes (e.g. image) of the target customer. Corporate or umbrella branding can reduce the marketing investment required to develop a portfolio of independent brands. However it can also reduce the flexibility of response of the single branded company and can increase its risk profile unless all the brands sheltering under the umbrella fit completely with the key brand attributes.

Brand loyalty is a critical but complex subject; it is very important that marketing research establishes the real level of, and reasons for, brand loyalty as this has important consequences for the specific focus of the marketing strategy that should be implemented.

A key element in the marketing finance system for a brand-based strategy is a brand evaluation process. This sensibly applies the strategic investment decision criteria to evaluating alternative brand development expenditure levels, so as to allocate marketing investment resources as effectively as possible. It is not designed to produce an accurate brand valuation at a point in time; this can only be established by actually selling the brand to a willing buyer, the price achieved equals its market value.

Introduction

Brand-based strategies can be built around brands that emphasise either cus-tomers or products. Therefore, it is logical to consider the implications for marketing finance of such brand-based strategies before, in the following chap-ters, examining the specifically relevant issues arising from a customer-led strategy and a product-based strategy.

A *product-based branded* strategy looks to build on the current strengths of a particular brand with its existing customers by finding new customers for the existing products sold as the brand, as is shown in Figure 8.1. This is the basis of the many famous global 'product brands', such as Coca-Cola, Marlboro, Intel and Microsoft. Their original success was normally achieved in their domestic market and, from this very strong base, the product branding was developed internationally. The key factor is that the brand is integrally associated with one particular product or relatively tightly focused range of products, e.g. Shell- and oil-based products.

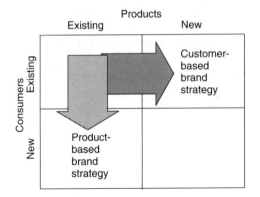

Figure 8.1 *Brand-based strategies*

A relatively newer branding strategy is to base the brand around a particular group of customers and to generate future growth by identifying other things that can be sold, under the same branding, to this same group of customers. Thus the future brand development is based on increasing *the range* of relevant products sold rather than necessarily expanding the markets or segments in which the existing products are sold. Not surprisingly, these customer-based brands have been extensively utilised by companies in industries that have great difficulty in developing sustainable product-based brands.

Thus many retailers have focused on investing to create very strong brands in order to build strong loyalty from their existing customers. This loyalty has enabled these retailers to expand significantly the range of products sold under the retailer's own brand to these customers. In the UK, the ultimate example of this was Marks & Spencer because all the goods sold in its stores were, for many very successful years, exclusively labelled St Michael, its own in-house retail brand. This retailer developed such immense loyalty and trust from a whole generation of customers that it was able to move into a wide range of goods and even services. Thus, in addition to selling food, other grocery products, and clothes, the group launched home furnishings, furniture and even financial services. Indeed at the time of its initial launch, Marks & Spencer's first retail investment products received a higher level of consumer uptake than any previous similar launches. This may have been helped by a few high-profile collapses of 'investment schemes' at around the same time, with the result that investors were very keen to place their money with someone they knew and could trust to deliver 'good value for money'. (However, it is interesting to note that this was achieved even though Marks & Spencer could not extend their famous 'no quibble, moneyback' guarantee to these new financial services products!)

Of course, the relevance of a particular brand may change over time; it will be argued through this chapter that brands do have life cycles, it is simply that some very strong brands have very long life cycles. If, and when, this happens, the company can get into financial difficulties very quickly, particularly if the brand name is also the company name. This happened quite spectacularly to Marks & Spencer at the end of the 1990s when their products, particularly their clothes, were no longer seen as appropriate to their core, loyal customers. As one generation of loyal customers gets older and their children turn into adults, these new young adults do not necessarily want to wear the same brand as their parents *still do*; this is illustrated in Practical Insight 8.1.

Practical Insight 8.1

Levi's – re-engineered for a new generation

Levi Strauss developed a very strong brand in casual clothing that became an icon for the young generation in the 1960s and 1970s as they rebelled against the staid formality of the clothes worn by their parents. Levi's continued to flourish as this generation grew slightly older, because they modified the product: fuller figure jeans, relaxed comfort fit jeans, etc.

However, eventually this still loyal group of customers had teenage children of their own and they wanted their own brand. Levi's faced a significant loss of sales (their ageing original customers bought less jeans and kept each pair for longer) if they failed to win the next generation. A combination of re-inventing the product ('engineered to fit'), modifying the sales process (customised fitting, with made to measure jeans, plus a 'shrink to fit' bath in some stores) and completely new youth-focused advertising (no more 1950s heritage allusions) has effectively extended the brand life cycle; but, at one point, it was a very close thing.

Marks & Spencer has had both to reinvest in its core brand and to modify a key element in its original marketing strategy; *now* premium products that do not bear the St Michael branding are available in its stores. The strength of a good brand can therefore sometimes ultimately become a weakness; if all loyal customers associate the brand with a certain price and quality position it can be impossible to incorporate, within the brand, products that fall well outside this very clearly defined positioning.

Another industry that has based many of its marketing strategies on customer-led branding is financial services. This has proved critical in achieving a sustainable competitive advantage in a very competitive marketplace where the economic life of any new product-based advantage can be measured in days or weeks. As soon as any new financial product is marketed, competitors can reverse engineer how it works and thus normally can launch their own versions incredibly quickly. So quickly that the innovator cannot generate a sufficient financial return on its R&D costs and launch marketing expenditure. Unless, that is, it can develop a reputation for innovation with a large body of potentially loyal customers. Such a customer-based branding strategy can be applied in several different ways; product innovation, quality of service, low costs and hence low prices, tailored services for specific market segments, etc. A classic example of such a customer-led brand is Virgin, as is illustrated in Practical Insight 8.2.

Practical Insight 8.2

Virgin – stretching a brand

Richard Branson founded Virgin as a small record label, which grew rapidly following the spectacular success of a few previously unknown artists. The business then moved into music retailing with Virgin stores, and then into an airline, Virgin Atlantic. The airline competed on the North Atlantic route with the major dedicated airlines such as BA, but its branding appealed to a younger traveller. Thus it offered a different seating mix of mainly cheap seats with no frills and 'Upper Class', which even had its own bar area on the upper deck of the aeroplane.

The brand was further extended into Cola and alcoholic drinks (vodka) and then financial services and mobile telephones. The brand positioning in these services was to offer an uncomplicated product explained in language the consumer could understand. All of these brand extensions were consistent with the image of non-conformity, slight irreverence, and a desire to get things done in your own way that was epitomised by Sir Richard Branson's own lifestyle.

Virgin then moved into branding inter-city train services; a move that personally I cannot relate back to the brand values and consumer segmentation that had proved so successful in the past.

Brands as intangible assets

Whatever specific form the branding strategy takes, the marketing expenditure required to develop and then maintain the resulting brand must be rigorously financially evaluated and controlled. Indeed the key financial justification for developing any brand-based strategy is that the resulting brand(s) will *create shareholder value*. As the normal accounting treatment for all marketing expenditure is to write it off (i.e. expense it) in the year in which the expenditure is incurred, brands do not normally feature as assets on the balance sheets of brand-based companies.

This means that these companies should, if their branding strategies have been financially successful, be earning a *super profit* on the more tangible assets that *they do include* on their balance sheets. I find it extremely interesting that many companies that claim to own several *very valuable* brands *do not* in fact deliver any *excess financial return* on their exclusively tangible assets (e.g. factories, etc.) that support these 'valuable' brands.

Of course it is true that a strong brand really is an intangible asset of the business and should be managed as such. Indeed in many businesses the brand portfolio is undoubtedly the most valuable asset owned by the group. However before considering how we should financially evaluate, control and manage such a potentially valuable asset it is important to understand clearly where the brand value comes from. Many of the brand valuations that I have reviewed and seen over recent years do not value only the 'brand', as they include all the future cash flows expected to be generated from future sales forecasts; i.e. they also include the return required on the tangible assets that enable the underlying product to be produced and sold. As is discussed in more depth below, a proper brand evaluation exercise should ideally only include those additional financial returns that are attributable to the brand, which should be distinguished from the underlying product.

In any brand marketing textbook, it is immediately made clear that a brand is more than the underlying product (i.e. good or service). A *brand* is a product with a *distinctive* (preferably unique) *proposition* that is *consistently delivered* through time and place. Brands may also convey something more representational (e.g. emotional) about its users rather than just reflecting the relative functionality of the product. Indeed a successful brand creates or articulates the sustainable differential advantage of the underlying product. If the specific attributes of this successful brand can be identified an appropriate brand evaluation procedure can be developed, which separates out the true value added by the branding process. The main features of successful, and hence valuable, brands are: innovation, differentiation, service and quality. If this cannot be properly achieved, the financial evaluation must ensure that proper allowance is made for the required rate of return on the additional tangible assets that are required to produce the 'brand'. This is considered again later in the chapter, when the details of brand evaluation are discussed.

Realising the asset value

A true brand asset should enable a level of super profit to be earned, and this can in reality only be achieved in a few ways, as is shown in Figure 8.2.

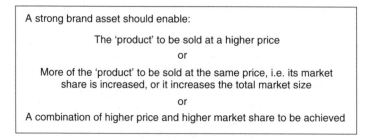

Figure 8.2   *Brand assets; realising the asset value*

Conceptually the simplest way of exploiting a strong brand is through premium pricing of the branded product, when compared to its unbranded equivalent. However in the real world, this comparison is often far from simple. The premium priced branded product will often have added functional benefits for customers that are not available on the lower priced versions. The additional costs incurred in adding these features/benefits must be taken into consideration, as was discussed in Chapter 4 when discussing competitor analysis. The added value gained from any premium pricing is clearly net of these additional costs.

However as mentioned in Part One, the strength of the brand probably resulted from a substantial investment in marketing expenditure over a number of years. This increased marketing investment should have been regarded as quite high risk as, if it did not succeed in building a successful sustainable brand, there would be no financial return at all. Thus the financial evaluation should have required a compensating high level of financial return if the investment proved successful. Alternatively the expenditure would have needed to be phased so that relatively small amounts were committed until the probability of a successful outcome was increased to an acceptable level; as was discussed in Chapter 7.

A second way of achieving super profits from a branded strategy is if the brand enables a greater volume of sales to be achieved than would have been the case with an unbranded equivalent product. Thus the brand is sold at the same price as its unbranded competition, but more is sold because of its branding. This may be due to it gaining an increased market share or the branding could actually increase the total market size. Of course, the challenge for any brand evaluation is to establish what the market share of an unbranded equivalent product would have been; in order to assess the value added by the branded strategy.

As these brands sell at the same price as other products in the market they are often described as 'value for money' brands. We all know what is meant by the phrase but it still annoys me because to their purchasers all brands must be, by definition, 'good value for money'; even if I am paying a premium price for the brand!

Obviously these two ways of realising the brand asset value can be used in combination; a slightly higher selling price together with a better market share. Indeed a great deal of the marketing research effort in brand-led companies should be directed towards trying to identify the optimal pricing and volume mix for each brand. It is important that the financial evaluation and control process understands and focuses on the specific brand strategy. In all these cases, the brand increases the financial return that can be generated from the product and the financial evaluation, which must obviously be done before the marketing investment expenditure is committed, compares the expected present value of that increased financial return against the total financial expenditure required.

However a strong brand could reduce the volatility of the future cash flows produced by the product. This might be through developing strong customer loyalty, so that less switching takes place with alternative products. The strong brand image might mean that, in times of volatility in total demand in the industry, a flight to 'quality' or 'good value for money' makes the sales revenues of the brand less volatile than its competition. These less volatile cash inflows clearly reduce the risk associated with the brand and should result in a lower required rate of return.

Ideally a very strong brand should generate higher future returns that are less volatile, thus generating shareholder value by moving in the optimal value-adding strategic direction, i.e. increasing returns while reducing risk as was shown by direction D in Figure 1.6. The selected source of shareholder value creation clearly has an important impact on the brand evaluation process that should be carried out for all brands. However before considering this, it is necessary to summarise brand development.

Brand development

There are a number of stages involved in developing, and then maintaining, a brand. Space does not allow a truly comprehensive coverage of this area and, anyway, this is already done in most good marketing texts. Thus it is more than adequate for our purposes to consider the specific stages in the development of a repeat purchase consumer brand. A successful, sustainable 'repeat purchase' consumer brand normally has achieved some degree of success in all of the stages shown in Figure 8.3; however, the level of success may not be uniform across all the stages.

The first challenge is to create some level of awareness of the brand among consumers. This awareness can be created, and tested, at different levels such as unprompted, spontaneous awareness of the initial advertising used to launch the brand. Thus targeted consumers can be asked whether they are aware of the product category and, if so, what brands they know about. Respondents can also be prompted by giving them brand names or story lines from adverts, etc. This type of marketing research can be done both before a further burst of advertising takes place and then repeated afterwards; enabling the impact of the new advertising to be assessed in terms of changing awareness.

As will be shown in this section, each stage in the brand development process can be subjected to this kind of marketing research through which the effectiveness of each particular item of marketing expenditure can be assessed. The vital gap, and hence a crucial role for marketing finance, is to link these marketing effectiveness measures and techniques back to the overriding objective of creating shareholder value. In other words, to demonstrate how creating additional brand awareness can contribute to generating a super profit; this can only be done by developing both the marketing and financial effectiveness

A successful, sustainable 'repeat purchase' brand has achieved success in the following stages (The level of success may not be uniform across all areas however)

☐ Awareness

☐ Propensity to purchase

    ☐ i.e. interest and desire are created

☐ Ability to purchase

    ☐ at least a minimum level of distribution is achieved

☐ Level of trial

    ☐ targeted purchasers actually buy the product

☐ Repurchase

    ☐ an adequate proportion of triallists repurchase the brand, indicating satisfaction in use

☐ Level of usage

    ☐ these repurchasers adopt a satisfactory level of regular usage of the brand

Figure 8.3 *Brand development*

measures into an integrated set. The old 'I know I waste half my advertising expenditure, but I don't know which half' must be seen, in the twenty-first century, as unacceptable given the capabilities of a good marketing finance system.

Creating awareness is only a very first stage in developing a sustainable brand and the impact of this awareness needs to be researched. Consumers may all recall your advertisements but this is not helpful if the adverts made them less likely to try the brand. Thus attitudinal research can be carried out to see whether the awareness created is positively inclined towards the brand. The awareness research should also check that consumers can actually associate *your* advertisements with your *brand*; there have been a number of classic examples of extremely creative, award winning advertisements that actually 'enhanced' the awareness of a competitor's brand. On a very silly personal level, I have always assumed an inverse correlation between the number of advertising awards won by a marketing team and the effectiveness of their advertising campaigns. This is not too surprising from someone who used to work for companies like Mars, whose 'A Mars a day, helps you work, rest and play' has over the past 50 years won no advertising awards, but has helped to sell many millions of Mars bars.

We have now created a willingness on the part of some consumers to try the brand so that our next task is to make it readily available. For a consumer product, this can be measured through the distribution in retail outlets or other appropriate channels of distribution. The best measure of distribution is the 'value weighted' level of distribution, as this adjusts for the rate of sale through the different shops rather than simply showing the proportion of shops that stock the brand. Also we can track the effective distribution which highlights 'out of stocks' in retail outlets that are supposed to stock the brand.

During the launch and development of a brand, it may be very important to gain distribution in very specific channels of distribution; e.g. where opinion formers and early adopters do their shopping, as getting them to try the brand may be critical to its long-term success. In such a case, this specific element of distribution can be targeted and monitored closely. Again, this is already done in most marketing-led companies but the financial evaluation of the optimal level of distribution is much less common.

Many fast moving consumer goods companies track their value-weighted level of distribution for each of their brands on a regular basis, normally monthly. The normal target is to achieve as high a level as possible and levels of 95–100 per cent are not at all unusual in this sector. However with the increasing level of concentration in retailing, a relatively high level of value-weighted distribution can be achieved with a much lower level of numeric-weighted distribution; i.e. your brands are available in the larger shops that sell more. This can mean that, in order to gain an additional 5 per cent in value distribution, you need to deliver to another 10 per cent or 15 per cent of the total retailers. The additional costs involved may not make it financially worthwhile to do this, particularly as the rate of sale in these much smaller retail outlets may be very low indeed. This could mean that consumers buying for the first time from such outlets could obtain a less than perfect product, which could put them off the brand forever.

However, as discussed in more detail in Chapter 9, there may be other strategic reasons for wanting to obtain distribution in smaller outlets that do not, at first sight, make financial sense. It may be a way of creating brand awareness through communicating directly at point of purchase (as is done by cigarette companies now that most mass media advertising is unavailable to them) or of stimulating trial by key consumers who we know happen to shop in these specific outlets. Many FMCG companies also classify retailers in terms of the profile of their customers so that they can focus their marketing expenditure on those channels of distribution that have the highest proportion of target consumers.

The objective of both awareness creation and distribution is obviously to get targeted consumers to actually buy and use the product. Therefore tracking the rate of trial by new users is a critical piece of marketing research; however, this really requires very carefully focused marketing research. Most new successful brands have very specific target groups of consumers, for whom the particular brand attributes should be especially relevant; see the case study at the end of the chapter. It is therefore potentially much more beneficial if one of these targeted consumers tries the brand, as they should be much more likely to be converted to a regular user. Also consumers have very different profiles when it comes to trying new products and they bring distinctive personal approaches to purchasing decisions. At one end is a group that will basically try any and every new brand that comes on to the market; they are often known as innovators. Thus gaining trial by this group may not be too difficult but, as they will then move on to try the next new brand, achieving any degree of brand loyalty from them may be next to impossible. At the other extreme are the very slow adapters, who need a long time to be convinced of the benefits of changing from their existing buying routines. However once they have been converted to your brand, they will need an equal amount of convincing to move away to a competitor's offering. In between, according to Kearton's Adaptive Innovative Index, there are a group of early adapters who could be convinced to try the new brand quite quickly and may be influential in getting others to try it, as long as they like it. Of course, if they don't like it, they may be equally influential in stopping the later adapters from ever trying the brand. These concepts of consumer loyalty are developed later in the chapter, but it should already be clear that trial by particular groups of new consumers may be financially worth much more than purchases by another potentially less loyal group.

For certain consumer product segments it is very important that trial is obtained from the innovators, even though they themselves may never become truly loyal to the brand. They may be extremely influential on the subsequent purchases made by their followers, who look to see what has been tried by their leading opinion formers. This question of achieving and assessing the rate of trial is a good illustration of how financial evaluation and control should be integrated with marketing strategy and marketing research. The initial brand development strategy should have considered what level of trial by which relevant consumer segments was needed to make the brand launch successful. The marketing plan should then have set out what level of awareness (with corresponding attitudinal assessments) was required in each important relevant consumer segmentation, and what level of distribution was needed to achieve this level of trial. Only when these have been established can the marketing launch budget for the brand be properly developed. Unfortunately it is still far too common to find brand launch plans that jump suddenly and mystically from very high launch advertising needs to high market shares. This makes it impossible to control the brand development in its early stages, as it is only after all the marketing expenditure has been spent that the company can see if the high eventual market share was achieved.

Sensible financial control over brand developments requires measurable targets to be set for each phase of the process and ideally for each of these phased targets to be put together in an overall marketing plan that will, if each phase works, result in the ultimate market share desired by the company. As the brand develops, problems can then be identified early and the weak points in the implementation process can be rectified. For example, it is not enough to know that the rate of trial for a new brand is not on target; is it caused by lack of awareness, low propensity to purchase, or lack of product availability? Only by knowing which element of the marketing mix is not working, can the resource allocation decision be properly made. There is little point in spending still more money on taking brand awareness up to 65 per cent from its existing 50 per cent, if the low level of distribution at 20 per cent means that the willing triallists are finding it very difficult to buy the product. Astonishingly I am aware of several 'leading' FMCG branded companies that are only now beginning to use this sequential success assessment process to identify the weak links in their brand development (or customer relationship development) chain.

The importance of this phased financial control process at the next stage in brand development is even more clear-cut; the next stage is getting an adequate proportion of triallists to re-purchase the brand. Clearly re-purchasing the brand indicates a degree of satisfaction in using the product for the first time. Equally too low a level of re-purchase should lead to a fundamental reassessment of the brand's development plan. There are a number of possible explanations but most of them are not good news! The worst situation is that trial was by exactly the targeted group of consumers and they simply don't like it; there is then little point in gaining further trial until the product has been fixed. In fact having more consumers try the brand before it works properly could damage it irretrievably, as they may never come back to try any subsequent 'new, improved' offering.

Another common cause of this conversion rate problem is that the wrong consumers have been trying the brand. This indicates that either the marketing is being badly targeted or that the current channels of distribution are inappropriate; again these need to be rapidly reviewed against the original specific targets that were set before significant additional marketing expenditure is committed to try to create additional trial.

The final stage in the brand development process for our repeat purchase consumer brand is achieving a satisfactory rate of regular usage among these converted triallists. Our targeted consumers may like the brand when they try it, but, if they only adopt it as a small part of their total consumption of the product category, the whole brand development may not have proved financially worthwhile. Thus, prior to the brand launch and prior to the commitment of any significant launch marketing expenditure, an overall model of how the required ultimate market share will be achieved should be developed. This model should highlight both the overall risk associated with the brand launch and the critical elements in the development process that need to be monitored most closely. If the initial risk assessment is unacceptably high, the company may need to undertake some pre-launch marketing research, including possibly carrying out a test market. Remember that the main role of marketing research is to reduce risk, not to increase returns!

Thus the model should indicate what proportion of the total potential user population is predicted to try the new proposed brand and what level of conversion into regular users is anticipated, together with the expected average level of consumption per such regularly using consumer. Clearly the higher the proportion needed at each stage to make the brand launch financially viable, the higher is the associated risk; I am a great believer in using the reverse break-even method in evaluating this type of project. You calculate the minimum level of market share that is required to 'just' financially justify the marketing investment required, and so on back through the model for each stage in the development process; you then assess the probability of achieving each of these levels. This technique was developed as a result of some personally painful learning experiences, one of which is illustrated in Practical Insight 8.3.

Practical Insight 8.3

Marketing success, but financial disaster

One of the most successful brand launches that I was ever involved in unfortunately also turned out to be probably the greatest financial disaster. We had evaluated a new specialist catering brand of canned-meat products using the new technology discussed in the case study at the end of Chapter 6. As was discussed in that case study, the new technology was not itself a sustainable competitive advantage because it could be copied by competition. The sustainable advantage therefore was in being the first to build the 'technology owning' brand in this market.

This increased the risk because it meant that it was not possible to carry out any really meaningful marketing research (such as a test market) prior to launching the new brand. However we were confident that the new branding offered significant customer benefits and a sustainable differential advantage should be achievable.

The financial evaluation showed a super profit level of return if a market share of above 15 per cent was achieved, and this seemed conservative. Following the brand launch, all customer reactions were very positive and we achieved virtually a 100 per cent repeat purchase rate from those customers that tried the brand; unfortunately our rate of sale indicated a market share of just over 5 per cent.

After some additional research, we came to the conclusion that we had, in fact, achieved an astonishing 60 per cent market share within 9 months of launch. However the total market was therefore only one tenth the size that we had originally estimated!

Development versus maintenance expenditures

The discussion regarding brand development is clearly based on the belief that brands can be long-term assets of a business that can produce ongoing sizeable future cash inflows, if they are properly developed. However this 'full potential' will, as with most long-term assets, only be realised if these brands receive significant investments during their development periods. These marketing investments, normally in the form of advertising and promotional expenditure, develop the brand attributes that are the source of the long-term sustainable cash inflows from the brand.

Hence the financial return from these marketing investments may be several years into the future, and they must be financially evaluated using the discounted cash flow techniques covered in Chapter 7. Unfortunately, as discussed in Part One, the normal accounting treatment for marketing expenditure does not classify even such long-term marketing activities as true financial investments. This means that it can be possible to improve the short-term financial performance of a business by cutting back on development marketing activities, even though this probably means that the brands will never come anywhere near to their full potential values.

It is therefore critically important that marketing budgets are split between development activities and maintenance activities, rather than being meaninglessly classified between above-the-line and below-the-line. If development marketing budgets are reduced in an attempt to boost short-term profits, the long-term indicators that *must* be part of the overall performance measurement process should be reassessed. For brand development, these would be specifically developed brand health indicators that show the relative future strength of the key elements of the brand.

However it must also be remembered that brands are developed in a competitive environment and the effectiveness of marketing expenditure is significantly affected by competitors' level of spending. This is shown diagrammatically in Figure 8.4, where the curve drawn is an extreme version to make the point clearly.

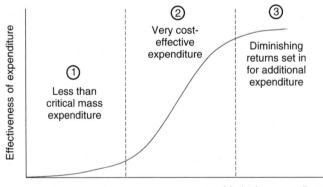

Figure 8.4   *Relationship of marketing expenditure and effectiveness*

If a company spends too little on brand development in a heavily supported industry, the effectiveness of its spend will be minimal. Unless a critical mass of marketing support is spent, the company will not overcome the level of 'noise' that already exists in the market place and the targeted customers will not register the desired messages. The effectiveness may be very low due to the relatively higher level of competitive expenditure or other general marketing activity that drowns out the company's specific marketing message. Clearly this critical mass level can be reduced if the targeted group of customers can be so highly segmented that they can be very specifically (e.g. individually) addressed. This is area 1 on the left hand side of Figure 8.4. Once this critical mass point is passed there is normally a very strong positive correlation between increasing marketing expenditure and its effectiveness, area 2 in Figure 8.4. However there is a point where the law of diminishing returns sets in and incremental marketing expenditure has almost no additional impact; some observers believe that the curve in area 3 can actually turn down, as additional expenditure annoys existing customers so much that they switch away from the brand. The particular shape of the S-curve for any industry is obviously dictated partially by the nature of the product and the degree of involvement of its customers, but it is also significantly impacted by the level of competitive marketing activity in the industry at the time.

Not surprisingly this has led to the development of a relative marketing expenditure measure: share of voice. Share of voice (SOV) refers to the proportionate share of the total marketing expenditure spent by the company's brand. One increasingly common relationship compares this SOV to the relative share of market achieved by the brand (i.e. its value market share, SOM). As shown in Figure 8.5, the ratio of SOV/SOM can be greater than 1, equal to 1 or less than 1.

If a brand is proportionately outspending its share of market (i.e. SOV/ SOM > 1), then the company is investing in developing the attributes of the brand. This investment should have been rigorously financially evaluated before commitment and should be controlled by monitoring changes in the brand attributes, or other leading brand health indicators. Once the brand has been fully developed, the level of marketing support should be designed to maintain

$$\frac{SOV}{SOM} > 1 \implies \text{A development/investment strategy}$$

$$\frac{SOV}{SOM} = 1 \implies \text{A maintenance/holding strategy}$$

$$\frac{SOV}{SOM} < 1 \implies \text{Normally a cash-/profit-extracting strategy}$$

Figure 8.5   *Share of voice compared to Share of market*

the brand at its current position. The required level of maintenance marketing expenditure should still be assessed by reference to competitive levels of expenditure; the objective may well be to achieve an SOV/SOM ratio of 1. However this required expenditure must still be financially justified by evaluating the sustainable level of cash inflows that can be generated by maintaining the brand.

There is potentially one brand in any market that may be able to sustain its current market share while spending proportionately less on marketing support than its share of market (i.e. having an SOV/SOM ratio < 1). This is the brand with the dominant market share, because such a brand often achieves economies of scale in its marketing expenditure that are not available to its smaller competitors. Thus, due to its dominant market share, it can still significantly outspend, in absolute terms, all of its competitors, while spending proportionately below its market share. If it actually spent at its proportionate rate it would find itself in area 3 of Figure 8.4, i.e. in the area of rapidly diminishing returns.

Notwithstanding this specific powerful sustainable competitive advantage, in most cases, an SOV/SOM ratio below 1 indicates that the brand is not being properly maintained and will, in the long term, decline in strength. This may be the appropriate strategy if the brand and/or the market are coming to the end of their life cycles. However one particular strength of brands is that it is often possible to transfer the brand attributes to another product before the decline of the original product has irretrievably damaged the brand attributes. If the brand is successfully transferred to another product, the economic life of the brand has clearly been extended. This transfer of brand attributes should be financially compared with the alternative strategy of developing a new brand specifically designed for the new product. Similar financial justifications should be done for all brand umbrella and brand extension strategies, which are discussed below, as they involve significant risks that must be taken into account, as well as the benefit of reducing the brand investment needed for developing a new brand.

I have come across some brand-led companies that maintain they are developing a particular brand even though it is very clear that their SOV/SOM ratio is below 1 for this 'development' brand. The only possible explanation is that their marketing expenditure is being spent significantly more effectively than the competition is. Unfortunately I have yet to find such a company that can demonstrate this greater effectiveness; as already mentioned, this can be achieved by better market segmentation and more specific targeting of customers (this area is developed in the next chapter).

Brand attributes

So far in this chapter I have made several references to brand attributes; it is now time to discuss this concept in more detail. Some brands deliberately

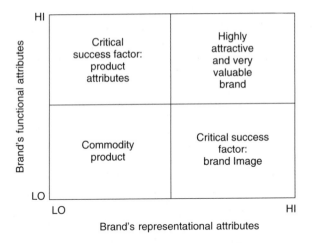

Figure 8.6 *Brand attributes: functional or representational*

convey something very positive about how well the product works or the technical characteristics of the product; the marketing emphasises the functional attributes of the brand. Other brands do not try to 'be functionally better' than the rest, but they create an image that is attractive and relevant to the targeted customer. This image may be emotional (trusting or caring, etc.), prestigious, rebellious, young, creative, intelligent, etc.; the emphasis is on the representational attributes of the brand. The differences are shown diagrammatically in Figure 8.6 and are illustrated in Practical Insight 8.4.

Practical Insight 8.4

Whisky-segmented brand attributes

The alcoholic drinks industry is dominated by brand-based strategies and the few large global players all have a wide range of brands. Some of these brands are very image-focused while others deliberately emphasise the specific functional characteristics of the underlying product. Unsurprisingly in the whisky industry, these different brand positions appeal to specific segments of the total whisky-drinking population.

Whisky can be produced as a blend of different malts, with the blending process being designed to ensure that the final product quality and taste is completely consistent from year to year. Most branded blended whiskies therefore emphasise their representational attributes; e.g. premium brands are associated with a rich and exciting lifestyle image (wind surfing across an exotic sun-filled bay).

However whisky can also be produced as a single malt brand from a specific very small distillery located on one single river in Scotland or Ireland. The product

---

Whisky-segmented brand attributes (*Continued*)

characteristics differ significantly from area to area and from year to year (depending on the peatiness of the soil through which the water passes and the level of rainfall). Many whisky drinkers express very strong preferences for their particular favourite single malt brand and its very strong functional characteristics.

The importance of brand attributes is that the marketing communications should emphasise the critical success factors, whether they are image-related or product-related. This, of course, means that the marketing research must be similarly focused. A successful image-oriented brand may only need to be 'as good as' the competition in terms of its underlying product's performance, as long as its image attributes create sustained customer loyalty.

If a brand can outperform the competition in terms of both functional attributes and representational attributes, it has the potential to be a very valuable brand indeed. However it may still face potential attack from more specialised brands that emphasise only one dimension, but move further along their chosen axis in Figure 8.6. This is what happened to IBM during its period of decline from the world's third most valuable brand to bottom of the league table, as was discussed in the case study in Chapter 3. No single company took over IBM's position as a risk-reducing, high-quality computer manufacturer, but a range of companies established much more focused positions within the computer industry. IBM's use of a single brand across the whole industry made it very difficult for it to adapt its position to reflect the increasingly different requirements of its new more sophisticated and more segmented customers.

Many companies have used the concept of corporate or umbrella branding in order to reduce the marketing cost of developing a range of separate, standalone brands. When it works well, the linked brandings can reinforce each other but, even so, it must be remembered that each new brand extension can put at risk the existing overall brand franchise. Very good examples of this come from the car industry where many manufacturers try to link their various models together under the corporate name. Thus the Mercedes brand has a very strong brand image and also very good functional attributes, which have enabled it to achieve good market shares in its chosen premium segments alongside a premium price position. Therefore using this brand umbrella to launch smaller cars into more volume-oriented market segments (the 190 range, the 'A' Class and the Smart car) must be viewed as high risk and be financially evaluated accordingly. If Maserati and Lamborghini owners perceived themselves as driving very expensive Fiats, the price premium obtainable might fall dramatically.

All the brands placed under the umbrella should therefore share the same attributes and brand positioning. In some industries, companies go to significant lengths to avoid customers realising that many of the brands in the market are actually supplied by the same company; each brand having its own distinct identity and often its own direct competitor, this is illustrated in Practical Insight 8.5.

Practical Insight 8.5

A plethora of washing powders

The washing powder industry is dominated globally by Procter & Gamble and Lever Bros (part of Unilever). However these two dominant companies each have a wide range of washing powder brands; most of which compete directly against a specific brand of the other company. It is difficult to justify this plethora of brands on the premise that this significantly increases the size of the total market. People presumably wash their clothes when they are dirty. Also, the brands are supported individually without strong direct linkage back to the owning business, so that no real group identity is developed with the consumer.

Thus there is little economy of scale involved in the marketing messages being sent to the end consumer. However, a wide range of existing brands will mean that retailers don't want to stock any more brands in this category. This makes it very difficult for any new entrant to gain distribution for their new brands. Without strong retail distribution, any other brand development expenditure will be ineffective as potential triallists are unable to find the new brand.

However this competitive marketing strategy can still be effective even if the new competitor gains some retail distribution. In a mature consumer market, some consumers are inherently loyal to their existing brand, while a proportion will be willing to try something new; this new choice may be made almost on a random basis, just to buy something different. Hence if the existing market is made up of only two brands, any new brand will have a chance of gaining one-third of these 'floating' consumers. If there are already over thirty existing brands, the random trial factor falls dramatically to around 3 per cent; thus the new brand will find it tougher to achieve trial and hence a viable market share.

Branding is normally designed to create some form of customer loyalty, as there is a lot of research to demonstrate that loyal customers are much more profitable than new ones (this is used in Chapter 9). There is some very interesting research into customer loyalty for consumer goods by Knox and Walker that is summarised in Figure 8.7, which resulted in their diamond of loyalty that is shown as Figure 8.8. The right hand side of the diamond shows the level of brand support shown by different consumers; brand support is demonstrated by the brand's relative share of the consumer's total purchases in this category. The left hand side of the loyalty diamond shows brand commitment that reflects the attitude of the consumer towards the brand. Technically brand

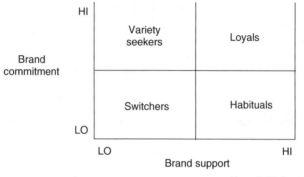

Knox & Walker 1994

Figure 8.7   *Customer loyalty classifications*

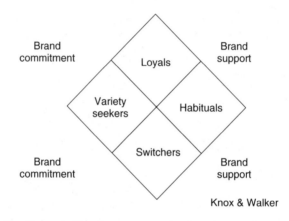

Knox & Walker

Figure 8.8   *The diamond of loyalty*

commitment is a combination of product involvement and perceived brand risk. Without getting into too much detail, product involvement describes the level of interest that the consumer has in the particular product category and the perceived brand risk reflects the relative degree of willingness/reluctance to switch to another brand. These combinations of product involvement and perceived brand risk that result in each consumer category's overall brand commitment are shown in Figure 8.9.

These four classifications of different types of loyalty have quite significant implications for the marketing strategy of any business involved in this sector, and therefore for the focus of the marketing finance process within such a business; these implications are summarised in Figure 8.10. The switchers classification shows low brand support together with low product involvement and low brand risk perception; basically they will decide what brand to buy depending upon what is on special offer as they walk round the supermarket, etc.

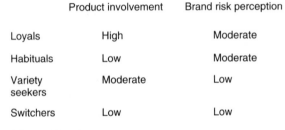

	Product involvement	Brand risk perception
Loyals	High	Moderate
Habituals	Low	Moderate
Variety seekers	Moderate	Low
Switchers	Low	Low

Figure 8.9 *Drivers of loyalty*

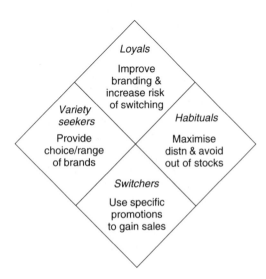

Figure 8.10 *Implications for marketing strategy*

The product category holds very little interest for them and each company needs to do something different to grab their attention albeit temporarily. The implication is that the marketing strategy to gain these consumers should emphasise specific promotions to gain immediate short-term sales opportunities but these promotions will not develop loyalty from these consumers. They will switch to the best special offer next time they go out to buy this product category; therefore each promotion must be financially worthwhile on its own account, there will be no long-term benefit.

The variety seekers are much more involved in the product category but will, on principle, always buy a range of brands over time; they have no problem in changing from one brand to another. However it is possible to build some brand support so that one specific brand can become a regular *part* of the range that they buy. If a company wants to increase its longer-term share of this consumer segment, it needs to develop a range of brands that provide these variety seekers with the choices that they crave; maintaining a range of relatively similar brands can obviously be very expensive.

The habituals group of consumers show a high level of brand support in that they regularly buy only one brand, but they demonstrate a low level of involvement and interest in the product category. In other words they buy this particular brand out of habit, simply because they always have done. This represents a significant risk because if they are forced to buy another brand, they may become habitually loyal to their new brand. The implications are that the company must ensure that their habitual consumers are never forced to experiment with a competitive brand. This can be done by avoiding out of stocks and ensuring that effective distribution is achieved to enable these habitual consumers to always find their regular brand; some consumer goods companies even obtain distribution in popular holiday destinations if they have large consumer groups from this classification.

The true loyal segmentation will buy other brands if forced to but they will return to their favourite brand as soon as possible. They do care about the branding and show this through long-term brand support. It is important that the branding company maintains the brand attributes that have generated this strong loyalty. In some cases, inappropriate brand extensions have significantly weakened the loyalty of this very valuable group of customers.

It should be clear that the brand marketing strategies need to be tailored to the needs of each of these different loyalty segmentations. This requires marketing research to establish the relative importance of each of these classifications to any specific brand; if most consumers of the brand are habituals, the strategy required is quite different than if they are mainly true loyals or variety seekers. If most are switchers, marketing finance should challenge whether the company really has a brand-based strategy.

Brand evaluation process

In a brand-led business the marketing finance system should include a brand evaluation process, which evaluates the relevant brand value drivers and brand attributes and arrives at the brand asset value. The process is deliberately called brand evaluation because it is not the absolute value of the brand that is really important. All such valuations that are based on discounting expected future cash flows are subject to the exercise of large degrees of judgement and are somewhat subjective. The important issues are the movements in the brand value and its trend over time and, as long as the process is applied consistently, these are much less subjective, even though any single valuation at a point in time may be debatable. Unfortunately several of the brand-based companies that have implemented a brand *evaluation* exercise have suffered from it being regarded exclusively as developing the brand *valuations*; this is highlighted in Practical Insight 8.6.

Practical Insight 8.6

A brand evaluation exercise?

One very large global FMCG group with a very large range of brands decided to carry out a brand evaluation exercise as a key input to their brand marketing resource allocation process. Unfortunately this was not properly communicated to the end markets that were actually implementing the process. They simply received an instruction from head office to complete yet 'another time-consuming and irrelevant exercise'.

Most of these countries decided that high valuations were obviously better than low valuations, because nobody wanted to be in charge of poor quality brands. Thus all the possible judgements were exercised to generate very high values and these were duly forwarded to the corporate centre. When they were added together, the total brand valuations came to more than ten times the current market capitalisation of the company.

My whimsical advice was to sell off as many brands as possible and return the money to the shareholders immediately. Needless to say, this advice was neither appreciated nor followed.

The basics of a brand evaluation process are to generate the expected future cash flows from the brand but, as mentioned earlier in the chapter, the cash flows should be directly attributable to the brand itself, rather than the under-lying product. For premium-priced brands this is quite often practical, but it is more difficult to separate the cash flows in a brand that sells at the same price as unbranded equivalents but generates increased market share. A practical solution is therefore to include all the expected cash inflows, but also to deduct a charge representing the required rate of return on the tangible assets required to produce the brand's cash inflows. This is being generous to the brand as it assumes that all of any super profit is attributable to the brand, rather than to other sources of sustainable competitive advantage. If other sources of shareholder value *have been* identified, such as economies of scale result-ing in lower cost levels, then these values can be built in to the brand evalu-ation process.

These expected cash flows then need to be discounted to their present values, and this requires the selection of an appropriate discount rate. As discussed in Chapter 7, the discount rate should not be too far away from the company's cost of capital, and significant risk differences should be handled by using probability estimates to adjust the expected cash flows. Also the value of any flexibility that can be achieved in the brand development strategy should be built in by using some form of real options, etc.; e.g. a test market that validates the fundamental branding proposition without giving competi-tors the opportunity to launch at the same time nationally.

However the first set of expected cash inflows is not the answer, it is merely the start of the brand evaluation process. The model should be re-run using alternative levels of brand development support expenditure in order to assess the optimum brand value; this represents the full potential value of the brand. It may not be possible to invest to this full extent in all of the brands in the company's portfolio, but such a brand evaluation process highlights the different levels of shareholder value that can be created by equal incremental marketing investments in alternative brands. Therefore it is a key element in the critical resource allocation decision process. This is why it is so important that the process is implemented consistently through time and across the organisation, and why the exercise discussed in Practical Insight 8.6 was such a wasted opportunity.

It also highlights why marketing budgets should be split between development and maintenance activities. Development expenditures should be justified by the increase in the value of the brand asset; i.e. by using discounted cash flow techniques to evaluate the net present value of the incremental investment. The expected economic life of the super profits from the brand (i.e. the competitive advantage period) should be assessed and regularly reviewed and specifically reviewed whenever the competitive situation changes significantly. The analysis phase of our continuous process covered in Part Two should have highlighted likely changes in the competitive environment, and early warning indicators of such critical changes should be developed. A good example of this is the petrol retailing case study in Chapter 5, where the commoditisation of a product-based brand rendered previous valuable brand attributes such as quality, availability and reassurance relatively worthless as they became taken for granted by customers, and made the value for money branding of the retailers much more relevant.

Maintenance marketing expenditures are designed to keep the brand at its current level of brand strength, e.g. keep the brand attributes at their existing levels. It is now very well established that both most brand value drivers (e.g. awareness, trial, etc.) and specific brand attributes (e.g. image) will decay quite rapidly unless they are properly maintained. Consistency in the marketing communication process (e.g. advertising copy strategy) and in the brand positioning can decrease this rate of decay (mathematically we can describe this in terms of increasing the half life of the geometric decay rate) but, nevertheless, development marketing expenditure cannot create an infinite impact. Thus the level of maintenance expenditure that is required should be established; as already mentioned, this requires an assessment of the level of competitive spending, and therefore may need reviewing if actual levels differ significantly from that anticipated. The consequences of under spending on maintenance activity will probably be quickly felt in short-term market performance but if sustained should also be reflected in a reduction in the brand asset value.

Over the life cycle of a brand, the proportionate mix of marketing expenditure will switch from virtually all development activity during the brand launch (there is nothing to maintain) to all maintenance activity once the brand has been fully developed. If a brand is reaching the end of its economic life, the level of marketing support may be reduced below the level required for complete maintenance of the brand attributes. This should be done so as to maximise the total cash generation over the remaining economic life. However, as already mentioned, it is sometimes possible to transfer the brand attributes, before the brand is irreversibly damaged, to another product. Thus the original 'product' may die more quickly but the brand can continue on a new, longer economic life cycle.

An overall perspective

A well-designed brand-focused marketing finance system will help to establish the full potential economic value of a brand. It will also assist in establishing and monitoring the effectiveness of additional brand expenditure by reference to each brand attribute.

It should also help to establish the optimum mix of brand value drivers (often also known as brand health indicators) that should be aimed for, given the overall potential for the brand (e.g. the mix of brand awareness and effective distribution).

Such a marketing finance system should assist in the financial justification of brand development expenditure and in establishing the required level of brand maintenance expenditure.

Case study – Philip Morris versus BAT plc

As already discussed in the case study in Chapter 4, Philip Morris has had a very successful product-based branding strategy built around its key brand Marlboro which still accounts for over half the cigarettes it sells worldwide. BAT plc, which is now a totally focused tobacco group following the demerger of its financial services businesses, has a vision statement 'to achieve leadership of the global tobacco industry in both a quantitative and qualitative sense'. Unfortunately for BAT it has no single brand that can come close to challenging either the total sales volumes of Marlboro, or its geographic spread of markets where it is the brand leader.

However there are alternative branding strategies that do not have to be based around a 'one size fits all' philosophy. Therefore BAT is implementing a brand portfolio approach based around its greater in-depth understanding of the smoking consumer. It is seeking to ensure that its 'brands are differentiated from each other and from the competition and directed at meaningful consumer segments'.

It is also looking to develop 'competitively superior products, that enhance the unique consumer positioning of the differentiated brand portfolio', including aspiring to be the first to launch a cigarette 'that will, over time, be recognised by scientific and regulatory authorities as posing substantially reduced risks to health'. Thus product differentiation is being allied with consumer segment-ation and this is to be made available through 'world-class customer service'. They state that they aim 'to provide superior service to their trade customers while improving supply chain productivity'.

The above quotations are extracted from BAT's 2001 Annual Report in order to demonstrate that this very clearly different marketing strategy has been publicly communicated to its shareholders, and therefore to its competitors including Philip Morris. It is a very good example of how you cannot expect to takeover from the existing leaders by doing the same things that they are already doing; identifying an alternative strategy may well increase the chances of success. However it may also be much less risky, albeit much more boring, to stay as a highly profitable No. 2 in a strongly shareholder value-creating industry.

9 Customer-Led Strategies

Overview

A customer-led strategy is built around the existing customers, and growth is generated by identifying new products which can be successfully sold to these customers. A key task for marketing finance therefore is to identify those customers from which the company can generate shareholder value. In any customer-led strategy, the marketing strategy is based on a market segmentation, but this can be done in a variety of ways. The objective is to identify financially viable groups of similar customers for whom tailored differential positionings can be developed. Marketing finance needs to be involved in the financial evaluation of the identified segments and in the prioritisation of those with the greatest potential to generate super profits.

The financial analysis of these customer groupings is a critical element in customer-led strategies; thus a relevant customer-account profitability analysis process is essential. This should only include attributable costs to the customer groupings, which results in the need to do a tiered financial analysis; as the groupings get broader, more of the costs become directly attributable.

The fundamental idea behind customer-led strategies is that customers can be regarded as long-term valuable assets; thus the relationship with the customer should be invested in, developed to its full potential, and then maintained for the duration of its economic life. The concepts of development and maintenance marketing expenditure are therefore once again important.

A long-term relationship should be mutually beneficial and the company must therefore also create value for the customer; the balance between the value created for the customer and the value created from the customer should be carefully managed.

Companies that are serious about relationship marketing should be evaluating the life cycle profitability of their customers as this should assist in focusing investment resources on the most financially attractive segments. There are techniques that link the different key strategic thrusts at each stage to the tailored financial evaluation and control process that should be used. However long-term customers can also provide indirect benefits and these should also be valued. Referrals and referencability, together with innovation and learning, can mean that certain relationships are financially worthwhile despite generating apparently less than required direct returns. These contingent benefits should be valued using the conditional probability, simulation and real options techniques discussed in Chapter 7.

Introduction

As stated in Chapter 8, brands can be built around products or customers, but a customer-based brand is designed to encourage existing loyal customers to try new products that are launched under the same brand (e.g. retailer brands such as Tesco, Aldi, Carrefour, etc.).

Indeed any customer-led strategy is, by definition, built around the existing customers of the business. As is shown in Figure 9.1, the development process is to identify new products that can be successfully sold to these existing customers. A critical question in the financial evaluation of such a growth strategy is therefore 'which customers should form the basis for future growth'. If the company has an overall financial objective of creating shareholder value, the obvious answer is to base the strategy around those customer groupings from which the company can generate sustainable super profits.

This requires a strategically oriented, long-term customer account profitability (CAP) analysis to be carried out. This CAP analysis should indicate the relative profitability of different groups of customers, but it should not be used as an attempt to apportion the net profit of the total business among the different customers. In fact, apportioning (or 'spreading') costs among customers can destroy the main benefits from the CAP analysis. The analysis should support important strategic decisions regarding which customer segments should be invested in, etc. The resulting information produced must be relevant to these decisions and this will not be the case if a large proportion of indirect costs is apportioned to these customers.

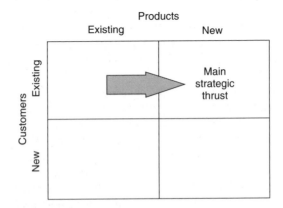

Figure 9.1 *Focus on existing customers*

As is explained in the body of the chapter, the key phrase is direct attributable costing, where the real cost drivers for each customer-related cost are identified. These cost drivers are what cause the cost to be incurred by the business and what make the level of the cost change. Once they are identified it normally becomes clear as to how customers should be grouped together. Many companies now operate quite sophisticated CAP analysis systems but, if the strategy is to be based around customers, the analysis needs to be done on a long-term basis. Such long-term CAP analyses are less common. The idea is to evaluate which types of customers are worth investing in because, over their economic life cycle, the business expects to be able to generate a positive net present value from the investment. This type of marketing strategy is commonly referred to as relationship marketing, because the business tries to develop (i.e. invests in) a long-term relationship with the customer. If this type of marketing strategy is in use, the company needs to tailor its marketing finance system to treat these customer relationships as a long-term asset of the business. Thus development and maintenance marketing expenditures are as relevant here as they were in the earlier discussion on brands.

Indeed, in a relationship marketing-based strategy, attention shifts towards customer retention and development rather than being exclusively focused on customer acquisition. The key priority is retaining the most valuable long-term customers, who will more than repay the required marketing investment. However, in order to attract and retain these valuable long-term customers, the company must create more value *for* these customers than the competition; any sustainable long-term relationship must be mutually beneficial.

Customer value can be defined as the perceived benefit obtained by the customer less the price paid and other 'costs' (e.g. time, inconvenience) incurred in order to own the good or service. Customers who do not perceive that they are getting value from a relationship are likely to defect. If this happens, the original marketing investment in acquiring this customer has failed to create shareholder value.

Experience has taught me that discussions regarding 'customer values' can result in a great deal of confusion. A company seeks to achieve value *from* the customer for itself, but a sustainable long-term relationship requires it to deliver value *for* the customer. In this chapter, customer value will be used to describe *value for* the customer (i.e. from the customer's or buyer's perspective) and customer account profitability (or customer profitability, etc.) will be used for *value from* the customer (i.e. from the supplier's or vendor's perspective).

Marketing segmentation

In any customer-led strategy, the marketing strategy process starts with carrying out a market segmentation exercise. The appropriate differential advantages for each of these market segments are identified and the business defines its positioning strategy for those attractive segments that it decides to target. A relationship management process is then developed for the customers in these segments.

Thus it all starts with market segmentation, but this segmentation can be done in many different ways. As is shown in Figure 9.2, there are several stages on the road to true market segmentation starting with 'one size fits all'. The classic example of mass production was, of course, the Model T Ford which was reverse engineered so that it could be sold at a price that the target consumers could afford. Thus to bring the cost down it was available only in black, with no optional extras. This product made Ford Motor Company into the largest car company in the USA, and hence in the world at that time, but this leadership did not last all that long. General Motors decided that consumers wanted some choice in the car that they bought, and so they differentiated their products with some relatively small changes but these were also marketed under several different brand names that still persist today. Ford stuck with its standard product concept for some years and rapidly became, and has stayed, the No. 2 car company in the world.

Product differentiation is still not really market segmentation because it has been described as 'bending demand to the will of supply' in that it is still production-oriented. The product is made to look different and these differences are then offered to the market. It is what I refer to as a sales approach (i.e. we sell what we have got) rather than a true marketing approach (i.e. we make what you want). Therefore true market segmentation seeks to identify what customers really want and then matches the company's products to these specific requirements. This can quite easily result in over segmentation or fragmentation of the market where almost every customer wants something unique. Some industries are trying to satisfy this 'mass customisation' concept, which results in virtually individual segmentation. Of course for many industries this is a matter of cost, but the car industry and the computer industry have moved a long way along this process, as is illustrated by Practical Insights 9.1 and 9.2.

From	One size fits all	Mass production (Model T Ford)
Through	Inside out planning	Product differentiation
To	Outside in planning	Market segmentation
And possibly	Mass customisation	Individual segmentation

Figure 9.2 *Trends in marketing strategies*

Practical Insight 9.1

A long way from the Model T Ford

The car industry has progressed a long way from selling a standard product that was made in millions. It is now perfectly possible to design your own personalised car from a massive range of options. The key is that your car is obviously not made until after you have confirmed exactly what you want; this means that you may only be able to see a computerised simulation of your 'dream' car, before it arrives as a living nightmare!

The challenge for the car industry is to modify its supply chain processes so that there is an acceptable gap between placing your individualised order and the car being delivered to you. This is still creating major conflicts within many of the largest car manufacturers, as operations managers want long, efficient production runs while marketing managers want to offer increasingly tailored products.

The solution is, as discussed in Rudolph and the Elves in Chapter 2, to put great flexibility into the supply chain where it is needed and will add value; flexibility is normally very expensive. Standard and efficient processes can still be used elsewhere in the supply chain of this market-segmented business. For car companies they use great flexibility in their assembly plants and paint shops, where each successive car may be different. They do not need it in their engine manufacturing plants, where all 1.6 litre diesel engines should be the same. The marketing strategy *must* dictate how operations and supply chain processes are structured.

Practical Insight 9.2

Dell Computers: a new business model

Dell Computers has been the fastest growing and most profitable personal computer company almost from its launch. It was started with a new business model of how personal computers should be sold to customers. First it is based on direct marketing, rather than distributors, dealerships or retailers. Second, and even more importantly, Dell do not hold any finished goods inventory. They assemble (i.e. they buy in the components) your computer once you have ordered it. This enables customers to specify exactly (within the range of options provided by Dell) what their computer will contain.

This requires Dell to have a very responsive supply chain because order to delivery cycles must be very short in this industry (consumers may be willing to wait several months for their new Mercedes to be manufactured. but they will not wait 2 weeks for their new desktop or laptop). A measure of their success in this area is that in some markets, their delivery lead times for a uniquely tailored product are less than buying a competitor's standard product from a distributor.

For most industries, mass customisation equals over-fragmentation of the market and would be financially disastrous. Therefore market segmentation is really an aggregation process of grouping together similar customers. A market is defined as 'the actual and potential buyers of a product', and it should be remembered that by segmentation, or even product differentiation, we are automatically redefining markets. Marketing finance has an important role in ensuring that each of these redefined market segmentations is financially attractive, and to highlight those that have the greatest potential for generating super profits.

Segmentations can be objective or subjective. Objective means that it is fact-based and hence less debatable but, often, also much less useful and relevant. For business to business industries, classic *objective* segmentations are geographic (e.g. regionally), size (e.g. total sales revenue), organisation type (e.g. international, national, regional, local); these tend not to help in directing future strategic investments. More relevant, but still hard data-based, segmentation criteria can be based on: the degree of compatibility with us on the buying criteria they use, their buying methods (e.g. central buying decision versus local negotiation), their delivery/distribution requirements (e.g. delivery to central warehouse or to multiple individual locations), the level of importance of the product to the customer (e.g. key input versus standard non-essential commodity). There are also softer more judgmental segmentation criteria that can be strategically very relevant; these include: level and importance of innovation and flexibility, style of key decision-makers (e.g. risk-taking professional or risk averse family member), degree of loyalty, stage of development (e.g. high growth versus mature or declining), degree of systems compatibility.

For business to consumer industries the range is even greater. Objective segmentations clearly include age, gender, socio-demographics (the normal a, b, c_1, c_2, d, e classifications) but these have now been developed into geo-demographics and biographics. Geo-demographics analyses clusters of similar people and families living in particular localised areas, so that consumer-focused companies can tailor their distribution of specific products to the particular needs of the consumers that are likely to use the shops in the area. Biographics has really grown out of the data capture capability of bar scanning in that it classifies consumers based on their retail transactions; in the modern world, you are what you buy! This has led to some classic examples where retailers have changed their store layouts at certain times of the day in response to this information; they not only know who you are and what you buy, but when you buy it.

However the more rapidly growing method of segmenting consumer markets is based around psychographics; these relate to life styles, personality types and self-concepts. Lifestyle segmentations focus on activities, interests and opinions while personality groupings emphasise things like inner versus outer directness, degree of self-monitoring and level of innovativeness. Self-concept measures focus on 'how we are', 'how we want to be' and 'how we perceive ourselves to be' (which can, of course, differ significantly from how we actually are). The important issue in psychographic segmentation is that there is no right or wrong answer, the segmentation is try to group together similar types of consumers; the problem is that people can try to give you the answer that they 'feel' is 'better'.

There are also still other forms of segmentation that are particularly relevant to certain industries; these include: occasions for purchase or use (known as situational context), where some consumers will drink different brands when they are at home than they do when out with friends or work colleagues; buying/usage intensity, where some high usage consumers will use more than one brand (possibly in distinct situations) so that share of usage may be an important piece of marketing information.

It should be clear from this very summarised review of the vast range of segmentation methods that the basis of segmentation that is to be used requires careful thought; particularly if it is to be used as the basis for major strategic marketing investment decisions.

Customer account profitability analysis

A well thought through market segmentation should provide a vertically structured grouping of customers that enables a comparison of their relative profitabilities to be made. As already stated, a soundly based CAP analysis is an essential pre-requisite for a customer-led strategy, in that it enables the company to identify those most profitable customers on which the strategy should be based.

Such a soundly based CAP system must be designed to take account of all the significant differences in the way customers are dealt with. Thus the analysis of relative customer contributions should compare all the areas of significant difference; the customer groupings (i.e. the identified market segments and sub-sets of these) should be made by reference to their significant similarities, so that the consistent differences from other groups are highlighted.

An illustrative example of a CAP analysis is shown as Figure 9.3 for an FMCG company selling through different types of retailers; the key issues are the same for this type of CAP analysis in any other industry. The objective is not to try to arrive at a net profit for each customer or customer grouping; as mentioned in the introduction to this chapter, apportioning costs to customers can destroy the decision support relevance of the analysis. The aim is to high-light the financial impact of the different characteristics of these market segments and of the different ways in which customers are serviced.

Hence the attributable costs of all the significant differences must be ascertained and charged to the relevant customer groups. In Figure 9.3, it is therefore not by chance that each heading is titled 'customer-specific', 'direct', or 'customer-attributable'. If the cost is not incurred directly because of the customer, it should not be included in the analysis. For this to be successfully achieved, it is essential that the *real cost drivers* are identified for each such

Illustrative example for an FMCG products company selling through retailers

	£		
Gross sales by customer			x
Less sales discounts & allowances			x
Net sales by customer			x
Less direct cost of sales			x
Gross customer contribution			x
Less customer specific marketing expenses	x		
Direct sales support costs	x		x
Less customer specific direct transaction costs			
Order processing	x		
W/Housing & distribution	x		
Invoice processing	x		
Inventory financing	x		
A/Cs receivable processing & financing	x		
Specific sales support	x	x	
		x	
Less customer attributable overheads		x	
Net customer contribution		x	

Figure 9.3   *Customer account profitability analyses*

Attributable customer costs

Customer-related discounts

Selling and order processing

Warehousing and distribution

Operational costs

Marketing, including advertising

General administration and fixed costs

These costs can differ among different customer groups by more than the business' profit

Hence there is the likelihood of substantial differences in relative customer profit contributions

Figure 9.4   *Customer account profitability analyses*

area of cost. There is a mass of research evidence from CAP analyses in many industries that, as is shown in Figure 9.4, there are significant differences in the attributable cost levels in many of these areas among different customer groupings. These differences inevitably result in substantial differences in the relative net customer contributions.

The problem for many companies is that they have sophisticated costing systems that are primarily based around allocating costs to products, rather than to customers. Thus in many cases the total charges to the CAP analysis are built up from the product-costing system depending upon the actual mix of products purchased by each customer grouping. This is clearly unsatisfactory, particularly when a number of these costs are actually directly attributable to customers, as is demonstrated by Practical Insight 9.3.

Practical Insight 9.3

Freight & warehousing: a customer-led cost

The case study on Knight Foods in Chapter 6 mentioned a distribution costing problem. Knight Foods sells a range of food products that have very different warehousing and freight characteristics. Thus some canned catering products were packed in heavy cases and full pallets could be stacked on top of each other, right up to roof level; whereas some cases of retail products (dehydrated potato, etc.) were very light and the bulk product needed specialised pallet racking in the warehouse. The company had developed a very complex apportionment system for spreading both the budgeted and the actual freight and warehousing costs across this range of products. Some of the costs were spread on weight, some by pallet and still others by number of cases or time spent in the warehouse.

The input of these costs into the CAP analysis required applying each of these costing bases to the actual product sales made to each customer so as to build up the total freight and warehousing cost for the segment. In no way could this cost be described as 'attributable' to the customer, or be used as the basis for strategic or even tactical decision-making.

However, the company actually sent trucks, carrying a mixed load of product, direct to these customers, so that the *directly attributable* freight costs per customer *could be objectively* calculated. In the warehouse most of the costs were fixed apart from in the order picking area, where the bulk stored product had to be broken down and repacked for shipment to the customers. This was necessary because customers did not order in the same quantities that the company produced and stored in. There were potentially significant savings to be generated if this 'bulk splitting' activity could be reduced, and more full pallets and cages could be shipped to customers.

Again this cost is *directly attributable* to the way customers order and it is perfectly possible to offer customers a discount for ordering in full pallet multiples; rather than, as was done at Knight Foods, for ordering more than 250 cases in total. As is discussed later in the chapter, the level of the discount should be set as a proportion of the saving; a long-term relationship should be mutually beneficial.

It should also be clear that the level of directly attributable costs differs depending upon the size of the customer grouping. Thus, in some industries, there may be relatively few directly attributable costs at the individual customer level but, as these individual customers are grouped together, more meaningful levels of directly attributable costs are identified; and, hence more significant differences among groups of customers are revealed. This is diagrammatically shown in Figure 9.5 as a smooth continuous curve; in practice, the curve normally has a number of dysfunctional step points in it, which highlight the key levels at which CAP analysis should be focused.

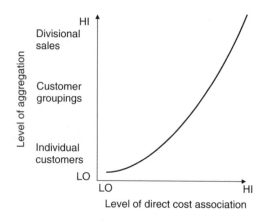

Figure 9.5   *Customer account profitability analyses: cost levels directly associated with different levels of customer aggregation*

Relationship marketing

A customer-led strategy is based on the belief that the customer is the key intangible asset (i.e. source of sustainable competitive advantage) of the business. Hence this key asset should be managed so as to maximise the net present value that can be generated over the asset's economic life. Such long-term asset management would normally involve three types of expenditure:

- Research type expenditure: to identify the characteristics of the most attractive customer groupings or market segments.
- Investment (development) expenditure: to win business from these target groups of customers and then to develop a long-term relationship with them.
- Maintenance expenditure: to defend this long-term relationship against competitors while ensuring that its full potential is fulfilled.

A strategically oriented marketing finance system would therefore have financial evaluation and control processes that assist in justifying and then managing these development and maintenance levels of marketing expenditure.

This idea of investing in customers in order to develop a long-term relationship that will then be defended has now become known as relationship marketing. In a relationship marketing environment, the focus changes from the individual current transaction to the value of the longer-term relationship with the customer. A transaction-led strategy, where no assumption of repeat business can be made, emphasises the profitability of each individual sale to the customer; hence any ongoing customer-based analysis is really only a series of individual transactions.

The financial analysis under a relationship marketing strategy is fundamentally different; the company may quite deliberately not try to recover all of its costs during the early stages of the relationship, these costs are seen as part of the investment in the customer. Thus the question of long-term customer retention and development becomes much more important; these must be subjected to a proper financial justification, because it is not worth retaining a customer at any cost.

In any growth strategy based on customers, an obvious constraint on the rate of growth is the level of customers lost in any period, as new sales have to be generated to make up for those lost. However it is also well established that new customers are generally much less profitable than existing customers, particularly in a number of industries where the costs of customer acquisition are very high. There is also research by Bain & Co., a firm of strategic consultants, that demonstrates that long-term customers increase their level of purchases over time. Further, as is discussed later in the chapter, long-term customers can be an attractive source of business referrals, both from other parts of their own organisation and other companies. Equally negative publicity from dissatisfied ex-customers is avoided if more customers are retained.

However the greatest source of value enhancement from retaining and developing customers is that customer service costs decrease substantially over time in most industries. Many companies have very expensive new business teams (e.g. advertising agencies, insurance brokers, accountants and lawyers) that target the prospective new customers.

Once these targets become actual customers they are passed over to their ongoing account management team, and the 'heavy hitters' move on to the next target. However this is by no means the only area where costs reduce significantly; in many industries it is an expensive process simply to set up a new customer in the accounting and sales administration systems. Also there is a very steep learning curve for both organisations as they start to understand how the other party's processes really work. Therefore administrative support time and hence costs normally reduce substantially for a period before, like all learning curves, starting to flatten out.

It should be clear that, if a company is serious about implementing a relationship marketing strategy it should understand how its internal costs change over time with different groups of customers. Unfortunately very few companies have costing systems designed to give them this information even though, in practice, the data collection problems are relatively trivial. Even more important is what should be done with the information when it is collected. The cost savings should be shared with the customer because it is their loyalty and continued business that has generated them; also it reinforces the concept of a mutually beneficial relationship. At the same time and even more importantly, it builds an entry barrier against competitors that will be targeting these customers; by definition, your loyal, long-term customer is your competitor's target or prospect.

In order to highlight the importance of these long-term customer relationships, it is very useful if the whole organisation is focused on 'satisfying' these customers' expectations and requirements. Some very common terms in this area now are 'surprise' or 'delight' the customer, i.e. exceed their expectations by giving them something that they were not expecting. I have a problem with these ideas unless the surprise and delight can be achieved at no cost to the supplier. If the customer was not expecting or requiring something, it is probable that they will place a low value on whatever 'extra' has been delivered. This means that it is quite possible that the vendor has added more cost into the relationship than the perceived added value to the customer; this is definitely not shareholder value enhancing. Therefore I happily accept the term 'anticipate' customers' expectations, because this will demonstrate a good understanding of and concern for these long-term customers and should be more fully valued by the customers. All areas of the business (operations, quality control, supply chain and distribution, customer administration, as well as sales and marketing) must all understand the target customers' needs. All of these areas should also have key performance measures that relate to how well they have satisfied these customer needs and expectations. This is discussed in Part Four but one example is given in Practical Insight 9.4.

Practical Insight 9.4

When is a complaint not a complaint?

Customer complaints are a good area to examine to get a perspective on different companies' attitudes to relationship marketing. One financial services company set itself a performance measure of speed of response to a complaint; their benchmark was 'same day reply in the same medium'. Thus, if a customer e-mailed a complaint, they would e-mail back the same day, and similarly for telephone calls, faxes, etc. They regularly achieved a 100 per cent score and thought that was good! Unfortunately this measure said nothing about resolving the customer's complaint so that a lot of their 'same day' responses were really just acknowledgements (e.g. thank you for your complaint received today!). Of course, when the customer rang up to complain that no one had done anything about their complaints, they would ring back *on the same day*.

Another financial services company used the number of complaints as its measure of customer service. This resulted in members of staff going to great lengths to avoid actually recording that a *complaint* had been made; they introduced a complicated complaints form that had to be completed, with lots of detailed information to be filled in by the 'complaining' customer.

At the other extreme, an FMCG company measured its success in dealing with complaints by tracking whether the complaining customer was *still* a customer 6 months after their complaint had been resolved. This was applying the logic that a customer that complains is giving you the chance to rebuild the relationship; a customer that is past this stage simply ceases to be a customer, and often tells lots of their contacts what they have done, and why.

One way of achieving this critical focus on customer retention is therefore to ensure that everyone in the organisation regards these key customer relationships as being worth their full life-cycle potential. My favourite example of this is Wal-Mart, which now has an incredible 1.3 million employees; all of whom go through an induction training programme instituted by Sam Walton, the founder. He said, 'I tell all my staff to see all customers as having $50 000 written across their forehead', as this should make the employee smile and try to be helpful; they are talking to 'serious money'. The $50 000 was Sam Walton's estimate of the life-cycle purchases by the average Wal-Mart customer and was established nearly 50 years ago. Now we are more sophisticated, but even I would not suggest that anyone tried to picture a customer with, written across their forehead, the words, 'present value of the expected super profits over the customer's life cycle'.

Customer value

We have already said a long-term relationship should be mutually beneficial and that, therefore, in order to attract and retain customers, a company must create more value for these customers than its competitors. Customer value is the perceived benefit obtained by the customer less the price paid or other sacrifices of time, convenience, etc. that the customer makes to own the product. Where the perceived benefit derived by the customer is greater than the sacrifices made, customer value is created. It is well established that customers' perception of value is based on more than specification, features and price and that value perceptions are formed over time and can be affected by outside influences.

At first sight, increasing customer value seems to increase the seller's shareholder value as well. New customers are acquired if high customer value is generated, and existing customers are retained and developed; thus total customer account profitability should grow as sales revenues increase. However, beyond a particular critical point, further increases in customer value will actually reduce the seller's shareholder value; in other words, the customer value package has now been made too good. The company is not now 'capturing' enough of the total value that is being 'created' by the ongoing relationship. Marketing finance needs to be able to identify where this critical turning point is; in order to make decisions about those marketing strategies that will create shareholder value, as well as generating sufficient customer value for those segments targeted for long-term relationship management. This is why it is so critically important that companies are able to value customer relationships and manage customers appropriately at the different stages in their life cycle.

Customer life cycle profitability analyses

CAP analyses are now quite common and, in some companies, do highlight the relative profit contributions of differing customer groupings in a way that assists in some resource allocation decisions. However an even more important development in profitability analyses for customer-led strategies is the idea of life cycle profitability of customers. This type of analysis should assist in concentrating resources on those customer groupings where the greatest long-term super profits can be generated.

A good way of structuring such a life cycle CAP analysis is by using a variant of the directional policy matrix, as is shown in Figure 9.6. The horizontal axis represents the relative customer compatibility rating for different individual customers or customer groups. This should be evaluated from the customer's perspective by considering the factors that are taken into account by the customer when deciding which supplier to buy from. Normally a points factor scoring system is used where each factor (usually a maximum of five factors are used) is given a weighting and the company is ranked against its competitors on each factor so that an overall score results. The key question is whether the relative strengths of the company are relevant to this particular group of customers. Thus if a company has built up a strong branded image, with a reputation for quality and a high level of service, potential customers that are looking for a low cost, adequate product would be considered incompatible. However as this evaluation is done from the customer's perspective their perception of the potential supplier may be incorrect and could possibly be changed by the supplier.

The vertical axis normally shows the business potential of the customer, where business potential is the share of the customer's total business that the

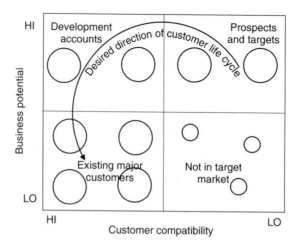

Figure 9.6   *Directional policy matrix (customer variation)*

company at present does not have. Thus a prospective customer is at the top of the vertical axis, because everything is business potential. The overall size of the customer or grouping is indicated by the size of the circle used, with the current positioning being represented by the centre of the circle.

Customers logically follow a life cycle as is shown by the curve in Figure 9.6; they start in the top right hand box as prospects and targets. Clearly they have high business potential at this stage as they are not yet customers, and the reason no business is being done with them yet may well be due to a perceived low level of compatibility. The top left hand box contains development accounts that still have a high business potential because the company only has a small share of their total potential business. However these accounts are considered compatible customers, so that they should progress downwards into the bottom left hand box as the company gains an increasing share of the available business. The bottom right hand box is not part of the target market because it contains possible customers that are incompatible and have been assessed as having low business potential; many of these will be small circles, where the total business is not worth the investment required.

This initial analysis enables the company to develop specific strategic thrusts for each stage of the life cycle, and marketing finance should be developing similarly tailored financial evaluation measures and control techniques. The key strategic thrusts are shown in Figure 9.7 and the marketing finance measures in Figure 9.8; the easiest way to explain the model is to follow a particular customer through its life cycle.

This customer starts off in the top right hand box (high business potential but low customer compatibility); this means that the customer thinks that the

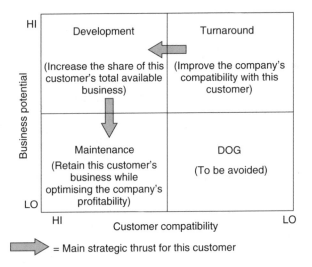

Figure 9.7 *Customer life cycle profitability analyses – strategic thrust*

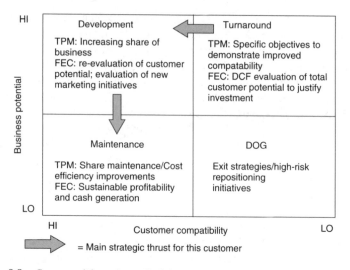

Figure 9.8   *Customer life cycle profitability analyses – tailored performance measures (TPM) and financial evaluation and control techniques (FEC)*

company is an unsuitable supplier. Before a long-term relationship can be developed, this customer's compatibility rating must be improved. This becomes the key strategic thrust for these turnaround accounts; the performance measures used should not include sales targets or profit measures at this stage. However marketing finance should have done an evaluation of the potential value of this customer in order to assess whether it is worth trying to change the perceived incompatibility. In some cases, such a DCF evaluation will be difficult but it may be possible to regard the first marketing investment as acquiring an option (as discussed in Chapter 7) to get to know the customer better. Certainly, at this initial stage, any DCF evaluation of the potential customer asset value will be done using the probability assessments and risk management techniques discussed in Chapter 7. Marketing finance should also use modelling techniques to assess the potential impact of different marketing approaches to this prospective customer.

In some cases, the reasons for the apparent lack of compatibility are in fact perfectly valid; what the customer wants does not match with the marketing strategy of the supplier. This should move the customer down to the bottom right hand (dog) box, as there really is now very low business potential from this customer.

Once the compatibility rating has been improved, the key strategic thrust should be to increase the share of this customer's total available business; the maximum potential share that can be obtained should be assessed carefully, as many customers would never consider going to a single supplier position. This means that the tailored performance measure for these development accounts is the increase in the share of the customer's business; still not current customer account profitability. The focus for marketing finance at this stage of the customer life cycle is to reassess the DCF evaluation of the long-term potential of this customer; by now, a much more accurate evaluation should be possible as better knowledge of the customer is gained. Also the proposed marketing investments should be assessed prior to implementation and closely monitored to learn their relative effectiveness, as a learning process for the future; this will involve using short-term techniques (such as payback periods) in addition to the long-term DCF technique.

As the company's share of this customer's business increases, the customer moves down into the maintenance category, where the key strategic thrust is to retain this customer's business while optimising the customer account profitability. This is the stage when the financial return on the earlier investment in the customer is realised and so the financial measurement focus moves to sustainable customer account profitability and positive cash generation (there should be no further need for significant additional investments in specific fixed assets or working capital for this customer once the level of business is fully developed). The tailored performance measures used for maintenance customers should be to monitor the share of this customer's business (a decline in share should be taken as an indication of loss of customer loyalty) and the customer compatibility rating, as well as the achievement of cost efficiency improvements in the way in which this customer is serviced. Part of these cost efficiency gains can be retained so as to boost the customer's profitability but, as mentioned earlier, part should be shared with the customer so that they receive a benefit for their loyalty and to make it more difficult for competitors to make this valuable customer a better offer that they can't refuse.

There are a number of books and articles on relationship marketing that state that long-term customers will pay a premium price because over time they develop higher switching costs. This really worries me as you are effectively 'ripping off' your most valuable asset, simply because they are slightly more reluctant to leave you. Over time they should automatically become more profitable due to cost efficiencies and your increasing share of their business; you should charge them a *lower* price, not a *higher* one. Marketing finance should be evaluating the potential risk of a competitor stealing this customer and trying to identify and evaluate loyalty reinforcing marketing activities; the financial justification of such initiatives is clearly not an increase in return but a reduction in the risk of losing this continuing income stream.

An increasing number of companies are now trying to evaluate customer lifetime values and are using increasingly sophisticated tools to do so. Data warehouses and data mining tools assist organisations in measuring the economic value of customers. Predictive modelling techniques can be used to predict the remaining lifetime of the customer relationship and the likely result-ant future stream of cash flows from this customer. One insurance company discovered that customers who had defected exhibited characteristic behaviour patterns; it inserted a function into its data warehouse to identify these behav-iour patterns as they emerged and set up a team to manage those customers that might otherwise have been lost.

True relationship marketing suggests, however, that even this lifetime eco-nomic value does not necessarily reflect the total value of the customer to the company. There may be other indirect relationship benefits, which seem to be of four types. Referrals (word of mouth) and referencability can both reduce the cost of acquiring other customers; product innovation for, and learning from, these relationship customers may benefit the whole company. These indirect relationship effects can mean that certain customer relationships do create shareholder value, even though the direct financial returns do not generate a positive net present value.

However, because these indirect benefits are more contingent upon the continuing strength of the relationship, different valuation techniques need to be adopted. Three techniques are particularly useful for financially evaluating and controlling these indirect customer relationship benefits: conditional prob-ability, simulation and real options. Real options are particularly interesting as there is some evidence from Lynette Ryals, a leading researcher in this area, to suggest that options thinking explains some significant marketing decisions in this field.

CAP analysis is complicated even further when the business sells through an indirect channel of distribution to the ultimate user of the product, e.g. as is done by many consumer goods companies that sell directly to whole-salers, distributors or retailers, which then sell on to the final consumers. Increasingly, this type of business wants to have sound financial analysis on both its direct customers and its ultimate but indirect consumers. Thus, many FMCG companies, particularly in the USA, have invested very large sums of money in developing very extensive *consumer* databases. This enables them to know much more about who eventually uses their product, even though they bought it indirectly. Clearly if their strategy is to develop new products that will appeal to these same consumers, this knowledge is critical. However it also illustrates a significant competitive advantage for the indirect channel of distribution (e.g. the retailer), as they can gain even more detailed customer information much more cost effectively. This is being used very proactively by the major retailers through their significant investments in retailer brands and customer loyalty programmes (store cards, etc.), that enable them to develop very appropriately designed and targeted new products. As the old saying goes, information is power when it comes to customer-led strategies.

Case study – D & M Confectionery Ltd

Background – The original business

D & M Confectionery Ltd was a regionally based, privately owned company that specialised in marketing and distributing cakes. Its initial success was based on focusing on the smaller retailers (i.e. individual shops and small chains, that tended to be owner-managed) where its product expertise added significant value to the customer. It added further value through developing its own regional brand (Country Style was the brand name), which helped to create consumer loyalty for the product range that was actually sourced from a number of locally based bakeries.

The owner and managing director, Mike Ato, had considerable skill in identifying and specifying new products and this expanding product range was a key element in the profitable growth of the business. At this stage, the company had cash on deposit at the bank as it collected the cash from its customers before it had to pay its suppliers, and its needs for capital investment were relatively low. This meant that the financial risk of the business was low but the business risk was relatively high.

D & M supplied a branded product to a range of retailers, who relied heavily on the product expertise of D & M and its van sales people. This customer relationship meant that any unsold retailer stock would be picked up by D & M at the sell-by-date, in order to safeguard their brand. In effect D & M was renting space in the retailer's shop and paying variable rental based on sales achieved. D & M also controlled the shelf life remaining when the cakes were physically delivered to the retailer but, as D & M was bearing the product risk, it regarded its field force more as sales people than delivery drivers. Its delivery system was therefore not very efficient, but it was customer-oriented and very flexible, and its relatively high profit margins meant its early growth was financially successful.

The new business opportunity

Mike was ambitious and wanted to grow. He identified a potential demand for a new range of high-quality cakes that could be sourced from Danish bakeries. He modified their existing products to his exact specifications and started importing into the UK. The success was astonishing and this new product range (all branded as Country Style) brought D & M to the attention of the major supermarket chains. Mike saw this as the chance to move into a much bigger league and enthusiastically entered negotiations with several chains.

It soon became clear that these national supermarkets wanted only the imported product, and they wanted to brand it themselves. They also intended to order centrally so that D & M's van sales force would be merely delivery drivers, and they wanted an efficient and effective distribution service from D & M. This represented a big change in D & M's existing business strategy and current sources of value-added, as well as requiring significant investments in warehousing, more and larger trucks and new computer systems to cope with the dramatically increasing volumes and tighter delivery timing require- ments. There was also a significant increase in the working capital tied up in the business, as the supermarkets demanded much longer credit terms than had been granted to D & M's original smaller customers, many of whom had paid in cash at the time of delivery. Also the increased volumes from the Danish suppliers led them to seek faster payment for their goods; consequently D & M became heavily reliant on bank debt financing.

Also the big supermarkets negotiated substantial volume discounts on their already reduced prices; they were not buying D & M's branded goods, and their selling out price was much more important to them than to the much smaller retailers that D & M was used to dealing with. However D & M was no longer bearing the entire product risk because, as long as it delivered the cakes with an agreed period of shelf life remaining, the supermarket now bore this risk (they had decided how much to order and it was packaged as their own brand). Clearly this new business had dramatically different value drivers to the existing business and a financial evaluation of the impact before starting followed by up-to-date monitoring thereafter was essential.

Unfortunately D & M had always relied on overall financial data and during the very rapid changes even this became more and more out-of-date (no man- agement accounts at all were produced for the months during which the new computer system was implemented). The new system did include a CAP analysis, and this eventually highlighted that some of these new major accounts were being operated at a loss.

Also during this period of dramatic change, D & M decided to concentrate all its Danish sourcing with one supplier in order to simplify the administrative processes and operational issues. Clearly the mutual dependence between the two increased as the sales of Danish cakes continued to grow. When D & M revealed its lack of profitability (i.e. when the new computer system came into operation) to its bank, the bank became concerned about its level of exposure and asked questions about the timing of future payments to this Danish supplier. The supplier agreed to extend its credit period (which it had previously reduced), but wanted to be reassured 'about the strength of D & M's customer relation- ships' by meeting these key customers. Within 3 months, the Danish supplier had agreed with these supermarkets to deliver to them direct, bypassing D & M completely.

Inevitably D & M went into liquidation because its original business could not possibly support the dramatically increased fixed cost base taken on for the new market segment. Obviously there are many reasons contributing to the collapse of the company and it would be far too simplistic to suggest that a good CAP system would have prevented this happening; but it certainly would have helped.

10   Product-Based Strategies

Overview

A product-based strategy generates growth by identifying new markets in which existing, financially successful products can be sold. Such a strategy should clearly be built on those existing products that have the potential to produce super profits and this makes a system of direct product profitability (DPP) analysis a critical area for marketing finance.

The objective of such an analysis is to highlight the relative profitability of existing products; this normally requires products to be grouped together if the analysis is to be both practical and relevant to strategic decisions. As the classifications of product become more detailed, less costs can be directly attributed to each separate product classification and the DPP analysis becomes less useful in its key decision-support role.

The DPP analysis should be tailored to the attributes of the product. A product with a cost advantage should be subjected to rigorous comparative cost analysis but this is much less relevant where the product attributes are based on differentiation and value-added. Ideally this DPP analysis should be done on a long-term basis over the remaining product life cycle; so that the future potential of the product can be included as well as its current financial performance.

There are two very different marketing strategies for product-based strategies where the costs of the product reduce over its life cycle; a quite common phenomenon known as the experience curve. In one case, selling prices today are set based upon the anticipated long-term costs associated with the product; the current loss on sales can be regarded as an investment in attempting to develop a long-term cost advantage. The other pricing strategy seeks to generate profits more quickly, either by setting very high initial selling prices or by reducing selling prices at a significantly slower rate than that at which costs are reducing. These high early profits may attract in new competitors or may delay the development of the market.

Many product-based strategies also have the added complexity associated with trying to sell a range of products to the same customers; there can often be an element of cross subsidisation among the products. Any such discount or rebate granted to a customer should be attributed to the real cause (i.e. its true cost driver) rather than being apportioned across all the products sold to this customer.

All competitive advantages have finite economic lives, and therefore a key strategic investment decision is whether the company should reinvest part of the super profits being generated from an existing advantage, in trying to develop a replacement competitive advantage. Such reinvestment decisions clearly require rigorous financial evaluation and the risk assessment will be highly influenced by the relevance to the proposed new competitive advantage of the existing core competences of the company.

There are many product costing techniques available and marketing finance should look to apply them more strategically before trying to invent completely new ones. This argument applies to standard costing where the traditional application of variance analysis does not necessarily lead to economically sound decisions. If the method of calculating efficiency/usage variances is modified, it becomes possible to base operational decisions on the most up-to-date cost information available rather than using the standard costs that may well be over a year old.

Transfer pricing is another common area of problems for product-based strategies because, far too often, it is seen as a method of cost apportionment or cost recovery, rather than a genuine pricing mechanism between different parts of the same business. The system should follow the same principles whether the transfer price is for a core process within a vertically integrated group or for the provision of support services. Resource allocation decisions should focus on the use of the critical limiting factor within the business (i.e. the factor that is constraining the future growth of the business) and measure the relative contributions of different products and processes in terms of 'per unit of the limiting factor'.

Introduction

In the previous chapter, the issues relating to marketing strategies built around existing customers were considered. An alternative, but possibly equally attractive, strategic thrust is to base future growth around existing products. These products may also be strongly branded, as was discussed in Chapter 8, but the critical element in a product-based strategy is that the growth objectives are delivered by finding new markets, new segments, or new customer groups to which to sell these existing products, as is diagrammatically shown in Figure 10.1. Obviously, the specific existing 'success' attributes of the product should be directly relevant to these new customers.

Not surprisingly, this strategic thrust should normally be based on those products that can achieve a sustainable level of super profit in their existing markets. This should give marketing finance a head start in such product-based strategies because most businesses have lots of product costing

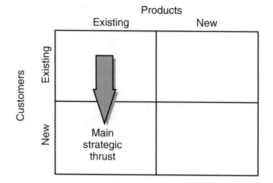

Figure 10.1   *Focus on existing products*

information; almost all costing systems are structured around allocating and apportioning costs to products. However what is needed is a soundly based, decision-focused, long-term DPP analysis and unfortunately many sophisticated costing systems do not meet any of these criteria. They are not soundly based, nor decision oriented, and focus on month to month comparisons.

As with the customer profitability analysis developed in Chapter 9, the objective of DPP is to indicate the relative profit contributions from the different product groups. Therefore, yet again, apportioning a lot of indirect costs in an attempt to arrive at a 'net profit' for each product can destroy the validity of the analysis and lead to disastrous decisions being taken. Many costing systems include incredibly complex methods of apportioning costs, often to other indirect areas of the business, so that part of these apportioned costs then has to be reapportioned before it finally ends up in a 'product cost'. Equally many costing systems try 'to recover' fixed costs by treating them as if they are variable, so that a recovery rate per unit of output (or some other variable recovery basis, such as per machine hour, etc.) is applied. This can result in the wonderful term 'over recovery' or 'under recovery' of the cost, depending on the actual level of output. My personal favourite, which I still see regularly in companies' management accounts, is 'an over recovery of the overhead costs', meaning presumably that more overheads have been charged to the product costings than were actually spent. Does this mean that overheads have become a source of profit? If so, perhaps we should spend more on them, so that we can increase the absolute amount of the over recovery! In most cases the company has actually spent at around the level of the fixed cost that it forecast; that is, after all, the nature of fixed costs.

Another potential problem with a traditional approach to product costing can be with the definition of what constitutes 'a product'. The objective of DPP in a product-based strategy is to highlight which 'products' should form the basis for the future; e.g. for international expansions, for line extensions, for repackaging for sale to different segments or through different channels, etc. In many companies, the same basic product may be packed in different sizes and sold under different brands, each of which offers a specific value proposition to its respective customers. A good DPP analysis should enable marketing finance managers to 'cut and slice' the financial information in the most appropriate and relevant way and at the right level for the particular strategic decision that is under consideration. This normally results in products being classified into a hierarchical structure, with differing degrees of financial information being required at each level, as is illustrated by Practical Insight 10.1.

Practical Insight 10.1

One product or many?

One of the main products sold by Knight Foods, the subject of the main case study in Chapter 6, was dehydrated instant mashed potato (IMP). The company had two main consumer brands, but manufactured retailer brands for a number of major supermarkets, and also sold the product into the catering and industrial sectors. Thus the finished product was packed into a wide range of pack sizes, different case configurations, etc.

However the initial part of the manufacturing process was common to all those products, i.e. raw potatoes were processed into a dehydrated powder that was then quality graded. The secondary process varied with different additives being mixed into some products, and the premium brand going through a re-agglomeration process, so as to form the powder into small pieces of potato. These different formulations then required separate bulk storage facilities, although common bulk storage by quality grade was used at the end of the primary process.

Packaging machines were dedicated to specific pack sizes, rather than formulations, and the distribution channel, again not the formulations, dictated the tertiary supply chain costs (i.e. distribution, key accounts and trade marketing) that were attributable to the product.

Clearly most of the marketing costs were directly attributable to the brand or the customer (for retailer brands) level in the product hierarchy.

Thus the product costings were a complex mixture of common and shared resources, with specifically direct costs by brand, pack size, distribution channel, manufacturing process and quality grade. Clearly some business decisions could have impacts at any or several of these levels, and it is therefore important that the DPP system provides accurate timely and relevant information to support decisions at all these possible levels.

Direct product profitability

As already stated, a product-led strategy should be based on the existing successful products that are already achieving, or are capable of achieving, sustainable super profits in their current markets or market segments. A growth strategy based on these products seeks to find new markets or segments in which the key differential attributes of these successful products should be similarly appropriate and relevant and, hence, financially successful.

Consequently an essential element in implementing a product-based strategy is a good DPP analysis, in order to indicate the relative profitability of the product portfolio. DPP analysis has been in use by leading companies for many years, having been developed originally by Procter & Gamble (P & G) as a means of defending the shelf space allocations given to some of their leading products. In the 1960s supermarkets were becoming more contribution-oriented and were looking at the rate of contribution generated from each square metre of shelf space (they now use cubic capacity, so as to take account of stacking height) in the store. At first sight this placed bulky, relatively low-priced items at a significant disadvantage; the classic contrasts were always between washing powders and razor blades. As P & G was (and still is) a leading player in washing powders it set out to demonstrate that, if the rate of sale was included in the financial analysis, the overall direct profit contribution from washing powder was at least as good as the smaller, more highly priced, but less frequently purchased alternative products.

Not surprisingly this DPP analysis has been developed since these early days but, perhaps more surprisingly, the most sophisticated versions of the analysis have been developed by retailers. Many retailers now allocate individual product facings, as well as the total space for a whole category of goods, based on a detailed DPP analysis; clearly it has become very important for manufacturers selling through these retail channels of distribution to carry out their own, equally rigorous, DPP analyses. This immediately highlights one of the issues discussed in Chapter 9 on relationship marketing and customer value; the manufacturer needs to do a DPP analysis to understand its own relative profitability, but it also needs to understand the profitability of its direct customers from the various components of its total product range. This issue, which may result in cross-subsidisation, is discussed later in the chapter.

An illustrative example of a DPP analysis for a manufacturing company is given in Figure 10.2 and immediately comparisons can be made with the customer account profitability (CAP) analysis shown in Chapter 9. In a CAP analysis, all the costs that are included are directly attributable to the customer whereas, in a DPP analysis they should be directly attributed to the product. Thus, all the headings in Figure 10.2 are 'product specific', 'direct product costs', 'product attributable overheads', with the result being to arrive at validly comparable 'direct product profitability' totals. (The actual heading should, of course, be direct product contribution but P & G originally christened the analysis DPP and the name has stuck!)

As before, the objective is not to apportion the total costs of the company in order to arrive at a completely meaningless net profit by product. Unfortunately I still come across companies doing this with sometimes quite disastrous

	£	
Gross sales by product		x
Less product-specific discounts & rebates		<u>x</u>
Net sales by product		x
Less direct costs of product		<u>x</u>
Gross product contribution		x
Less product-based marketing expenses	x	
Product-specific direct sales support costs	x	<u>x</u>
		x
Less product-specific direct transaction costs		
Sourcing costs	x	
Operations support	x	
Fixed assets financing	x	
Warehousing & distribution	x	
Inventory financing	x	
Order, invoice & collection processing	x	<u>x</u>
		x
Less product attributable overheads		<u>x</u>
Direct product profitability		x

Figure 10.2   *Direct product profitability analyses: illustrative example of a manufacturing company's DPP analyses*

results. It is quite common to find, after apportioning all costs including the CEO's salary, etc., that one or two products make 'a loss'. If this information is used as the basis for decision-making, the company may decide that it would be better off financially if it stopped selling these 'loss-making' products. Of course, once these products are de-listed it then has to reapportion these shared costs (unless the CEO is willing to take a proportionate cut in salary, etc.) to the remaining products. This can result in new products becoming 'loss making' and hence candidates for termination. Before long we could, using such 'financial analysis', have justified closing down what was previously a profitable business.

The DPP analysis should only include decision relevant costs, and these are the directly attributable costs at the level of the product segmentation that is being analysed. This is one of the key challenges of DPP analysis; if there are too many product classifications, there will be a very low level of directly attributable costs and the analysis will not be very helpful as a decision support tool. However, if there are too few product groupings, the analysis which will be much more comprehensive will be of even less use in decision-making. Clearly, as highlighted in Practical Insight 10.1, different types of strategic decision will require different levels of product grouping. As was true for CAP analysis, the challenge is to identify the true cost driver for each type of cost and to use this cost driver to *allocate* the cost to the appropriate product level in the DPP analysis; this cost driver should not then automatically be used to apportion the total cost down to lower levels in the analysis. Identifying the 'causes' of costs being incurred is therefore critical, as is illustrated by Practical Insight 10.2.

Practical Insight 10.2

Excess warehouse stock: who bears the cost?

Continuing to use Knight Foods as an example, it had very high finished goods stocks of one product group in its IMP range. The catering range of products was packed in 5-kg cans, which were sealed while being flushed with nitrogen, and these were packed in cases of six cans. These cases were stacked on pallets and the pallets could, quite safely, be stacked in the warehouse four high without damaging the product. Also because it was canned and nitrogen flushed, this product had by far the longest shelf life in the entire product range.

However most of the orders for catering products were large (full truck loads) and had significant delivery lead times. Thus these products could have been manufactured to order so that finished goods stocks of this range would have been minimal. Yet the warehouse was full of catering IMP.

The explanation was not too unexpected. Production used this product as a way of balancing their production efficiencies due to its long shelf life and ease of storage; in other words, it was the classic fall back product beloved of production schedulers everywhere.

Consequently the production department should be allocated the excess storage costs for this catering product, as they are getting the benefit in improved production utilisations and recoveries, etc. They are the real cost driver and not the catering sales and marketing team who didn't ask for the inventory, and would prefer not to have had it, as it continually generated questions from top management who assumed that they were not selling enough.

This issue makes the grouping of products very important. The grouping should produce a manageable number of product categories, at each horizontal division of the total, without destroying the decision relevance of the DPP analysis. A good DPP system should take account of all the significant differences in the ways products are developed, sourced, produced, marketed, sold and distributed. Thus the analysis should compare all the relevant areas of the business. As a result product groups will often emphasise shared technologies, raw material inputs, processes, fixed assets, brand names, packaging formats and delivery mechanisms.

Product attributes

In addition to designing the DPP system around the specific product groupings required by any business, the analysis needs to take account of the particular

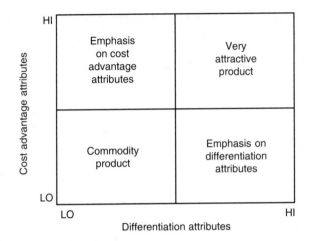

Figure 10.3   *Product attribute matrix*

product attributes present in the organisation. The simplest way of distinguishing product attributes is, as we have done before, to separate them between cost advantage attributes and differentiation attributes, as is done in Figure 10.3.

If a product has neither differentiation nor cost advantage attributes, it is really a commodity product. As has previously been discussed, commodity products sell exclusively on price, but no one creates any sustainable shareholder value from producing a pure commodity product. When a product possesses both cost advantage and differentiation attributes, the company has a very attractive product and should be able to generate substantial, sustainable super profits.

However, in most cases, products possess one or other set of attributes and the different types of product attributes require very different DPP systems. (This analysis is very similar to some of the issues considered in Chapter 5 when the details of competitor analysis were discussed.) If the product has a strong cost advantage but little differentiation capability, the strategic focus is on the relative product cost; hence, cost benchmarking against competitive products is essential.

A cost advantage means, by definition, being able to produce an equivalent product at a lower cost than competitors. This requires a precise definition of what *customers* perceive as an equivalent product; remember that your competitors are defined for you by your customers in terms of their 'alternative suppliers'. Once the equivalent product has been established, an appropriately detailed cost comparison against this competition needs to be undertaken. These competitive cost comparisons should indicate all the sources of existing and *predicted* cost advantages and disadvantages, and their likely sustainability. The analysis is meant to be decision-oriented and therefore it should be forward looking to suggest actions that are required to remove or reduce any existing cost disadvantages and to prevent potential cost disadvantages. More positively, the analysis may highlight potential actions that could build new sustainable cost advantages for the future.

A differentiation advantage indicates that customers perceive some value added in the product that makes it preferable to competitive offerings; as was discussed in the chapter on branding, this preference may be due to the functional characteristics of the product or to its more representational attributes. Any financial analysis of this differentiation attribute requires a clear understanding of the cause of these customer perceptions of value-added. In most cases, there will be cost implications of this value added and the DPP analysis must include any additional costs incurred in generating these value-added attributes, and a comparison must be made of these costs against the value perceived by the customers. When products have differentiation attributes therefore, the DPP system should focus on analysing value-added rather than carrying out excessively detailed relative cost comparisons. The objective is to value the specific differentiation attributes of the company's own products and competitive products from the customers' perspective; what is now normally known as 'value in use' pricing, so as to distinguish it from visual comparisons of selling prices. The DPP should try to identify the relative costs that either are actually incurred or would need to be incurred by the company and its competitors in delivering each such differentiation attribute.

Alternatively it may be possible to change customers' perceptions by creating a new differentiation attribute, or strengthening an existing attribute; in which case, the financial analysis should estimate the investment required to do this and highlight the risks involved in such an investment strategy.

Product life cycle profitability analysis

As stated earlier, DPP analyses are now quite common and, in some companies, are carried out with a high degree of both sophistication and decision relevance. Importantly this means that they do indicate the *relative* profit contributions of differing product categories.

However if the long-term strategy of the organisation is to be structured around the most attractive products, it is critical that the segment profitability analyses are done over the life cycle of the products. Otherwise a mature product may be directly compared with a newly launched product that has much better long-term potential but dramatically lower current profitability. Thus a product life cycle profitability analysis should assist in concentrating resources on those products from which the greatest long-term super profits can be generated.

This is particularly true for the wide range of products that are subject to the impact of the experience curve during their life cycles. The experience curve, which is illustrated in Figure 10.4, shows how the unit cost (expressed in real

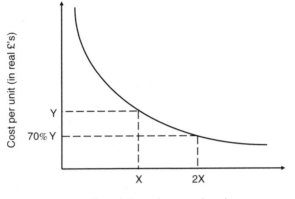

Figure 10.4 *Experience curve*

terms, thus excluding inflationary impacts) reduces as the cumulative volume produced increases. The normal convention is to describe these experience curves in terms of the percentage unit cost reduction generated by the doubling of cumulative output; thus the illustration in Figure 10.4 is a 70 per cent experience curve, which is more steeply downward sloping than a 80 per cent one but less so than a 60 per cent curve. The factors driving these unit cost reductions are primarily the learning curve element, whereby efficiencies improve as a workforce becomes more used to doing something, plus the economies of scale and technology benefits, through which as volumes increase, better and cheaper processes can be utilised.

An asymptotic exponential curve is somewhat difficult to use in practice but, by changing the dimensions of each axis to a logarithmic basis, this curve becomes a nice straight line, as is shown in Figure 10.5. This issue of cost levels changing with the volume produced raises an important strategic question because usually the volume demanded is determined by the selling price established, but the selling price is itself normally established by some reference to the expected cost level, as is diagrammatically shown in Figure 10.6.

Traditionally selling prices in these industries have tended to be reduced more slowly than costs are reducing during the rapid growth stages of the product's development; normally, at the time of launch, selling prices are set at or below the initially very high unit costs, as is shown in Figure 10.7. This means that profit margins per unit are increasing while sales volumes are also increasing rapidly; the industry should therefore be highly profitable during this period. Unfortunately this has frequently ended in tears because the combination of high profits and rapidly growing demand has either attracted in a large number of new entrants or has resulted in dramatic capacity expansion

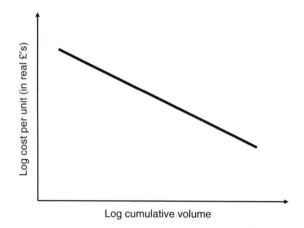

Figure 10.5 *Experience curve (using log: log axes)*

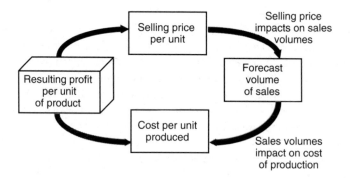

Figure 10.6 *Life cycle costing techniques – pricing strategy in an experience curve environment*

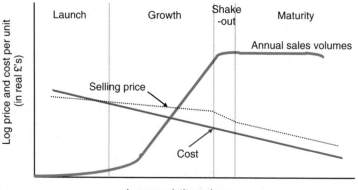

Figure 10.7 *Life cycle costing technique: experience cost curves and selling prices*

by the existing businesses within the industry. This surge in productive capacity has often resulted in the short, sharp shake-out phase in the industry that is shown in Figure 10.7 as the dip in the selling price line; i.e. fierce price competition takes place until the industry moves back towards a more balanced position between supply and demand. Quite frequently, of course, the selling price has to fall well below the unit costs during the intense price war that may be needed to resolve the excess capacity problem. Once stability is restored, the selling price and cost per unit should move in parallel as is shown in Figure 10.7, and illustrated in Practical Insight 10.3.

Practical Insight 10.3

Technology products and experience curves

Many consumer technology products have exhibited exactly the pricing and cost characteristics discussed above. The high initial selling prices established at their launch for most of these products (video recorders, dvd players, wide screen and plasma TVs, third generation mobile phones, etc.) severely limit demand to the very wealthy plus those individuals that must have the latest innovation. As selling prices are reduced, the products become more mainstream and the demand increases dramatically, thus fuelling the reduction in unit costs that comes with increased cumulative volumes. Indeed the companies themselves often manage this process as is currently the case with the latest video mobile phones, where companies are already actively forecasting dramatically reducing prices over the next 12–18 months.

Setting a high initial price can be part of a skimming pricing policy, as is discussed later, but it can also be part of developing the aura around the product. 'Last year it sold for £1000 but today you can buy it for £250'; as long as you do not seriously annoy all the people who paid £1000, this may work well.

However there is, not surprisingly, an alternative way of using such a predictable cost reduction linkage with volume. Instead of setting today's selling price by reference to today's costs, the price today is established by reference to the long-term cost level that will be achieved once the product achieves its full potential. This clearly will give a much lower initial selling price and should stimulate demand much more quickly than if the selling price starts high and is reduced progressively. Diagrammatically this is shown in Figure 10.8, where it is clear that the selling price is based on the expected long-term cost per unit, *plus* a required rate of return per unit *plus*, hopefully, a super profit level.

The strategy behind such a pricing move is to try to develop a long-term sustainable competitive cost advantage by moving much faster down the experience curve than competitors. Thus, if successful, the short-term 'loss' per unit can be regarded as an investment in developing this sustainable cost advantage; hence, producing the hoped for super profit level of return once costs do come down to their long-term expected level. Clearly there are a number of

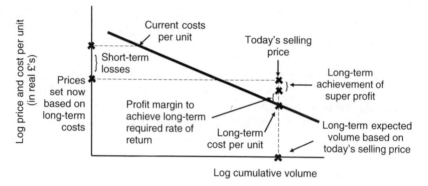

The 'short-term loss per unit', if successful, is really an investment
in developing a long-term sustainable cost advantage

Figure 10.8   *Life cycle costing techniques: strategic use of experience curves in setting prices*

risks associated with such a strategy, one of which is that it depends critically on the slope of the experience curve for this product (if it is actually an 80 per cent curve, but the strategy assumed a 60 per cent curve, it will be a financial disaster as costs will never reach the anticipated level).

Also it assumes that reducing the selling price immediately will stimulate demand dramatically; for some products, it may be necessary for consumers to see their key influencers (i.e. role models) buying the early expensive models before the product becomes accepted. However the greatest risk is probably the assumption that this will build a *sustainable* cost advantage. It may be that competitors find a completely new way of producing the product once demand has become so large; the cost advantage assumes that competitors will follow the leader down the normal industry experience curve. Another possible risk is that the total demand is simply not large enough to generate the cost savings needed to make the initial selling price profitable; a variant on this is illustrated in Practical Insight 10.4.

Practical Insight 10.4

Aeroplane demand – experience curve driven

One industry that has, for many years, applied the experience curve logic is aerospace. The whole philosophy of developing new aircraft is the linkage between the potential demand and the cost per unit. This explains why the major aerospace companies are so keen to sell options, long-term fleet orders, etc. to their major potential customers as early in the development cycle as possible; anything that helps to define the long-term potential demand for the new aeroplane reduces the risk significantly.

An extreme and slightly silly example of this is that the only thing wrong with the financial evaluation of Concorde was that they didn't sell the 000's of them that were needed to make it financially viable. A much higher volume would have reduced the direct manufacturing cost per unit dramatically, plus enabling the very sizeable development costs to have been recovered over such increased volumes.

Unfortunately the world demand was never going to be that big and the dramatic increases in fuel prices not too long after Concorde's launch further curtailed any sizeable potential demand. It is still slightly sad to learn, while finishing the book, that Concorde is to be pensioned off at the end of the year.

Penetration versus skimming pricing strategies

This use of long-term cost projections as the basis of current pricing decisions is a good example of a 'penetration pricing' strategy. Prices are initially set at low levels (e.g. below current costs) in an attempt to stimulate growth in demand and to gain substantial early market share. Thus early losses are expected but the strong market share, if it can be retained, and the rapidly growing total market *should* enhance the long-term profitability of the business. Indeed a penetration pricing strategy can be used as an entry barrier to keep potential competitors from entering a rapidly growing industry. If selling prices are set below current costs, any new entrant faces the prospect of making losses on their early sales in addition to all the normal investment costs associated with entering a new industry or market. This potential for loss making may at least lead to a deferral of any competitive entry, until more knowledge regarding the rate of growth and full potential of the market has been gained. Unfortunately for this potential competitor, such a delay will normally result in more sustained losses when they do enter, as the original company will already be progressing down its experience curve, and approaching the long-run cost position at which it will start to make good profits.

However, in many cases, the first company in the market looks at the short-term opportunity and so takes advantage of its early dominant position and the low initial demand to set selling prices at a level that enables it to show good profits initially. This 'skimming' type of pricing strategy may seem attractive in the short term but the high selling prices will delay the rate of growth in sales volumes. The lower sales volumes reduce the cost advantage that the business can build up over prospective competitors, because its cumulative volume will be less and it is the cumulative total volume that gives rise to the major benefits of the experience curve. Also the early high profit margins may attract new competitors. If the cost structure of the industry is one of high fixed costs and low variable costs, a subsequent change to much lower selling prices once the competitive capacity has been installed will not prove successful; such potential competitors must be kept out if at all possible.

Cross subsidisation

Many companies now use DPP analysis in conjunction with their CAP analysis in an attempt to show how advantageous it is for a customer to buy their whole range of products, rather than selecting only the top few brand leaders. This strategy can be enhanced, where financially justifiable, by giving the customer an additional discount if the whole range of products, including any new product launches, is stocked. This is a variation on the logic of giving discounts based on the total sales revenue generated from a customer over a specified period (normally the financial year of the supplier, when it is referred to as an overriding discount), and should also be rigorously evaluated by marketing finance. The problem is that the discount is usually given on all the business done with this customer, rather than only on the incremental business. Consequently the product mix bought by the customer may be significant if the net contributions vary considerably across the range.

The extra discount for full stocking is normally beneficial to innovative companies, that are regularly launching completely new products, additions to existing products, range extensions, etc. Such a discount can be used to guarantee a critical mass of distribution immediately upon launch, so that the launch advertising is not wasted due to an absence of effective distribution. This can be particularly cost effective if the discounts are only given to leading customers that are likely to influence the buying decisions of the majority of remaining potential customers. Gaining immediate distribution for new products in these leading customers may almost guarantee initial orders from the rest. However it is critically important that marketing finance understands the true cause of such discounts being given so that the cost can be properly attributed, rather than being spread across all products, or charged directly to the leading customers with a consequent reduction in their relative profitability.

Another quite common marketing strategy that creates complications for any product profitability analysis is to use one product as a 'loss leader' in order to sell other more profitable products to the same or related customers. Obviously if the majority of customers only purchased the subsidised loss leader product, the overall profitability of the business would disappear although growth in sales revenues might be substantial. It is also quite possible that a change in the external competitive environment (such as the development of more focused competitors) could make the existing cross subsidisation strategy unsustainable in the future; the computer industry illustrates this point.

Initially most computer manufacturers regarded themselves as producing and selling hardware boxes, and the size of the box was determined by the data processing requirements of the customer. Almost coincidentally the customer needed software to operate the hardware and technical support to maintain the complex kit. As processing volumes increased, the customer needed more and more hardware, and add-on memory and extra central processing units were bought to plug into the existing hardware. If one company supplies all of a customer's computer needs (hardware, software, maintenance), the customer is only really interested in the total price charged, and the relative pricing of individual elements within the package does not really matter.

However, as soon as new competitors enter the industry with different, more focused strategies, this relative pricing becomes critical. If the prices of hardware are set relatively high, with software and maintenance being provided almost at cost, the potential for new hardware suppliers to enter the industry is clear. This is particularly true if they specialise in one particular peripheral device (such as printers, disk drives, etc.) so that they can quickly gain the maximum economies of scale and produce very good quality products. These new competitors can severely affect the overall profitability of the main computer companies if they reduce these original companies' share of the previously highly profitable add-on markets. One potential strategic response by the original computer companies could be to alter the relative pricing strategy of the component elements; reducing the selling prices of hardware peripherals, but increasing software and maintenance. This clearly reduces the attractiveness of the industry to focused hardware manufacturers, but increases it to independent software houses and third party maintenance companies. The cross subsidisation almost inevitably makes it attractive for a more focused competitor to concentrate on the product that is showing the excessively high profit margin and to ignore the product that is being heavily subsidised. It is therefore vitally important that the relative pricing strategies for related products are only established after careful examination of the potential competitive responses.

Reinvesting to replace an existing competitive advantage

Clearly it is possible for one company to maintain its own relative pricing strategy when it is a monopoly supplier but, as has been argued throughout the book, monopoly positions are unlikely to be sustainable in the long term, particularly if super profit rates of return are achieved by the monopolist. Therefore a company with any existing strong competitive advantage must analyse both the remaining economic life of the existing competitive advantage and what it can eventually be replaced by. As has already been made clear, most protectable competitive advantages are the result of significant high-risk investments, and these investments need to be rigorously financially evaluated; this is just as true when the required expenditure is a reinvestment of part of the super profits being generated by a current advantage.

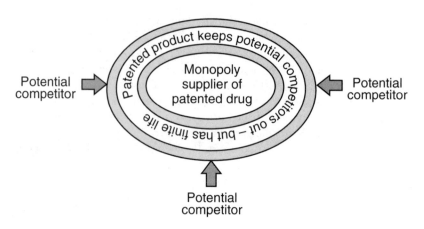

Figure 10.9   *Reinvesting to replace an existing competitive advantage: competitive position during the life of the original SCA – e.g. a patented drug*

This can be illustrated by an example from the pharmaceutical industry of a patented drug. Pharmaceutical companies spend vast amounts on R&D in an attempt to develop new molecular entities from which new drugs can be developed. The return from such successful new drugs can be protected by the granting of a patent, which normally has a finite life of 20 years; part of this economic life is used up during the development and testing period of the drug, before the company is licensed to sell it. This is shown diagrammatically as Figure 10.9.

During this monopoly supplier period, the patent owner can generate a high return in order to justify its earlier high-risk research investment. However part of this super profit can be reinvested in an attempt to create a new replacement competitive advantage for the period following the expiry of the patent. Although its competitors are not allowed to produce and sell the patented drug, they will all be able to reverse engineer its clinical properties and thus will be ready to launch their own much cheaper versions at the known end of the patent period. They can be quite willing to sell at a cheaper price because *they* did not spend the money on high risk R&D and the risk associated with the drug is significantly lower as the total market potential has by now been precisely defined. It is by no means unusual, in this industry, to find selling prices falling by 80–90 per cent in the year following a patent expiry.

However the patent owner can seek to pre-empt this position by a variety of new marketing strategies, as are shown in Figure 10.10; the decision will be significantly influenced by the core competences of the particular drug company. One possibility is to use a version of the penetration pricing strategy discussed earlier, so that selling prices are reduced towards the end of the patent life.

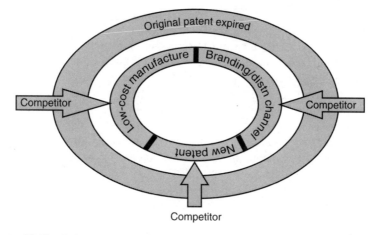

Figure 10.10 *Reinvesting to replace an existing competitive advantage: competitive position after the expiry of the original SCA – competitors are now able to launch their version of the previously patented product*

This increases total demand and could enable the company to retain the position of the lowest cost manufacturer of the drug even after its patent has expired. Unfortunately there is an almost inevitable conflict between a very 'lean and mean' low-cost culture and the high R&D expenditures with equally high profit margins of a patent-focused pharmaceutical company.

An alternative strategy therefore is to try to develop a new patent related to the same product, so that the entry barrier is preserved for several more years. Classic examples from the industry include new delivery formulations, slow release versions of the drug and stronger, or weaker, versions of the original; each of these needs careful evaluation of the probability of success prior to any significant expenditure being incurred. Another increasingly common strategy is to develop the product into a brand during its patented period; this does not increase the financial return during this period as it is, by definition, the only product available. However the branding, particularly when combined with access to a new distribution channel (such as the 'over-the-counter' drug market) before competitors are able to respond, can generate a high level of consumer loyalty. This can mean that the originator does not have to drop its selling price even though much cheaper generic versions eventually become available.

Strategic use of standard costing

There are already many product costing techniques that have been developed. Therefore a marketing finance approach does not need to develop lots of new techniques, it simply needs to use the existing ones more strategically. An excellent example of this is standard costing which has been very widely used for over 50 years but, in many companies, causes more problems than it solves.

In many companies, there are a wide range of 'engineering' type relationships where, for any given level of input, the amount that will be produced can be predicted with relative confidence; indeed, the amount that *should* be produced can often be predicted with absolute certainty. Any difference from this expected level can be attributed to the efficiency of the production process, rather than the accuracy of the predictive relationship. Conversely for any required level of output, the inputs needed can also be calculated. These relationships are by no means restricted to the production or engineering environment; examples are common in sales force planning, distribution and logistics, and advertising awareness creation and maintenance.

However the 'true' engineering relationships, apply to physical quantities (e.g. tonnes of steel, hours worked, calls made, deliveries made, 'opportunities to see' advertisements) but for financial decision-making these physical items have to be turned into monetary values. Standard costing does this by calculating a 'standard' rate per unit (e.g. per tonne, per hour, etc.), and this is where the problems start. Clearly any business wants its managers to be motivated to make the best economic decision for the company, and all decisions should be based on up-to-date, forward-looking information; yet 'standard costs' are normally calculated for the whole of next year, before the year has even started and are often based on the current year's actual costs. Also if costs fluctuate significantly away from the standard cost, our perception of managers' actual performance may be distorted and they may be motivated to act against the economic interests of the business. A numerical example may make this clearer, once the fundamental logic underpinning standard costing has been summarised.

A standard cost consists of two basic elements: a standard usage per unit and a standard price per unit, together they produce the standard cost. Thus, as shown in Figure 10.11, for labour, a standard cost is calculated by multiplying the standard time allowance for some specified process or output by the standard rate for that grade of labour. Therefore a standard cost is the level of cost that *should* be incurred for a given level of activity and is normally governed by some measurable input–output relationship. Of course, it is most unlikely that, in reality, the standard cost will be achieved and one of the great strengths of standard costing is that it enables a detailed analysis of the causes of the differences between (i.e. variances from) actual and standard costs. The traditional approach to variance analysis, which is set out in Figure 10.12, splits these differences into a usage or efficiency variance (the normal nomenclature is usage for materials, etc. and efficiency for labour) and a price or rate variance (with rate being used for labour). The objective is quite logically to allocate accountability with controllability and any price or rate variance is often

$$\begin{array}{ccc}
\text{Standard} & & \text{Standard} & & \text{Standard} \\
\text{cost} & = & \text{usage per} & \times & \text{price per} \\
& & \text{unit} & & \text{unit}
\end{array}$$

e.g. for labour processes

$$\begin{array}{ccc}
\text{Standard} & & \text{Standard} & & \text{Standard} \\
\text{labour} & = & \text{time} & \times & \text{rate per} \\
\text{cost} & & \text{allowance} & & \text{hour}
\end{array}$$

$$\begin{array}{c}
\text{(for this} \\
\text{grade of labour)}
\end{array}$$

Figure 10.11 *Strategic use of standard costing techniques: components of a standard cost*

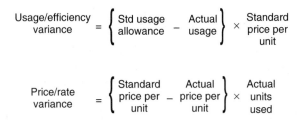

$$\begin{array}{ccc}
\text{Usage/efficiency} & & \left\{ \begin{array}{ccc} \text{Std usage} & & \text{Actual} \\ \text{allowance} & - & \text{usage} \end{array} \right\} & \times & \begin{array}{c}\text{Standard}\\\text{price per}\\\text{unit}\end{array} \\
\text{variance} & = &
\end{array}$$

$$\begin{array}{ccc}
\text{Price/rate} & & \left\{ \begin{array}{ccc} \text{Standard} & & \text{Actual} \\ \text{price per} & - & \text{price per} \\ \text{unit} & & \text{unit} \end{array} \right\} & \times & \begin{array}{c}\text{Actual}\\\text{units}\\\text{used}\end{array} \\
\text{variance} & = &
\end{array}$$

Figure 10.12 *Strategic use of standard costing techniques: standard costing – the traditional approach to variance analysis*

outside the direct control of operational (e.g. production) managers. My silly example in this area is from the car industry; if the price of steel suddenly increases by 25 per cent, the manager responsible for body assembly cannot really offset this increase by sending out four-door cars with only three doors fitted! Thus the usage/efficiency variance is traditionally calculated using the standard price per unit with all the price/rate variance being separately identified.

This appears fine until the full ramifications are evaluated in a period of volatile prices, particularly where there are alternative ways of working. Most business outputs can be achieved in a variety of ways ranging from 'fast and furious' to 'slow and steady'; i.e. a rapid rate of output giving good labour efficiency but higher raw material usage or a slower speed with less wastage. If line managers are to make the best possible economic decisions, they must be based on the latest possible costs and not on standards that may now be wildly out-of-date. This can actually be achieved by a very minor, but significant, change in the way variances are computed, as is shown in Figure 10.13. The usage/efficiency variance is still based on the difference in physical usage between the actual and the standard allowances but this difference is now turned

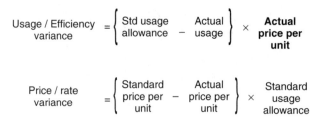

$$\text{Usage / Efficiency variance} = \left\{ \text{Std usage allowance} \ - \ \text{Actual usage} \right\} \times \textbf{Actual price per unit}$$

$$\text{Price / rate variance} = \left\{ \text{Standard price per unit} \ - \ \text{Actual price per unit} \right\} \times \text{Standard usage allowance}$$

Figure 10.13   *Strategic use of standard costing techniques: standard costing – the strategic approach to variance analysis*

into a financial value by multiplying by the actual (i.e. latest) price per unit. In fact, if it is available it is better still to use the replacement price (i.e. the forecast, or any outstanding order value, price per unit), as this is the best estimate of future costs.

Case study – Sub-assemblers Inc.

Sub-assemblers Inc. had built up a good reputation for the efficient contract production and assembly of a broad range of relatively labour intensive products. It did not develop any new products itself and focused on being a low-cost contractor for other companies. As the company was normally producing a constantly changing range of products, production managers needed quite wide discretion in the way they ran the operations area. This required up-to-date, relevant financial information from the standard costing system.

However, although weekly detailed variances were produced, the company was losing out on the renewal of some contracts; customers had indicated that competitors were quoting lower prices on established product lines. A common factor in these lost orders was a high degree of volatility in raw material prices and consequently large price variances. Sub-assemblers had increased the proportion of self-employed workers used on these contracts with a resulting change in the labour rate away from the standard established before the beginning of the year.

One particular contract illustrated the problem; the standard cost per unit was based on 4 hours of labour with an allowance of ten units of raw material, as shown in Figure 10.14. However if more care was taken, the raw material usage could be reduced to eight units but this way of working would require 6 hours of labour. The standard costing system showed, as in Figure 10.15, that this alternative would be more expensive.

The weekly variance analysis also seemed to indicate that operations were being run effectively as there were net favourable efficiency variances; the favourable labour efficiency variances of £12 500 more than compensating for the adverse raw material usage variance of £10 000. Unfortunately this £2500

Required weekly output = 1000 units
Standard costs per unit:

Labour cost	=	Standard time of 4 hours	×	Standard rate per hour of £12.50	=	£50
Standard raw material cost (material Y)	=	Standard units allowed of 10	×	Standard price per unit of £10	=	£100
				Total standard cost		£150

Actual costs for week were:

Labour rate per hour	£10
Material Y price per unit	£15
Actual labour used	3000 hours
Actual units of material Y used	11 000
Actual units of X produced	1000

Total costs for week:

Labour 3000 hours @ £10	= £30 000
Material Y 11 000 units @ £15	= £1 65 000
	£1 95 000
but standard cost for 1000 units	£1 50 000
i.e. total adverse variance of	£45 000

Figure 10.14   *Base data for product X*

per '000 units of X

	Existing method	Slower more careful method
Labour costs	4 × £12.50 × 1000 = £50 000	6 × £12.50 × 1000 = £75 000
Material costs	10 × £10.00 × 1000 = £1 00 000	8 × £10.00 × 1000 = £80 000
Total costs	£1 50 000	£1 55 000

i.e. The alternative method of production would increase costs per 1000 units of X by £5000.

Figure 10.15   *Production trade-offs at standard prices*

positive variance was far outweighed by the adverse raw material price variance of £55 000; even after allowing for a favourable labour rate variance of £7500, there was still a net £45 000 adverse variance on the week's activities. These calculations are set out in Figure 10.16.

However Figure 10.14 showed that the actual costs per unit were a long way from those predicted in the standards; the labour rate per hour was only £10 compared to £12.50, while the raw material price per unit was a massive £15 compared to only £10 in the standard. This meant in reality savings in labour times were worth less, while using excess raw material was much more expensive. Re-computing the efficiency variances using actual prices, as is done in Figure 10.17, shows that the real efficiency impact is an adverse £5000 rather than the previously calculated favourable £2500.

Furthermore these changes in relative input prices mean that the alternative way of working should also be reassessed, as is done in Figure 10.18. This

Labour variances:
Labour rate variance

(Standard rate – Actual rate)	× Actual hours		
i.e. (£12.50 – £10.00)	× 3000 Hours	= Favourable	£7500

Labour efficiency variance

(Standard usage – Actual usage)	× Standard rate		
i.e. (4 × 1000 – 3000)	× £12.50	= Favourable	£12 500
	Total favourable labour variance		£20 000

Raw material variances
Price variance

(Standard price – Actual price)	× Actual units		
i.e. (£10.00 – £15.00)	× 11 000	= Adverse	£55 000

Usage variance

(Standard usage – Actual usage)	× Standard price		
i.e. (10 × 1000 – 11 000)	× £10	= Adverse	£10 000
	Total adverse labour variance		£65 000

Figure 10.16   *Company's variance analysis*

Favourable labour efficiency
$(4 \times 1000 - 3000) \times £10.00$ per hour $= £10 000$

Adverse material usage
$(10 \times 1000 - 11 000) \times £15.00$ per unit $= £(15 000)$
Net adverse variance $£(5000)$

Figure 10.17   *Real efficiency variances using actual prices*

per '000 units of X

	Existing method	Slower more careful method
Labour costs	$4 \times £10.00 \times 1000 =$ £40 000	$6 \times £10.00 \times 1000 =$ £60 000
Material costs	$10 \times £15.00 \times 1000 = £1 50 000$	$8 \times £15.00 \times 1000 = £1 20 000$
Total costs	£1 90 000	£1 80 000

Figure 10.18   *A strategically oriented variance analysis: re-computing the tradeoff at actual prices but standard usages*

shows that the increased actual raw material costs mean that it would be beneficial to use less raw material even though this requires more of the now cheaper labour input. Clearly it makes sense that such decisions should use the most up-to-date cost inputs rather than the now irrelevant and out-of-date standard prices. The strength of standard costing rests on the engineered input–output relationships, but these do not extend to the input price relationships; hence actual costs make for a more decision-based form of analysis, yet disappointingly few companies have made this small alteration to their standard costing systems.

Clearly if a competitor has a more rationally based management accounting process (or no standard costing system at all!), its managers may be motivated to adjust their relative usage levels to take account of the actual costs being incurred. This revised method of analysis is not trying to hold operating managers responsible for price changes that they do not control, but it is trying to make them take into account the economic realities that the company is facing.

Transfer pricing

Another area of product costing that can create great problems in many companies is transfer pricing. Transfer prices should be primarily used to enable economic decisions to be taken regarding the allocation of resources within a vertically integrated group, including whether a particular process should be carried out internally or outsourced. Thus these internal *prices* must use the appropriate level of relevant costs, whether incremental or avoidable, rather than reflecting an apportionment of the total costs incurred by the business. This is particularly important where a major use of transfer prices is likely to be in selecting which of a range of products is the most financially attractive. In overall terms, any business should want to concentrate its resources on those opportunities with the greatest potential for generating super profits; the question is how to identify those opportunities.

However all businesses suffer from some constraints that restrict their ability to expand infinitely. The key to the financial analysis of resource allocation decisions is to identify the critical limiting factor that is currently constraining the future growth of the business, such as the cubic capacity of shelf space in its stores for the retailers mentioned earlier in the chapter. If the company then focuses on those products with the greatest contribution achieved per unit of this limiting factor it will, in the short term, also maximise its overall profitability; in the long term, the company can invest to remove the current constraints on its growth! A case study should make this much clearer.

Case study – Tissues Unlimited

It is very common for companies in the pulp and paper industry to be vertically integrated; indeed, several Scandinavian forestry products companies have moved downstream by acquiring paper, packaging and nappy producing companies because of their high usage of wood pulp. Tissues Unlimited has a large tissue mill producing bulk tissue from wood pulp and recycled waste paper. It also has converting plants to which much of the bulk tissue is transferred, where it is transformed into toilet rolls, facial tissues and kitchen towels, which are then sold to retailers. Both the tissues mill and the converting plants are run as separate investment centres, so that a system of transfer

```
Fixed costs of tissue mill        =    £12m
Budgeted division profit for year  =   £  4m
                                       £16m

Budgeted output in tonnes         =  80 000
∴ Required contribution per tonne =   £200
```

Thus transfer prices were

Type of tissue	Variable cost/tonne	Required contn/tonne	Transfer price per tonne
White facial	250	200	450
Coloured facial	230	200	430
White toilet	225	200	425
Coloured toilet	205	200	405
White kitchen towel	210	200	410
Coloured kitchen towel	195	200	395

Figure 10.19   *Existing tissue transfer pricing system*

pricing is required. This system is complicated because there is an internationally traded market place for bulk tissue; thus the tissue mill can sell in bulk and the converting plants could buy in from outside suppliers. In order to avoid unnecessary buying and selling, these transactions are handled at the centre of the group, by using the internal transfer price as a benchmark.

This internal transfer price starts with the variable cost per tonne of each particular product to which is added a contribution per tonne to recover the fixed costs of the tissue mill and its required rate of return on its investment base; this is shown in Figure 10.19 for a small but representative sample of products.

However, with this transfer pricing system the tissue mill managers currently find themselves being asked for an increasing proportion of facial tissue production, with the consequent shortage of kitchen towel and toilet tissue being made up by purchases on the bulk tissue market. This is illustrated by Figures 10.20 and 10.21.

	Budgeted output tonnes	% age	Actual proportion
Facial	25 000	31.25	50%
Toilet	35 000	43.75	37.5%
Kitchen towel	20 000	25.00	12.5%
	80 000	100.00%	100%

Figure 10.20   *Tissue mill production tonnages*

	Buy-in opportunities		Sell-out opportunities		
	Tonnage	Price/tonne	Tonnage	Price/tonne	Decision
White facial	100	£500	750	£460	Sell out
Coloured facial	300	£480	–	–	No deal
White toilet	–	–	200	£400	No deal
Coloured toilet	330	£400	–	–	Buy in
White kitchen towel	–	–	275	£375	No deal
Coloured kitchen towel	550	£380	–	–	Buy in

Figure 10.21   *Latest market price*

Comparing these available market prices against the internal transfer prices highlights the trend towards the production of facial tissues. The group has an opportunity to buy in white facial at £500 per tonne and coloured facial at £480 per tonne; but its own transfer prices are £450 and £430 respectively, thus these deals are unattractive. However there is the chance to sell out 750 tonnes of white facial at £460 per tonne, which is attractive as it is £10 higher than the required transfer price. The tissue mill can free up capacity to produce this by buying in the coloured toilet tissue (at £400 compared to a transfer price of £405) and the coloured kitchen towel (at £380 compared to a transfer price of £395). At first glance this strategy should be increasing the tissue mill's divisional profits.

However, the tissue mill is well below budget even though the mill is operating 24 hours per day, 7 days a week. Preventive maintenance is carried out during the two factory shutdowns during the year, with the result that the maximum available hours per machine are 8000 per year ($24 \times 7 \times 47.62$ weeks). Since the mill has five similar machines the total production time is 40 000 hours. Unfortunately for the current transfer pricing system, the outputs per machine hour are not the same for the range of products due to their significantly different basis weights in grammes per square metre, as is shown by Figure 10.22. Also with the heavier products, such as kitchen towel, the machines can be run faster without holes appearing in the tissue.

As the proportion of facial tissue being produced increases, the total potential tonnage output of the mill decreases; indeed it is physically impossible for the mill to produce 80 000 tonnes given the projected actual mix in Figure 10.20. The tonnage outputs of producing exclusively each specific type of tissue are shown in Figure 10.23; these illustrate that the mill is not actually constrained by tonnage, as this changes with the product mix.

	Basis weight (gms per sq. metre)	Output in tonnes per machine hour *
White facial	16	1.5
Coloured facial	16	1.5
White toilet	19	2.2
Coloured toilet	19	2.2
White kitchen towel	24	2.75
Coloured kitchen towel	24	2.75

*Assumes economic runs for each product

Figure 10.22 *Product weights*

	Tonnes per hour	Total hours	Maximum output (tonnes)
100% Facial tissue	1.5	40 000	60 000
100% Toilet tissue	2.2	40 000	88 000
100% Kitchen towel	2.75	40 000	110 000

Figure 10.23 *Tissue mill potential tonnage outputs*

Product	Output per hour in tonnes	Contn per hour*	Contn per tonne	Variable cost/tonne	Transfer price/tonne
White facial	1.5	£400	266.67	250	516.67
Coloured facial	1.5	£400	266.67	230	496.67
White toilet	2.2	£400	181.82	225	406.82
Coloured toilet	2.2	£400	181.82	205	386.82
White kitchen	2.75	£400	145.45	210	355.45
Coloured kitchen	2.75	£400	145.45	195	340.45

*Contribution per hour is given by:–

Fixed costs   = £12 m

Budgeted profit = £4 m

£16 m

Maximum available hours 40 000

$$\therefore \text{ Required Contn per hour } = \frac{£16\,m}{40\,000} = £400$$

Figure 10.24   *Transfer prices using contribution per hour*

Product	New transfer price	Buy-in price	Sell-out price	Decision
White facial	516.67	500	460	Buy in
Coloured facial	496.67	480	–	Buy in
White toilet	406.82	–	400	No deal
Coloured toilet	386.82	400	–	No deal
White kitchen	355.45	–	375	Sell out
Coloured kitchen	340.45	380	–	No deal

Figure 10.25   *Impact of new transfer prices*

The real current limiting factor for the tissue mill is the available machine production hours, as these cannot be increased from the current 40 000 hours without acquiring another machine. Thus the transfer pricing system should be based around the contribution per machine hour that is required to achieve the returns required for the tissue mill; this new calculation is shown as Figure 10.24.

The impact of this change in transfer pricing is quite significant as can be seen by reviewing the latest market prices against these new transfer prices as is done in Figure 10.25. The increased required transfer prices of facial tissues reverse the trend towards manufacturing this product for external sale in bulk. Given the longer time needed to produce a tonne of facial tissue, it is important that facial tissue is 'charged' for its relatively high usage of this critical limiting factor. Conversely the higher tonnage outputs per hour of kitchen towel and, to a lesser extent, toilet tissue mean that the required contributions per tonne are reduced, so that opportunities to sell out in bulk become more attractive. The capacity required can be 'freed up' by buying in facial tissue, a reversal of the previous trend.

This case study illustrates the key issue in designing a transfer pricing system; use the limiting factor of the business as the driving force of the transfer prices. If this is done, any decisions involving allocating this critical limiting resource will be soundly based. Managers will logically concentrate their resources on those products that generate the maximum contribution per unit of the limiting factor. In practice, an optimum solution can only be achieved when the product contributions per unit of limiting factor are equalised; otherwise profits can be improved by reallocating resources from a lower contributing product to a higher one.

This logic for establishing transfer prices can be applied just as effectively to the provision of internal services within a business; the critical factors from the customer's perspective must be set out in the service level agreement between the customer and the internal supplier.

Part Four

Control

11 Exercising Control over the Future

Overview

No one can control the past, it can only be explained. The main value from explaining the past is if any 'learning' from the past can be applied to make the future better; thus historical analysis should be used as a learning process to indicate how things should be done differently in the future. The performance measures used by a business must therefore be tailored to the key strategic thrust of that business and should highlight the potential future impact on the key assets of the business of any new strategic move.

The control process must be completely integrated in the planning process (I try to avoid using the term 'planning' without attaching the words 'and control' to it). Therefore businesses should not regard 'planning marketing' and then 'controlling their marketing plans' as distinct roles or sequential processes. Marketing finance must be totally involved in both planning and controlling marketing activities.

Analysis of the past can be very useful if it is applied to improve decision-making in the future; all feedback loops should be treated as a learning process. Unfortunately many management accounting processes overemphasise the purely historical reconciliation aspect of reporting.

Where internal business units are created and transfer pricing systems are implemented, there needs to be a service level agreement (SLA) between the supplier and the internal customers. SLAs facilitate the allocation of responsibility within the business and thus make good control much easier.

There are a number of critical success factors that can be identified for sound control to be achieved by a marketing finance system. The marketing finance system must focus on strategic decisions that should have been predicted in advance by the linkages between the system and the objectives and strategy of the business. The relevant decision support information should be communicated to the strategic decision-makers in a user friendly (i.e. immediately usable) format. Marketing finance must measure the intangible assets of the business, and this is facilitated by splitting marketing expenditure into development and maintenance categories. As control can only be exercised over the future, marketing finance should control the commitment process rather than focusing on the actual physical payment for, or expensing of, the marketing activity. Control requires a degree of choice to be possible and thus 'engineered' cost relationships should be identified; particular emphasis should be placed on the truly discretionary activities that marketing managers can undertake prior to any commitment being made.

Introduction

It should by now be clear that 'controlling' marketing involves far more than recording and analysing the accounting transactions that result from marketing activities. In other words marketing finance is not simply 'accounting for marketing'. It should be regarded as a two-stage process involving the pre-commitment financial evaluation of proposed marketing expenditure, as well as the ongoing control over these expenditures as they take place.

The objectives of these varied marketing activities are very diverse, but marketing has itself developed a range of tailored evaluation processes and non-financial effectiveness measures. The challenge for finance is to find equally tailored and value-adding ways of controlling marketing expenditures, which link these activities to the overall objectives of the organisation.

As already discussed, this requires a high degree of integration between marketing and finance, and a substantial level of tailoring in the marketing finance system and the resulting performance measures used by the business. Ideally, if the marketing strategy changes significantly, this should lead to a corresponding change in the tailored marketing finance system. If such a change is not made, it is quite likely that the business will be using inappropriate performance measures, that may motivate marketing managers to act against the long-term interests of the overall business. Another potential risk is that the marketing finance system does not provide adequate timely decision support information for the new, key strategic decisions that the business faces as a result of the change in marketing strategy. Many organisations are taking critical marketing decisions with very little strategic financial evaluation, because they do not have suitably tailored marketing finance systems. In such businesses there is no real 'strategic control over marketing'.

This part of the book tries to indicate how such strategic control over marketing can be achieved. This chapter focuses on how control can only be exercised over the future and how feedback loops should be used as a learning process, rather than as a method of 'apportioning blame'. The following chapter then considers how strategically relevant performance measures should be developed for the whole business before being appropriately 'cascaded' down through the organisation, so that an inter-linked pyramid of key performance indicators is put in place.

There appear to be many reasons for the lack of sound financial controls in the marketing area. Almost all marketing expenditure is written off (i.e. expensed) to the profit and loss account in the year in which it is spent, irrespective of the time frame over which the returns may be generated. This is, as previously stated, in accordance with the so-called 'prudent' view underlying financial accounting (tell that to investors in Enron and WorldCom!), because the returns from these marketing expenditures cannot be 'guaranteed'. However there is no way that a brand launch, new market entry or major new product development is financially justifiable by considering only the returns generated in the first year. *All* long-term investments must be financially evaluated by comparing the expenditures required against the future expected returns. Where these financial returns are only expected to occur well into the future, they should be included at their present value equivalent, as was discussed in Chapter 7. The actual accounting treatment should be irrelevant to this decision evaluation process, as economic business decisions should be based on the future differential cash flows arising from the decision; this is illustrated in a numerical example later in the chapter. More businesses now follow this sound logic in their decision evaluation process but then revert to using accounting measures to 'control' the implementation of the originally soundly based decision.

This reversion can often result in long-term disaster, even though the short-term performance measures have been achieved. The rapid growth of retailer brands that has been mentioned earlier in the book is a good example of this. Many companies that sell through retailers would regard themselves as having 'brand-based' strategies as was discussed in Chapter 8; thus it would be illogical for these companies to do anything that damaged their brands. However in many cases that is exactly what they have done!

One initial problem seems to have been caused by their brands not being included on their balance sheets as valuable assets. This meant that the potential change in brand values resulting from any strategic moves was not as readily visible as it might have been. Also many of these companies used the very common accounting return on investment (ROI) ratio as a principal financial performance measure but, once again, the brand values were not included in this calculation. Consequently it was quite easy to justify utilising some 'spare' productive capacity to manufacture 'modified' products for existing customers, i.e. large retailers. These 'modified' products were often almost the same as the company's branded products, except for the packaging; this 'avoided' any extra product development costs. However the pricing was normally dramatically different. This was justified on the argument that it was marginal business (e.g. up to 10 per cent of the company's total volume) and would be 'turned off once demand for the branded products picked up again'. Pricing was therefore often done on a 'contribution basis' (i.e. variable costs plus a margin to contribute towards existing fixed costs), so that no fixed costs were directly allocated to these incremental sales. In the short term, this extra sales volume even with its low-profit contribution would improve the return on net *tangible* assets, but the company was also creating a lower priced competitor for its own branded products.

The retail customers were happy as they were getting a good quality product at a very good buying-in price. This enabled them to sell out at an advantageous price, even after taking a higher retail margin than on the equivalent branded products; logically, the retailer should make a greater margin as it is creating a higher proportion of the total value chain by now 'doing the branding'. The next stage of this saga is depressingly predictable; the retailer's products were selling very well and it wanted to increase its orders. This was 'good news' to the manufacturer because its brands were selling less well and therefore it had more spare capacity available.

However this size of order could no longer be regarded as 'marginal' to the manufacturer, and finance departments often now wanted to allocate some overheads to this growing segment of the total business. This meant that the manufacturer wanted to increase its selling price to the retailer. You are now entering one of the most interesting, and frequently shortest, discussions you will ever come across in business; a major retailer wants to (say) double its order levels and its supplier wants to increase its selling price for this increased order! Not surprisingly the retailer normally expects its buying-in price to come down as volumes increase.

Clearly the retailer's response was to threaten to take away all the *volume* to another manufacturer and also there could be significant risk attached to the volume of branded products still sold through this retailer. It is important to remember that the retailer's branding strategy was based around its customers; hence, the actual supplier of this retailer's brand was largely irrelevant as long as the quality and pricing can be maintained. Hence the manufacturer was now selling much more of a commodity product with the 'differentiation' being added by the retailer branding, which was of course owned by the retailer. Thus many of the branded manufacturer's core competences were not relevant to this new business and its performance measures and control processes should also have been very different, as is illustrated by Practical Insight 11.1.

For many branded manufacturers the growth of retailer brands has dramatically changed both their profit margins and their marketing strategies. In many FMCG industries there has been a significant downward trend over many years in the profitability of manufacturers that has been inversely mirrored by the increase in profitability of the major retailers through which they sell their branded products.

Practical Insight 11.1

Fast moving consumer goods: different strategies

Having worked at both ends of these FMCG industries marketing strategies, it is very clear to me that there are significant differences in culture and philosophy and hence the requirements for control systems and performance measures.

Mars' philosophy is to seek to create consumer demand through brand marketing so that retailers *need* to stock the brand; this is the normal definition of a 'power' brand. This does not mean that retailers are not important, but it means that the consumer is *even more* important. There should therefore be more performance measures that focus on consumers than on the direct retail customers.

As Financial Director of Sterling International, the basis of the Tissues Unlimited case study, I saw that this position was totally reversed. The group focused on producing retailer branded products, a broad range of small brands for smaller retail groups, and bulk tissue for the branded products of other tissue manufacturers (otherwise known as competitors). The most important element therefore was the direct customer (the retailer, etc.) as the interface with the end consumer was very indirect and relatively vague. Thus quality was dictated by the direct customer and deliberately ranged from excellent (for other manufacturers' premium-branded products) to adequate (for some retailer brands and most industrial customers).

If these branded manufacturers had had a brand evaluation process in place, as advocated in Chapter 8, they would have needed to take into account the potential impact on these brand values of starting to produce equivalent retailer branded goods. At the very least the relative strength of the brands (as shown by their brand health indicators), and hence their capability to withstand this new form of competition, should have been reviewed. In some cases, this position was made even more difficult as these new 'contracts' for retailer own labels (as they used, somewhat disparagingly, to be called by manufacturers) were not even under the direct control of the branded sales and marketing teams.

The performance measures used for manufacturing and operations areas of many groups also create increasing pressures to fill machines and maximise throughputs, even at marginal prices; e.g. machine utilisation measures, total output measures, outputs per employee, etc. normally without any reference to profit margins let alone shareholder value measures. As will be repeated through this part of the book, the performance measures used in the business must be tailored to the key strategic thrust of the business; in the above example, the original branded products strategy of the manufacturers. Moreover these tailored performance measures should indicate the potential impact on the key drivers of this strategy (e.g. the brand health indicators of the current brands) of any new proposed strategic move (e.g. the move into producing retailer brands). It is potentially less dangerous to sell incremental volumes of products that are available from utilising spare capacity into a new export market than to sell it to an existing customer merely packaged in a different format, however even this can cause problems as is illustrated in Practical Insight 11.2.

Practical Insight 11.2

Exports or re-imports?

One food company I worked for decided to increase output by launching two existing branded products into Scandinavia. The total market potential was not huge and so launch costs were kept to a minimum. The existing pack designs were retained and simply translated, and distributors were appointed for the market segments identified.

This meant that British consumers would readily identify the packs but would not understand the cooking and preparation instructions. The pricing strategy was to make the products highly competitive in order to encourage trial, etc., and this could be justified because it was 'marginal business'.

Soon after launch, one particular distributor was doing much better than all the others and its volumes far exceeded our estimates of the market segment. Also this distributor suggested that rather than us delivering the containers of product to its port of entry (and including the transportation cost in our selling price), the distributor would collect the product from our factory, for a discounted selling price obviously.

Further investigation revealed that this change would actually save this distributor 2 lots of costs for crossing the North Sea as the product was being re-imported into the Eastern region of England and sold, at a large discount to our UK selling prices, to retailers in that region!

Another marketing activity that can create many control problems is promotions. The confusion in many companies seems to be caused by the application of a single financial evaluation and control process to all promotional activities. Unfortunately the marketing justifications for and consequent objectives of different types of promotions can be quite diverse and this should result in more tailored financial control processes. The normal financial justification itself can often be too simplistic even when applied to those promotions where it is relevant. The most common form of financial control is simply to analyse whether the additional sales generated by the promotion more than outweigh the loss of profit margin caused by the effective reduction in the selling price. This evaluation and control process assumes that the key objective for the promotion is a short-term increase in sales volumes but, even if this is true, many such promotions have a steal effect from the periods just before and after the promotions.

As an example, let us take the case of a 1-month price reducing 'on-pack' promotion of a branded FMCG product sold through retailers, where the entire cost of the promotion is to be borne by the manufacturer. This manufacturer will clearly need to sell the promotion into the retailers in the period prior to its 1 month duration and the retailers may, quite deliberately, reduce their stocks of the standard product during this period; ideally, retailers would want zero stocks of the standard product on the day the price reducing promotion starts.

This will reduce standard product sales before the promotional period and, of course, these sales would have been made at a full rate of contribution.

Also, hopefully consumers will increase their purchases during the promotional period and thus retailers should increase their purchases correspondingly. However consumers may increase their purchases but not their rate of usage, which would mean that consumers will buy less in the period after the promotion as they use up the cheaper inventories they have built up. Thus the promotional assessment must take account of the impact on sales levels, at their relative contribution rates, both before and after such a value-increasing promotion.

Another classic example of this type of problem is illustrated by the recent promotional activities of banks and building societies in the UK retail mortgage market. Many financial services companies launched promotional offers of discounted mortgage lending rates of interest to *new* customers. This encouraged lots of existing homeowners to switch mortgage suppliers in order to get a lower rate of interest; in many cases, these people were at the same time able to increase their total borrowings for the same monthly repayment as the value of their property had increased since their original purchase. This spate of re-mortgaging created a massive level of 'churn' in the market as each participating bank and building society won many new customers and lost lots of existing customers. There was obviously a very high cost associated with this promotional bonanza due to the high administration costs of processing new mortgage documentation and closing existing accounts, in addition to the reduction in the interest rate spread on these new accounts.

More importantly, the impact of this activity has been to reduce significantly customer loyalty to any specific bank or building society. Most of these promotional rates were only available to 'new' customers and thus an existing customer did not qualify for a reduced borrowing rate on their existing mortgage, where the administration costs would be negligible. They were 'forced' to move their account to get the best deal available, and this was done in an industry that claims to have 'customer-led' strategies where building customer loyalty is important!

A value-increasing promotion is normally regarded as any promotion that reduces the effective selling price; e.g. a directly lower selling price, a buy some get some free offer, a larger pack size for the normal selling price, etc. Value-adding promotions offer something else other than a reduced purchase price to the customer; this can take the form of a loyalty programme, some form of collectible, a prize giving competition, etc. Different types of promotion can be used to achieve a wide range of both tactical and more strategic objectives. An appropriately tailored, particularly in terms of the time period covered, financial evaluation and control process should therefore be used for each specific promotional activity.

This is becoming even more important as, for an increasing number of industries, the fragmentation of mass channels of communication (e.g. the explosion in the number of television channels) and the increasing advertising overload of consumers mean that more and more companies are using promotional activities as key elements in their brand-building strategies (the phrases 'retail media' and 'new world of marketing' are becoming increasingly common in FMCG companies).

Integrating control into the planning process

That was quite deliberately a long introduction to this chapter as it attempted to show how the control process must be properly integrated into the total analysis and planning process of the business. Some readers may remember that, in Part One, I made the statement that planning and control are equally important and both are more important than analysis. Yet a glance at the balance of this book (three chapters on analysis, five chapters on planning, and only two chapters on control) does not seem to bear out this initial statement. This is because, throughout the chapters on analysis and planning, I have kept referring to the control issues that need to be considered. Indeed the more important statement from Part One is that analysis, planning and control is a continuous, iterative process and the boundaries between each stage and the next should become very blurred.

It is therefore illogical to use the term planning without linking it to the appropriately tailored control process that will be applied to monitor how successfully the plans are being implemented. The critical aspect about any control process is that it must focus on the future because, as has already been stated, the past can only be explained not controlled. Unfortunately this is a classic example of the Pareto 80:20 rule being applied the wrong way round; in most companies, at least 80 per cent of the management accounting reports produced are reconciliations and explanations of what has already happened. Thus endless analyses are produced of last month's actual performance versus budget, latest forecast, the same month last year, the previous month, and then similar comparisons are done on a year to date basis.

Obviously these analyses and explanations can be useful but only if they are applied in a positive manner in order to improve decision-making in the future. Thus *all feedback loops should be treated as a learning process*, and explanations of actual events are a key feedback loop as long as there is potential future relevance. This means that a totally different focus needs to be applied to the financial analysis of actual results and outcomes. The most important areas for analysis are those that are most likely to recur frequently in the future, and these are frequently in the marketing area of the business: price changes, competitor initiatives, tax and regulatory changes, exchange rate movements, economic condition changes including business cycles. Even though the exact set of circumstances will never be replicated, there can often be key learnings to be gained about the reactions of customers, competitors and suppliers to particular types of change in the business environment.

These learnings for the future are of much greater value than an incredibly detailed analysis of the specific events that happened last month; unfortunately the emphasis still tends to be on producing accurate, precise 'facts' that are of little use in driving the business towards its long-term objectives. The role of marketing finance is to help the organisation to achieve its goals and objectives, not to provide a detailed explanation of why and how it failed to meet them. Even worse is when the role includes 'who' screwed up as well as the why and how of underperformance. A culture of 'blame apportionment' in financial reporting leads to the absence of risk-taking within the organisation.

Thirty years ago as a young management accountant, one of my roles was to write the notes that accompanied the monthly set of management accounts that I was responsible for preparing. All the major variances from the plan and the latest forecast had to be explained and, in order to do that, I went and talked to the managers of each area of the business. In other words, these notes were prepared with (in reality, by) these line managers because they had the detailed information on what had actually happened in the previous month. In my terms, if anything I had produced in my monthly accounts for their area of responsibility came as a surprise to them, they were not properly in control of their part of the business. The benefit and value-added of this process was not therefore in producing the actual notes to last month's accounts, which told the responsible managers nothing that they did not already know, it was in providing a very valuable input to the re-forecast for the rest of the current year and for future medium- and long-term planning. An example of a good linkage between a control process and future decisions is given in Practical Insight 11.3.

Practical Insight 11.3

Short-run pricing decisions

Using the Tissues Unlimited case study of Chapter 10, the tissue mill faced a regular problem of how to set a selling price for short run, urgent orders for bulk tissue. The tissue production process goes from light colours to dark and then the machines are stopped, the tanks washed out and machines cleaned down and the cycle starts again. Interrupting this process therefore increases machine downtime and also the production efficiency is lower on a short run as the machines never get to run optimally.

Prior to the change in the basis of transfer pricing, the responsible manager made an educated guess as to how much extra to charge per tonne for these small uneconomic quantities. However the new transfer pricing system focused on the limiting factor of output which was identified as available machine hours, and a required contribution per machine hour was established.

This made the pricing of any special orders quite straightforward. The start point was obviously the variable cost per tonne for the specified quality of tissue. The next required input was an estimate of the total production time required for the order in terms of machine hours; i.e. this included any downtime required to

> **Short-run pricing decisions** (*Continued*)
> changeover to this colour and furnish, the total time to produce the ordered tonnage, and then to switch back to the normal production schedule. This total time multiplied by the required contribution per hour gave the minimum acceptable total contribution that needed to be added to the variable cost for the particular order.

Another key element for a good control process is that it should indicate the sustainability of the present situation and what events will indicate, in advance, that this situation is likely to change. This is particularly true for an existing differential advantage held by a business; the car industry competitor analysis example from Chapter 4 can be expanded to illustrate this point. The marketing finance question is whether an existing differential advantage held by our company, or by a competitor, is really a sustainable competitive advantage. It is easiest to explain this by using two sets of very simplified numbers for a hypothetical example of one advantage held by us and one held by the main competitor; these values are set out in Table 11.1.

The values in Table 11.1 highlight that our current differential advantage is a relatively small value enhancer, but it is sustainable; it would cost the competitor more to add it into their product than the customer considers that it is worth, therefore it would be value destroying for them to do so. At present the competitor holds an apparently much greater value-enhancing advantage; perceived use value of 200 with a cost to the competitor of only 140. However, the cost to us of matching the competitor's current offering is even less than the competitor's current cost level. This shows that this position can immediately be attacked by us adding in the same offering into our product, and thus matching the competitor. If we do this our value creation will be greater than that generated by the competitor; same perceived use value (200) but a cost of 130 instead of 140. The next marketing decision is whether we want to be more aggressive by reducing the selling price to the customer because of our cost advantage; i.e. we could include this current option as a standard

Table 11.1   *Differential advantage: sustainability evaluation*

	Advantage held by us	Advantage held by competitor
Perceived use value to customer	100	200
Cost to current provider (i.e. us/competitor)	90	140
Cost to competitor/us to match current offering	110	130

fitment on our product, because it would cost the competitor more to do the same. In this case the narrow cost differential relative to the high perceived value by the customer makes this unlikely, but there are some extremely good examples of this being done in the car industry.

A classic example was the Japanese car industry looking to create an additional advantage out of their superior manufacturing quality; this quality meant that their cars did not go wrong as often as their competitors' cars. Unfortunately this was not valued very highly by the customer at the time of buying a new car. The first phase was to offer an optional extended warranty that could be purchased at the same time of buying the car; the uptake on these was not very high as they were seen by customers as expensive. Indeed they were expensive as they represented a source of super profits to the car companies, particularly Japanese car companies that needed to spend less on repairing their cars during this extended warranty period. The next phase was much more significant as the Japanese manufacturers included 'for nothing' an extended 3 year unlimited mileage (or restricted mileage) warranty on many of their cars. This tried to force customers to value this benefit when they compared cars from competing manufacturers. The Japanese companies also knew that it would cost their competitors far more to match this product enhancement. Obviously it forced the USA- and European-based manufacturers to focus on their build quality so that their warranty claims costs would be reduced significantly. (As an aside this had an adverse impact on the profitability of the car dealerships, for which warranty work had represented an important source of profits.)

Impact of organisational structure

As has been discussed before, many companies are breaking their businesses down into smaller parts with the aim of making each sub-division focused on profitability and, in some cases, even shareholder value. This does not create many major problems when each business division represents a relatively stand-alone organisation with its own external customers, products and ideally assets; what was defined in Part Two as a strategic business unit. However many groups want to go much farther than this and seek to create 'internal' business divisions through the use of transfer pricing mechanisms.

The key aspect of transfer pricing as a genuine pricing system between willing buyers and sellers, rather than a cost apportionment exercise, has already been covered but, for truly internally focused divisions, an equally important factor is the establishment of SLAs. An SLA sets out exactly what is being supplied by one part of the organisation to another and thus what is being paid for. In other words it is exactly the same as the contract that would be agreed with an outside supplier if this activity was to be outsourced. The benefits of this are self-evident in terms of clarifying exactly what the transfer price represents but the main benefits are in terms of control.

If a good SLA has been drawn up, and therefore is agreed between the supplier and its internal customer(s), the separate accountabilities for performance should also be clearly understood. This is where many SLAs fall down because either they do not specify precisely what each party is responsible for or the responsibilities stated do not match with the factual controllability of future events. The accountability of the supplier in any internal SLA is to perform to the terms of the SLA and the supplier should then be paid accordingly. It is therefore the responsibility of the customer side of the SLA to ensure that this level of performance is what is actually required and that the transfer price represents good value for money. In many cases there will be some involvement from the centre to facilitate or arbitrate but the outcome still needs to be between a willing buyer and a willing seller; if not the transfer pricing process can introduce a significant accountability and controllability gap that is covered in detail in the next chapter.

Critical success factors of a marketing finance process

For several years I headed up a research centre in Cranfield School of Management that concentrated on marketing finance issues and we developed some common 'critical success factors' for control of this area. These have been more recently refined and I include them, here as a way of drawing together the control issues faced by marketing finance departments and managers.

CRITICAL SUCCESS FACTOR (1)
Validate the linkages between objectives, strategies and marketing
finance systems.

As emphasised throughout the book there must be clearly established links between the goals and objectives of the business, and the strategies that are selected to achieve them. Further these overall strategies must be linked to the detailed tailored competitive and functional strategies that are implemented by the sub-divisions of the business. Marketing finance should validate these links for the sales and marketing strategies and develop appropriate leading indicators of whether the objectives will be achieved.

More importantly, the marketing finance system should highlight the key strategic decisions that will have a significant impact on the successful outcome of these strategies. Indeed marketing finance must be focused on decision support and particularly on supporting the key strategic marketing decisions. The system has to be able to assist not only in the initial strategic marketing decisions but also in monitoring, updating and, quite possibly, revising those decisions as the marketing strategies are implemented.

CRITICAL SUCCESS FACTOR (2)
Close the communication gap between marketing and finance managers.

The marketing finance system must communicate the necessary information to the marketing managers making these key strategic decisions. This communication process must take into account the potentially significant differences in the way that different types of managers assimilate information. If the information is provided in a non-user friendly way or even simply an unfamiliar way, at worst it will not be used at all while, at best, it may delay the decision as it will require further processing by the decision-maker. If this additional processing is not done properly, it could even result in an incorrect decision being taken.

It is still quite common to find that internal financial information is produced in formats designed by accountants for accountants. Many marketing managers find large tables of financial numbers both incomprehensible and very boring; given the flexibility and processing power of modern computers, it is perfectly practical to provide all strategic decision-makers with individually tailored reporting formats. The important issues in designing each such format are to remove the risk of misunderstanding by the decision-maker and to reduce the time required to assimilate the information before the decision can be taken.

CRITICAL SUCCESS FACTOR (3)
Identify the likely types of strategic marketing decisions.

The tailored communication process is based on the simple but immensely useful logic of providing 'the right information to the right manager at the right time'. Given the common 'one-off' nature of strategic decisions, it may be very difficult to deliver relevant useful financial information in time for it to be used in the decision-making process, unless marketing finance can predict, sufficiently well in advance, what types of marketing decisions are likely to be made.

Fortunately it is relatively straightforward to characterise strategic marketing finance decisions into four main types. The positive 2 decisions involve entering a new area of business and expanding on an existing area; both these decisions normally involve the allocation of financial resources to implement the decision. The financial evaluation of these types of decision should be based on the *incremental* costs and benefits that are expected to result from the decision.

The more negative 2 decisions are forms of exit evaluations; either to exit completely or to stay in but on a reduced scale of activity. The exit decision may involve direct closure or sale to another business but the financial evaluation should be carried out by comparing the financial cost or benefit that is expected to derive from staying in, with the best alternative method of exiting.

It should be remembered that both of these financial outcomes can be negative so that the least cost alternative would be selected. The benefits of closure are clearly the realisable values of any assets that can be sold plus the savings that can be achieved by ceasing to pay for certain existing costs. Thus the relevant costs are the *avoidable* or *severable* costs that will be saved as a result of the decision.

The problem for marketing finance is not only that different financial information (i.e. incremental or avoidable future cash flows) is needed for the different types of strategic decision, but also these decisions do not require the normal financial information produced by most management information systems. These systems concentrate on historic cost analysis and these costs tend to include sophisticated bases of apportionment that often destroy their decision relevance.

CRITICAL SUCCESS FACTOR (4)
Provide the relevant information for the particular decision.

Strategic decision-makers do not have time to sort through masses of irrelevant financial information. First, information, not data, must be provided so that additional processing or combining of pieces of information is unnecessary. Second, it is critical that only relevant financial information is provided to the decision-maker. This means producing specific tailored reports to support particular decisions. If the traditional accounting logic of including lots of apportioned costs is followed, as mentioned above, the resulting financial analysis will serve only to confuse the decision-maker. Decision-makers require supporting financial information that shows how the *economic* returns are expected to change as a result of the decision.

CRITICAL SUCCESS FACTOR (5)
Focus on, and measure, the intangible marketing assets of the business.

Using the adage 'what gets measured, gets done', marketing finance must develop an *evaluation* process for measuring the key marketing assets of the business. Thus brands, customers, channels of distribution should be treated as the major assets that they are for most organisations. This evaluation should include both those marketing assets that are currently being exploited and those that are currently being developed for future exploitation.

This requires marketing expenditure to be split between development activities (designed to improve the long-term value of a marketing asset) and maintenance expenditure (designed to keep an existing marketing asset at its current level). The financial impacts and the appropriate financial evaluation and control processes are different for these types of marketing expenditure.

CRITICAL SUCCESS FACTOR (6)
True financial control can only be exercised in advance of financial commitment.

Most management accounting reports reflect the actual activities of a particular period (e.g. the monthly profit and loss account), but marketing finance should be focused on decision support. The actual decision is taken at the time of *committing* to the expenditure, not when the activity actually takes place (the example of booking advertising months in advance was used earlier in the book). Thus the main emphasis of a marketing finance system should be on commitments, not on accounting expense or even expenditures (i.e. when the physical payment leaves the company).

CRITICAL SUCCESS FACTOR (7)

Identify where management discretion is restricted through engineered cost relationships.

In many marketing activities, even before formal financial commitment, managers have very limited discretion due to the physical input to output relationships that rule the activities. These 'engineered' costs enable the physical relationships to be used as the control mechanism, rather than the less predictable financial relationship. This is applying the genuine form of standard costing that was discussed in Chapter 10, and an example applying this to sales force control is given in Chapter 12.

CRITICAL SUCCESS FACTOR (8)

Marketing objectives and the engineered relationships may both change over time.

Although these 'engineered' relationships can greatly enhance the control of many marketing activities, they tend not to be based on any immutable laws of physics. Changes in the external environment, changes in technology, the entry of a new competitor, changes in the attitudes of key customers could make the old physical relationships no longer relevant. Equally the marketing objectives of the business are not set in stone and may change over time.

The marketing finance system, at the very least, needs to be flexible enough to cope with such changes when they occur. However a good marketing finance system should highlight the possibility of such changes and indicate the likely consequences of these possible changes. Modelling techniques, sensitivity analyses, etc. can be of great value in this area.

CRITICAL SUCCESS FACTOR (9)

Identify appropriate financial and non-financial performance measures for all levels of the business.

It has already been stated that the business needs both economic performance measures and managerial performance measures. These measures should distinguish between committed and truly discretionary expenditures, development and maintenance expenditures, and incorporate any physically engineered relationships.

As this area is the main focus of the following chapter, it will not be discussed in depth here.

CRITICAL SUCCESS FACTOR (10)

Develop an overall marketing investment planning and control process.

Ideally the marketing finance system should develop into an overall marketing investment planning and control model that enables competitive initiatives and external environment changes to be simulated, as well as evaluating internal marketing strategies. Such an overall model would link with the overriding corporate objectives and the resulting economic performance measures. However it would also incorporate and validate the appropriateness of the varying levels of managerial performance to ensure that they were all in line with the corporate objectives and the economic return targets for the business.

It would be used to evaluate specific key elements of marketing plans and the model would obviously be updated using actual outcomes to improve the predictions of the future. In other words it would genuinely use its feedback loops as a learning process, rather than as an apportionment of blame.

I have to say that I have not yet come across such a comprehensive marketing finance model.

A rapidly changing competitive environment

As a way of trying to illustrate how a marketing finance system needs to be both tailored and responsive to the changing needs of a business, I am using another structured example; like the previous such examples, this one is based on reality but the numbers have been changed to protect both the innocent and the guilty, and to keep the analysis relatively straightforward.

Asurething plc, a risk averse large diversified group, develops a new product but, in order to minimise its perception of the associated risk, it only initially invests in capacity for 50 000 units p.a. It takes the view that it could subsequently invest in additional capacity if demand for the product really takes off. Its cost structure and original financial evaluation (using its cost of capital of 20 per cent as the discount rate) are shown in Table 11.2. In order to create shareholder value, the company needs to achieve a rate of return in excess of 20 per cent that, according to the figures in Table 11.2, this project should do.

The problem for Asurething is that the technology used in this new product is generally available and its product is not strongly branded. Once the potentially high 'super profits' become known, other companies are likely to be attracted to this new market, particularly as demand is forecast to grow rapidly.

Table 11.2 *Company A's initial cost structure and project evaluation*

Capacity invested in – 50 000 units per year.
Investment required – Plant £5 00 000.
(It is assumed that this product is neutral in terms of working capital investment.)
Plant life is estimated to be 10 years with nil residual value. (All companies use straight line depreciation.)

		Per unit		*Per year*
		£		(£000's)
Selling price		10		500
Variable cost		4.50		225
Contribution		5.50		275
Fixed costs – exc. depn	1.5		75	
– depreciation	1	2.50	50	125
Profit		3		150
Investment at cost –				£500

Year 1 accounting ROI = 30% (using cost of fixed assets)
Discounted cash flow analysis (@ 20%)

Year	Cash flow	Discount factor	Present value
0	(£500k)	1	(£500k)
1–10	£200k	4.192	£838.4k
			NPV +£338.4k

(Note: The DCF analysis uses the cash flow generated each year, ignoring any time lags, as being profits plus depreciation. Nil residual value for the plant at the end of 10 years has been assumed.)

Indeed the marketing director of Asurething is soon hired by some venture capitalists to start a direct competitor! The new company, Becopied Ltd, is started one year later to produce the same product with exactly the same plant specification as A.

However, as a small focused company, B is able to keep its manufacturing costs lower than A, although its fixed cost base per unit is slightly higher (as it is a completely stand-alone business). In order to generate demand for the increased industry total of 1 00 000 units annual output, selling prices have to be reduced to £9; A has no real choice but to follow this reduction in general selling prices. Becopied's cost structure and initial financial evaluation are shown in Table 11.3; as before its financial projections indicate a positive impact on shareholder value, even with the assumption of the reduced selling price.

Asurething has generated some efficiency gains during its first year of operations so that its variable costs per unit have reduced to £4 (from £4.50). Unfortunately this gain is more than offset by the reduction in selling prices

Table 11.3   *Company B's cost structure*

Capacity invested in – also 50 000 units per year (Year of entry – Year 2)
Investment required £5 00 000.

		Per unit £			*Per year* (£000's)
Selling price		9			450
Variable cost		4			200
Contribution		5			250
Fixed costs – exc. depn	2.00			100	
– depreciation	1.00	3		50	150
Profit		2.00			100
Investment at cost –					£500

First year accounting ROI = 20%
Discounted cash flow analysis (@ 20%)

Year	Cash flow	Discount factor	Present value
0	(£500k)	1	(£500k)
1–10	£150k	4.192	£628.8k
			NPV +£128.8k

(Note: This positive net present value is based on the important assumption that the selling price remains at £9 per unit throughout the 10 years, or that it only reduces in line with efficiency improvements.)

caused by Becopied's entry into the market, as is shown in Table 11.4. A's efficiency gains give it the same variable costs as B; the learning curve advantage of being first in the industry. Thus, given its lower fixed cost base, A is making a higher net return than B and still should be creating shareholder value over the product's life cycle; albeit not as much as originally predicted.

Table 11.4   *Company A's revised cost structure (after the entry of B, i.e. Year 2 of production)*

		Per unit				*Revised*
		Original		*Revised*		*per year*
Selling price		10		9		450
Variable cost		4.50		4*		200
Contribution		5.50		5		250
Fixed costs – exc. depn	1.5		1.5		75	
– depreciation	1	2.50	1	2.5	50	125
Profit		3.00		2.5		125

* The variable cost per unit has reduced due to the experience curve effect, e.g. learning curve benefits gained during the first year of production.

Table 11.5 *Updated project evaluation for Company A's investment (@ 20%)*

Year	Cash flow	Discount factor	Present value
0	(£500k)	1	(£500k)
1	£150k	0.833	£125k
2–10	£125k	3.359	£420k
			NPV + £45k

Indeed, even if the reduction in selling price to £9 in Year 2 had been predicted, the project would still have been financially attractive, as is shown in Table 11.5.

However, the changed competitive environment may make Asurething want to review its future strategy. The entry of one new competitor may make it concerned about the possibility of further new entrants particularly given the price elasticity of this product; demand has doubled for a 10 per cent decrease in selling price. In future investments, Asurething may seek to develop strong entry barriers more quickly or review its launch pricing strategies when experience curve benefits can be expected. A lower, more aggressive penetration pricing policy at launch may have discouraged B from entering the industry so rapidly. It is now clear that A's initial financial evaluation was over simplistic and over optimistic.

Unfortunately neither A nor B reviewed their strategies quickly enough as Costcutter Inc enters the industry at the beginning of Year 3. This new entrant focuses on the rapid growth in demand caused by small price reductions. Also quadrupling output capacity only doubles the required capital investment, so that C is able to generate economies of scale on its investment in 2 00 000 units of annual capacity. Thus despite having to reduce the unit selling price to £7 (in order to generate demand for the industry total output of 3 00 000 units), Costcutter is able to generate a very significant level of shareholder value, as is shown in Table 11.6.

This more substantial decline in selling prices affects Asurething, as is shown in Table 11.7. Clearly the financial return is now unattractive and, if this position had been forecast before making the initial investment, the decision to launch would not have been taken. However A now faces a possible exit decision, not a hypothetical entry decision. The net realisable value of the plant is only its scrap value, which is £50 000. And the original investment cost of £5 00 000 is now irrelevant as is the net book value of £4 00 000 (£5 00 000 less 2 year's straight line depreciation). Asurething should include the opportunity cost on this scrap value in its exit decision evaluation; it foregoes the receipt of a £50 000 cash inflow if it decides to stay in the industry. However the company has identified some fixed cost savings, and should achieve further experience curve reductions in its variable costs over the next year.

Table 11.6   *Company C's cost structure*

Capacity invested in – 2 00 000 units per year
(Year of entry – Year 3)
Investment required £10 00 000.

		Per unit £		Per year (£000's)
Selling price		7		1400
Variable cost		3.2		640
Contribution		3.8		760
Fixed costs – exc. depn	0.8		160	
– depreciation	0.5		100	
		1.3		260
Profit		£2.5		£500

Investment at cost – £10 00 000
First year accounting ROI = 50%
Discounted cash flow analysis (@ 20%)

Year	Cash flow	Discount factor	Present value
0	(£1000k)	1	(£1000k)
1–10	£600k	4.192	£2515k
			NPV +£1515k

Note: This DCF computation also ignores the prospect of reducing variable costs and selling prices over the life of the project.

These restated costs, as is shown in Table 11.8, show that Asurething is still better off staying in the industry rather than exiting; however, the expectations of shareholder value creation have disappeared.

Worse is to come for Asurething and its existing competitors, as Developments GMBH enter the scene at the beginning of Year 4 with a new patented

Table 11.7   *Company A's revised cost structure (after C's entry)*

		Per unit		Per year (£000's)
Selling prices		7		350
Variable cost		4		200
Contribution		3		150
Fixed costs				
– exc. depn	1.5		75	
– depreciation	1.0	2.5	50	125
Profit		0.5		25

Table 11.8 *Company A's exit decision computation*

	Per unit £	Per year 000's
Selling price	7	350
Variable cost	3.6*(1)	180
Contribution	3.4	170
Fixed costs	1.2*(2)	60
Net Contribution	2.2	110

Exit evaluation
Present value of opportunity cost of salvage value = £50 000
Benefit of future cash flow by staying in industry
Years 1–7 £1 10 000 p.a. × 3.605 = £3 96 000
        (Annuity factor)
Decision is clearly to stay in the industry
*(1) The variable cost will reduce due to the experience curve effect.
*(2) Fixed costs are included at their avoidable level only, some costs
      are now shared with other products.

method of making the product, thus creating a potentially sustainable competitive advantage. This technology significantly reduces both variable costs and capital costs through large economies of scale; hence Developments also decides to go for high volume with an initial investment in 2 50 000 units of annual capacity. Its cost structure is shown in Table 11.9, which also shows that the selling price is now driven down to £5 per unit. This reduction has dramatic impacts on all the existing competitors in the industry, none of whom could have justified their initial investment if this prospect had been foreseen.

Asurething and Becopied should now rework their exit decision evaluations, as is done in Table 11.10. Becopied should leave the industry because of its higher fixed cost base, which is dedicated to its only product and is hence fully avoidable if the business closes down. This would be the best financial decision even if the plant had no residual value; however, as previously discussed, some industries have net costs associated with exiting, and this can make it *less* financially *unattractive* to stay in an industry even though cash flows are negative.

Asurething is somewhat in a dilemma because, if Becopied closes down, the selling price may rise sufficiently to make it just worthwhile to stay in. It decides to stay in for a year and see what happens; B leaves the industry and the selling price rises to £5.50, thus temporarily vindicating its decision. However at £5.50, Developments may expand its capacity as this would be shareholder value-creating for it.

Before this can happen, in Year 5 Everlasting Far East Ltd enters the industry with another large scale investment. It is using a cheaper version of the original technology and has much lower production costs than even the

Table 11.9   *Company D's cost structure (new patented technology)*

Capacity invested in – 2 50 000 units per year
(Year of entry – Year 4)
Investment required – £7 50 000

		Per unit £	Per year (£000's)
Selling price		5.00	1250
Variable cost		3.00	750
Contribution		2.00	500
Fixed costs – exc. depn	0.70		175
– depreciation	0.30	1.00	75	250
Profit		1.00	250

Investment at cost – £7 50 000
First year accounting ROI = 33.3%
Discounted cash flow analysis (@ 20%)

Year	Cash flow	Discount factor	Present value
0	(£750k)	1	(£750k)
1–10	£325k	4.192	£1362.4k
			NPV +£612.4k

Table 11.10   *Companies A and B – exit options after D's entry*

	A		B	
	Per unit	Per year	Per unit	Per year
Selling price	5	250	5	250
Variable cost	3.6	180	3.2	160
Contribution	1.4	70	1.8	90
Fixed costs	1.2	60	2.0	100
Net contribution	0.2	10	(0.2)	(10)

Discounted cash flow @ 20%
Scrap value – present value now £40 000.
Benefit of future cash flows Years 1–6
£10 000 × Annuity factor of 3.326 = £33 260
On this cash flow analysis, A is also better off
leaving the industry,
However:
  (1) Its variable cost will continue to decline.
  (2) If B leaves the industry, the capacity will be
      reduced and the selling price will rise – thus
      giving A an incentive to stay in.

B is clearly better off
leaving as it is generating
a negative cash flow at a
£5 selling price.

Table 11.11   *Company E's cost structure (cheaper version of original technology and longer-term view)*

Capacity invested in – 2 50 000 units per year (Year of entry – Year 5)
Investment required – £7 50 000
(Life of assets assumed to be 15 years)

		Per unit £		Per year (£000's)
Selling price		4.00		1000
Variable cost		2.50		625
Contribution		1.50		375
Fixed costs – exc. depn	0.8		200	
– depreciation	0.2	1.00	50	250
Profit		0.50		125

Investment at cost – £750k
First year accounting ROI = 16.67%
Discounted cash flow analysis (@ 15% – lower cost of capital)

Year	Cash flow	Discount factor	Present value
0	(£750k)	1	(£750k)
1–15	(£175k)	5.847	£1023.2k
			NPV + £273.2k

patented process of D. Also it is prepared to take a longer-term view. Thus it uses a 15-year timescale (compared to 10 years for all the existing companies) and it has a lower cost of capital (15 per cent versus 20 per cent); the result is shown in Table 11.11. As is shown, this drives the selling price down to £4 per unit and this forces Asurething to follow Becopied out of the industry; A's cash flow is now negative as well. A's departure does not affect the selling price as it had already been predicted by Everlasting in deciding on the scale of its investment; i.e. it knew that it would force the selling price down below A's exit point.

The relative positions of the three remaining players after A & B's departures are shown in Table 11.12. Costcutter is making a small loss but will stay in the industry until its plant needs replacing; its cash flow (i.e. in this example profit excluding depreciation) is still slightly positive. Developments is not generating the shareholder value that it hoped for from its patented technology but it will certainly not leave and could try to segment the market. Everlasting has therefore selected an entry strategy that should produce a period of stability for the industry, until it is potentially supplanted as the low-cost producer by an even lower cost-based competitor!

Table 11.12   *Relative cost structures (after departure of Companies A and B)*

Company		C		D		E	Total
Capacity (000s)		200		250		250	700
Per unit data (£s)							
Selling price		4		4		4	
Variable cost (inc. learning curve for C & D)		2.75		2.8		2.50	
Contribution		1.25		1.20		1.50	
Fixed costs							
– exc. depn	0.8		0.7		0.8		
– depn	0.5	1.30	0.3	1.00	0.2	1.00	
Net profit		(0.05)		0.20		0.50	

This example has tried to illustrate the critical need both to include potential competitor reactions and to use the decision relevant financial information in any strategic marketing finance evaluation. It also highlights the need to develop a truly sustainable competitive advantage; even D's patented technology left it open to pure price competition. This chapter ends with a brief case study to try to bring together some other important elements of a good marketing finance control process.

Case study – McDonald's

Background

McDonald's was founded by Ray Kroc in Illinois, USA in 1955 when he opened the first restaurant. Now the chain has 30 000 restaurants in over 100 countries and total annual sales revenues, including franchisees' sales, of over $40 billion. Ray Kroc initially built a dominant domestic market share and then took the successful product formula international; the first British restaurant was opened in 1974.

The use of franchisees to own and operate the vast majority of the restaurants made this rapid growth much easier to finance. However McDonald's is unusual in that it owns many of the sites that are occupied by its franchisees; rental income thus supplementing the franchise fees paid by operators, as well as safeguarding these now prime locations, whose potential McDonald's was often the first to identify. During the 1990s McDonald's was still opening over 1500 new stores per year but some markets, most notably the USA, were becoming saturated. Thus new store openings had an increasing cannibalisation effect on existing restaurants in the same area.

One of the keys to the group's success was the development of the brand as epitomised by the 'golden arches' and Ronald McDonald (supposed to be second only to Santa Claus in terms of children's recognition). However the brand also meant the product, i.e. 'burgers and fries'. This enabled competitors to enter the market with look-alike products, Burger King and Wendy's, or with variants on the concept of fast food; KFC, Taco Bell and a variety of Pizza chains. Of course, Burger King and Wendy's would argue that they have a better product than McDonald's but they still focus on 'burgers and fries'.

McDonald's has launched different products but the last really successful true innovation was Chicken McNuggets in 1983, with the Big Mac having been around since 1968. The problem for the group is that its business is maturing and the previous high rates of growth are no longer achievable. Indeed USA sales per store have not been rising for over 10 years and actually started to fall in 2002. The international growth has not been able to fill this gap and earnings fell in 2001; then for the last quarter of 2002, the group announced a loss of $343.8 million.

This led to the removal of the chief executive officer and the recall from retirement of Jack Cantalupo as chairman and chief executive officer. At the time of writing he is developing his plans for the group; it will be interesting to see how well his proposals (based on his 28 years experience with the company) fit with a marketing finance-based analysis.

Strategic analysis

McDonald's was very clearly developed as a brand-based business; its strong brand was used to attract good quality, well-trained franchisees (all Hamburger University graduates) and made it an attractive, anchor occupant for new retail and leisure developments. The corporate centre set out very strong rules as to how each restaurant should look, be laid out and be run, as well as providing access to centralised sourcing of key raw materials. Most importantly though, it managed the brand and its initial key differentiation attributes were consistent product quality (whether or not an individual likes the product, it has to be accepted that it is consistent) and service. Service was a key element and this meant minimal waiting for customers to be achieved without serving up a product that had been sitting around being kept warm for ages. It could achieve all this by keeping its product range incredibly simple, compared with a pizza restaurant with vast numbers of different toppings, etc.

It took competitors some time to catch up with these brand attributes, and most of the individual fast food restaurants were forced out of business by the expansion of the branded chains. Also during this period, the overall fast food sector was growing rapidly in many countries and this clearly helped with McDonald's overall rate of growth. It was, at this stage, a major advantage for McDonald's to be seen as overtly American, the home of the hamburger and fast food in general; writing this book during the Iraq invasion means that this strong USA connection is causing different issues for the chain at present.

As the industry started to mature in the USA and competitors became better organised, McDonald's earlier brand advantages had less significance and the market became much more price conscious; for some time now, McDonald's and Burger King have been competing with each other to discount their burgers to lower and lower prices. This introduces product cross-subsidisation because most of the profit from each customer is then generated from the 'fries' that they buy. In 2002 sales of fries in the USA *fell* for the first time, with a correspondingly amplified impact on McDonald's profitability; possibly customers who are buying a heavily discounted burger are not prepared to pay out for 'full priced fries' to go with it.

This could also be caused by a trend towards 'healthier eating'; there are now more sandwich shops in the USA than burger restaurants. If this is true it signals a longer-term problem for the group because its 'product' may have moved into the decline phase of its life cycle. McDonald's has tried to reduce its dependence on this 'burger, fries and service' mix, but none of the new 'product concepts' has really been successful.

Indeed it can be argued that McDonald's have been under a false impression that it owns a customer-led brand, which would enable it to launch new products that its existing loyal customers would be willing to buy. The alternative view is that these new products appeal to completely different customers (e.g. chicken sandwiches and 'bacon butties') from the regular McDonald's burger eater; thus the branding is less relevant and also less appropriate as it is associated with 'burgers and fries' and children (through Ronald McDonald) in the minds of these potential new customers.

Even worse this product range diversification may have reduced the appeal of McDonald's to its traditional customers (rather like the earlier illustration of Levi's, 'why are old people sitting in my restaurant?') and also it could reduce the previously key benefit of service quality. There is no doubt that consumers' perception of the service level in McDonald's has declined significantly and, in the USA, it now regularly ranks not only below its direct competitors but also below many other industries that are certainly not known for their customer service excellence.

The most logical strategic option is therefore for McDonald's to go back to its core strategy (burgers, fries and service), which would mean that its future growth prospects are reduced. The key question that it needs to answer is whether its brand is still a potential source of super profits or whether price competition has become the norm for its end of the industry. McDonald's does have another much smaller business, Partnership Brands, that owns other restaurant groups. To most consumers these are not associated with McDonald's and the combination of McDonald's original management skills (location identification, franchisee development, brand building, and consistent service delivery) together with more modern branding and product concepts could be a potentially powerful strategic option, using the profits and cash flow from a re-focused and possible rationalised McDonald's restaurant chain.

However whatever marketing strategy it does follow, there is a definite need for McDonald's to implement an appropriately tailored marketing finance control system. The issues of developing appropriately tailored control measures for different stages of the life cycle are discussed in the following chapter, which also concludes with a case study on a very closely related branded products company, Coca-Cola.

12   Establishing Performance Measures

Overview

Performance measures are needed at three levels, each with a different focus, and this makes it virtually impossible for any single measure to work effectively in all these roles. A wide range of performance measures can be used in most businesses; some should be externally focused and may require the objective and consistent application of managerial judgement.

A hierarchy of performance measures is required so that each level in the organisation is given specifically relevant measures; it is critically important that such a hierarchy is internally consistent, so that everyone is aiming at the same set of objectives.

Economic performance measures are very important to shareholders as they indicate whether shareholder value is being created. However they are not normally a good indicator of managerial performance; this requires a relative performance measure. At the very top of a company, e.g. the main board of directors, it may be reasonable to use primarily economic performance measures but, even here, they should be placed in an appropriate context by referencing them against a peer group of other companies, or the stock market in total, etc.

As you go lower down the organisation, there are greater restrictions on managerial discretion and it is important that there is a direct linkage between effective managerial control and the performance measures used. It may seem more *efficient* to use the same performance measure (e.g. ROI) for all managers, but it normally has a dramatically adverse impact on the *effectiveness* of the performance measures in influencing managerial behaviour. Managerial performance measures require the true cost driver for all costs to be identified and the accountability should stay at this level of the organisation. Far too often this identified cost driver is then used as the basis for apportioning the total costs across lower levels in the organisation, thus destroying the direct accountability/controllability linkage.

Key performance indicators (KPIs) are leading indicator measures of performance that focus on the key strategic thrusts at the particular level of the business. There should be a limited number (maximum of five) of KPIs for each manager because no one can focus on a vast range of measures. The challenge for the organisation is to develop an interlinked set of KPIs for each level in the business so that each set is consistent with the overall objectives of the company but relates to decisions and actions relevant to each managerial level.

Products, customers and brands all follow some form of life cycle and different performance measures may be needed for each stage. These tailored performance measures should include both financial and non-financial measures that should be clearly linked to the key strategic thrusts at each stage.

If all these different ways of looking at the business are put together, a unique set of performance measures can be developed for each business. However this set fits the current strategy and the current business environment; if either of these changes significantly the set of performance measures should be reviewed and modified if necessary.

Introduction

As stated at the beginning of the book, the strategic challenge for most businesses is changing and becoming more demanding. Increasingly the focus for businesses is changing away from 'outperforming the internally established performance measure' (what I have referred to as the 'budget, actual, variance' syndrome) to 'outperforming the external competition' in order to *create shareholder value*. As discussed in more detail in this chapter, this requires each business to develop tailored performance measures at three levels in order to indicate:

1 The economic attractiveness of the industry or sector
2 The relative competitive performance of the business
3 The performance of each key strategic thrust of the business

Unfortunately there are no simple solutions to this challenge, as no single performance measure performs well at all three levels. A further complication is that even more specifically tailored performance measures are required at each decision-making level of the organisation.

Alongside this challenge for business, the finance function faces its own strategic challenges. Finance functions can often be perceived, particularly by their marketing colleagues, as *constraining* due to an excessive emphasis on internally focused, hierarchically determined financial control procedures. They are also often regarded as *uninvolved* and *uncommitted*, because their objectivity and emphasis on rigorous evaluation and control can be interpreted as aloofness, arrogance or just disinterest. Also the financial controls applied within many businesses are almost completely unaffected by major changes in other areas of the business. As a consequence, the overall view of financial control is that it is *cost increasing* rather than value-adding, where unnecessary controls are imposed that often increase the workloads of parts of the business that do not receive (or perceive) any direct benefits.

However if a well-designed marketing finance system is put in place, at least part of finance (except that it is now likely to be regarded as part of marketing) can be regarded as *enabling*, rather than constraining, through its positive contributions to strategic decision-making. The desired integration into marketing makes marketing finance much more *participative* because marketing finance managers are closely involved in marketing decisions, and physically work alongside marketing managers, most particularly the marketing research manager. This should make marketing finance a genuinely *value-adding* activity for the organisation, where the benefits of having active finance involvement in marketing decisions clearly outweigh the cost incurred. Such a value-adding, strategically enabling, participative marketing finance role must obviously be achieved without losing financial control of the business. This is why the development of a tailored set of performance measures is so critical.

New performance measures

A wide range of performance measures can and should be used to assess the overall performance of a business, its component elements and its key strategic thrusts, and the managers who are running the business. The three levels of performance measurement require both internal and external comparisons to be incorporated. Some of these comparisons will inevitably require the exercise of judgement in the absence of absolute factual information; these required judgements should be, and should be seen to be, objectively and consistently applied.

All the performance measures should be decision-oriented and any comparisons should highlight actionable differences. The very practical 'so what?' question should always be asked; so what action do we take if the performance measure is not what we expected? If there is no action, we have either selected the wrong performance measure or it is being applied at the wrong level in the organisation.

Both financial and non-financial performance measures are needed, but they should be designed to complement each other rather than repeat the same measure in financial values as well as physical terms. Innovative measures should be used whenever they add value; this added value can be because attention is now focused on the most strategically relevant area of the business, rather than on the most obvious and easiest area to measure. This issue is illustrated in Practical Insight 12.1.

The set of performance measures used by any business should therefore not only be integrated with the specific marketing strategy of the business, but also tailored to the particular needs of the process that is being measured. The challenging 'so what' question means that these performance measures should primarily be leading, rather than lagging indicators and there must be a balance of long-term and short-term measures. This is relatively simple to state in theory but much more difficult to achieve in practice.

Practical Insight 12.1

Refocusing attention away from tonnage

The Tissues Unlimited case study from Chapter 10 introduced a need to alter the performance measures used, and the associated bonus system, for the employees at the bulk tissue mill. In the past the emphasis had been on the total tonnage of tissue produced each week, as this was felt to be the most controllable and measurable output from the tissue mill. Unfortunately it was too controllable!

This performance measure meant that, due to the very different machine output rates per hour depending on the type of tissue being manufactured, the mill employees were delighted whenever the production schedule showed that high outputs of kitchen towel were to be produced. They were therefore getting very depressed about the trend towards producing more and more facial tissue that was discussed in the case study. This made it very difficult for them to achieve their production targets and hence their expected bonus payments. Ideally production departments should be motivated to produce all products with similar levels of enthusiasm; if there is a difference, it should be motivated by the super profitability of the product rather than its weight! Further this tonnage-based performance measure encouraged behaviour that was against the interests of the company. Almost all automated manufacturing processes have a tolerance built into the system (in this case, each product had a specified basis weight per square metre of tissue, but there were acceptable ranges either side of this target). It was clearly in the interests of the tissue mill to set their machines at the heavier end of this acceptable range, thus maximising the total tonnage produced. 'Running the machines heavy' also meant that the machines could be run at slightly faster speeds, again giving an increased tonnage output.

The basic performance measure and bonus system did not include variable cost levels and so these were of much less interest. Profits were a performance measure for the senior managers at the mill, but they also participated in the tonnage-based system.

The new transfer pricing system based on contributions per hour provided a perfect opportunity to introduce a new performance measurement system (and bonus scheme) for the tissue mill. The objectives of the new system were to motivate the mill employees and managers to optimise the time for which the machines were available for production (as production hours were the limiting factor at present), to produce the required tonnages in the shortest times possible while maintaining the required quality levels, to minimise changeover times between products (some quite minor capital investment achieved significant reductions and corresponding improvements in flexibility) and to minimise controllable variable costs per unit of output. Some of these measures are mutually conflicting which forces the mill managers and senior operators to make the tradeoffs that they should understand better than anyone else in the organisation. An example is whether to increase the weight setting on a particular product; the machines could be run at faster speeds, thus reducing run times but variable costs would be increased. The standard costing system also had to be amended to ensure that up-to-date costs of raw materials were used in assessing the economics of this tradeoff; pulp prices and particularly waste paper prices are highly volatile.

Another key issue for the performance measures used within any business is the concept of 'goal congruence'. As has been mentioned before, this simply means that each part of the organisation should be motivated to act in the best interests of the total organisation. Clearly motivating the tissue mill to increase the weight of the bulk tissue that it produces is not goal congruent if the group sells the converted product externally based on length, sheet count, etc.; I have yet to find a consumer who buys a toilet roll, box of facial tissues or kitchen towel based primarily on how heavy it feels! Similarly incentivising a sales force to sell volume (e.g. cases, tonnes, millions of units, etc.) is not necessarily goal congruent with an overall objective to create shareholder value. It is frequently easiest to sell the 'best value' product in the range and this, not surprisingly, is often the one that generates the lowest rate of contribution. However transfer pricing systems in large groups are probably the greatest source of dysfunctional behaviour by specific parts of an organisation. Acting in line with the transfer pricing rule does not necessarily make for optimal performance for the overall group, particularly when the transfer pricing system is established primarily for external fiscal (e.g. tax authority acceptability) reasons, as is illustrated by Practical Insight 12.2.

Practical Insight 12.2

Not for cost plus 10%!

One very large multinational, like many others as has been mentioned before, had established a global transfer pricing system for products produced by one business for eventual sales by another business unit in a different end market. The system, which had agreement from the tax authorities, was that goods should be sold at cost plus 10 per cent. There were obviously rules that established how 'cost' was to be calculated (although there were many examples of different interpretations of these rules). The objective of the tax authorities was to ensure that taxable profits were generated in both the producing country and the external sales country.

However most of this group's products generated far higher cost markups than 10 per cent and therefore internal transfers within the group were relatively unattractive. This was particularly true for the USA-based subsidiary, whose main strategic focus was on its high-volume domestic business. It found the relatively small export orders very costly, particularly as its manufacturing process was geared to long production runs, and changeovers were very time-consuming. The 'costs' allowed in the transfer pricing system did not fully enable the USA operation to recover all of these added inefficiencies although, in reality, its costing system could not calculate the true costs of production of these small export quantities.

Therefore the USA business, which was under severe profit pressure from the group centre, unilaterally decided that it would no longer produce small order quantities for other parts of the group. Although small by USA market standards, some of these quantities were both significant and highly profitable to the ultimate sales countries. Consequently this decision made the USA's performance look potentially marginally better (in fact it got worse as it could not reduce its fixed costs), but adversely affected the group's performance.

Accountability and controllability

As stated earlier in the book, it is a fundamental tenet of good management practice, and hence of sound performance measures, that managers should only be held accountable for matters over which they can exercise some degree of control. However shareholders want managers to be motivated to create shareholder value, and this is only achieved by a better than required economic performance. Economic performance assessment must take into account all the relevant internal and external factors impacting on this performance, whether or not these factors can be controlled by the organisation.

This means that, in many cases, economic performance is not a good indicator of relative managerial performance. In an economically attractive industry, all the players in the industry could generate super profits and thus create value for their shareholders. Conversely, in an economically very depressed industry, all the companies may fail to deliver the return required by their shareholders; in fact, the best company may simply make a smaller loss than all the rest. Therefore from a shareholder value perspective, it is much better to have invested in a below average performing company that happens to be in a very financially attractive industry, than to have selected the best company in a very depressed industry.

Economic performance measures are thus very important to shareholders and should form part of the total performance measures used by any company, particularly at the very top of the company. Shareholders feel that they have the right to hold the board of directors accountable for the economic performance of the total business, even though the directors cannot control all aspects of the external environment. However, shareholders seem to believe that as the directors do, in theory at least, control what areas of activity their company chooses to operate in, they should be able over time to move the business away from any unattractive current areas of activity into more likely sources of shareholder value creation; clearly, life is not really quite as simple as that because of exit and entry barriers, relevance of core competences, etc. The end result, nonetheless, is that very senior managers are often largely judged by economic performance measures.

In an increasing number of cases, this economic performance measure is placed into a relative context by comparing the particular company's performance against an appropriate peer group, e.g. the industry sector or comparable alternative stock market investments in the case of a publicly quoted company. This still leaves the question of what actual form of economic performance measure should be used. Throughout this book the focus has been on creating shareholder value; i.e. making super profits rather than merely making a profit. However in Part One I explained that economic profit, which shows the annual excess return achieved after allowing for the required rate of return on the capital invested in the business, is not necessarily a good indicator of the long-term health of the business. From the shareholders' perspectives the most

relevant economic measure is total shareholder return for the year (i.e. dividend yield plus or minus the annual change in share price) as this represents
their actual economic return. This obviously needs to be adjusted by the required
rate of return for the particular company but, even then, this is not necessarily
a measure of the performance of the top management team, as discussed earlier
in the book.

Unfortunately the very common use of stock (i.e. share) options in publicly
quoted companies can make this problem even worse. The normal system is
that senior executives are given the right to buy shares (but not the obligation
to buy the shares, because it is an option) in the company at a fixed price
during some future time period (e.g. starting 3 years from now and expiring in
5 or 7 years time). The idea is fairly obviously that if the share price grows
during this period, the executives will gain from exercising their options and
this puts them in a similar position to the shareholders. There are of course
some quite serious differences between an executive stock option holder and
a current shareholder. The current shareholders have invested money in buying their shares and therefore require a return on those funds (the opportunity
cost concept); part of this return may be received in the form of dividends
which are not paid to option holders. This can be taken into account simply by
setting the exercise price of the executive stock options above the current
share price; the percentage increase for each year is the total required rate of
return for equity in the particular company less the annual dividend yield paid
in those years. Very few companies make this simple correction, preferring to
set stock option exercise prices at or near today's share price so that executives get all of the upside in the share price performance.

However they do not suffer all of the downside if there is any, they simply
would not make a gain on their options and therefore they do not exercise
them. This is where the long-time period over which these options can be
exercised is of significant value; the share price may fall below today's price
for a while, but it might be back well above this level before the stock options
have expired. Indeed, as discussed in Chapter 7, a key value driver for stock
options is the volatility of the share price; a more volatile share generates a
more valuable option. It seems slightly perverse that shareholders should incentivise senior executives for increasing the volatility, i.e. the risk profile, of the
company that they are running on the shareholders' behalf.

Is there a sensible alternative? The problem is, as stated way back in
Chapter 1, that shareholder value is calculated using discounted cash flows
over long periods of time and this can make it difficult to translate it into a
periodic (e.g. annual) measure of performance. This is why companies, and
their remuneration committees, fall back on total shareholder return measures,
stock options and, heaven forbid, accounting measures such as earnings per
share and return on investment (ROI). *It is possible* to carry out a full shareholder
value calculation for the company on an annual basis, i.e. an economic valuation

of the business using the discounted value of the expected future cash flows. The shareholder value created in the year is clearly the adjusted net difference between two successive such calculations; as discussed in Chapter 1, this calculation may give a significantly different answer to the total shareholder return generated for that year. The concern that most people have with using such a measure as the basis for assessing performance is that it is based on forecasts of future expected cash flows. However it is actually based on the *difference between* two forecasts of future expected cash flows and therefore, as long as both forecasts are done on a consistent basis, the movement should be much more meaningful than either absolute value. This is reinforced because a high value this year (thus apparently showing good shareholder value creation) becomes the start point for next year's calculation.

The important issue about considering such a process, which would obviously only be used internally within the company by the remuneration committee of the board, is that it starts to focus attention on the real value drivers of the business. The analysis of each year's evaluation should concentrate on the changes in existing and potential future sustainable competitive advantages, rather than on the resulting cash flows. The logical next stage therefore is to use these leading indicators of future shareholder value creation as the basis of performance evaluation. It is these key value drivers that shareholders should really want the top management team to build and then exploit, while developing their replacements; these top managers should not be able to claim that these areas are outside their control, even if 'their true value' is not currently reflected in the share price.

Certainly as performance measures are designed further down the organisation, normally starting with the business divisions' management teams and central functional areas, it is critically important that this linkage between accountability and controllability is clearly maintained. As stated above, if managers are to be held accountable for a certain level of performance, they should be able to exert influence on the outcome.

Accountability/controllability gaps frequently occur as a result of sophisticated cost apportionment or cost recharging systems, as opposed to proper 'pricing systems'. The ultimate recipients of such a shared out cost may be held *accountable* for their proportions of the total cost (e.g. €1 00 000 being 20 per cent of a total cost of €5 00 000), but they do not *feel responsible* for this cost as they cannot influence it. In many cases, the major arguments regarding such costs revolve around the proportion (i.e. the 20 per cent) of the cost that a particular department or area is being charged for rather than the actual amount; managers feel that they may have some influence over this element if they complain loud and long enough. Of course reducing their proportion (to say 15 per cent) does not actually save the company money (it is still spending €5 00 000) and usually results in someone else within the company being charged a higher proportion.

A real concern is that such a system can end up with no one feeling responsible for the total amount spent (i.e. the €5 00 000); the total is recharged out to a range of managers who do not feel it is their responsibility and the managers who spent it in the first place feel that it has all been recharged so they have no net responsibility or, possibly and worryingly, accountability. It is important that no such gaps are allowed to develop in the cost structure where an 'its not my responsibility' attitude can be expressed.

These gaps can be avoided if the true cost driver is identified for all the costs incurred by the business. These direct causes of the costs (remember that a cost driver causes the cost to be incurred and changes the level of the cost) must be held responsible, and thus the appropriate managers must be held accountable for the total level of the costs. If the accounting system confuses or hides these cost driver relationships, as can be achieved through apportioning out the total costs, managers may not be motivated to challenge the total cost levels or take up all the potential opportunities for cost reductions. Sometimes it may not be immediately obvious what the controllable cost driver is in a particular area, but this must be identified and then used as the focus of a performance measure for that area.

Sales force performance measures can provide two examples of this type of problem. Any sales manager with responsibility for a normal field sales force has quite surprisingly little discretion in terms of the total cost of that sales force. Sales force total costs are made up of a large number of different items, as illustrated in Table 12.1. At first sight therefore, it appears that the

Table 12.1   *Field sales force cost structure*

Salaries	x
Other employment costs	x
Commission	x
Recruitment	x
Car expenses	x
Telephones	x
Petrol	x
Accommodation	x
Subsistence	x
Entertaining	x
Samples	x
Consumables	x
Training	x
Support costs	x
	£10 million

At present, 100 sales people are employed by the company.

accountable manager can influence the total costs of £10 million in a number of ways. However, on closer examination it becomes clear that there is only one real cost driver for the field sales force.

If salaries per employee are reduced to levels below those prevailing in the industry, this is likely to result in the loss of the best sales people. Similarly, attempting to reduce petrol or car expenses per head, or accommodation and subsistence per sales person will also reduce the effectiveness of the sales force, if these relationships have been properly established in the past. There is a quite well-defined 'engineered cost' relationship for many of these costs; this relationship is itself slightly dynamic as the engineered costs per employee will change if the size of the sales force changes significantly. This highlights that the only real controllable variable is actually the number of sales people employed by the company. For the illustration in Table 12.1, it costs £1 00 000 per year to have a properly equipped, effective field sales person; the key question, therefore, is 'is it worth that much money to have *all these people?*' rather than 'can we make the people cheaper?' The marketing finance evaluation and control process should focus on justifying the actual number of sales people by considering the relative financial contributions that would be generated by different sized sales forces, and on validating the engineered cost relationship being used for this sales force.

The other performance measure issue for this field sales force is how the performance of an individual sales person should be assessed. In many companies this is done by setting sales revenue targets or sales volume targets against which each sales person is measured. The problem is that such an exclusive focus on short-term sales revenues or volumes may be counter productive to the achievement of the long-term objectives of the business. The performance measures used need to be specifically tailored to the particular aims and objectives of the sales force, as is illustrated in Practical Insight 12.3.

Practical Insight 12.3

Product specialist or account manager?

In financial services, most large banks have had 'account managers' for their corporate and business customers for many years. In theory this role is to provide a single point of contact for the customer with the bank, and thus the account managers should facilitate the sale of the whole range of banking services to their customers.

However, in practice, most of these account managers were credit specialists (i.e. they knew a lot about debt products, such as overdrafts, term loans, etc.) and so they were more comfortable selling what they knew. This behaviour was reinforced by their performance measures which, in most cases, heavily emphasised their sales of these debt products; they possibly got some small credit if the customer actually bought some other services from the bank. Still worse, in several

---

Product specialist or account manager? (*Continued*)

banks, these account managers saw their customers as 'theirs', and so acted as 'gatekeepers' effectively controlling access to their customers by other product groups within the bank. This made it very difficult for many other services (foreign exchange, cash management, corporate advisory, securitisation, etc.) to generate business from existing customers; hence they tended to develop their own customer relationships, which goes totally against the logic of a 'customer-led' strategy.

More recently most banks have recognised the problem, and now include the cross-selling of products to key customers as an important performance measure for their account managers; some are now deliberately using account managers who do not have a debt product specialism.

For branded fast moving consumer goods companies there is a slightly different form of the same problem. Many such companies consider improving the quality of the product received by the consumer as being very important to their long-term success. For many product categories such as food, the freshness of the product is a significant factor in the overall perception of its quality, but many of these companies still incentivise their sales forces to sell as many goods as possible. Where these sales forces do not sell directly to the consumer, but to the channel of distribution (e.g. retailers or wholesalers) that then supplies the consumer, there is the risk of 'stuffing the pipeline' that has been referred to in earlier case studies. More sales *into* the channel of distribution do not automatically lead to more purchases *out* of the channel by consumers; thus there is the potential for holding increasing stock levels in the channels and consequently delivering less fresh, poorer quality product ultimately to the consumer. Once effective distribution has been achieved, there needs to be a target for trade stock levels *in* the channel expressed in days or weeks of sales *out* of the channel. This would stop the sales force achieving their sales targets by overfilling the trade pipeline. Their focus should be on increasing off-take by consumers but, if they are given the wrong performance measure, it should not come as a surprise if they try to achieve their objectives. What is needed is a set of performance measures that are completely in line with the long-term objectives of the business.

Key performance indicators

The third level of performance measures is therefore very specific to the particular business and its long-term objectives. These measures must be appropriately tailored to the business and the level within the business at which they are being applied. It has already been established that there is a vast range of potentially successful competitive strategies that are based on a specific mix of sustainable competitive advantages. Several of these different strategies may be implemented in various segments of the same industry at the same time; this means that different companies in the same industry may need very different performance measures, and that the same company may need different performance measures in various parts of its organisation.

Also the assessment of managerial performance at different levels in an organisation requires the development of an interlinked set of appropriate managerial performance measures. At each level, these measures should identify and focus on the key areas over which the managers exert control or have discretion. However the levels must be integrated to ensure that no accountability/controllability gaps are created and that the overall objectives of the organisation are not compromised by these hierarchical performance measures.

In order to create real focus at each level in the business, all organisations need to develop a cascading pyramid of interlinked key performance indicators. KPIs are meant to be *leading* indicators of the success or failure of the critical strategic thrusts at each particular level in the business. No level, area, manager or individual employee can focus on a vast array of performance measures and I have found over many years that a maximum of five KPIs at each level is optimal. Recently I have been working with a large group that is trying to introduce this concept of a cascading pyramid of KPIs; the problem is that they have developed an initial set of 37 measures for their top management team to focus on. This is better than the company that, in all seriousness, presented the 147 KPIs that were used in the sales and marketing area of the business.

It is, in fact, quite possible to have a large number of KPIs in use across a business but no person should be focusing on more than five of these. The trick is to link each of the levels together, and ideally this should be done by moving progressively back along the leading indicator causality factors. As is shown in Figure 12.1, the 5 KPIs used at the top of the business (by the main board or executive committee) can *each* be expanded into five more KPIs for

A cascading pyramid

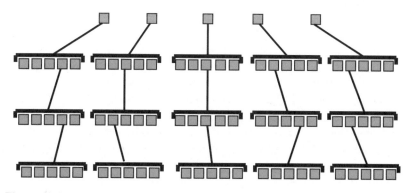

Figure 12.1   *Key performance indicators – creating focus*

the level below and so on down the organisation. Theoretically this means that, even at the third level down the pyramid, any business could be using 125 KPIs (i.e. 5^3). However, in practice the total number will be significantly lower as many of the KPIs at each lower level will be relevant and interrelated to several KPIs in the level above.

However no individual manager is focused on more than five of these KPIs. For any manager's performance assessment, the 5 KPIs that are selected need not all come from the same level in the pyramid and will probably not all come from one particular grouping of KPIs. They must all, at least partly, be controllable by the individual whose performance is being assessed. This means that more than one individual can have the same KPI and that different people can have KPIs that relate to different aspects of the same strategic thrust. In business many responsibilities are shared, and objectives can only be achieved by a team effort; this reality should be reflected in the KPIs used within the business.

What is meant by linking each of the levels and moving backwards in terms of leading indicators? I have already stated that high profits are a lagging indicator of the success of a marketing strategy; i.e. a business makes a profit because its marketing strategy has proved successful. Yet high profits, particularly super profits, can be a leading indicator of shareholder value creation if they lead to increasing share prices as the stock market comes to expect these super profits to be achieved in the future. Thus measures can be lagging indicators at one level but leading indicators at another level. It is also true that possible management action differs at the various levels within any business; the top management team establish the mission, the long-term objectives and set out the overall strategy, but they cannot micro-manage all the details of how this strategy is implemented. Therefore there can be leading indicators of how the overall strategy is going that are lagging indicators at a more detailed level of implementing this strategy. We need a leading indicator at each particular level of the business that is being considered; so what tells us in advance that the marketing strategy is going to work, and then what tells us that that factor will be successful and so on! An example may make this clearer, and one is shown as Figure 12.2.

This example uses a repeat purchase, branded consumer product sold through retail distribution where the business has a key overall objective of increasing its market share. At the top of the company this value market share becomes one of the five KPIs because, if it is achieved, it is expected to lead to increased profits and hence shareholder value creation; i.e. it is a leading indicator of shareholder value creation. However using the achievement of an objective to control achieving that objective is counter-intuitive; it is, by definition, a lagging indicator because you only know after the event if the objective was achieved, and we cannot control the past. Therefore the next stage is to try to identify what will lead to this desired increase in market share. For this

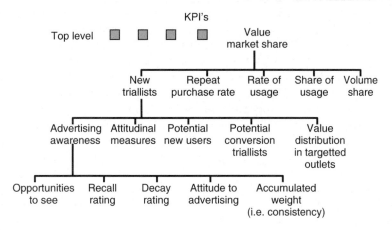

Figure 12.2 *An example for a particular FMCG company; with a key objective to increase market share*

company the five key factors are shown as the next level of KPIs. If market share is to grow, this company needs to win new consumers and this requires new triallists, who must re-purchase the product after trying it and then adopt it as part of their normal consumption. Targets for each of these factors can be established that, if achieved, should result in the overall value market share objective also being achieved; they are leading indicators of the ultimate objective. Of course the relative overall usage rate of these new consumers and our share of this usage will influence the ultimate market share gained, and winning new consumers could be outweighed by losing more existing consumers; this explains the other three KPIs at this level. Each of these five KPIs would then be further analysed into its own leading indicators, some of which may be common. Taking one element, the critical new triallists KPI, it is possible to analyse how new triallists are acquired in this market. One important factor is the total potential new user population, which is a factor of our existing market share (how many consumers can we get to switch from competitive offerings) and the rate of new entrants into this market. Another linked element is the proportion of this potential new user population that is actually trying our product; these are linked but one is much more controllable than the other and consequently the conversion ratio to actual triallists is a better managerial performance measure. How are these potential triallists won over is a mixture of knowing about the brand, wanting to try the brand and then being able to buy the brand; each of these is again linked, but different sales and marketing managers will have specific responsibilities for only one element of this mix.

Breaking down advertising awareness shows that there are again still more specific leading indicators of whether the advertising message will work and hence whether enough new triallists will be achieved so that the desired market share growth will be achieved. If many consumers have seen the adverts, remember them but do not like them (i.e. we get a poor response on the attitude to advertising), there is no point in increasing advertising spend because overall trial rates are below plan; the company needs to fix the problem with its advertising communication. It should be clear that this process enables a much clearer focus at each level in the organisation but also shows managers where their KPIs fit into the overall objectives of the organisation. This can be far more motivating than giving all managers the KPI of increasing profit by 10 per cent simply because that is the organisation's overall objective; for most managers, the only direct action they can take to affect that measure is to reduce their own levels of expenditure which may, or may not, be in the long-term interests of the business. Managers need to be given performance measures where their possible actions are in line with the long-term interests of the organisation, as is illustrated in Practical Insight 12.4.

Practical Insight 12.4

An annuity stream of future profits

Life Assurance is a classic example of an industry where current and future profit levels are largely the result of strategic actions taken some considerable time in the past. When a long-term life assurance policy is sold, the future premium income is known as is the actuarially calculated probability of paying out early on the policy; life assurance is all based on the law of large numbers of policies so that statistical distributions do apply. Thus life assurance companies can normally predict very accurately what their profit contributions will be each year from existing business; it is just an unwinding of the discounted cash flow calculation done at the inception of the policy.

This means that current profit levels are not a meaningful measure of real performance this year. One focus should be on the level of new business generated this year, net of policy cancellations and maturities, as this indicates the long-term sustainability of the business. However, for certain types of life business, the very high up-front commissions paid to generate new business mean that new policies can actually produce an accounting loss in their first 1 or 2 years, despite being highly profitable over the life of the policy. If the performance measures over-emphasise this year's level of profitability, a bonus-focused manager may decide to curtail the writing of these long-term profitable classes of business in order to achieve the short-term target.

Tailored financial control measures

As already stated, a strategically focused marketing finance system should be tailored to the specific requirements of the organisation's competitive strategy.

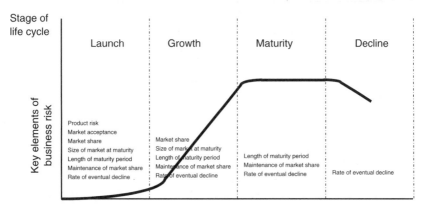

Figure 12.3   *Changing business risk profile over the product life cycle*

If the competitive strategy changes, the marketing finance system and its associated performance measures should be reviewed and amended accordingly. This clearly means that businesses that have customer-led strategies should use different performance measures from those used by businesses that are implementing product-led strategies; also brand-based strategies (which can be used by both customer and product-led businesses) require their own tailored performance measures. Each of these strategic thrusts requires that the performance measures focus on the key long-term assets of the business; i.e. customers, products or brands.

However there is one type of change that will eventually affect all competitive strategies and that is the progress of the business, over time, through the life cycle for its industry. The normal phrase used is 'product' life cycle, and this will be used in this section of the chapter, but the life cycle concept is equally applicable to customer and brand-led strategies. As shown in Figure 12.3, the risk profile of a business reduces over its life cycle, as the main risks (i.e. volatilities) are associated with the launch and growth stages. To many people, this seems counter-intuitive because in the decline phase the business is getting smaller, but it is predictably getting smaller, and thus the perceived risk is reduced because of this level of expectation. This idea of a reducing risk profile over the life cycle is simply represented by a 2×2 matrix in Figure 12.4 as this makes the diagrammatic development of the argument easier.

The key idea now is to identify how the critical success factors change as the business moves through the life cycle and this is shown in Figure 12.5; this concept was developed for customer-led strategies in Chapter 9. In the very high-risk launch stage, the focus should clearly be on developing and launching the product. A critical success factor for many new product-based businesses is 'time to market'; i.e. how long does it take to turn a concept or idea into a saleable product. There is a significant risk that a competitor may get its product launched more quickly but in any case an excessive delay is normally

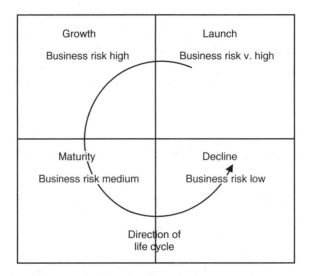

Figure 12.4   *Business risk – as it* will *change over the life cycle*

Growth Business risk high CSF: Growth in market share and development of total market	Launch Business risk v. high CSF: Development and launch of new product
Maturity Business risk medium CSF: Maintenance of market share at minimum cost	Decline Business risk low CSF: Cost minimisation and/or asset realisations

Figure 12.5   *Changing critical success factors over the life cycle*

using up the limited competitive advantage period during which super profits can be generated. Once the product is launched this risk is removed and the business passes into the growth phase; as previously discussed the key objective is to grow market share to its optimum level during this rapid growth period, as competitive responses to share gains are likely to be less aggressive.

However if the company was first to launch the product it should start out as market leader and its strategy will normally be to maintain this market leadership during the growth stage. As previously discussed, it is the responsibility of the market leaders to ensure that the total market fulfils its full potential, and this gives two critical success factors for this phase: growth in market share and development of the total market.

Once the product matures, the focus of the strategy should change as aggressive market share growth can result in value destroying responses from competitors (i.e. the start of price wars resulting in a lose–lose game for the industry). The critical success factor for the market leader is to maintain its market share at the minimum cost possible, without opening up opportunities for competitors to steal significant share; Chapter 9 showed that it was during this maturity phase that the benefit of sharing cost savings with customers was particularly valuable. Of course, smaller competitors may be less worried about entering into value destroying competition, as they have a smaller share of the existing industry value chain, but it is still in the interests of the market leader to manage the profitability of the total industry. Eventually the product will move into its decline stage where sales volumes reduce, albeit slowly, and it is important that the business does not try to avoid this by over-investing in marketing activities. The focus should be on downsizing the business to match the new levels of demand, so that asset realisations and cost reduction activities become more important. It is quite common that, by this stage, the basis of competition has become selling price, so that the relative cost levels will be of increasing importance. These critical success factors can themselves be translated directly into tailored leading indicator performance measures with a particularly valuable measure being a leading indicator of when the product is moving into the next phase.

However these non-financial measures also help to highlight what type of financial control measures should be applied to each stage of development. It is only during the maturity phase, as shown in Figure 12.6, that the very common accounting-based ROI is at all valid. Even here, I much prefer the residual income measure discussed earlier in the book although, as shown in Figure 12.7, the best financial performance measure for mature products is sustainable operating cash flows as it avoid the potential confusion that can be caused by 'Mickey Mouse' accounting presentations. The reason that ROI is acceptable for mature businesses is that the business is focused on producing good profits now while maintaining the asset base for the future, and ROI gives a reasonable view as to whether that is being achieved. Unfortunately it is still a lagging indicator for the current year but this year's profits can be used as a reasonable leading indicator for future sustainable profit levels.

None of the other stages is either steady state or stable and therefore using ROI will either overstate or understate the future potential of the business. During the launch phase there is almost no meaningful financial control measure due to the very high business risk and associated very high level of volatility.

Growth	Launch
FCM:	FCM:
DCF evaluation of investments in growth in market and market share	R&D milestones, decision focused reviews, probability assessments
Maturity	Decline
FCM:	FCM:
accounting return on investment or residual income	free cash flow from operations

Figure 12.6 *Tailored financial control measures over the life cycle*

The financial evaluation that should have been done prior to committing the funds to develop, and launch the product would have been based on the expected future cash flows but, as discussed in Chapter 7, these 'expected' cash flows will probably have a very wide range of possible outcomes. Typically

Growth	Launch
CSF: market dominance	CSF: time to market
Focus: marketing	Focus: R&D/market research
FCM: DCF of marketing investments	FCM: R&D milestones decision-focused reviews risk management
Maturity	Decline
CSF: maintenance of position	CSF: controlled exit
Focus: supply chain	Focus: asset management & cost control
FCM: sustainable operating cash flows/ROI/RI	FCM: total free cash flow including asset realisations

Figure 12.7 *Illustration of matching financial control measures to strategic thrusts over time*

this would include some chance of complete failure with no resulting cash inflows and some chance of very high cash inflows if the product ultimately proves to be very successful. Thus, while the 'expected' cash flows can and indeed must be used for evaluating the investment, they cannot be used as a meaningful 'control' measure during the development and launch stage. Control should instead focus on managing the very high-risk profile of the project and this includes using milestones for the research and development activities and marketing research, carrying out decision-focused reviews before committing the next phase of expenditure and, as discussed in depth in Chapter 7, trying to increase the probability of success of later stages before committing significant amounts of money to the project.

Once the growth phase has been reached, much more information on the market and the relative strength of the company's product will have been obtained. Thus the total range of the expected outturns should have reduced significantly so that the discounted cash flow evaluations can now also be used as a meaningful financial control measure. It is vital that such a long-term control measure is used if the product is to achieve its full potential, as much of the marketing expenditure during this growth stage will be development spend which has a long-term return.

During the decline stage, the business is looking to reduce its investment in the product by recovering some working capital as volumes drop, and by not reinvesting all the accounting depreciation expense in new plant and machinery. This means that the cash generation from the product should be higher than its accounting profit level and this makes free cash flow from operations a good performance measure. The drawback is that actual cash flow is once again a lagging measure, but targets can be set both for releasing working capital and for the reinvestment rate in fixed assets, and this can produce a more leading indicator of the actual cash generation.

This process can therefore be developed to produce a balance of financial and non-financial measures that link together the critical success factors of the strategic thrust at each stage with the focus of the marketing finance system and the appropriate type of performance measure, as shown in Figure 12.7.

Another way of developing a set of tailored performance measures for different types of organisation has already been discussed in Chapter 6, where the Rainbow Model showed that the specific role of the corporate centre in large groups can have a significant impact on the performance measures that should be used across such a group.

If all the relevant various factors are combined for any particular business, it should become clear that a unique set of tailored performance measures can be developed for each business depending on its specific needs. Thus, as discussed in the Rudolph and the Elves case study at the end of Part One, these tailored performance measures may well have more in common with a business applying a similar strategic thrust in a completely different industry than with a business in the same industry that is employing a very different strategy.

Case study – Coca-Cola Inc.

It was very tempting to try to write a final case study that covered all the issues addressed in the book, but I soon gave this up as too ambitious. However I decided to finish by discussing a company that consistently delivered very high levels of shareholder value over quite a long period from a clear marketing focus; in other words it achieved the sub-title of the book by 'turning marketing strategies into shareholder value'. Its challenge is to continue to do this in the future.

Background

Coca-Cola Inc. was able to grow, initially in the USA, very rapidly by focusing on the manufacture of its syrup concentrate and the brand advertising for its soft drink product. The actual production of the finished consumer product was outsourced to bottlers spread across the USA. These bottlers were set up with territorial exclusivity (by 1920s there were 1200 franchised Coke bottlers), perpetual contracts and a fixed syrup price. The bottlers did very well as the market grew rapidly but, as the USA market matured in the 1970s with volume growth rates of only 3 per cent, they looked on Coke bottling and distribution as a good profit generator but no longer a high potential business.

Also Coke's bottlers were, by definition, locally based and therefore were not structured to do regional and national deals with the rapidly expanding retail chains. Pepsi–Cola could do this as it owned many of its larger bottlers; by 1977 Pepsi had an equal share to Coke in the USA supermarkets. In the early 1980s Pepsi moved into snack foods and restaurants, acquiring Pizza Hut, Taco Bell and KFC; all of these chains, not surprisingly, switched to selling Pepsi. Coca-Cola already had McDonalds but then won Burger King and Wendy's as well. The restaurant sector and vending machines are highly profitable channels of distribution for soft drinks companies; pricing is high and so are consumption levels, thus exclusive distribution can be a major advantage. Unusually, grocery distribution in this industry is more a method of brand building rather than a source of super profits; it is in the grocery channel that both Coke and Pepsi have faced their most severe competitive pressure from retailer brands and generic competition.

Coca-Cola wanted to restructure its bottlers but the perpetual contracts and fixed price syrup made this potentially very expensive. The new CEO, Robert

Goizueta, used a product development to achieve this in 1981. The company had developed a high fructose corn syrup as an alternative to sugar in the syrup which reduced the cost by 20 per cent; Goizueta made the lower cost product available to bottlers on a condition of amending the original contracts. During the early 1980s Coke then acquired many of its bottling franchisees and focused on developing the areas of other good bottlers.

Unfortunately this significantly increased its asset base and made its return on equity look much lower, even though these bottlers were themselves highly profitable. In 1986, Coca-Cola Enterprises was set up as a holding company for these owned bottlers and a majority stake (51 per cent) was floated onto the USA stock market. This achieved two things; one, Coke no longer had to consolidate its remaining 49 per cent minority stake; so its return on equity rose back to its old levels and, two, it generated over $1 billion in cash that could be spent on acquiring more bottlers. This model was replicated as Coca-Cola grew rapidly internationally during the 1980s and 1990s with its large anchor bottlers that effectively controlled a region or large country being partially owned by Coca-Cola Enterprises (CCE).

By the mid-1990s Coca-Cola had a dominant share in the international (i.e. to them, non-USA sales) soft drinks market and 80 per cent of its $4 billion operating profit was made outside the USA. The growth rate outside the USA was still significantly greater than the now very mature USA market. Coke's market capitalisation had grown astronomically from under $5 billion in 1981 to around $150 billion in 1996. Coca-Cola had thus generated significant shareholder value over a 15-year period by being a focused branded beverage producer linked to a network of bottlers that are its key direct customers.

Pepsi–Cola, on the other hand, had moved into other product areas including snack foods (e.g. Frito Lay) and fast food restaurants (now sold off) but 90 per cent of its profits came from the USA; not least because it had less than half Coke's market share outside the USA (45 per cent versus 21 per cent). Pepsi has also now spun off its bottling operations.

In the second half of the 1990s Pepsi mounted an aggressive marketing campaign in the USA; it doubled its annual marketing spend, based on blind taste tests that indicated consumers actually preferred Pepsi to Coke. This closed the market share gap to its smallest level since 1980 and resulted in the launch of New Coke, which was supposed to taste better than either Old Coke or Pepsi. This well-documented disaster was rapidly replaced by Classic Coke (i.e. Old Coke again) but Coca Cola also faced other problems, not helped by the economic slowdown and its own quality issues: growth of competitor brands (e.g. Dr Pepper, now owned by Cadbury Schweppes), continuing growth of retailer brands and a growing range of alternative 'healthier' drinks.

Another new CEO, Douglas Ivester, tried to change the corporate culture and refocus the company on creating shareholder value. He introduced economic value as the group's main financial performance measure and radically over-hauled the company's planning and control process. This tried to bring about more creativity from lower level employees through a greater level of delegated authority so as to reduce the perceived arrogance and bureaucracy that had built up within the company. Unfortunately the stock market lowered its future growth expectations for the shares as the company showed that it could not sustain its previous sales growth rates. Its dominant market share meant that it could still achieve profit growth by not spending on its brand marketing (there were no high-profile marketing campaigns during this period), but this was also seen as a longer-term threat by stock market analysts. Ivester left in 1999 and was replaced by Douglas Daft; as stated earlier, he has recently curtailed Coke's short-term profit estimates in an attempt to ensure that the focus is on the long-term strategy.

Strategic analysis

Coca-Cola made a very early key strategic decision that was to try to gain a dominant market share while its market was in its infancy; hence, the use of exclusive franchised bottlers that gave it national coverage very quickly. It focused on controlling the brand imagery and the product quality (the syrup concentrate and the product's packaging, including its unique bottle shape). This enabled it to develop an incredibly strong consumer franchise despite having at least two intermediaries between it and the consumer (the bottler and the retail channel of distribution). The strategy also minimised its required investment in both capital and people, so that the rate of potential super profits was very high once strong market share was achieved.

However it also restricted its strategic flexibility if its bottlers were not as committed to the brand and the consumer as Coca-Cola was. It needed more negotiating power once the channels of distribution became more concentrated and its consumer branding potentially became less powerful. Exclusive distribution in restaurants, bars, clubs, etc. is a potentially double-edged marketing sword; it is a source of brand trial as many consumers will not leave just because the restaurant serves Pepsi rather than their normal Coke or vice versa; hence they get to try the competitive product and may get to like it. However a request for one brand which gets automatically replaced by the No.1 rival brand may damage the perceived brand differentiation; 'its all really the same stuff, but we happen to sell only Pepsi'.

Coca-Cola has proved several times, by launching other products, that it is virtually impossible to replicate the strength of a brand like Coke, which makes it a victim of its own success. The potential market for Coca-Cola may be very large but it is definitely finite and sustaining high growth when you have a dominant share of a maturing market becomes more and more difficult. The risk is that the brand strength and the pressure for profits lead to a strategy of trying to keep increasing profit margins; not surprisingly there are many similarities between the Coca-Cola story and Marlboro cigarettes. These increasing profit margins make it easier for competitors to offer better value for money products and still make a more than acceptable return. This is particularly true when the total size of the market makes it possible to be financially viable with only a very small market share. The consequence is that it is vital that the company can continually refresh its brand imagery, but this becomes increasingly difficult as the brand gets older, with the result that the age profile of Coca-Cola drinkers gets much broader. Also as the market share of the grocery channel increases, the visibility of the leading brand's price premium becomes greater and there is the significant additional risk that the economic buyer (the supermarket shopper) is not the actual end consumer, and he/she may decide to buy the much cheaper alternative cola brand 'because its all really the same stuff' and 'its probably made by the same people anyway'.

Another problem for the market leader in a maturing market is that it has the major role in defending and developing the total value of the market, while the small competitors can simply look to gain market share even at the risk of damaging the total return for the existing leaders.

For several years Coca-Cola offset its maturing USA market by growing internationally, eventually taking an even greater share of the world market outside the USA than it has inside the USA. While this overall market and Coke's share of it was growing rapidly, the overall group's profit could sustain a strong rate of growth. As this market slows, the future rate of growth becomes much more questionable and inevitably this would lead to a re-rating of the growth expectation that is incorporated into the share price. Shareholders tend to extrapolate existing growth rates into the future (sometimes seemingly to infinity) and accordingly bid up the share price. They then require that the company achieves these growth expectations that they have by now already paid for; if the company fails, the resulting fall in the share price can be both very rapid and very large. It is therefore important that the company manages the expectations of the stock market, so that its share price does not rise too far; i.e. well beyond what can actually be sustainably delivered by the company's long-term strategy.

Coca-Cola undoubtedly turned its fantastically successful original brand-based marketing strategy into a massive amount of shareholder value; the challenge is now to sustain and build on this in a much more mature market with a more sophisticated set of competitors, more aggressive other stakeholders, and potentially less loyal consumers. If it is to do this, it will need a very tailored set of marketing finance generated performance measures, but they will not be the same ones that served it so well in the past.

Index